GREAT BRITAIN & I

G000123267

TOURIST and MOTORING ATLAS / ATLAS ROUTIER et TOURISTIQUE
TOERISTISCHE WEGENATLAS / ATLANTE STRADALE e TURISTICO / ATLAS

Contents
Sommaire / Inhaltsübersicht / Inhoud / Sommario / Sumario

Inside front cover: key to map pages
Intérieur de couverture : tableau d'assemblage / Umschlaginnenseite: Übersicht / Binnenzijde van het omslag: overzichtskaart
-Copertina interna: quadro d'insieme / Portada interior: mapa índice

II - III

Channel Tunnel - Tunnel sous la Manche
Folkestone Terminal - Terminal de Calais (F)
Shipping Services
Liaisons maritimes / Schiffsverbindungen / Scheepvaartverbindingen / Collegamenti marittimi / Líneas marítimas

IV - XXI

Main road map
Grands axes routiers / Durchgangsstraßen / Grote verbindingswegen / Grandi arterie stradali / Carreteras principales
1 inch = 15.8 miles - 1:1 000 000 - 1 cm = 10 km

1 - 119

Key | **1**
Légende / Zeichenerklärung / Verklaring van de tekens / Legenda / Signos convencionales

Great Britain & Ireland | **2 - 119**
Grande-Bretagne & Irlande / Großbritannien & Irland / Groot-Brittannië & Ierland
Gran Bretagna & Irlanda / Gran Bretaña & Irlanda
1 inch = 4.75 miles - 1: 300 000 - 1 cm = 3 km

120 - 147

Index Great Britain | **120 - 138**
Index Grande-Bretagne / Register Großbritannien / Register Groot-Brittannië / Indice Gran Bretagna / Índice Gran Bretaña

Index Ireland | **139 - 147**
Index Irlande / Register Irland / Register Ierland / Indice Irlanda / Índice Irlanda

148 - 192

Key | **148**
Légende / Zeichenerklärung / Verklaring van de tekens / Legenda / Signos convencionales

Town plans Great Britain | **149 - 185**
Plans de ville Grande-Bretagne / Stadtpläne Großbritannien / Stadsplattegronden Groot-Brittannië
Piante di città Gran Bretagna / Planos de ciudades Gran Bretaña

Town plans Ireland | **186 - 191**
Plans de ville Irlande / Stadtpläne Irland / Stadsplattegronden Ierland / Piante di città Irlanda / Planos de ciudades Irlanda

Eochair / Allwedd / Comnarthai ar phleanna bailte / Symbolau ar gynlluniau'r trefi | **192**

Back of the guide: distances
En fin de volume : distances / Am Ende des Buches: Entfernungen / Achter in het boek: afstanden
Alla fine del volume: distanze / Al final del volumen: distancias

Channel Tunnel
Tunnel sous la Manche

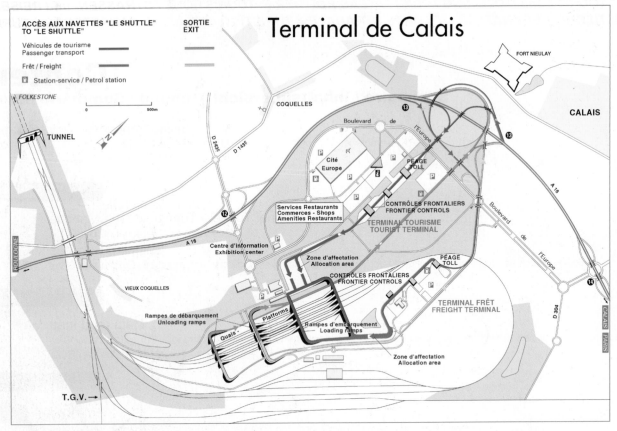

Terminal de Calais

ACCÈS AUX NAVETTES "LE SHUTTLE"
TO "LE SHUTTLE"

SORTIE
EXIT

Véhicules de tourisme
Passenger transport

Frêt / Freight

Station-service / Petrol station

FOLKESTONE

0   500m

TUNNEL

N

COQUELLES

CALAIS

FORT NIEULAY

Boulevard   de   l'Europe

Cité
Europe

PÉAGE
TOLL

CONTRÔLES FRONTALIERS
FRONTIER CONTROLS

TERMINAL TOURISME
TOURIST TERMINAL

Services Restaurants
Commerces - Shops
Amenities Restaurants

Centre d'information
Exhibition center

Zone d'affectation
Allocation area

CONTRÔLES FRONTALIERS
FRONTIER CONTROLS

PÉAGE
TOLL

TERMINAL FRÊT
FREIGHT TERMINAL

VIEUX COQUELLES

Rampes de débarquement
Unloading ramps

Quais - Platforms

Rampes d'embarquement
Loading ramps

Zone d'affectation
Allocation area

T.G.V. →

BOULOGNE

A 16

D 245E   D 143E

Boulevard   de   l'Europe

A 16

D 304

CALAIS PARIS

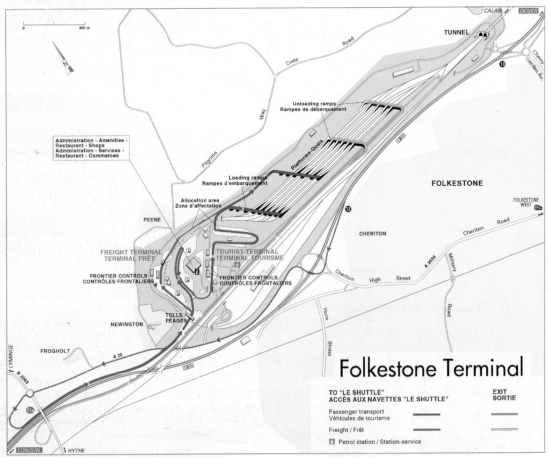

CALAIS   DOVER

TUNNEL

Crete   Way

Road

Unloading ramps
Rampes de débarquement

Administration - Amenities
Restaurant - Shops
Administration - Services -
Restaurant - Commerces

Platforms-Quais

FOLKESTONE

FOLKESTONE
WEST

Pilgrims

Loading ramps
Rampes d'embarquement

Allocation area
Zone d'affectation

PEENE

CHERITON

Cheriton   Road

FREIGHT TERMINAL
TERMINAL FRÊT

TOURIST TERMINAL
TERMINAL TOURISME

Cheriton   High   Street

A 2034

FRONTIER CONTROLS
CONTRÔLES FRONTALIERS

FRONTIER CONTROLS
CONTRÔLES FRONTALIERS

Military   Road

Horn   Street

TOLLS
PÉAGES

NEWINGTON

FROGHOLT   A 20

LYMINGE   B 2065

LONDON   HYTHE

Folkestone Terminal

TO "LE SHUTTLE"
ACCÈS AUX NAVETTES "LE SHUTTLE"

EXIT
SORTIE

Passenger transport
Véhicules de tourisme

Freight / Frêt

Petrol station / Station-service

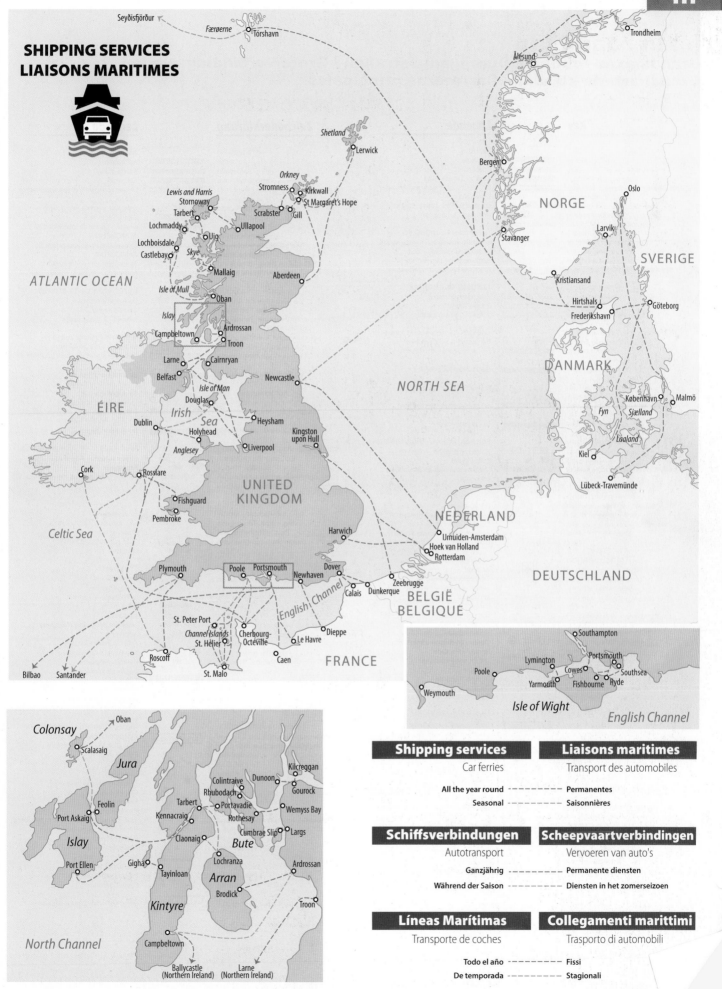

SHIPPING SERVICES
LIAISONS MARITIMES

Seyðisfjörður
Færøerne
Tórshavn
Trondheim
Ålesund
Bergen
NORGE
Oslo
Shetland
Lerwick
Larvik
Stavanger
Orkney
Stromness
Kirkwall
St Margaret's Hope
Gill
Lewis and Harris
Stornoway
Scrabster
Tarbert
Ullapool
Lochmaddy
Uig
Kristiansand
SVERIGE
Lochboisdale
Skye
Hirtshals
Göteborg
Castlebay
Mallaig
Aberdeen
Frederikshavn
ATLANTIC OCEAN
Isle of Mull
Oban
Islay
Ardrossan
DANMARK
Campbeltown
Troon
København
Malmö
Larne
Cairnryan
Newcastle
NORTH SEA
Fyn
Sjælland
Belfast
ÉIRE
Isle of Man
Laaland
Douglas
Kiel
Irish Sea
Heysham
Dublin
Holyhead
Kingston upon Hull
Anglesey
Liverpool
Lübeck-Travemünde
Cork
Rosslare
UNITED KINGDOM
NEDERLAND
Fishguard
DEUTSCHLAND
Pembroke
Harwich
IJmuiden-Amsterdam
Celtic Sea
Hoek van Holland
Rotterdam
Plymouth
Poole
Portsmouth
Newhaven
Dover
Zeebrugge
BELGIË
BELGIQUE
St. Peter Port
Calais
Dunkerque
Channel Islands
Cherbourg-
Octeville
St. Hélier
Dieppe
English Channel
Roscoff
Le Havre
Bilbao
Santander
St. Malo
Caen
FRANCE

Isle of Wight detail
Southampton
Lymington
Portsmouth
Poole
Cowes
Southsea
Weymouth
Yarmouth
Fishbourne
Ryde
Isle of Wight
English Channel

Scotland inset
Colonsay
Oban
Scalasaig
Jura
Kilcreggan
Colintraive
Dunoon
Rhubodach
Gourock
Tarbert
Portavadie
Feolin
Kennacraig
Rothesay
Wemyss Bay
Port Askaig
Claonaig
Cumbrae Slip
Largs
Islay
Bute
Lochranza
Ardrossan
Port Ellen
Gigha
Tayinloan
Arran
Kintyre
Brodick
Troon
North Channel
Campbeltown
Ballycastle
(Northern Ireland)
Larne
(Northern Ireland)

Shipping services	Liaisons maritimes
Car ferries	Transport des automobiles
All the year round -------	Permanentes
Seasonal - - - - -	Saisonnières

Schiffsverbindungen	Scheepvaartverbindingen
Autotransport	Vervoeren van auto's
Ganzjährig -------	Permanente diensten
Während der Saison - - - - -	Diensten in het zomerseizoen

Líneas Marítimas	Collegamenti marittimi
Transporte de coches	Trasporto di automobili
Todo el año -------	Fissi
De temporada - - - - -	Stagionali

Main road map
Grands axes routiers / Durchgangsstraßen / Grote verbindingswegen
Grandi arterie stradali / Carreteras principales

Key	*Légende*	*Zeichenerklärung*	*Legenda*
Roads	**Routes**	**Straßen**	**Strade**
Motorway	Autoroute	Autobahn	Autostrada
Motorway: single carriageway	Route-auto	Autostraße	Strada-auto
Motorway (unclassified)	Autoroute et assimilée	Autobahn oder Schnellstraße	Autostrada, strada di tipo autostradale
Dual carriageway with motorway characteristics	Double chaussée de type autoroutier	Schnellstraße mit getrennten Fahrbahnen	Doppia carreggiata di tipo autostradale
Interchanges:	Échangeurs :	Anschlussstellen:	Svincoli:
complete, limited, not specified	complet, partiels, sans précision	Voll - bzw. Teilanschluss, ohne Angabe	completo, parziale, imprecisato
Interchange numbers	Numéros d'échangeurs	Anschlussstellennummern	Svincoli numerati
Recommended MICHELIN main itinerary	Itinéraire principal recommandé par MICHELIN	Von MICHELIN empfohlene Hauptverkehrsstraße	Itinerario principale raccomandato da MICHELIN
Recommended MICHELIN regional itinerary	Itinéraire régional ou de dégagement recommandé par MICHELIN	Von MICHELIN empfohlene Regionalstraße	Itinerario regionale raccomandato da MICHELIN
Road surfaced - unsurfaced	Route revêtue - non revêtue	Straße mit Belag - ohne Belag	Strada rivestita - non rivestita
Motorway/Road under construction	Autoroute - Route en construction	Autobahn/Straße im Bau	Autostrada - Strada in costruzione
Road widths	**Largeur des routes**	**Straßenbreiten**	**Larghezza delle strade**
Dual carriageway	Chaussées séparées	Getrennte Fahrbahnen	Carreggiate separate
2 wide lanes	2 voies larges	2 breite Fahrspuren	2 corsie larghe
2 lanes - 2 narrow lanes	2 voies - 2 voies étroites	2 Fahrspuren - 2 schmale Fahrspuren	2 corsie - 2 corsie strette
Distances (total and intermediate)	**Distances** (totalisées et partielles)	**Straßenentfernungen** (Gesamt- und Teilentfernungen)	**Distanze** (totali e parziali)
On motorway in kilometers	Sur autoroute en kilomètres	Auf der Autobahn in Kilometern	Su autostrada in chilometri
Toll roads - Toll-free section	Section à péage - Section libre	Mautstrecke - Mautfreie Strecke	Tratto a pedaggio - Tratto esente da pedaggio
On road in kilometers	Sur route en kilomètres	Auf der Straße in Kilometern	Su strada in chilometri
On motorway (GB)	Sur autoroute (GB)	Auf der Autobahn (GB)	Su autostrada (GB)
in miles - in kilometers	en miles - en kilomètres	in Meilen - in Kilometern	in miglia - in chilometri
Toll roads - Toll-free section	Section à péage - Section libre	Mautstrecke - Mautfreie Strecke	Tratto a pedaggio - Tratto esente da pedaggio
On road in miles	Sur route en miles	Auf der Straße in Meilen	Su strada in miglia
Numbering - Signs	**Numérotation - Signalisation**	**Nummerierung - Wegweisung**	**Numerazione - Segnaletica**
European route - Motorway	Route européenne - Autoroute	Europastraße - Autobahn	Strada europea - Autostrada
Other roads	Autres routes	Sonstige Straßen	Altre strade
Destination on primary route network	Localités jalonnant les itinéraires principaux	Richtungshinweis auf der empfohlenen Fernverkehrsstraße	Località delimitante gli itinerari principali
Safety Warnings	**Alertes Sécurité**	**Sicherheitsalerts**	**Segnalazioni stradali**
Snowbound, impassable road during the period shown	Enneigement : période probable de fermeture	Eingeschneite Straße: voraussichtl. Wintersperre	Innevamento: probabile periodo di chiusura
Pass and its height above sea level	Col et sa cote d'altitude	Pass mit Höhenangabe	Passo ed altitudine
Steep hill - Toll barrier	Forte déclivité - Barrière de péage	Starke Steigung - Mautstelle	Forte pendenza - Casello
Ford	Gué	Furt	Guado
Transportation	**Transports**	**Verkehrsmittel**	**Trasporti**
Airport	Aéroport	Flughafen	Aeroporto
Transportation of vehicles: year-round - seasonal	Transport des autos : permanent - saisonnier	Autotransport: ganzjährig - saisonbedingte Verbindung	Trasporto auto: tutto l'anno - stagionale
by boat	par bateau	per Schiff	su traghetto
by ferry	par bac	per Fähre	su chiatta
Ferry (passengers and cycles only)	Bac pour piétons et cycles	Fähre für Personen und Fahrräder	Traghetto per pedoni e biciclette
Motorail	Auto/Train	Autoreisezug	Auto/treno
Administration	**Administration**	**Verwaltung**	**Amministrazione**
Administrative district seat	Capitale de division administrative	Verwaltungshauptstadt	Capoluogo amministrativo
Parador / Pousada	Parador / Pousada	Parador / Pousada	Parador / Pousada
Administrative boundaries	Limites administratives	Verwaltungsgrenzen	Confini amministrativi
National boundary	Frontière	Staatsgrenze	Frontiera
Principal customs post	Douane principale	Hauptzollamt	Dogana principale
Secondary customs post	Douane avec restriction	Zollstation mit Einschränkungen	Dogana con limitazioni
Restricted area for foreigners / Military property	Zone interdite aux étrangers / Zone militaire	Sperrgebiet für Ausländer / Militärgebiet	Zona vietata agli stranieri / Zona militare
Sights	**Lieux touristiques**	**Sehenswürdigkeiten**	**Mete e luoghi d'interesse**
2- and 3-star	Sites classés 2 et 3 étoiles	Sehenswürdigkeiten mit 2 und 3 Sternen	Siti segnalati con 2 e 3 stelle
MICHELIN Green Guide sites	par le Guide Vert MICHELIN	im Grünen Reiseführer MICHELIN	dalla Guida Verde MICHELIN
Religious building	Édifice religieux	Sakral-Bau	Edificio religioso
Historic house, castle	Château	Schloss, Burg	Castello
Monastery	Monastère	Kloster	Monastero
Stave church	Église en bois debout	Stabkirche	Chiesa in legno di testa
Wooden church	Église en bois	Holzkirche	Chiesa in legno
Open air museum	Musée de plein air	Freilichtmuseum	Museo all'aperto
Antiquities	Site antique	Antike Fundstätte	Sito antico
Rock carving - Prehistoric monument	Gravure rupestre - Monument mégalithique	Felsbilder - Vorgeschichtliches Steindenkmal	Incisione rupestre - Monumento megalitico
Rune stone - Ruins	Pierre runique - Ruines	Runenstein - Ruine	Pietra runica - Rovine
Cave - Windmill	Grotte - Moulin à vent	Höhle - Windmühle	Grotta - Mulino a vento
Other places of interest	Autres curiosités	Sonstige Sehenswürdigkeit	Altri luoghi d'interesse
Scenic route	Parcours pittoresque	Landschaftlich schöne Strecke	Percorso pittoresco
Other signs	**Signes divers**	**Sonstige Zeichen**	**Simboli vari**
Recreation ground	Parc de loisirs	Erholungspark	Parco divertimenti
Dam - Waterfall	Barrage - Cascade	Staudamm - Wasserfall	Diga - Cascata
National park / Nature park	Parc national / Parc naturel	Nationalpark / Naturpark	Parco nazionale / Parco naturale

Signos Convencionales

Carreteras

Autopista
Carretera
Autopista, Autovía
Autovía
Accesos:
completo, parcial, sin precisar
Números de los accesos
Itinerario principal recomendado por MICHELIN
Itinerario regional recomendado por MICHELIN
Carretera asfaltada - sin asfaltar
Autopista - Carretera en construcción

Ancho de las carreteras

Calzadas separadas
Dos carriles anchos
Dos carriles - Dos carriles estrechos

Distancias (totales y parciales)

En autopista en kilómetros
Tramo de peaje - Tramo libre
En carretera en kilómetros
En autopista (GB)
en millas - en kilómetros
Tramo de peaje - Tramo libre
En carretera en millas

Numeración - Señalización

Carretera europea - Autopista
Otras carreteras
Localidades situadas en los principales itinerarios

Alertas Seguridad

Nevada:
Período probable de cierre
Puerto y su altitud
Pendiente Pronunciada - Barrera de peaje
Vado

Transportes

Aeropuerto
Transporte de coches:
todo el año - de temporada
por barco
por barcaza
Barcaza para el paso de peatones y vehículos dos ruedas
Auto-tren

Administración

Capital de división administrativa
Parador / Pousada
Limites administrativos
Frontera
Aduana principal
Aduana con restricciones
Zona prohibida a los extranjeros / Propiedad militar

Curiosidades

Lugares clasificados con 2 y 3 estrellas por la Guía Verde MICHELIN
Edificio religioso
Castillo
Monasterio
Iglesia de madera
Iglesia de madera
Museo al aire libre
Zona de vestigios antiguos
Grabado rupestre - Monumento megalítico
Piedra rúnica - Ruinas
Cueva - Molino de viento
Otras curiosidades
Recorrido pintoresco

Signos diversos

Zona recreativa
Presa - Cascada

Parque nacional / Parque natural

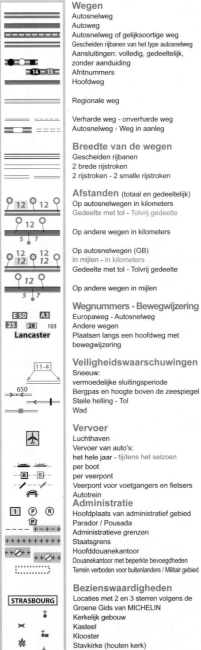

Verklaring van de tekens

Wegen

Autosnelweg
Autoweg
Autosnelweg of gelijksoortige weg
Gescheiden rijbanen van het type autosnelweg
Aansluitingen: volledig, gedeeltelijk, zonder aanduiding
Afritnummers
Hoofdweg

Regionale weg

Verharde weg - onverharde weg
Autosnelweg - Weg in aanleg

Breedte van de wegen

Gescheiden rijbanen
2 brede rijstroken
2 rijstroken - 2 smalle rijstroken

Afstanden (totaal en gedeeltelijk)

Op autosnelwegen in kilometers
Gedeelte met tol - Tolvrij gedeelte
Op andere wegen in kilometers
Op autosnelwegen (GB)
in mijlen - in kilometers
Gedeelte met tol - Tolvrij gedeelte
Op andere wegen in mijlen

Wegnummers - Bewegwijzering

Europaweg - Autosnelweg
Andere wegen
Plaatsen langs een hoofdweg met bewegwijzering

Veiligheidswaarschuwingen

Sneeuw:
vermoedelijke sluitingsperiode
Bergpas en hoogte boven de zeespiegel
Steile helling - Tol
Wad

Vervoer

Luchthaven
Vervoer van auto's:
het hele jaar - tijdens het seizoen
per boot
per veerpont
Veerpont voor voetgangers en fietsers
Autotrein

Administratie

Hoofdplaats van administratief gebied
Parador / Pousada
Administratieve grenzen
Staatsgrens
Hoofddouanekantoor
Douanekantoor met beperkte bevoegdheden
Terrein verboden voor buitenlanders / Militair gebied

Bezienswaardigheden

Locaties met 2 en 3 sterren volgens de Groene Gids van MICHELIN
Kerkelijk gebouw
Kasteel
Klooster
Stavkirke (houten kerk)
Houten kerk
Openluchtmuseum
Overblijfsel uit de Oudheid
Rotstekening - Megaliet
Runensteen - Ruïne
Grot - Molen
Andere bezienswaardigheden
Schilderachtig traject

Diverse tekens

Recreatiepark
Stuwdam - Waterval

Nationaal park / Natuurpark

Republic of Ireland: All distances and speed limits are signed in kilometres.

République d'Irlande: Les distances et les limitations de vitesse sont exprimées en kilomètres.

Irland: Alle Entfernungsangaben und Geschwindigkeitsbegrenzungen in km.

Ierland: Alle afstanden en maximumsnelheden zijn uitsluitend in kilometers aangegeven.

Repubblica d'Irlanda: Distanze e limiti di velocità sono espressi soltanto in chilometri.

República de Irlanda: Distancias y límites de velocidad están expresados sólo en kilómetros.

Key to 1:1 000 000 map pages
Légende des cartes au 1/1 000 000
Zeichenerklärung der Karten 1:1 000 000
Verklaring van de tekens voor kaarten met schaal 1:1 000 000
Legenda carte scala 1:1 000 000
Signos convencionales de los mapas a escala 1:1 000 000

ENGLAND

UNITARY AUTHORITIES

1	Bath and North East Somerset	43	North East Lincolnshire
	Bedford	44	North Lincolnshire
	Blackburn with Darwen	45	North Somerset
	Blackpool	46	North Yorkshire
	Bracknell Forest	47	Northamptonshire
	Brighton and Hove	48	Northumberland
7	Buckinghamshire	49	Nottinghamshire
8	Cambridgeshire		Nottingham
9	Central Bedfordshire	51	Oxfordshire
10	Cheshire East		Peterborough
11	Cheshire West and Chester		Plymouth
	City of Bristol		Portsmouth
13	Cornwall		Reading
14	Cumbria	56	Redcar and Cleveland
	Derby	57	Rutland
16	Derbyshire	58	Shropshire
17	Devon	59	Somerset
18	Dorset	60	South Gloucestershire
19	Durham	61	South Yorkshire
20	East Riding of Yorkshire		Southend-on-Sea
21	East Sussex	63	Staffordshire
22	Essex		Stockton-on-Tees
23	Gloucestershire		Stoke-on-Trent
	Greater London	66	Suffolk
	Greater Manchester	67	Surrey
26	Halton		Swindon
27	Hampshire	69	Telford and Wrekin
	Hartlepool	70	Thurrock
29	Herefordshire		Torbay
30	Hertfordshire	72	Tyne and Wear
31	Kent		Warrington
	Kingston-upon-Hull	74	Warwickshire
33	Lancashire	75	West Berkshire
	Leicester	76	West Midlands
35	Leicestershire	77	West Sussex
36	Lincolnshire	78	West Yorkshire
	Luton	79	Wiltshire
38	Medway		Windsor and Maidenhead
39	Merseyside		Wokingham
	Middlesbrough	82	Worcestershire
41	Milton Keynes		York
42	Norfolk		

SCOTLAND

UNITARY AUTHORITIES

1	1	Aberdeen City	17	17	Inverclyde
2	2	Aberdeenshire	18	18	Midlothian
3	3	Angus	19	19	Moray
4	4	Argyll and Bute	20	20	North Ayrshire
5	5	Clackmannanshire	21	21	North Lanarkshire
6		City of Edinburgh	22	22	Orkney Islands
7		City of Glasgow	23	23	Perth and Kinross
8	8	Dumfries and Galloway	24	24	Renfrewshire
9	9	Dundee City	25	25	Scottish Borders
10	10	East Ayrshire	26	26	Shetland Islands
11	11	East Dunbartonshire	27	27	South Ayrshire
12	12	East Lothian	28	28	South Lanarkshire
13	13	East Renfrewshire	29	29	Stirling
14	14	Falkirk	30	30	West Dunbartonshire
15	15	Fife	31	31	West Lothian
16	16	Highland	32	32	Western Isles

NORTHERN IRELAND

DISTRICT COUNCILS

1	1	Antrim	14	14	Down
2	2	Ards	15	15	Dungannon
3	3	Armagh	16	16	Fermanagh
4	4	Ballymena	17	17	Larne
5	5	Ballymoney	18	18	Limavady
6	6	Banbridge	19	19	Lisburn
7	7	Belfast	20	20	Magherafelt
8	8	Carrickfergus	21	21	Moyle
9	9	Castlereagh	22	22	Newry and Mourne
10	10	Coleraine	23	23	Newtownabbey
11	11	Cookstown	24	24	North Down
12	12	Craigavon	25	25	Omagh
13	13	Derry	26	26	Strabane

32
32 = UNITARY AUTHORITIES

WALES

UNITARY AUTHORITIES

1	1	Anglesey/Sir Fôn	12	12	Merthyr Tydfil/Merthyr Tudful
2	2	Blaenau Gwent	13	13	Monmouthshire/Sir Fynwy
3	3	Bridgend/Pen-y-bont ar Ogwr	14	14	Neath Port Talbot/Castell-nedd Phort Talbot
4	4	Caerphilly/Caerffili	15	15	Newport/Casnewydd
5	5	Cardiff/Caerdydd	16	16	Pembrokeshire/Sir Benfro
6	6	Carmarthenshire/Sir Gaerfyrddin	17	17	Powys
7	7	Ceredigion	18	18	Rhondda Cynon Taff/Rhondda Cynon Taf
8	8	Conwy	19	19	Swansea/Abertawe
9	9	Denbighshire/Sir Ddinbych	20	20	Torfaen/Tor-faen
10	10	Flintshire/Sir y Fflint	21	21	Vale of Glamorgan/Bro Morgannwg
11	11	Gwynedd	22	22	Wrexham/Wrecsam

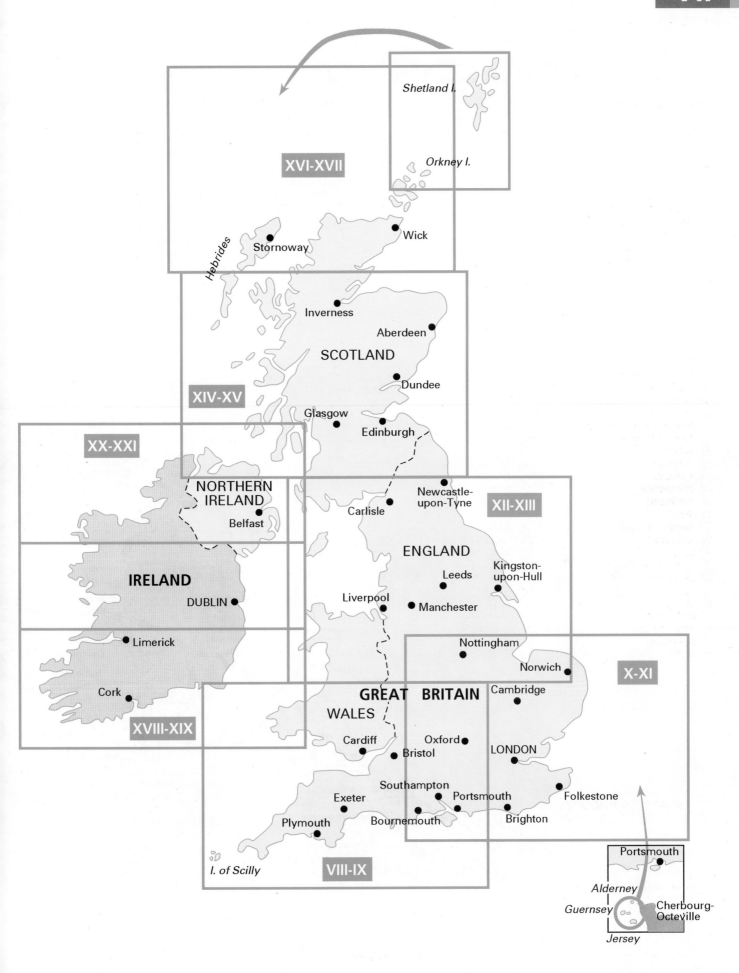

XVI-XVII

Shetland I.

Orkney I.

Hebrides

● Wick

● Stornoway

● Inverness

● Aberdeen

SCOTLAND

● Dundee

XIV-XV

● Glasgow

● Edinburgh

XX-XXI

NORTHERN IRELAND

● Belfast

Newcastle-upon-Tyne ●

XII-XIII

● Carlisle

ENGLAND

Kingston-upon-Hull ●

IRELAND

● Leeds

DUBLIN ●

Liverpool ●

● Manchester

● Limerick

● Nottingham

Norwich ●

X-XI

● Cork

Cambridge ●

XVIII-XIX

GREAT BRITAIN

WALES

● Cardiff

Oxford ●

LONDON

● Bristol

● Folkestone

● Southampton

● Exeter

● Portsmouth

● Bournemouth

● Brighton

● Plymouth

I. of Scilly

VIII-IX

Portsmouth ●

Alderney

Guernsey

Cherbourg-Octeville

Jersey

St. George's Channel

Saltee Islands
Point
e Harbour/
Ros Láir

Llanrhystud
A 485
Bridge
593
Elan Val
7
Aberaeron
A 482
Tregaron
New Quay
58
93
Synod Inn
Aberporth
Lampeter
Cardigan
A 487
Strumble Head
Newport
Fishguard/
Abergwaun
Newcastle Emlyn
Llandysul
Llandovery
Crymmych
St. David's Head
Pembrokeshire Coast
National Park
6
537
Carmarthen/
Caerfyrddin
85 Llandeilo
Black Mountain
Breco
Nati
802
St. David's
A 487
16
B 4329
16
74
46
21
Llangadog
Sennyb
Haverfordwest/Hwlffordd
Narberth
St. Clears
16 53
St. Bride's Bay
Whitland
23
30
48
Cross
Hands
Ammanford
68
42
Me
Aber
Milford Haven/
Aberdaugleddau
Pembrokeshire
Coast National
Park
32
52
Kidwelly
Pontarddulais
19
Pontardawe
14
Neath/
Castell Nedd
PembrokeDock
Pembroke
A 4139
Neyland
Saundersfoot
Pendine
Burry
Port
Tenby/
Dinbych-y-pysgod
SWANSEA/
ABERTAWE
Maesteg
St. Govan's Head
Carmarthen Bay
Rhossili
Llanelli
Port
Talbot
53
33
Worms Head
The
Mumbles
Port
Eynon
Porthcawl
Bridge
Pen-y-

BRISTOL CHANNEL

Lundy
Combe
Martin
Lynton
Lynmouth
Ilfracombe
A 39
Po
Exmoor
519
National
Croyde
Simonsbath
Braunton
Tarr
steps
Barnstaple
493
35
56
Hartland Point
Northam
South
Molton
Clovelly
Bideford
Great
Torrington
Cliffs of
Morwenstow
Kilkhampton
17
Tiv
Stratton
Holsworthy
Hatherleigh
Winkleigh
Bude
Crediton
Tamar
Okehampton
EX
621
High
Willhays
Moretonhampstead
Tintagel
Launceston
Lydford
Gorge
Dartmoor
Bovey
Tracey
Camelford
National
177
109
420
Tavistock
Princetown
Park
Ashburton
Newton
Abbot
Padstow
13
Wadebridge
113
182
Callington
Buckfastleigh
Bodmin
Liskeard
Buckland Abbey
78
126
Saltash
Plympton
41
66
Newquay
Lostwithiel
Totnes
Fraddon
West
Looe
PLYMOUTH
Plymstock
Modbury
St. Austell
Fowey
Torpoint
Newton
Ferrers
Dartmou
Truro
Trewithen
Polperro
Kingsbridge
Camborne
Mevagissey
St. Ives
Tregony
Trelissick Garden
Salcombe
St
Redruth
Penryn
St. Just
Penzance
Hayle
St. Mawes
252
Falmouth
Helston
Glendurgan
Garden
Land's End
St. Michael's
Mount
Sennen
Mount'sBay
St. Keverne
Subtropical
Gardens
Lizard
Tresco
St. Martin's
Lizard Point
Isles of Scilly
St. Mary's

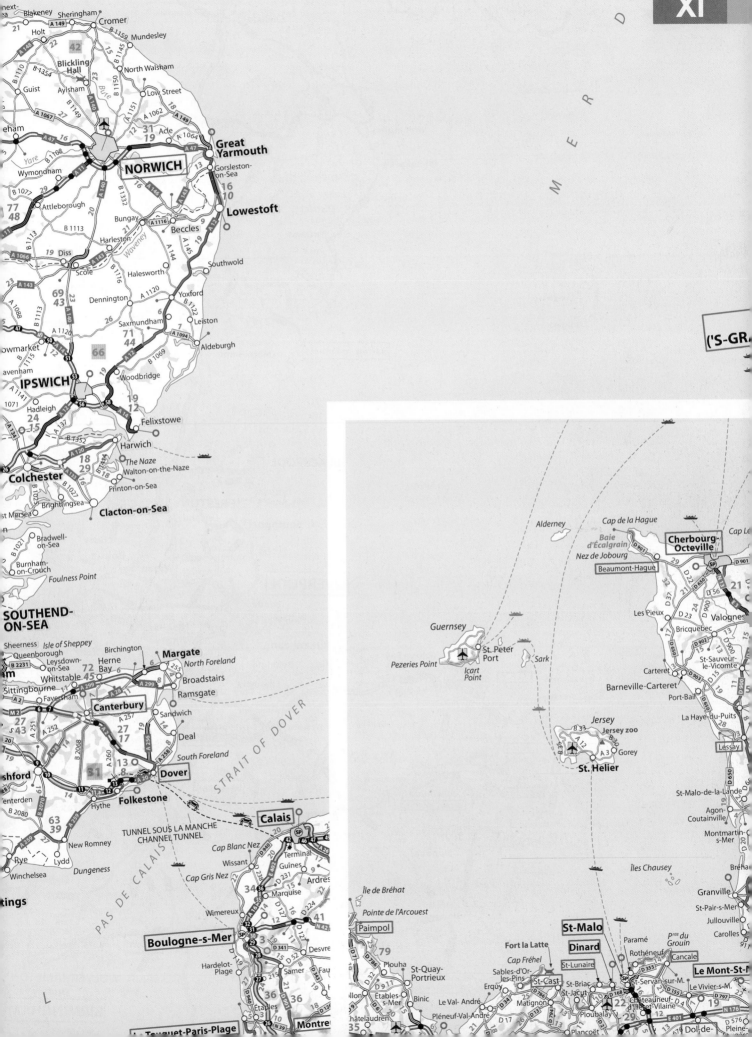

South Shields
SUNDERLAND
Jarrow
Tynemouth
Washington
Stanley
Chester-le-Street
Durham
Seaham
Houghton-le-Spring
Horden
Hartlepool
Peterlee
Sedgefield
Spennymoor
Redcar
Marske-by-the-Sea
Saltburn-by-the-Sea
Brotton
Billingham
Newton-Aycliffe
Stockton-on-Tees
Eaglescliffe
Loftus
Guisborough
Whitby
MIDDLESBROUGH
Darlington
Northallerton
Cleveland Hills
North York Moors National Park
Scalby
Scarborough
Bedale
Thirsk
Rievaulx Abbey
Helmsley
Pickering
Filey
Flamborough Head
Ripon
Easingwold
Boroughbridge
Malton
Norton
Bridlington
Knaresborough
Wetwang
Driffield
Beeford
Harrogate
Otley
Wetherby
Tadcaster
YORK
Market Weighton
Leven
Hornsea
Harewood
Selby
Barlby
Beverley
LEEDS
Garforth
Castleford
Howden
Goole
KINGSTON UPON HULL
Hedon
Withernsea
Dewsbury
Wakefield
Pontefract
Shaith
Thorne
Crowle
Scunthorpe
Barton-upon-Humber
Patrington
Kilnsea
Immingham Dock
Spurn Head
Ersfield
Barnsley
Bentley
Doncaster
Epworth
Brigg
Caistor
Immingham
Grimsby
Cleethorpes
Stocksbridge
Conisbrough
Bawtry
Rotherham
Market Rasen
Louth
Mablethorpe
SHEFFIELD
Maltby
Gainsborough
Wragby
Sutton-on-Sea
Castleton
Dronfield
Staveley
Retford
Alford
Chesterfield
Tuxford
Lincoln
Horncastle
Partney
Skegness
Bakewell
Chatsworth House
Hardwick Hall
Ollerton
Woodhall Spa
Spilsby
Haddon Hall
Mansfield
Southwell
Leadenham
Matlock
Alfreton
Sutton-in-Ashfield
Newark-on-Trent
Boston
Holkham Hall
Wells-next-the-Sea
Blakeney
Holt
Ashbourne
Ripley
Heanor
Hucknall
Sleaford
Hunstanton
The Wash
Houghton Hall
Belper
Ilkeston
NOTTINGHAM
Bingham
Donington
Sutterton
Sandringham House
Fakenham
Guist
DERBY
West Bridgford
Grantham
Holbeach
Long Sutton
King's Lynn
East Dereham
Long Eaton
Belvoir Castle
Rempstone
Bourne
Spalding
Wisbech
Swaffham
Wymondham
Burton-upon-Trent
Loughborough
Melton Mowbray
Crowland
Outwell
Stradsett
Downham Market
Oxburgh Hall
Watton
Swadlicote
Ashby de la Zouch
Shepshed
Coalville
Stamford
Guyhirn
March
Mundford
Brandon
Thetford
Lichfield
Tamworth
Oakham
Oadby
Uppingham
Eye
Whittlesey
PETERBOROUGH
Sutton Coldfield
Hinckley
LEICESTER
Corby
Weldon
Oundle
Ely
Littleport
Nuneaton
Bedworth
Lutterworth
Market Harborough
Husbands Bosworth
Desborough
Boughton House
Ramsey
Kettering

Kinnairds Head
Fraserburgh
Loch of Strathbeg
Rattray Head
Peterhead
Buchan Ness
Cruden Bay
Newburgh
Ellon
Pitmedden Garden
Mintlaw
New Deer
Turriff
Banff
Macduff
Cullen
Buckie
Lossiemouth
Elgin
Fochabers
Keith
Rothes
Craigellachie
Dufftown
Huntly
Forres
Nairn
Alness
Invergordon
Cromarty
Black Isle
Fortrose
Tore
Inverness
Dava
Grantown-on-Spey
Dulnain Bridge
Carrbridge
Aviemore
Glenmore Forest Park
Cairn Gorm
Cairngorm Mountains
Ben Macdui
Kingussie
Carn Ban
Newtonmore
Laggan
Cairngorms National Park
Monadhliath Mountains
Tomintoul
Colnabaichin
Rhynie
Mossat
Alford
Oldmeldrum
Inverurie
Kintore
Craigievar Castle
Crathes Castle
ABERDEEN
Ballater
Aboyne
Banchory
Braemar
Balmoral Castle
Stonehaven
GRAMPIAN MOUNTAINS
Pass of Drumochter
Devil's Elbow
Glas Maol
Beinn a' Ghlò
Blair Castle
Blair Atholl
Kinloch Rannoch
Pitlochry
Schiehallion
Laurencekirk
Inverbervie
The Pleasance
Marykirk
Brechin
Montrose
Kirriemuir
Forfar
Glamis Castle
Glamis
Alyth
Rattray
Blairgowrie
Meigle
Coupar Angus
Arbroath
Carnoustie
DUNDEE
Monifieth
Tayport
Buddon Ness
Newport-on-Tay
Leuchars
St. Andrews
Fife Ness
Crail
Anstruther
Pittenweem
Saint Monans
Elie
Cupar
Newburgh
Auchtermuchty
Falkland
Glenrothes
Leven
Methil
Buckhaven
Kirkcaldy
Lochgelly
Kinross
Cowdenbeath
Burntisland
Firth of Forth
Aberfeldy
Dunkeld
Ben Lawers
Loch Tay
BenChonzie
Perth
Crieff
Lochearnhead
Ben Vorlich
Auchterarder
Ochil Hills
Sidlaw Hills
Callander
Dunblane
Doune
Bridge of Allan
Dollar
Alva
Stirling
Alloa
Dunfermline
Kincardine
Culross
Rosyth
Inverkeithing
FORTH BRIDGE
S. Queensferry
Grangemouth
Bo' Ness
Denny
Falkirk
Kilsyth
Kirkintilloch
Linlithgow
Hopetoun House
Cumbernauld
Bathgate
Armadale
Livingston
Airdrie
Whitburn
Coatbridge
Motherwell
Wishaw
Hamilton
East Kilbride
Strathaven
Carluke
Lanark
North Berwick
Aberlady
Prestonpans
Leith
Musselburgh
Tranent
East Linton
Haddington
Dunbar
EDINBURGH
Dalkeith
Loanhead
Rosslyn Chapel
Penicuik
Pentland Hills
Moorfoot Hills
Lammermuir Hills
Cockburnspath
St. Abb's Head
St Abb's Head National Nature Reserve
Eyemouth
Duns
Berwick-upon-Tweed
Holy Island
West Linton
Carnwath
Peebles
Innerleithen
Galashiels
Melrose
Lauder
Earlston
Mellerstain
Abbey Dryburgh
Kelso
Coldstream
Greenlaw
Newtown St Boswells
Selkirk
Jedburgh
Hawick
Broad Law
Biggar
Abington
Douglas
Muirkirk
Mauchline
Cumnock
New Cumnock
Sanquhar
Elvanfoot
Moffat
Beattock
Thornhill
Drumlanrig castle
Lochmaben
Lockerbie
Langholm
Carter Bar
The Cheviot Hills
The Cheviot
Wooler
Belford
Bamburgh Castle
Alnwick
Warkworth
Amble
Felton
Rothbury
Northumberland National Park
Kielder Resr.
Otterburn
Ashington
Newbiggin-by-the-Sea
Morpeth
Blyth
SOUTHERN UPLANDS

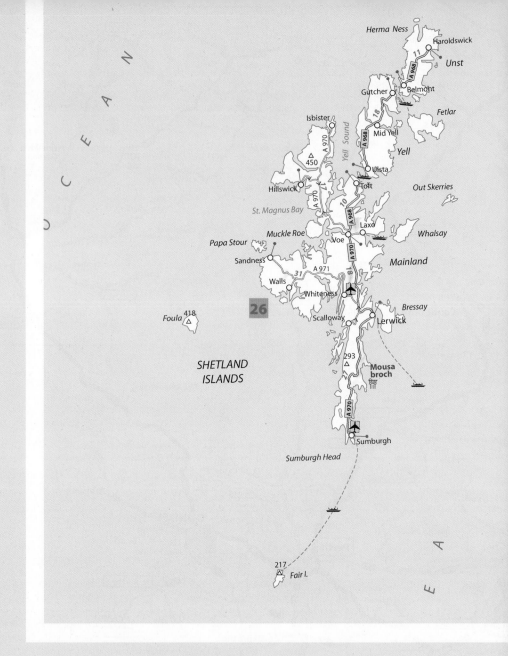

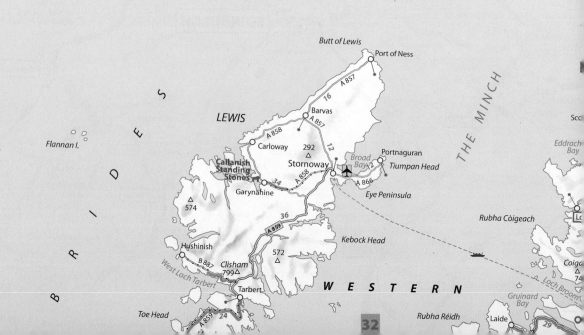

DUBLIN/BAILE ÁTHA CLIATH

LONGFORD
LOUTH
MEATH
FINGAL
WEST MEATH
OFFALY
KILDARE
S. DUBLIN
WICKLOW
LAOIS
NORTH TIPPERARY
KILKENNY
CARLOW
SOUTH TIPPERARY
WEXFORD
WATERFORD

Dundalk Bay
Castlebellingham
Ardee
Clogherhead
Drogheda/Droichead Átha
Balbriggan
Skerries
Rush
Lusk
Swords
Malahide/Mullach Íde
Portmarnock
Howth/Binn Éadair
Dún Laoghaire
Dalkey
Bray/Bré
Greystones
Enniskerry
Powerscourt
Russborough House
Hollywood
Laragh
Glendalough
Rathnew
Wicklow Head
Wicklow/Cill Mhantáin
Rathdrum
Aughrim
Arklow/AntInbhear Mór
Courtown
Gorey
Enniscorthy/Inis Córthaidh
Blackwater
Wexford/Loch Garman
Rosslare
Rosslare Harbour/Calafort Ros Láir
Carnsore Point
Cahore Point

Bailieborough
Kingscourt
Virginia
Ballyjamesduff
Oldcastle
Kells
Slane
Navan/An Uaimh
Newgrange
Old Mellifont
Monasterboice
Duleek
Ashbourne
Naul
Trim
Dunshaughlin
Athboy
Kilcock
Maynooth
Lucan
Clondalkin
Castletown House
Naas/An Nás
Newbridge/An Droichead Nua
Kildare
Kilcullen
Kippure 752
Poulaphouca Res.
Wicklow Mountains National Park
Lugnaquillia Mountain 924
Baltinglass
Tinahely
Carnew
Bunclody
Monasterevin
Portlaoise/Port Laoise
Emo Court
Portarlington
Athy
Castledermot
Tullow
Carlow/Ceatharlach
Bagenalstown
Borris
Graiguenamanagh
Kilkenny/Cill Chainnigh
Castlecomer
Freshford
Abbeyleix
Durrow
Rathdowney
Moneygall
Templemore
Thurles/Durlas
Holycross
Urlingford
Ballingarry
Callan
Thomastown
Jerpoint
New Ross
Wellington Bridge
Arthurstown
Cashel/Caiseal
Fethard
Clonmel/Cluain Meala
Carrick-on-Suir
Waterford/Port Láirge
Tramore
Dunmore East
Kilmore Quay
Saltee Islands
Hook Head
Waterford Harbour
Dungarvan Harbour
Helvick Head
Cappoquin
Lismore
Tallow
Dungarvan
Bunmahon
Ardmore
Youghal
Youghal Bay
Ballycotton

Mullingar/An Muileann gCearr
Kinnegad
Innfield
Edenderry
Tullamore/Tulach Mhór
Clara
Kilbeggan
Moate
Athlone/Baile Átha Luain
Clonmacnoise
Ferbane
Clonfert
Banagher
Birr
Kinnitty
Roscrea
Kilcormac
Slieve Bloom Mts. 527
Mountmellick
Mountrath
Longford/An Longfort
Granard
Edgeworthstown
Ballymahon
Castlepollard
Delvin
Derravaragh
Lough Ree
Strokestown
Elphin
Lanesborough
Ballymore
Ballyforan

Slievenamon 719
Comeragh Mts. 789
Knockmealdown Mts. 693
Cahir
Cloghen

ST. GEORGE'S CHANNEL
IRISH SEA

Pembrokeshire Coast National Park
St. David's Head
St. David's
Haverfordwest
St. Bride's Bay
Milford Haven
Aberdaugleddau
Stumble Head

Aran Island

Gweeb

Rossan Point — Glencolumbkille
R 263 17 Kill
Bunglass Cliffs

D o n e g

Inishmurray

Erris Head
Broad Haven
Ballycastle
Killala Bay
Easky
Strandhill
Slygo Bay
Rosses Point
65 40

Belmullet
Glenamoy
379 △
R 314 31 12 R 314 17
R 297
Inishcrone
Mountains △ 543 33
Ballysadare

12
R 313
M A Y O
R 315
Ballina/ Béal an Átha
The 20 R 294 R 294
SLIGO 18

Inishkea
Bangor
N 59 Oweniny
Crossmolina
R 294
47 29

BlacksodBay
670 Ballycroy
△ 720
19 R 312
R 316
Conn
Tubbercurry
R 294

Keel
Achill Island
R 319 17
Corraun △ 521
Nephin Beg Range
698
R 312
Nephin 804
R 310
Foxford
25 N 26 25 Charlestown
28

Mulrany 11 N 59
R 317
Pontoon
39 24
Swinford
R 320 15
Ballaghaderreen
R

Newport
17
Castlebar/ Caisleán an Bharraigh
R 310 N 5
Kiltimagh R 322
Frenchpa

C l e w B a y
R 311
18 11
Manulla
R 324 R 323 20
ROS

Clare Island
Westport/ Cathair na Mart
R 330
R 84 18
R 324
N 84 N 5

Louisburgh
14
Croagh 763 Patrick
Ballintubber
R 331
Ballyhaunis
12 N 60
N 5

Inishturk
R 335
66 41
Claremorris
10
22 R 360

Inishbofin
Mweelrea Mts
Murrisk
19
Robe
97 60
R 364

Inishshark
Killary Harbour
817
R 335
681
Lough Mask
Ballinrobe
Clare 22 R 360
B

RinvylePt.
Letterfrack
22
Leenane R 336 9
Kilmaine
R 332 19
Dunmore R 328
Glennama

The Twelve Pins
728
Maumturk Mts
Clonbur 19
R 345
Cong R 334
31
N 17

Clifden
701
N 59 22
Connemara
Lough Corrib
Headford
Tuam/Tuaim
R 332 17

49 79
Maam Cross
N 59
Oughterard 27
N 84
12
N 63 23
Mount Bellew

Slyne Head
R 341
13
R 359

Roundstone
R 340
Gortmore
G A L W A Y
9
Athenry
63 39 R 348

Carna
24
Galway/ Gaillimh
19 17 16 M 6

Lettermullan
Gorumna Island
R 336
Spiddal Barna Oranmore
Craughwell
Loughrea

Inishmore
Kilronan
Dún Aonghasa
Inishmaan
BlackHead
25
Ardrahan
R 350

A r a n   I s l a n d s
Inisheer
R 417
Kinvarra
R 353

Lisdoonvarna
Ballyvaughan
R 67 18
R 480
R 460
16
Gort

Key / Légende / Zeichenerklärung

Roads / Routes / Straßen

Motorway - Service areas	Autoroute - Aires de service	Autobahn - Tankstelle mit Raststätte
Dual carriageway with motorway characteristics	Double chaussée de type autoroutier	Schnellstraße mit getrennten Fahrbahnen
Interchanges: complete, limited	Échangeurs : complet, partiels	Anschlussstellen: Voll - bzw. Teilanschlussstellen
Interchange numbers	Numéros d'échangeurs	Anschlussstellennummern
International and national road network	Route de liaison internationale ou nationale	Internationale bzw.nationale Hauptverkehrsstraße
Interregional and less congested road	Route de liaison interrégionale ou de dégagement	Überregionale Verbindungsstraße oder Umleitungsstrecke
Road surfaced - unsurfaced	Route revêtue - non revêtue	Straße mit Belag - ohne Belag
Footpath - Waymarked footpath / Bridle path	Sentier - Sentier balisé/Allée cavalière	Pfad - Ausgeschilderter Weg / Reitpfad
Motorway / Road under construction	Autoroute - Route en construction	Autobahn - Straße im Bau
(when available: with scheduled opening date)	(le cas échéant : date de mise en service prévue)	(ggf. voraussichtliches Datum der Verkehrsfreigabe)

Road widths / Largeur des routes / Straßenbreiten

Dual carriageway	Chaussées séparées	Getrennte Fahrbahnen
4 lanes - 2 wide lanes	4 voies - 2 voies larges	4 Fahrspuren - 2 breite Fahrspuren
2 lanes - 2 narrow lanes	2 voies - 2 voies étroites	2 Fahrspuren - 1 Fahrspur

Distances (total and intermediate) / Distances (totalisées et partielles) / Entfernungen (Gesamt- und Teilentfernungen)

Toll roads on motorway	Section à péage sur autoroute	Mautstrecke auf der Autobahn
Toll-free section on motorway	Section libre sur autoroute	Mautfreie Strecke auf der Autobahn
in miles - en kilometers	en miles - en kilomètres	in Meilen - in Kilometern
on road	sur route	Auf der Straße

Numbering - Signs / Numérotation - Signalisation / Nummerierung - Wegweisung

Motorway - GB: Primary route	Autoroute - GB : itinéraire principal (Primary route)	Autobahn - GB: Empfohlene Fernverkehrsstraße (Primary route)
IRL : National primary and secondary route	IRL : itinéraire principal (National primary et secondary route)	IRL: Empfohlene Fernverkehrsstraße (National primary und secondary route)
Other roads	Autres routes	Sonstige Straßen
Destination on primary route network	Localités jalonnant les itinéraires principaux	Richtungshinweis auf der empfohlenen Fernverkehrsstraße

M 5   A 38
N 20   N 31
A 190 B 629 R 561
YORK

Obstacles / Obstacles / Verkehrshindernisse

Roundabout - Pass and its height above sea level (meters)	Rond-point - Col et sa cote d'altitude (en mètres)	Verkehrsinsel - Pass mit Höhenangabe (in Meter)
Steep hill (ascent in direction of the arrow)	Forte déclivité (flèches dans le sens de la montée)	Starke Steigung (Steigung in Pfeilrichtung)
IRL: Difficult or dangerous section of road	IRL : Parcours difficile ou dangereux	IRL: Schwierige oder gefährliche Strecke
In Scotland: narrow road with passing places	En Écosse : route très étroite avec emplacements pour croisement	In Schottland: sehr schmale Straße mit Ausweichstellen (passing places)
Level crossing: railway passing, under road, over road	Passages de la route : à niveau, supérieur, inférieur	Bahnübergänge: schienengleich, Unterführung, Überführung
Prohibited road - Road subject to restrictions	Route interdite - Route réglementée	Gesperrte Straße - Straße mit Verkehrsbeschränkungen
Toll barrier - One way road (on major and regional roads)	Barrière de péage - Route à sens unique	Mautstelle - Einbahnstraße
Height limit under 15'6'' IRL, 16'6'' GB	Hauteur limitée au dessous de 15'6'' IRL, 16'6''GB	Beschränkung der Durchfahrtshöhe bis 15'6'' IRL, 16'6' GB
Load limit (under 16 t.)	Limites de charge (au-dessous de 16 t.)	Höchstbelastung (angegeben, wenn unter 16 t)

7-12%   +12%

Transportation / Transports / Verkehrsmittel

Railway - Passenger station	Voie ferrée - Gare	Bahnlinie - Bahnhof
Airport - Airfield	Aéroport - Aérodrome	Flughafen - Flugplatz
Transportation of vehicles: (seasonal services in red)	Transport des autos: (liaison saisonnière en rouge)	Autotransport: (rotes Zeichen: saisonbedingte Verbindung)
by hovercraft - by boat	par aéroglisseur - par bateau	per Hovercraft - per Schiff
by ferry (load limit in tons)	par bac (charge maximum en tonnes)	per Fähre (Höchstbelastung in t)
Ferry (passengers and cycles only)	Bac pour piétons et cycles	Fähre für Personen und Fahrräder

Accommodation - Administration / Hébergement - Administration / Unterkunft - Verwaltung

Administrative boundaries	Limites administratives	Verwaltungshauptstadt
Scottish and Welsh borders	Limite de l'Écosse et du Pays de Galles	Grenze von Schottland und Wales
National boundary - Customs post	Frontière - Douane	Staatsgrenze - Zoll

Sport & Recreation Facilities / Sports - Loisirs / Sport - Freizeit

Golf course - Horse racetrack	Golf - Hippodrome	Golfplatz - Pferderennbahn
Racing circuit - Pleasure boat harbour	Circuit automobile - Port de plaisance	Rennstrecke - Yachthafen
Caravan and camping sites	Camping, caravaning	Campingplatz
Waymarked footpath - Country park	Sentier balisé - Base ou parc de loisirs	Ausgeschilderter Weg - Freizeitanlage
Safari park, zoo - Bird sanctuary, refuge	Parc animalier, zoo - Réserve d'oiseaux	Tierpark, Zoo - Vogelschutzgebiet
IRL: Fishing - Greyhound track	IRL : Pêche - Cynodrome	IRL: Angeln - Windhundrennen
Tourist train	Train touristique	Museumseisenbahn
Funicular, cable car, chairlift	Funiculaire, téléphérique, télésiège	Standseilbahn, Seilbahn, Sessellift

Sights / Curiosités / Sehenswürdigkeiten

Principal sights:	Principales curiosités :	Hauptsehenswürdigkeiten:
see THE GREEN GUIDE	voir LE GUIDE VERT	siehe GRÜNER REISEFÜHRER
Towns or places of interest, Places to stay	Localités ou sites intéressants, lieux de séjour	Sehenswerte Orte, Ferienorte
Religious building - Historic house, castle	Édifice religieux - Château	Sakral-Bau - Schloss, Burg
Ruins - Prehistoric monument - Cave	Ruines - Monument mégalithique - Grotte	Ruine - Vorgeschichtliches Steindenkmal - Höhle
Garden, park - Other places of interest	Jardin, parc - Autres curiosités	Garten, Park - Sonstige Sehenswürdigkeit
IRL: Fort - Celtic cross - Round Tower	IRL : Fort - Croix celte - Tour ronde	IRL: Fort, Festung - Keltisches Kreuz - Rundturm
Panoramic view - Viewpoint - Scenic route	Panorama - Point de vue - Parcours pittoresque	Rundblick - Aussichtspunkt - Landschaftlich schöne Strecke

Rye   (▲)
Ergol

Other signs / Signes divers / Sonstige Zeichen

Industrial cable way	Transporteur industriel aérien	Industrieschwebebahn
Telecommunications tower or mast - Lighthouse	Tour ou pylône de télécommunications - Phare	Funk-, Sendeturm - Leuchtturm
Power station - Quarry	Centrale électrique - Carrière	Kraftwerk - Steinbruch
Mine - Industrial activity	Mine - Industries	Bergwerk - Industrieanlagen
Refinery - Cliff	Raffinerie - Falaise	Raffinerie - Klippen
National forest park - National park	Parc forestier national - Parc national	Waldschutzgebiet - Nationalpark

KEELE

Verklaring van de tekens | Legenda | Signos convencionales

Wegen | Strade | Carreteras

KEELE

Verklaring van de tekens	Legenda	Signos convencionales
Autosnelweg - Serviceplaatsen	Autostrada - Aree di servizio	Autopista - Áreas de servicio
Gescheiden rijbanen van het type autosnelweg	Doppia carreggiata di tipo autostradale	Autovía
Aansluitingen: volledig, gedeeltelijk	Svincoli: completo, parziale	Enlaces: completo, parciales
Afritnummers	Svincoli numerati	Números de los accesos
Internationale of nationale verbindingsweg	Strada di collegamento internazionale o nazionale	Carretera de comunicación internacional o nacional
Interregionale verbindingsweg	Strada di collegamento interregionale o di disimpegno	Carretera de comunicación interregional o alternativo
Verharde weg - Onverharde weg	Strada rivestita - non rivestita	Carretera asfaltada - sin asfaltar
Pad - Bewegwijzerd wandelpad / Ruiterpad	Sentiero - Sentiero segnalato / Pista per cavalli	Sendero - Sendero señalizado / Camino de caballos
Autosnelweg in aanleg - weg in aanleg	Autostrada, strada in costruzione	Autopista, carretera en construcción
(indien bekend: datum openstelling)	(data di apertura prevista)	(en su caso: fecha prevista de entrada en servicio)

Breedte van de wegen | Larghezza delle strade | Ancho de las carreteras

Gescheiden rijbanen	Carreggiate separate	Calzadas separadas
4 rijstroken - 2 brede rijstroken	4 corsie - 2 corsie larghe	Cuatro carriles - Dos carriles anchos
2 rijstroken - 2 smalle rijstroken	2 corsie - 2 corsie strette	Dos carriles - Dos carriles estrechos

Afstanden (totaal en gedeeltelijk) | Distanze (totali e parziali) | Distancias (totales y parciales)

24 39   14 10

Gedeelte met tol op autosnelweg	Tratto a pedaggio su autostrada	Tramo de peaje en autopista
Tolvrij gedeelte op autosnelwegen	Tratto esente da pedaggio su autostrada	Tramo libre en autopista
in mijlen - in kilometers	in migla - in chilometri	en millas - en kilómetros
op andere wegen	su strada	en carretera

Wegnummers - Bewegwijzering | Numerazione - Segnaletica | Numeración - Señalización

M 5 A 38 N 20 N 31 A 190 B 629 R 561 YORK

Autosnelweg - GB: Hoofdweg (Primary route)	Autostrada - GB: itinerario principale (Strada «Primary»)	Autopista - GB: Vía principal (Primary route)
IRL: Hoofdweg (National primary en secondary route)	IRL: itinerario principale (Strada «National primary» e «Secondary»)	IRL: Vía principal (National primary et secondary route)
Andere wegen	Altre Strade	Otras carreteras
Plaatsen langs een autosnelweg of Primary route met bewegwijzering	Località delimitante gli itinerari principali	Localidad en itinerario principal

Hindernissen | Ostacoli | Obstáculos

7-12%   +12%   11'9

Rotonde - Bergpas en hoogte boven de zeespiegel (in meters)	Rotonda - Passo ed altitudine (in metri)	Rotonda - Puerto y su altitud (en métros)
Steile helling (pijlen in de richting van de helling)	Forte pendenza (salita nel senso della freccia)	Pendiente Pronunciada (las flechas indican el sentido del ascenso)
IRL: Moeilijk of gevaarlijk traject	IRL: Percorso difficile o pericoloso	IRL: Recorrido difícil o peligroso
In Schotland: smalle weg met uitwijkplaatsen	In Scozia: Strada molto stretta con incrocio	En escocia: carretera muy estrecha con ensanchamientos para poder cruzarse
Wegovergangen: gelijkvloers, overheen, onderdoor	Passaggi della strada: a livello, cavalcavia, sottopassaggio	Pasos de la carretera: a nivel, superior, inferior
Verboden weg - Beperkt opengestelde weg	Strada vietata - Strada a circolazione regolamentata	Tramo prohibido - Carretera restringida
Tol - Weg met eenrichtingsverkeer	Casello - Strada a senso unico (su collegamenti principali e regionali)	Barrera de peaje - Carretera de sentido único
Vrije hoogte indien lager dan 15' 6'' IRL, 16'6'' GB	Limite di altezza inferiore a 15'6'' IRL, 16'6''GB	Altura limitada (15'6'' IRL, 16'6''GB)

10

Maximum draagvermogen (indien minder dan 16 t)	Limite di portata (inferiore a 16 t.)	Limite de carga (inferior a 16 t)

Vervoer | Trasporti | Transportes

15

Spoorweg - Reizigersstation	Ferrovia - Stazione viaggiatori	Linea férrea - Estación de viajeros
Luchthaven - Vliegveld	Aeroporto - Aerodromo	Aeropuerto - Aeródromo
Vervoer van auto's: (tijdens het seizoen: rood teken)	Trasporto auto: (stagionale in rosso)	Transporte de coches: (Enlace de temporada: signo rojo)
per hovercraft - per boot	su idrovolante - su traghetto	por overcraft - por barco
per veerpont (maximum draagvermogen in t.)	su chiatta (carico massimo in t.)	por barcaza (carga máxima en toneladas)
Veerpont voor voetgangers en fietsers	Traghetto per pedoni e biciclette	Barcaza para el paso de peatones y vehículos dos ruedas

Verblijf - Administratie | Risorse alberghiere - Amministrazione | Alojamiento - Administración

Administratieve grenzen	Confini amministrativi	Limites administrativos
Grens van Schotland en Wales	Confine di Scozia e Galles	Limites de Escocia y del País de Gales
Staatsgrens - Douanekantoor	Frontiera - Dogana	Frontera - Puesto de aduanas

Sport - Recreatie | Sport - Divertimento | Deportes - Ocio

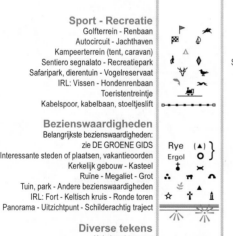

Golfterrein - Renbaan	Golf - Ippodromo	Golf - Hipódromo
Autocircuit - Jachthaven	Circuito Automobilistico - Porto turistico	Circuito de velocidad - Puerto deportivo
Kampeerterrein (tent, caravan)	Campeggi, caravaning	Camping, caravaning
Sentiero segnalato - Recreatiepark	Sentiero segnalato - Area o parco per attività ricreative	Sendero señalizado - Parque de ocio
Safaripark, dierentuin - Vogelreservaat	Parco con animali, zoo - Riserva ornitologica	Reserva de animales, zoo - Reserva de pájaros
IRL: Vissen - Hondenrenbaan	IRL: Pesca - Cinodromo	IRL: Pêche - Cynodrome
Toeristentreintje	Trenino turistico	Tren turístico
Kabelspoor, kabelbaan, stoeltjeslift	Funicolare, funivia, seggiovia	Funicular, Teleférico, telesilla

Bezienswaardigheden | Mete e luoghi d'interesse | Curiosidades

Rye (▲)   Ergol O

Belangrijkste bezienswaardigheden, zie DE GROENE GIDS	Principali luoghi d'interesse, vedere LA GUIDA VERDE	Principales curiosidades: ver LA GUÍA VERDE
Interessante steden of plaatsen, vakantieoorden	Località o siti interessanti, luoghi di soggiorno	Localidad o lugar interesante, lugar para quedarse
Kerkelijk gebouw - Kasteel	Edificio religioso - Castello	Edificio religioso - Castillo
Ruïne - Megaliet - Grot	Rovine - Monumento megalitico - Grotta	Ruinas - Monumento megalítico - Cueva
Tuin, park - Andere bezienswaardigheden	Giardino, parco - Altri luoghi d'interesse	Jardín, parque - Curiosidades diversas
IRL: Fort - Keltisch kruis - Ronde toren	IRL: Forte - Croce celtica - Torre rotonda	IRL: Fortaleza - Cruz celta - Torre redonda
Panorama - Uitzichtpunt - Schilderachtig traject	Panorama - Vista - Percorso pittoresco	Vista panorámica - Vista parcial - Recorrido pintoresco

Diverse tekens | Simboli vari | Signos diversos

Kabelvrachtvervoer	Teleferica industriale	Transportador industrial aéreo
Telecommunicatietoren of -mast - Vuurtoren	Torre o pilone per telecomunicazioni - Faro	Emisor de Radiodifusión - Faro
Elektriciteitscentrale - Steengroeve	Centrale elettrica - Cava	Central eléctrica - Cantera
Mijn - Industrie	Miniera - Industrie	Mina - Industrias
Raffinaderij - Klif	Raffineria - Falesia	Refinería - Acantilado
Staatsbos - Nationaal park	Parco forestale nazionale - Parco nazionale	Parque forestal nacional - Parque nacional

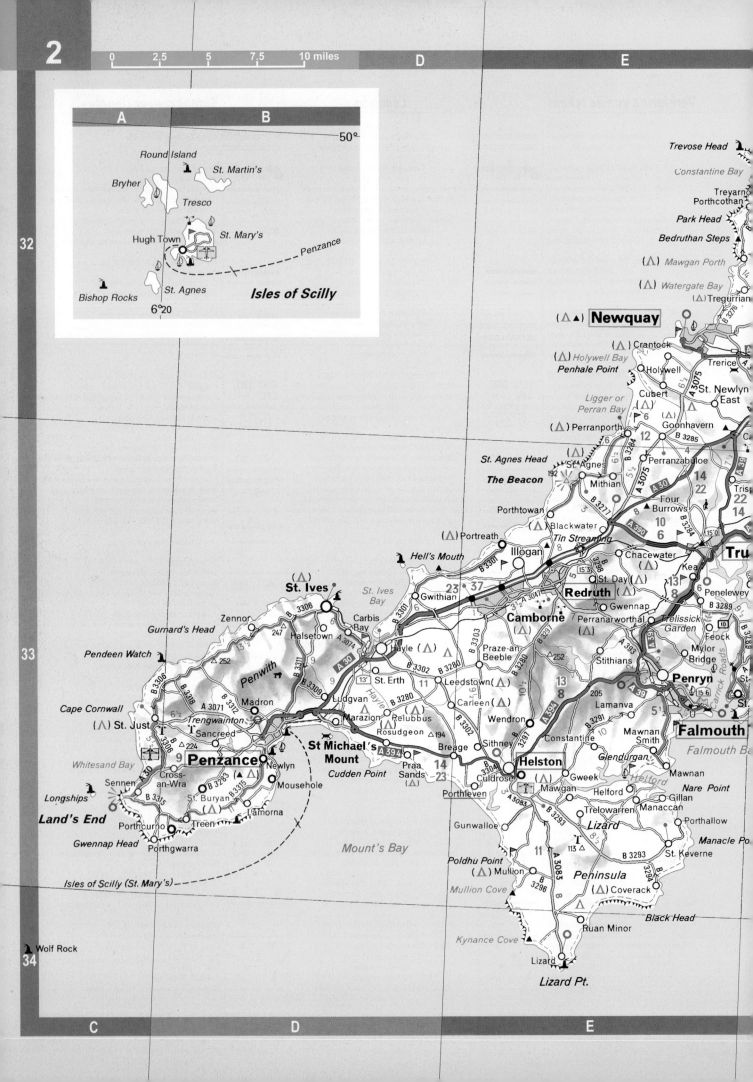

0 2.5 5 7.5 10 miles

D

E

Isles of Scilly

50°

A   B

Round Island

St. Martin's

Bryher

Tresco

Hugh Town   *St. Mary's*

Penzance

St. Agnes

Bishop Rocks

6°20

32

Trevose Head

Constantine Bay

Treyarnon
Porthcothan

Park Head

Bedruthan Steps

(Λ) *Mawgan Porth*

(Λ) *Watergate Bay*

(Λ) Tregurrian

(Λ▲) **Newquay**

(Λ) Crantock

(Λ) *Holywell Bay*   Holywell

Penhale Point

Trerice

St. Newlyn
East

Cubert

A 3075

*Ligger or
Perran Bay*

6½

6

(Λ)

Goonhavern

(Λ) Perranporth

B 3285

12

B 3284

Perranzabuloe

St. Agnes Head

St. Agnes

4

A 30

14

22

The Beacon

192

Mithian

A 3075

B 3277

Four
Burrows

22

14

10

A 390

6

B 3284

15·0

Tri

Porthtowan

3

Blackwater

Tin Streaming

(Λ) Portreath

Illogan

B 330

B 3298

15·3

St. Day

(Λ)

Chacewater

Kea

Tru

Hell's Mouth

23   37

Gwithian

A 3047

Redruth

5

(Λ)

13

8

*St. Ives
Bay*

B 330

6

Gwennap

Camborne

Perranarworthal

8

Penelewey

B 3289

St. Ives

Carbis
Bay

(Λ)

*Trelissick
Garden*

10

Feock

Zennor

B 3306

6

Hayle (Λ) Λ

B 3303

Praze-an-
Beeble

(Λ)

Stithians

252

Mylor
Bridge

Gurnard's Head

Halsetown

247

A 3074

St. Erth

B 3302 B 3280

13

A 393

Penryn

Pendeen Watch

B 3311

13'

11

Leedstown (Λ)

8

205

Lamanva

15 6

Carrick Roads

St

Penwith

B 3309

9

9½

Carleen (Λ)

A 394

Constantine

5½

0

A 3071

252

13

Mawnan
Smith

Falmouth

Cape Cornwall

Madron

Ludgvan

Hayle

Wendron

A 3291

10

Falmouth Ba

(Λ) St. Just

B 3312

Marazion

(Λ)

194

B 3302

Sithney

Glendurgan

6½

B
3306

A 224

Trengwainton

Relubbus

Breage

B 3297

Mawnan

Whitesand Bay

Sancreed

Rosudgeon

194

Helford

9

Penzance

Newlyn

14

Helston

Gweek

Nare Point

Sennen

Cross-
an-Wra

B 3283 B 3315

Praa
Sands

A 394

23

Culdrose

(Λ)

Mawgan

Gillan

Helford

Longships

St. Buryan

Mousehole

Cudden Point

(Λ)

Porthleven

A 3083

Trelowarren

Manaccan

Land's End

Porthcurno

Treen

Lamorna

(Λ)

Gunwalloe

Lizard

B 3293

Porthallow

Gwennap Head

Porthgwarra

113

St. Keverne

Manacle Po

Mount's Bay

11

A 3083

B 3293

Isles of Scilly (St. Mary's)

Poldhu Point

(Λ) Mullion

Peninsula

(Λ) Coverack

8½

Mullion Cove

B
3296

Black Head

Kynance Cove

Ruan Minor

Wolf Rock

34

Lizard

Lizard Pt.

C   D   E

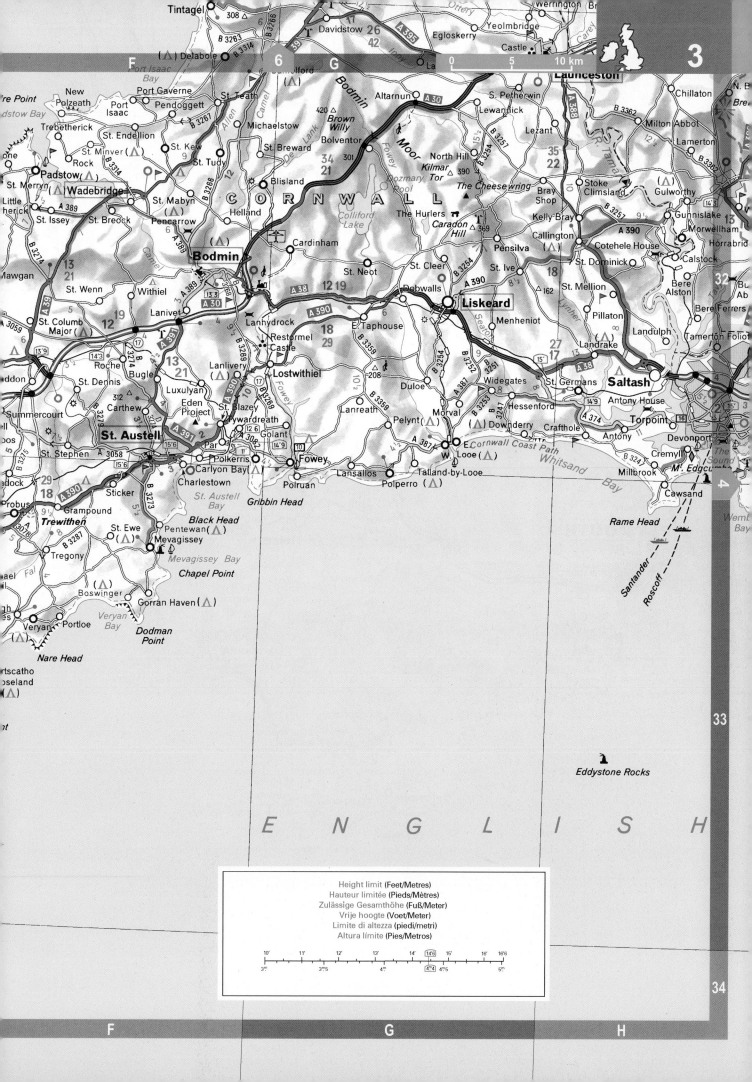

Weston
Feniton
Honiton
Fenny
Bridges
Cadhay
Ottery
St. Mary
Tipton
St. John
Sidbury
Sidford
Northleigh
Farway
Colyton
Colyford
Seaton
Axmouth
Rousdon
Branscombe
Beer
Salcombe Regis
Sidmouth (Λ)
Beer Head
Otterton
Budleigh
dleigh
lterton
Ladram Bay

Wilmington
Kilmington
Musbury
Uplyme
Axminster
Hawkchurch (Λ)
Marshwood
Charmouth
Chideock
Lyme Regis
West Bay
Burton Bradstock
S. Devon Coast Path

Parnham
Hooke
Netherbury
Symondsbury
Bradpole
Bridport
Askerswell
Winterbourne
Abbas
Swyre
West Bexington
Toller
Frampton
Stratton
Wolfeton
Charm

Litton
Cheney
Long
Bredy
Winterbourne
Steepletone
Martinstown
Hardy
Monument
Portesham
Abbotsbury
Swannery
Maiden
Castle
Broadwey
Chickerell

Chesil Beach (▲)

West Bay
Isle of Portland

Lyme Bay

N E L

CHANNEL ISLANDS

GUERNSEY
Pembroke Bay
l'Ancresse
Grand Havre
Vale
St Sampson
Cobo Bay
Castel
Vazon Bay
Belle Grève Bay
Herm
Lihou
Rocquaine Bay
St Saviour
St Peter-Port
Jethou
SARK
les Hanois
St Peter-in-the-Wood
St Martin
Forest
Fermain Bay
Grand la Seigneurie
Brecqhou
la Coupée
Icart Point
Jerbourg Pt
Little Sark

ALDERNEY
Renonpuet
Burhou
Swinge
Clonque Bay
Braye
The
Longy Bay
St Anne
Telegraph Bay

JERSEY
Grève de Lecq
Devil's Hole
Grosnez Pt
Bonne Nuit Bay
Bouley Bay
St John
Rozel
St Mary
Trinity
l'Etacq
St Lawrence
St Martin
St Peter
St Ouen's Bay
St Saviour
St Catherine's Bay
la Pulente
St Aubin
Grouville
Gorey
Corbière Pt
St Brelade
St Aubin's Bay
St Helier
St Clement
La Rocque
Noirmont Pt
Green Island
Royal Bay of Grouville

Weymouth
Poole
Portsmouth
Alderney
Herm
Sark
Guernsey
Cherbourg-Octeville
Jersey
St Malo

K *L* *M*

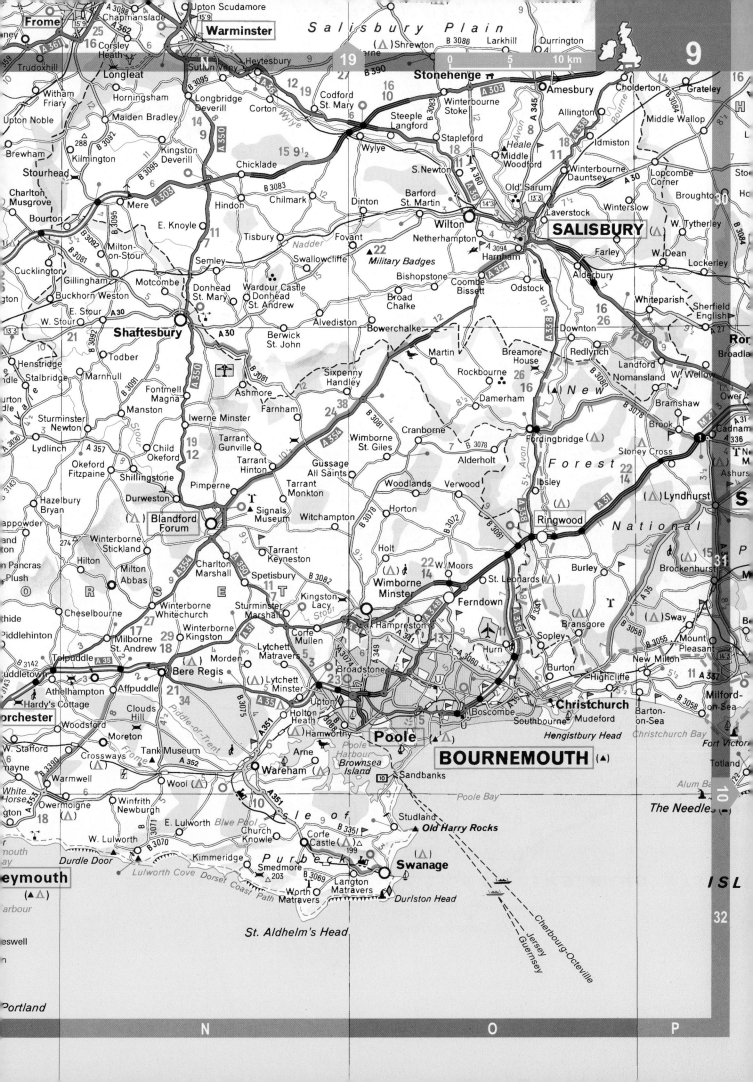

0   2.5   5   7.5   10 miles

Rosslare

Pembrokeshire Coast

Dinas Head

Strumble Head (▲)

213 △
Goodwick
Fishguard Bay
Bryn-Henllan
Dinas

St. Nicholas

Llanychaer

Fishguard

Ynysdeullyn
Abercastle
Mathry
Trecwn

Penclegyr
Trevine
Porthgain
Croes-goch
B 4331
Letterston
Punches
334

Abereiddy

St. David's Head (▲)

181 △ Carn Llidi
Bishop's Palace
Whitesand Bay
Bishops and Clerks
Ramsey Island
Ramsey Sound
St. David's
Tyddewi (△)
Solva
Newgale

P E M B R O K E
Llandeloy
Hayscastle
Wolf's Castle
Spittal
Scolton
51

Welsh Hook
15
24

Camrose
Rudbaxton
Wi

16
B 4330
A 487

A 40

St. Bride's Bay

Pembrokeshire Coast Path

Haverfordw
Hwlffordd
National P

Broad Haven (△)

Lit. Haven

B 4341
B 4327
13
10

The Smalls

Grassholme I.

Skomer Island (▲)
Martin's Haven

Broad Sound

St. Brides
St. Ishmael's
Marloes
Herbrandston
Steynton
Johnston
Rosemarket
Llangwm
Lawre

Skokholm Island (▲)

Dale

Milford Haven
Aberdaugleddau
Neyland

St. Ann's Head (▲)

Thorn I.
Angle

Pembroke Dock
Doc Penfro
Rhoscrowther
Pembroke
Penfro
Hundleton
Lamphey

Rosslare

Freshwater West
B 4319
Castlemartin
12

Linney Head
National Park
Stackpole
Bosherston
Stackpo

Stack Rocks
St. Govan Head (▲)

P e m b r o k e s h i r e

Brecon Beac

National Botanic Garden

Llandeilo

Llangathen

Trapp

Castle

Black Mountain Fore

Dan-yr-Ogof
Craig-y-nos

National Park

Cwm Taf
Pontsticill Resr.
Trefil

Merthyr Tydfil

Tredeg

Glanaman
Brynamman
Cwmllynfell
Abercraf (△)

Ammanford
Rhydaman
Gwaun-Cae-Gurwen
Ystradgynlais
Onllwyn
Penderyn
Garwnant
Forestry Commission Visitor Centre
Pontsticill

Trebel

Pontarddulais
Felindre
Clydach
Gurnos
Ystalyfera
Seven Sisters
Pontneddfechan
Glyn-neath
Hirwaun
Cefn-Coed-y-cymmer

Rhymney

SWANSEA

Pontardawe
Cilybebyll
Rhos
Crynant
Resolven

Vale of Neath
RHONDDA
Rhigos
Blaengwrach
A 4059
Aberdare
Aberdâr

Troedyrhiw
Merthy Vale

Gorseinon

Clydach
Sgiwen

Tonna
Glyncorrwg
Tynewydd
Treherbert
Maerdy
Cwmbach
Aberaman
Cwmaman
Mountain Ash
Aberpennar

Morriston

Neath   Castell-nedd
Cymmer
Abergwynfi
Treorchy
Rhondda
Abercynon
Nelson

Gowerton
Killay
Briton Ferry
Cwmafan
Afan Argoed
Nantyffyllon
Caerau
Nant-y-moel
Clydach Vale
Tylorstown
Ynysybwl

Three Crosses
Bishopston
Taibach
Maesteg
Blaengarw
Cymer Forest
Pontycymer
Ogmore Vale
Gilfach Goch
Tonypandy
Porth
Cymmer
Tonyrefail

SWANSEA
ABERTAWE

Margam
Margam Park
Llangynwyd
Llangeinor
BRIDGEND
Pontypridd
Beddau

The Mumbles
Port Talbot

Swansea Bay
Tondu
Bryncethin
Llanharan
Talbot Green
Llantrisant

Mumbles Head (▲)

Aberkenfig
Pencoed
Pontyclun
Llanharry
Miskin
Pentyrch

Kenfig
Pyle
Bridgend
Pen-y-bont
Coychurch

Nottage
Laleston
Ystradowen
Hensol
St-Brides-Super-Ely
Pendoylan
St. Nicholas

Porthcawl
(△)
Tythegston
Ewenny
Colwinston
Llysworney
Cowbridge
Bont-faen
Beaupre Castle
Bonvilston
Wenvoe

Ogmore-by-Sea
St. Brides Major
Llandow
Wick
Llantwit Major

Tusker Rock

Nash Point

GLAMORGAN
Eglwys Brewis
Penmark
St. Athan

St. Donats
East-Aberthaw
Rhoose
Porthkerry
CARDIFF AIRPORT

Breaksea Point

CHANNEL

Foreland Point

Lynton
Lynmouth
Somerset and N. Devon Coast Path

B 30

Woody Bay
Heddon's Mouth
Valley of the Rocks
Watersmeet
Culbone
Porlock Weir
Allerford
Selworthy
Minehead (△)

Berrynarbor
Combe Martin
Hunter's Inn
Parracombe
Oare
Doone Valley
Porlock
Luccombe
Dunster

Chambercombe
Exmoor Forest
Wootton Courtenay
Timbercombe
Watchet

W. Down (△)
Exmoor National Park

Arlington Court
Bratton Fleming
Challacombe
Simonsbath
Dunkery Beacon
Wheddon Cross
Bilbrook
Cleeve Abbey
Monksilver

Muddiford
Washford
Williton
W. Quanto

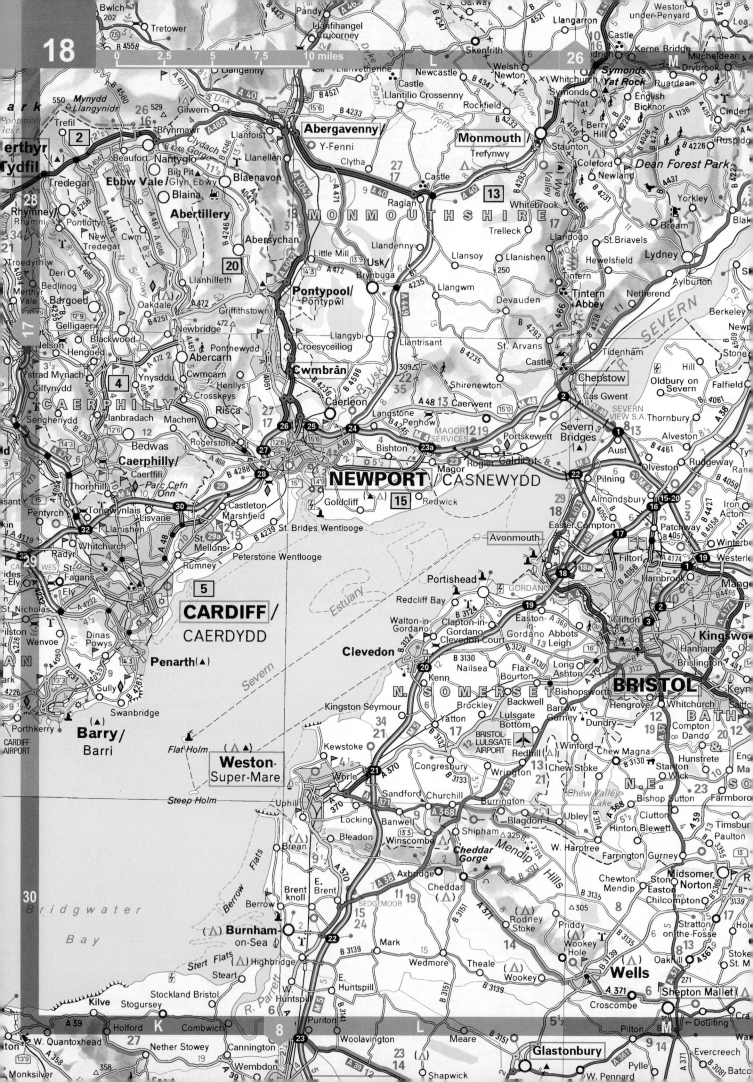

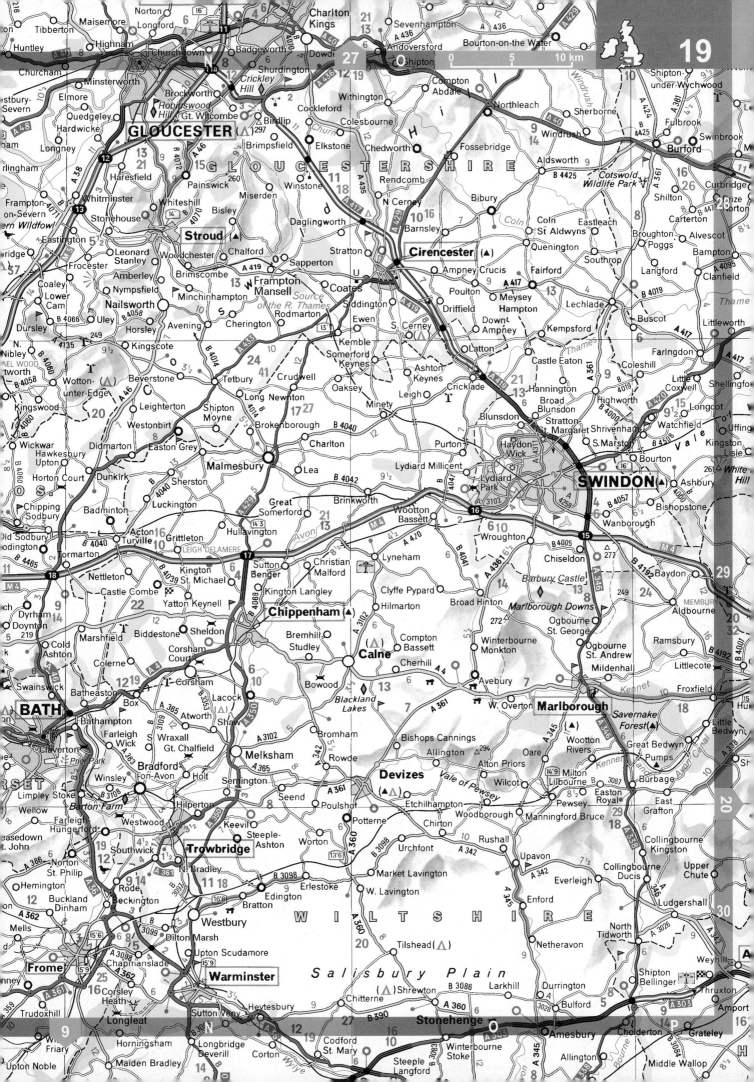

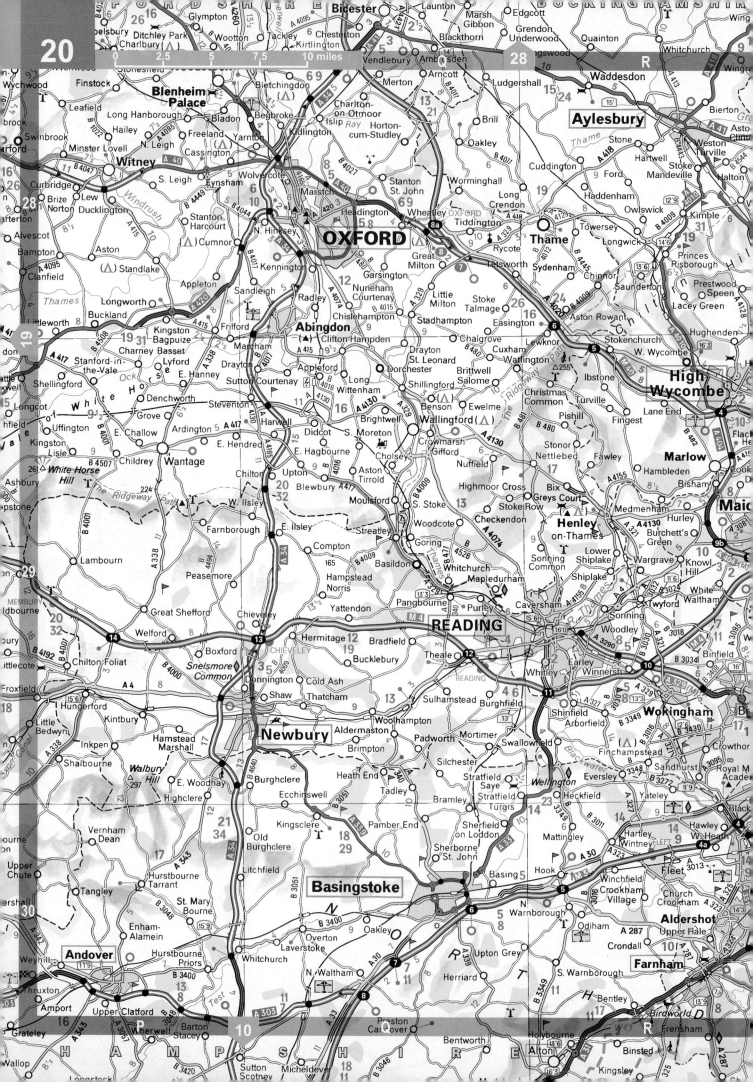

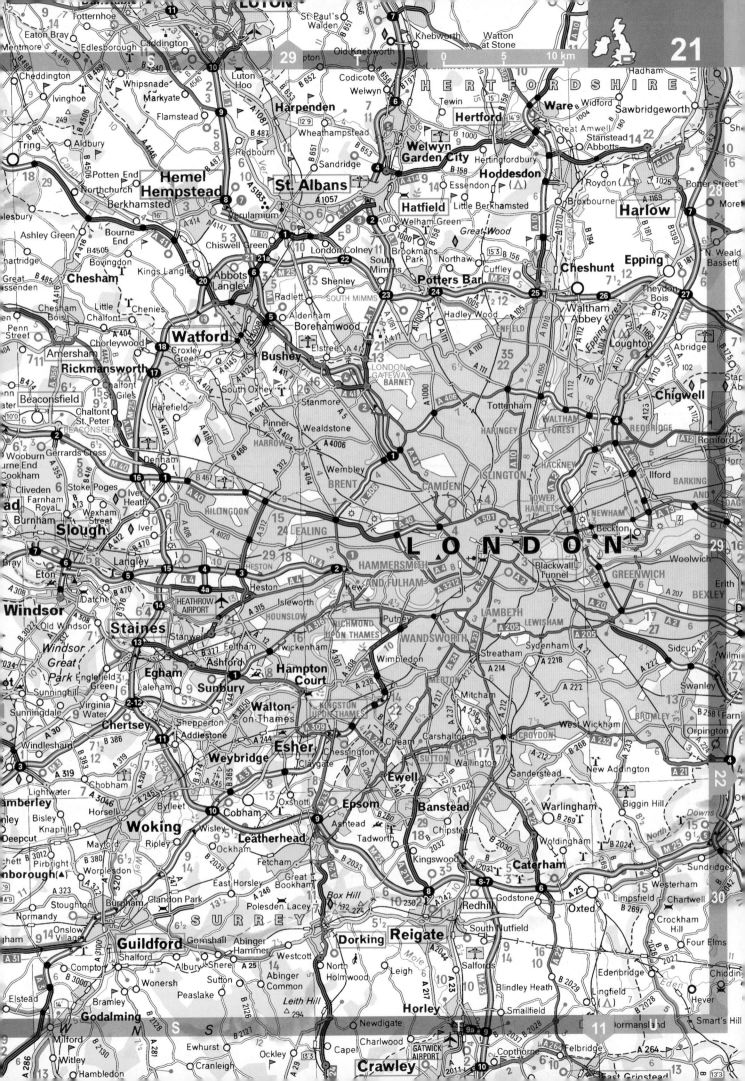

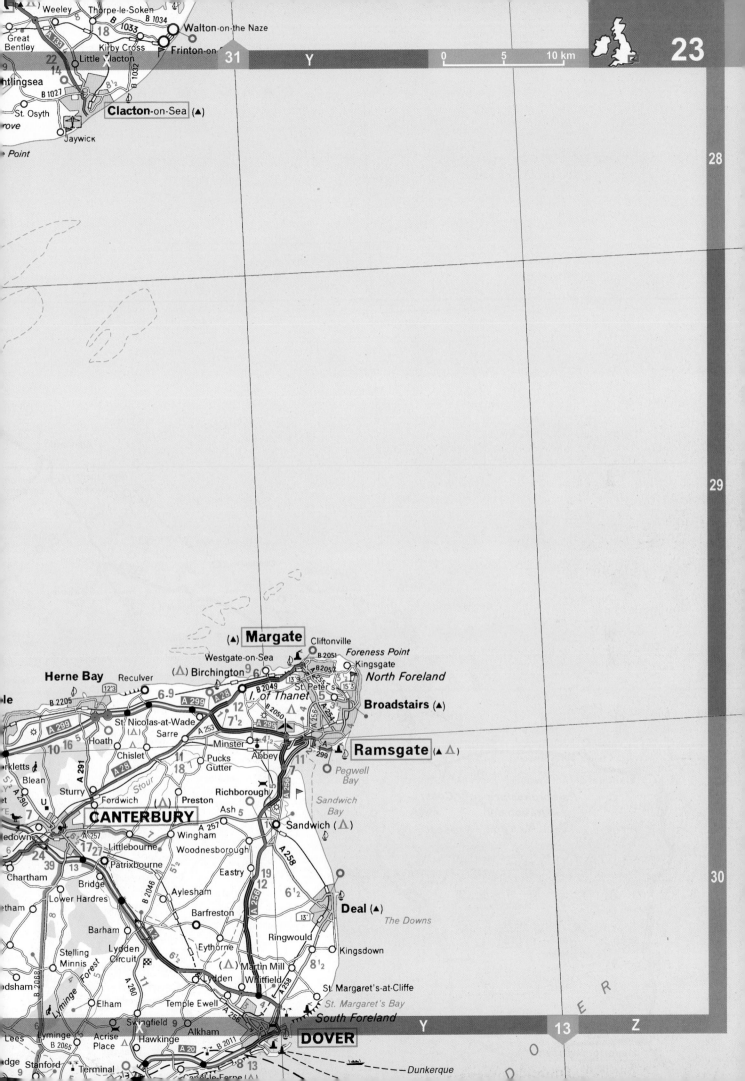

28

29

Weeley
Thorpe-le-Soken
Walton-on-the Naze
B 1034
B 1033
18
Kirby Cross
Frinton-on-
Great Bentley
22
14
Little Clacton
B 1033
Clacton-on-Sea (▲)
thlingsea
St. Osyth
B 1027
rove
Jaywick
Point

(▲) **Margate**   Cliftonville
Westgate-on-Sea   *Foreness Point*
B 2051
Birchington 9 6   B 205? Kingsgate
Herne Bay Reculver (△)   *North Foreland*
B 2205   12·3   13·9   St. Peter's   15·3
rkletts 6·9 A 299 A 28 St. Nicolas-at-Wade *I. of Thanet* 5 **Broadstairs** (▲)
le   B 2205   B 2049
10 16 5   Hoath   (△) A 253 Sarre   B 2050   4
Chislet   11   Minster 4½   **Ramsgate** (▲ △)
Blean   A 28   18 1   Pucks   Abbey   11   A 299
Sturry   Gutter   7   *Pegwell Bay*
A 291   Richborough   A 256
Fordwich (△) Preston   *Sandwich Bay*
CANTERBURY   Ash 5
A 257   Wingham   Sandwich (△)
ledown   A 257   7   Littlebourne Woodnesborough
24   17 27   Patrixbourne   A 258
39   13   Bridge   Eastry   19
Chartham   B 2046   5½   12
tham   Lower Hardres   Aylesham   6½
Barham   Barfreston   13'   **Deal** (▲)
Stelling Minnis   Lydden   Eythorne   *The Downs*
Circuit   Ringwould
dsham   B 2068   Lydden Whitfield   Kingsdown
Elham   (△) Martin Mill   8½   A 258
Temple Ewell   A 256
Lees   Lymige   Skingfield 9   Alkham   *St. Margaret's at-Cliffe*
B 2065   Acrise Place   Hawkinge   B 2011   *St. Margaret's Bay*
dge   Stanford   A 20   *South Foreland*
9   Terminal   **DOVER**   — Dunkerque

13

30

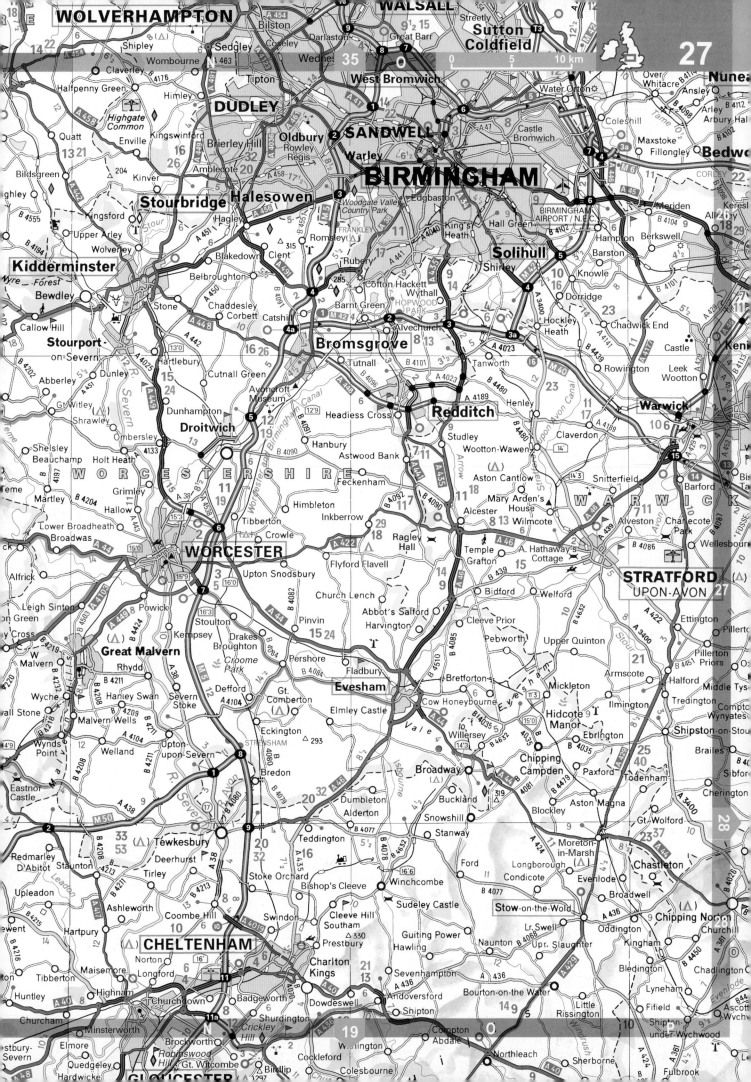

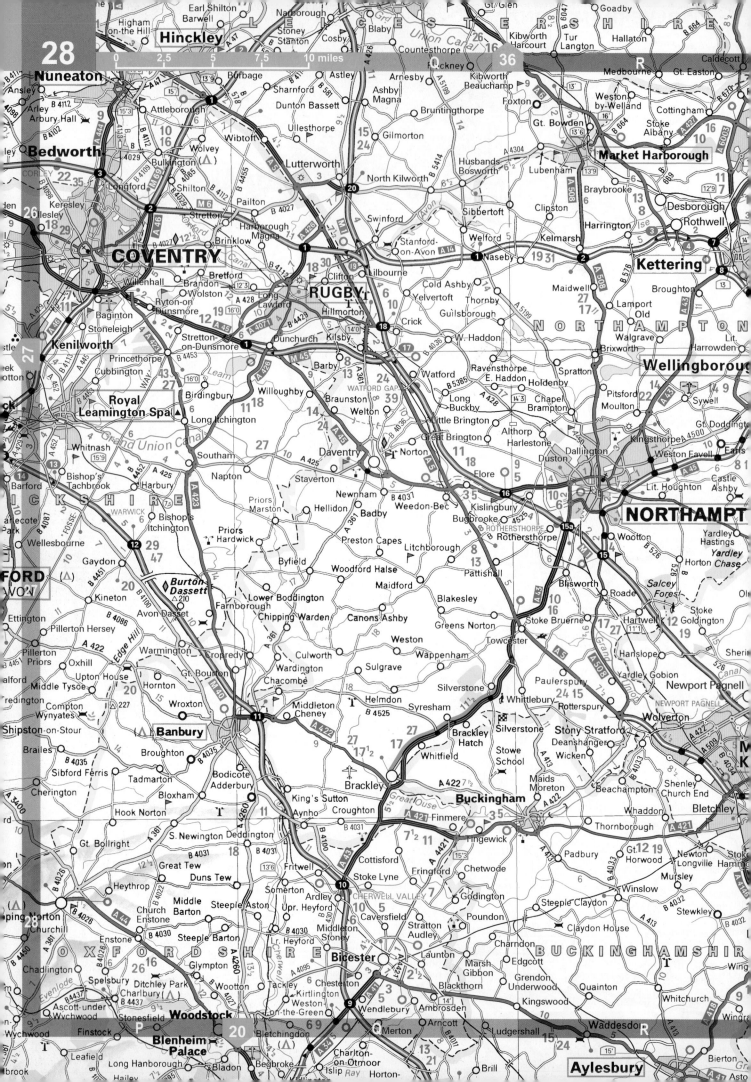

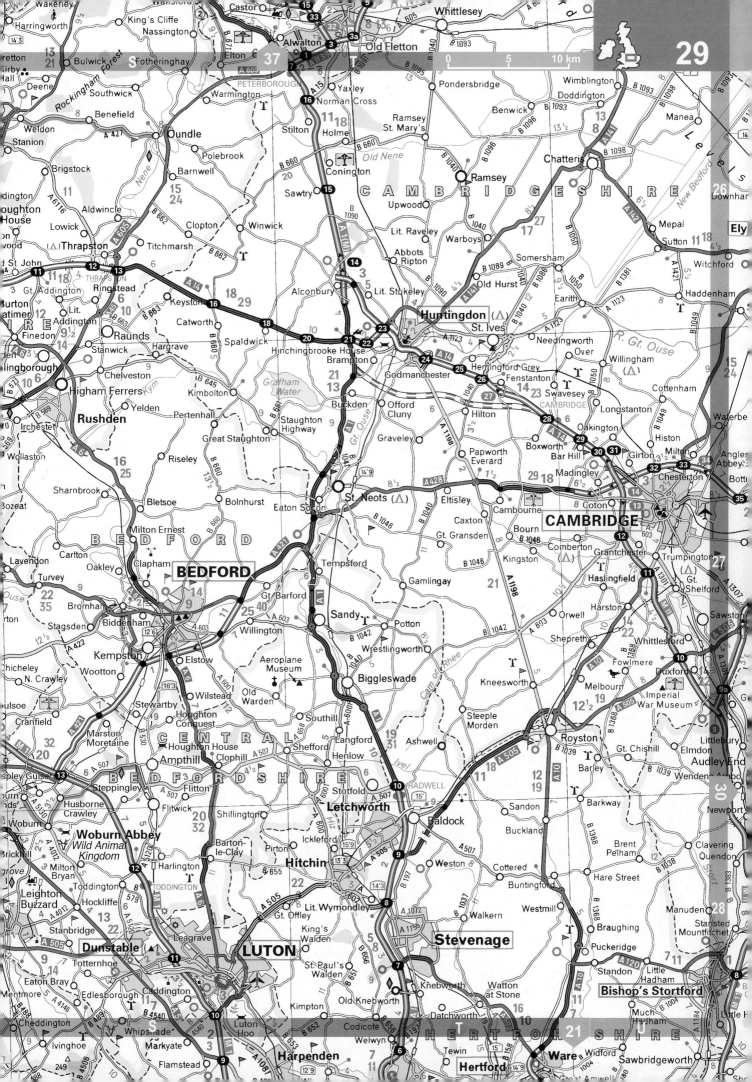

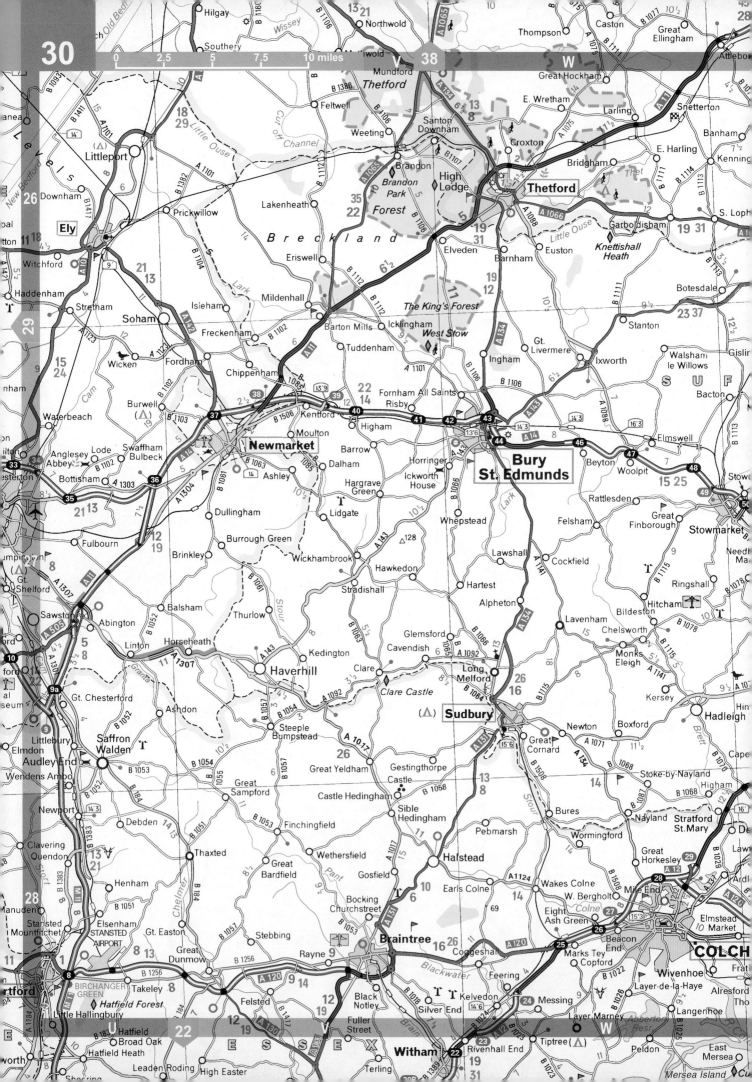

Shoteham
Ashwellthorpe
Flotman
Saxlingham Nethergate
Seething
Hales
Blundeston
B 1385
B 1074

Y
39
X
A 140
B 1135
Hempnall
Long Stratton
Ditchingham
Ellingham
Gillingham
Barsham
Beccles
Lowestoft (▲)
Pakefield

Aslacton
Shelton
(△) Bungay
Earsham
A 1116
A 144
21
9
Carlton Colville
A 12

Winfarthing
Pulham Market
Starston
Wortwell
Harleston
Flixton
Redisham
Henstead
Kessingland (△)

impling
Dickleburgh
A 143
Rumburgh
Metfield
B 1124
Brampton
3119
Wrentham
B 1127

Scole
Brockdish
B 1116
Fressingfield
B 1123
Halesworth
Holton
Blythburgh
Southwold
B 1387
Walberswick

Brome
Hoxne
Stradbroke
Walpole
Bramfield
Blythburgh
A 12
Dunwich

Eye
Occold
Laxfield
Heveningham
A 1120
Darsham
Westleton
Middleton
Theberton

Wetheringsett
Dennington
Badingham
Yoxford
Kelsale
Leiston (△)
Aldringham
Thorpeness

Debenham
Saxtead Green
Castle
Rendham
Saxmundham
A 1119
Aldringham
1353

Pettaugh
Earl Soham
Framlingham
B 1116
26
B 1121
B 1069
A 1094
Aldeburgh

Earl Stonham
Charsfield
B 1078
Marlesford
Snape
Tunstall
R. Alde

Otley
Wickham Market
B 1078
Sudbourne

Grundisburgh
Ufford
Butley
Orford
Orford Ness

Claydon
Melton
A 1152
B 1084

Whitton
Tuddenham
Woodbridge
Martlesham
Waldringfield
Shottisham
Hollesley
Hollesley Bay

IPSWICH
Kesgrave
Waldringfield

Belstead
Nacton
Levington
Kirton
Bawdsey

Woolverstone
Trimley Heath
A 154
R. Deben

Holbrook
B 1080
Shotley Gate
Felixstowe
(▲ △)

Mistley
Parkeston
R. Stour

Harwich
Dovercourt
Hoek van Holland

Ramsey
A 120

Wix
Great Oakley
The Naze

Tendring
B 1414

Weeley
Thorpe-le-Soken
Walton-on-the Naze

Great Bentley
Kirby Cross
Frinton-on-Sea

Clacton-on-Sea (▲)

0 5 10 km

0 2.5 5 7.5 10 miles

F A 40 *E S E Y*

Cymyran Bay

Rhosneigr
(△)

Llanfaelog

20 5
32

6

Pentre Berw

Cefn

B 4422

A 4080

Aberffraw

10½

B 4421

Llanfa
Bryn-C
do

Bordogan

A 4080

B 4422

Plas

A 4419

Brynsiencyn

(△)

Newborough

Mermaid Inn

Malltraeth Bay

Llanddwyn-
Island

Caernarfon

Bontnewydd

C a e r n a r f o n

24

B a y

Dinas Dinlle

(△)

53

Llandwrog
(△)

A 499

14

Pe

Pontlyfni
(△)

13½

Llar

Clynnog-
Fawr

22
35

21

Trevor

A 499

522

Yr Eifl

Trwyn y Gorlech

564

Llanaelhaearn

Llithfaen

B 4417

7½

A 497

Carreg Ddu

6

L i e y n   P e n i n s u l a

Morfa Nefyn

Nefyn

B 4354

Y Ffôr

(△)

Llanystu

Porth Ysgaden

B 4412

A 497

7

A 499

B 4354

Chwilog

(△)

10

Tudweiliog

Efailnewydd

A 497

9½

Cri

Llangwnnadl

B 4417

312

(△)

B 4415

L i e y n

Pwllheli

Tr eme

Penrhyn Mawr

103

Sarn Meyllteyrn

B 4413

13

Llanbedrog

B a y

25

B 4413

Botwnnog

305

B 4413

8½

6½

A 499

St. Tudwal's
Road

4

Y Rhiw

Llanengan

Abersoch

Mynydd Mawr

Aberdaron

160

Porth Neigwl
Hell's Mouth

Bwlchtocyn

Braich y Pwll

Bardsey Sound

Trwyn Cilan

St. Tudwal's Islands

Bardsey Island (▲)

26

C A R D I G A N   B A Y

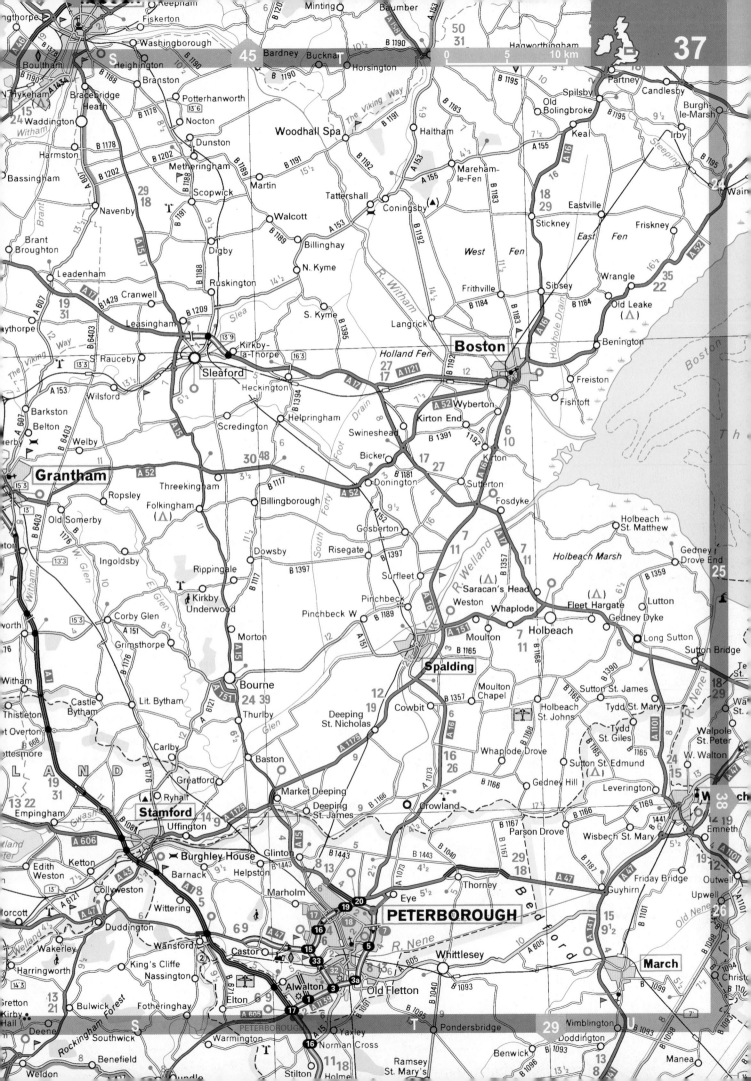

Chapel St. Leonards
A 52
Burgh-le-Marsh
A 158
Irby
Skegness
B 1195
ing
24
Wainfleet All Saints
A 52
sby

0   2.5   5   7.5   10 miles

Boston Deeps
Long Sand
Lynn Deeps
37

The Wash

Brancaster Bay
Holkham Bay

Holme-next-the Sea
Titchwell
17
Holkham
Wells-next-the-Sea
Cley-next-the Sea
9
21
A 149
Thornham
7
6
A 149
8
Blakeney
11
Brancaster
B 1155
Stiffkey
Hunstanton
(△)
Burnham Market
Holkham Hall
Wighton
Binham
Letheringset
B 1161
Ringstead
B 1153
6
B 1355
N. Creake
9
B 1105
Hindringham
12
22
Heacham
A 149
B 1454
Docking
Stanhoe
Little Walsingham
B 1388
35
Snettisham (△)
10
Creake South
10
Great Snoring
Lit. Snoring
(△) Barney
Briston
16
Great Bircham
Syderstone
B 1355
A 1067
Shernborne
B 1454
Sculthorpe
Thursford Green
B 1354
Dersingham
Houghton Hall
Tattersett
(△) Fakenham
Hindolveston
(△) Sandringham House
Hempton
Wood Da
Gedney Drove End
Castle Rising
East Rudham
Great Ryburgh
Guist
25
B 1439
A 148
Harpley
Colkirk
Foulsham
N. Wootton
Hillington
9
A 149
8
B 1153
22 35
14
S. Raynham
Whissonsett
13'9
S. Wootton
A 148
Grimston
Great Massingham
Brisley
N. Elmham
Sutton Bridge
Gaywood
Weasenham St. Peter
Wellingham
B 1145
Bawdes
utton
King's Lynn
4½
B 1145
Terrington St. Clement
Clenchwarton
12
N O R F O L K
Walpole St. Andrew
18
29
7
8
B 1145
E. Winch
Gayton
Litcham
Lyng
Walpole St. Peter
A 47
B 1145
26
Longham
Swanton Morley
Elsi
W. Walton
Tilney St. Lawrence
B 1163
16
Castle Acre
East Dereham
5
13
22 14
Priory
A 1065
B 1110
Wisbech
Wiggenhall St. Mary Magdalen
14
9
(△) Narborough
7
Gt. Dunham Little
A 47
B 1147
Emneth
12 19
Marham
Nar
Wendling
12 19
Yaxham
Matt
A 1075
Necton
W. Bradenham
Shouldham
A 1122
11
A 154
Swaffham
W. Winch
Garvestone
19 12
Stow-Bridge
11
18
Shipdham
Stradsett
46
Ashill
Cranworth
Kimberley
Outwell
A 1101
A 1122
Crimplesham
Gooderstone
B 1077
Saham Toney
Hingham
Upwell
26
Wereham
Hilborough
18
11
Watton
Wym
Nordelph
Denver
W. Dereham
Oxburgh Hall
B 1108
A 1075
10½
Christchurch
Hilgay
Stoke Ferry
Whittington
B 1108
45
28
h
B 1094
Southery
13 21
Caston
Great Ellingham
Welney
B 1386
Northwold
A 1065
Thompson
Methwold
Attlebor
30
Mundford
Great ickham
Feltwell
Thetford
13
E. Wretham
Larling
8
Snetterton
Weeting
Santon Downham
Banham

24

25

26

X   Y   0   5   10 km

Sheringham
W. Runton
(△)
Weybourne
Street (△)
A 148
A 1082
A 149
Cromer (▲ △)
Overstrand
Aylmerton
Baconsthorpe
Northrepps
B 1159
Roughton
Mundesley (△)
Aldborough
Thorpe Market
Trunch
ilgefield
Little Barningham
Honing
B 1145
Knapton
Bacton
tteringham
Erpingham
Felmingham
B 1150
Happisburgh
B 1159
Blickling Hall
6½
B 1145
North Walsham
(△)
B 1354
5
B 1149
Blickling
33 20
Swanton Abbott
Worstead
Honing
Sea Palling
Aylsham
B 1354
3
Scottow
Low Street
33
Stalham
B 1151
B 1159
Marsham (△)
A 149
Hickling Green
B 1145
8
Cawston
Buxton
15½
Neatishead
Hevingham
Catfield
Potter Heigham
Somerton
B 1152
Winterton-on-Sea
olk Wildlife Park
nwade
11½
B 1149
9½
A 140
Horstead
Coltishall
A 1151
Norfolk Broads
B 1152
Martham
B 1159
Hemsby
Felthorpe
Hainford
B 1150
Hoveton
Ludham
Bastwick
Thurne
8½
Ormesby St. Margaret
Attlebridge
12
Horsford
Wroxham
16
Horning
A 1062
Horsham St. Faith
Ranworth
S. Walsham
B 1152
9
Taverham
Drayton
Spixworth
Salhouse
Billockby
B 1140
Filby
A 1064
Caister-on-Sea
A 1067
Costessey
New Rackheath
B 1140
R. Bure
Sprowston
Catton
58
NORWICH
24 15
Acle
A 1064
8
Easton
Thorpe St. Andrew
A 47
Blofield
7
Bawburgh
A 1074
Brundall
GREAT YARMOUTH (▲ △)
B 1108
6 4
A 47
16'3
3 4,5
Surlingham
Freethorpe
Burgh Castle
Hethersett
Cringleford
R. Yare
B 1140
(△)
A 41
8 5
A 146
Caister St. Edmund
Cantley
Belton
21
A 143
A 12
Gorleston-on-Sea
Mulbarton
B 1113
75
East Poringland
10
Claxton
14 22
7
Reedham
13
Hopton
Ashwellthorpe
Newton Flotman
Thurton
Brooke
Loddon
Thurlton
Blundeston
10 16
B 1385
pooner Row
Saxlingham Nethergate
Seething
Hales
2½
B 1136
Haddiscoe
9½
A 1074
Oulton Broad
Bunwell
B 1135
A 140
Woodton
Hempnall
20 32
Burgh St. Peter
B 1113
Long Stratton
Ellingham
31
Lowestoft (▲)
Aslacton
Shelton
31 19
Ditchingham
(△) Bungay
Earsham
A 143
Gillingham
Barsham
A 1116
10 16
Beccles
A 146
31
Pakefield
Carlton Colville

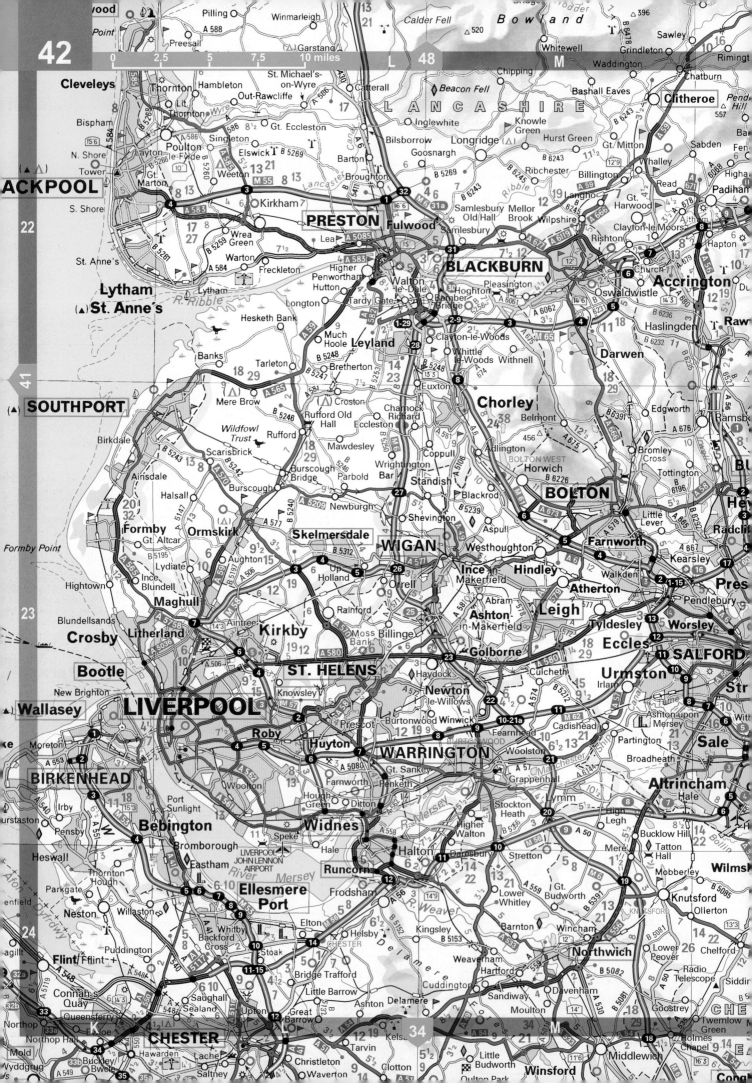

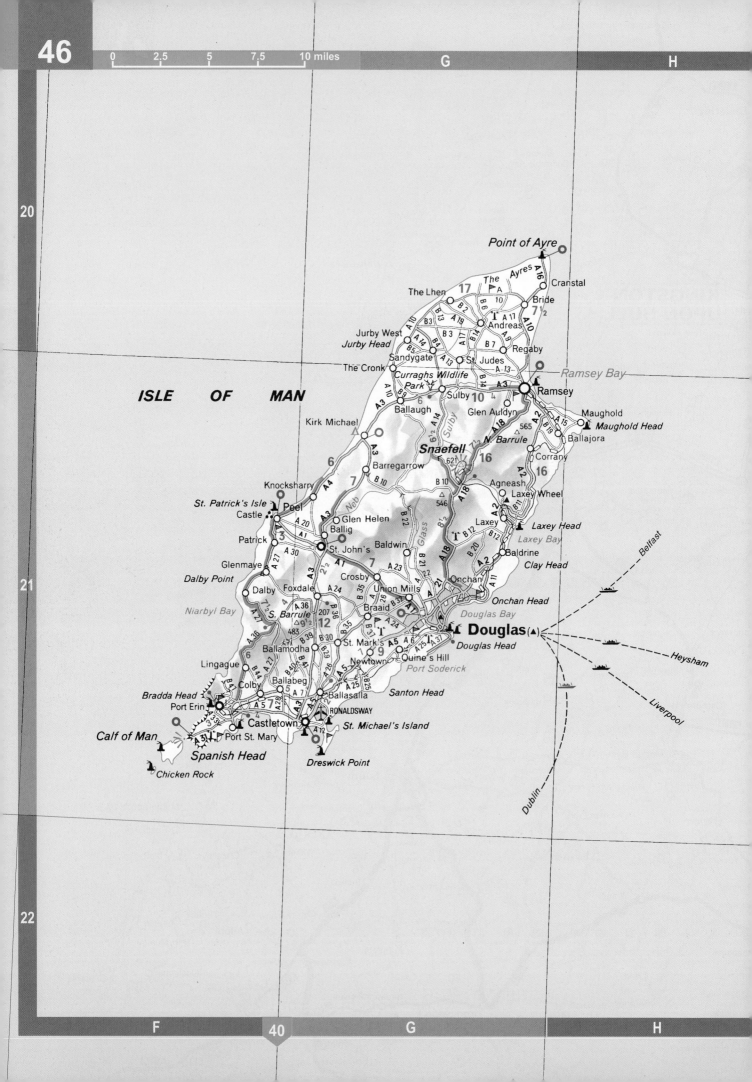

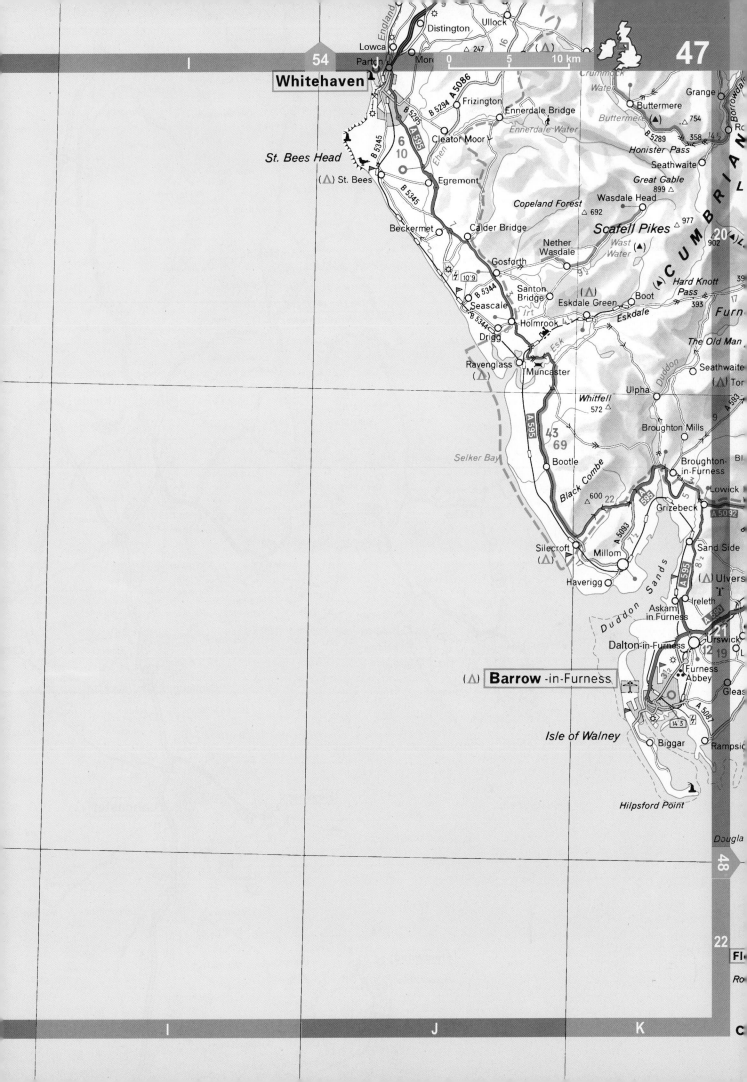

England

Distington   Ullock

Lowca

Parton

Whitehaven

Mor

0   5   10 km

Crummock
Water

Grange

Buttermere

Borrowda

B 5294   A 5086

Frizington

Ennerdale Bridge

B 5289   358   14

(A) 754

B 5295

Ennerdale Water

Honister Pass

A 595

6
10

Cleator Moor

Seathwaite

Ehen

St. Bees Head

B 5345

Egremont

Great Gable
899 △

Wasdale Head

CUMBRIAN

(A) St. Bees

B 5345

Copeland Forest
△ 692

Scafell Pikes   △ 977

20   (A) L
902

Beckermet

Calder Bridge

Nether
Wasdale

Wast
Water

Hard Knott
Pass   39

Furn

7

Gosforth

(A)

Boot

393   17

10·9

B 5344

Santon
Bridge

Eskdale Green

Eskdale

The Old Man

Seascale

Irt

Holmrook

Esk

Seathwaite

B 5344

Drigg

Ulpha

(A) Tor

A 595

Ravenglass

Muncaster

Whitfell
572 △

Duddon

(A)

9   A 593

Selker Bay

43
69

Broughton Mills

A 595

Bootle

Broughton-
in-Furness

Bl

Black Combe

600   22

Lowick

△ 600

Grizebeck

A 5092

A 595

Silecroft

A 5093   7½

Sand Side

8½

(A)

Millom

(A) Ulvers

Haverigg

Duddon
Sands

Ireleth

A 590

Duddon
Sands

Askam
in Furness

21
12   19

Dalton-in-Furness

Urswick

(A) **Barrow** -in-Furness

Furness
Abbey

Gleas

Isle of Walney

14·3

A 5087

Biggar

Rampsi

Hilpsford Point

Dougla

22

Fl

Ro

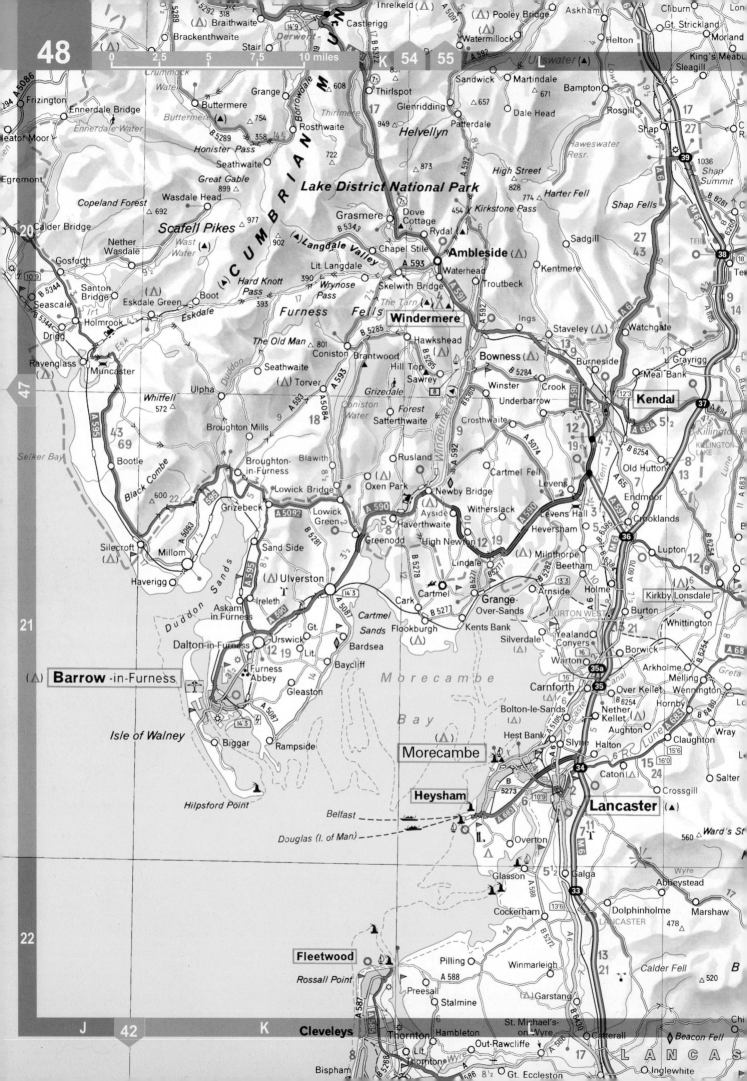

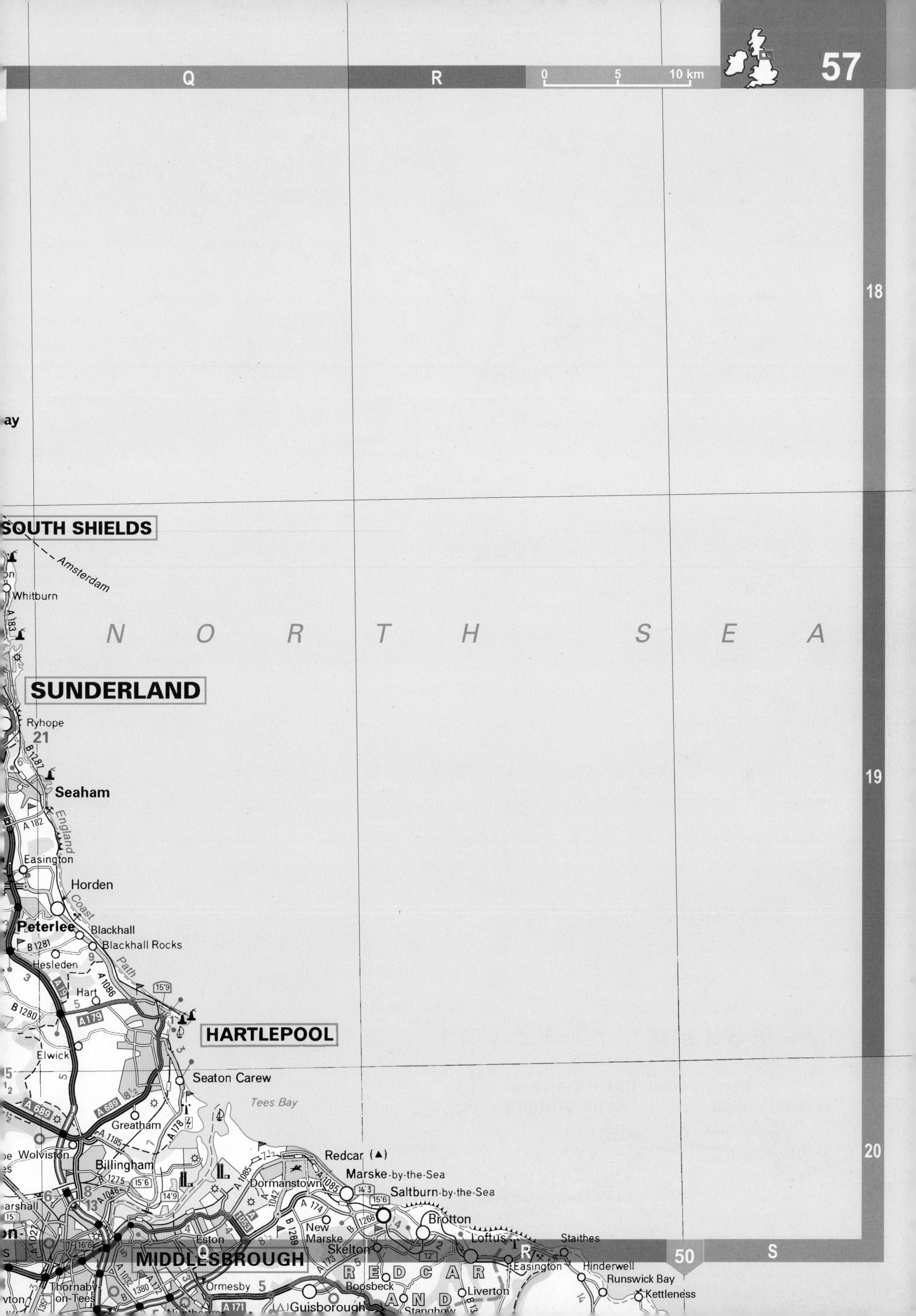

18

ay

SOUTH SHIELDS

— Amsterdam

Whitburn

N O R T H   S E A

SUNDERLAND

Ryhope
21

Seaham

England

Easington

Horden

Coast

Peterlee   Blackhall
            Blackhall Rocks

Hesleden   Path

A179   Hart   A1086

A179   15'9

HARTLEPOOL

Elwick

Seaton Carew

Tees Bay

A689   Greatham

A178

A1185

Wolviston   Billingham   15'6   Redcar (▲)

Marske-by-the-Sea

A689   Dormanstown   A1085   Saltburn-by-the-Sea

14'3

New   Brotton
Marske
Loftus   Staithes

Eston   Skelton

MIDDLESBROUGH   R E D C A R   Easington   Hinderwell

Ormesby   5   A N D   Runswick Bay

Thornaby-on-Tees   Boosbeck   Liverton   Kettleness

Guisborough   A171

19

20

50
S

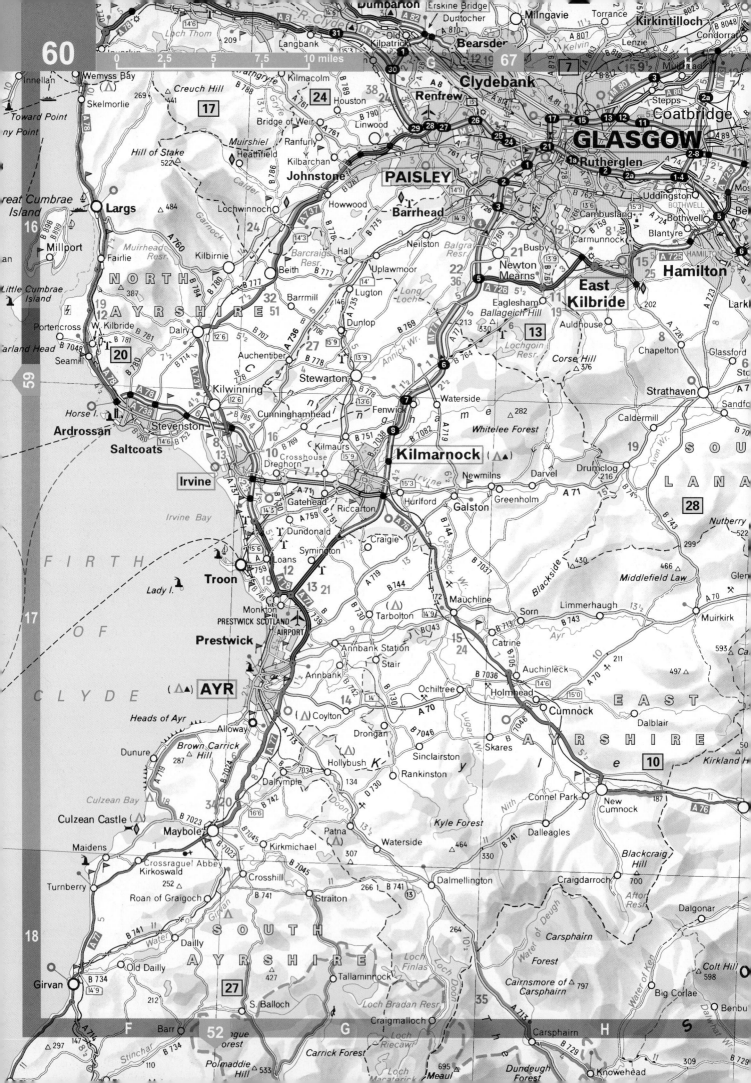

(▲) Calgary Bay

Clachan-Mór
Balephetrish Bay
Rubha Dubh
Treshnish Point
Ensay 342

Caoles
B 8069
B 8068
Haunn
176
B 8073
Achleck

A

B

(▲) Loch Tuath

Middleton
B 8065
Crossapoll
Tiree
B 8065
Cairn na
Burgh Beg
Fladda
Sound of Ulva

Balephuil
B 8067
Balemartine
Hynish Bay
Treshnish Isles
Lunga
Gometra
313

Rinn Thorbhais
B 8066
B 8068
Balephuil Bay
Hynish
Ulva

Lit. Colonsay

Bac Mór or
Dutchman's Cap
Staffa
Inch
Kenneth

Fingal's Cave

B

ISLE OF MULL

519

14

Rubha na
h-Uamha

Ardmeana
Tiror

erryvore

Eilean
Annraidh
L. na Làthaich
Loch Scrida

(▲) Iona
Baile
Mór

Fionnphort
A 849
9½
376

A 849

Bunessan
L. Assapol

Erraid
Soa I.
Ardchiavaig
R o s s   o f   M u l l

Eilean
a' Chalmain
Ardalanish
Bay

Rubh'
Ardalanish

W. Reef
Torran Rocks

15

Dubh Artach

Rubh' a'
Geodha

Kiloran Bay
143

139
Kiloran

An Rubha
B 8086
B 8087

A   N   T   I   C

Scalasaig
2½
Colonsay

Garvard
B 8085
Staosnaig

Rubha Dubh

93

Dubh Eilean
Oronsay

Eilean
nan Ron
Eilean
Ghaoideamal

E   A   N

Rubh' an

16

Rubha
a' Mhail

Nave Island
Sgarbh Breac
364

Ardnave
Point

Ardnave
Bunnahabhainn

An Clachan
Gortantaoid

Z
A
B Port Askaig
Feolin

Sanaigmore
B 8018
B 8017
Loch
Finlaggan
A 846

Saligo Bay
Loch
Gorm
Gruinart
Craigens
Ballygrant

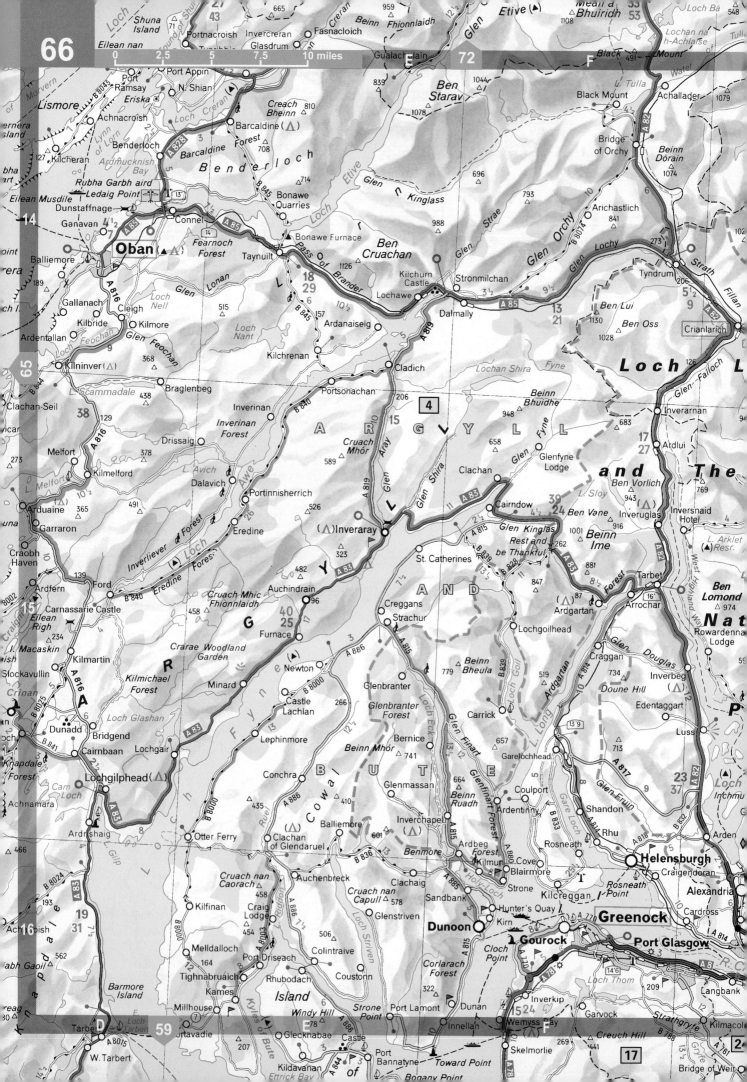

Mingary
Askernish
L. Snigisclett
Stuley
△ 374
L. Stulaval

0   2.5   5   7.5   10 miles

Daliburgh

76

T A   Y   T   H   E   Z   H   E

A 865
Lochboisdale

12

Boisdale
B 888
L. Boisdale
Calvay

Orosay
Easaval
△ 240

Pollachar
E. Kilbride
3
S. Glendale
Rubha na h-Ordaig

Sound of Eriskay

Sgeir a' Mhill

Fiaray
Sound of Fuday
Lingay
Rudha
Ban
△ 185

Scurrival Point
Sound of Barra

Eriskay

Eoligarry
Fuday
Orosay
Oitir Mhór
Stack Is.

Greian Head
Cleat
△

Gighay

Barra
7 ½
A 888
Bayhirivagh
Hellisay

Borve
5 ½ 1
Flodday

Doirlinn Head
333
3
Heaval
△ 383
Ersary
Fuiay
Bruernish Point

A 888
102
Castlebay

Caolis
△ 190

Vatersay

Vatersay
Muldoanich

Flodday
Sound of Sandray

Lingay
Sound of Pabbay
207
△
Sandray

13

Pabbay
△ 171
Rosinish

Sound of Mingulay

Mingulay
△ 273

Sound of Berneray

Berneray
Barra Head

14

Calgary Poin

Gunna

Urvaig

B   B

E

H

N   E   R

Balephetrish
Bay

Hough Skerries
Clachan-Mór
B 8068
Caoles
B 8069
5 ½

Rubha Chraiginis
119
△
Ballevullin
Kenovay
4 ½
Gott
Bay
Soa

Middleton
3
Scarinish
Tiree

B 8065
Crossapoll
Hynish Bay

Balephuil
B 8067
Balemartine

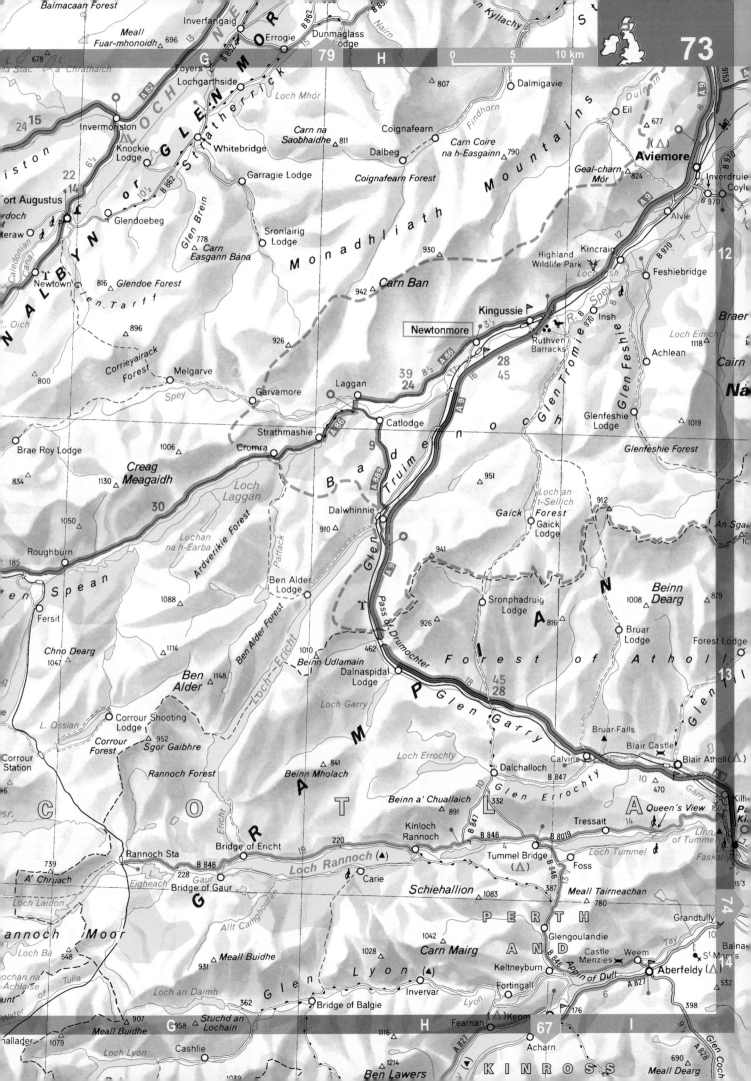

Balmacaan Forest
Inverfarigaig
Meall Fuar-mhonoidh 696
Errogie
Dunmaglass Lodge
n Kyllachy
807 Dalmigavie
Dulnain
Eil
677
Foyers
Lochgarthside
Loch Mhòr
Carn na Saobhaidhe 811
Coignafearn
Carn Coire na h-Easgainn 790
Aviemore
Inverdruie
Coylu
24 15 Invermoriston
Knockie Lodge
Whitebridge
Garragie Lodge
Coignafearn Forest
Geal-charn Mór 824
Alvie

22
14
Fort Augustus
Glen Brein
778 Carn Easgann Bàna
Sronlairig Lodge
930
Highland Wildlife Park
Kincraig
Feshiebridge

Newtown
816 Glendoe Forest
Carn Ban
942
Kingussie
Insh
Glen Feshie
Achlean
1118

896
926
Newtonmore
Ruthven Barracks
Glenfeshie Lodge
1019

Corrieyairack Forest
Melgarve
Spey
Laggan
39 24
28 45
Glenfeshie Forest

800
Garvamore
Strathmashie
Catlodge
Glentromie
951

Brae Roy Lodge
1006
Cromra
9
Gaick Forest
Lochan an t-Seilich
912

834
1130
Creag Meagaidh
30
Loch Laggan
Dalwhinnie
910
Gaick Lodge
An Sga

1050
Lochan na h-Earba
941
Sronphadruig Lodge
1008
Beinn Dearg
879

Roughburn
185
Ben Alder Lodge
1088
926
816

Fersit
Ardverikie Forest
1010
Pass of Drumochter
462
Dalnaspidal Lodge
Forest of Atholl
Bruar Lodge
Forest Lodge

Chno Dearg 1047
1114
Ben Alder 1148
Beinn Udlamain
18 45 28
Bruar-Falls
Blair Castle

Corrour Shooting Lodge
Loch Garry
Glen Garry
Calvine
Blair Atholl

Corrour Forest
952 Sgor Gaibhre
Loch Errochty
Dalchalloch
B 847
10
470

Corrour Station
Rannoch Forest
841 Beinn Mholach
Glen Errochty
Queen's View
150

Beinn a' Chuallaich 891
B 841
Tressait
14

Rannoch Sta
Bridge of Ericht
Kinloch Rannoch
220
B 846
Tummel Bridge
Loch Tummel
Foss

739
228 Gaur
Bridge of Gaur
Loch Rannoch
Carie
Schiehallion 1083
387
Meall Tairneachan

A' Chruach
Loch Laidon
Grandtully

annoch Moor
Meall Buidhe
1028
Carn Mairg
1042
Glengoulandie
Castle Menzies
Weem
Aberfeldy

Loch Bà 548
931
Glen Lyon
Invervar
Fortingall
Keltneyburn

907 958 Stuchd an Lochain
Bridge of Balgie
Lyon
Kenm
67
Grandtully

Meall Buidhe
1116
1214
Ben Lawers
KINROSS
Acharn
690

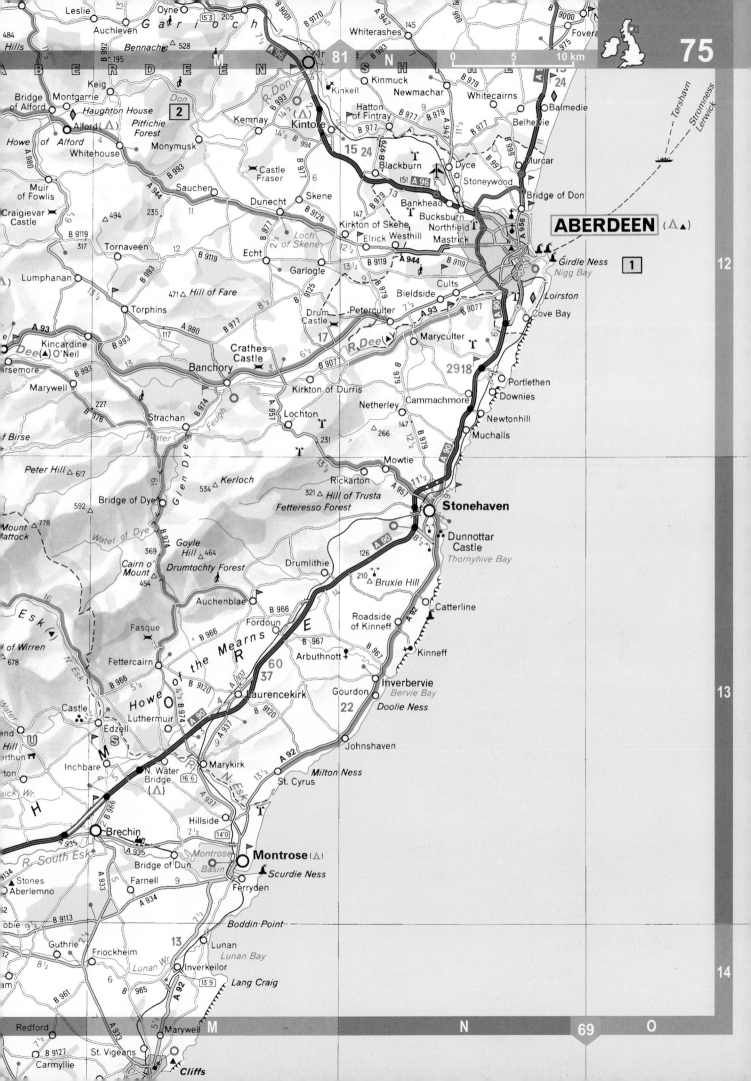

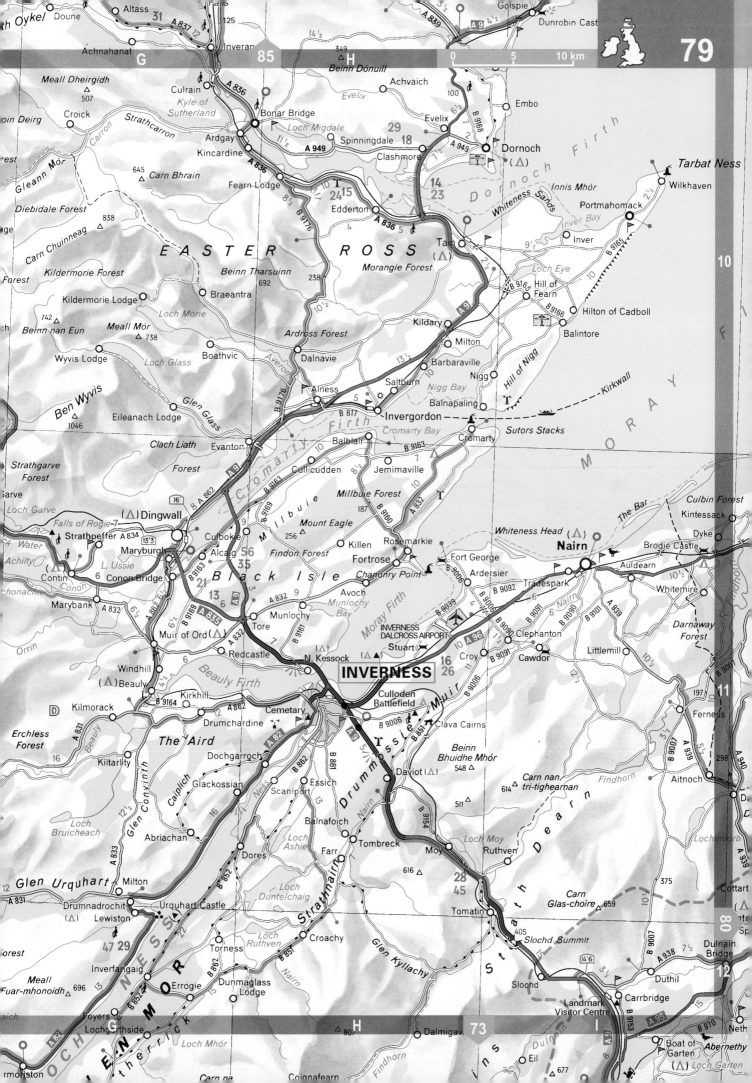

0   2.5   5   7.5   10 miles

Z A

ISLE OF LEWIS
AND HARRIS

8

H E B R I D E S

Galson

16

Borve

Shader

Barvas

Arnol

L. Urrahag

Bragar

12

50

Shawbost

Loch Breivat

28

A 858

261

Garenin

Carloway

Beinn Mholach

292

A 857

110

Little Bernera

Dun Carloway Broch

Gallan Head

West Loch Roag

Tobson

Tolsta Chaolais

L. Laxavat Ard

Aird Uig

Pabay Mór

Valtos

Breaclete

Breasclete

Newmarket

T

Miavaig

Great
Bernera

Eilean
Kearstay

Callanish

T

Timsgarry

Vuia Mór

Floday

Crulivig

Standing Stones

Garynahine

Stornoway

Camas Uig

Uig

Loch Roag

A 858

13½

A 859

B 887

9

Mangersta

LEWIS

Achmore

112

L. Orasay

B 887

9

574

Little Loch Roag

B 8011

Islivig

Enaclete

L. nam
Falcag

Leurbost

Aird Brenish

L. Grunavat

B 8059

L. Trealaval

Crossbost

Ranish

Brenish

Suainaval

20

Barkin Isle

Mealasta I.

Loch Airigh
na h-Airde

Laxay

Keose

Eilean Chaluim

Cromore

L. Tamanavay

Morsgail Forest

281

Balallan

L. Erisort

Kershader

Marvi

Kearstay

Braigh Mór

Loch Resort

Ulladale

303

Loch Langavat

Arivruaich

L. Sgibacleit

Glenside

Scarp

308

B 8060

A 859

36

Seaforth
Head

14

Gravir

L. Odhai

Gasker

Hushinish

Tirga Mór

Stulaval

492

401

Park
or
Pairc

Eishken

Lemreway

Hushinish Point

B 887

679

579

217

572

Crionaig

371

Ardvourlie

Seaforth
Island

467

Amhuinnsuidhe

13

Clisham

Beinn Mhór

Eilean Iubhard

Taransay Glorigs

Meavaig

799

Maaruig

Loch Shell or Loch Sealg

Soay Mór

North Harris

Loch Seaforth

10

HARRIS

West Loch Tarbert

Ardhasaig

Rhenigidale

Sound of Shiant

Taransay

Isay

267

Lo ch
Trollamarig

Eilean Mór
a'Bhaigh

Shiant Islands

N A N

506

Tarbert

Kyles
Scalpay

334

Luskentyre

Scotasay

Scalpay

L E S)

South Harris
Forest

A 859

Scalpay

104

Toe Head

Borv

76

Drinnishadder

Scalpay

Coppay

Scarista

South Harris

398

Shillay

365

Grosebay

Y Z A

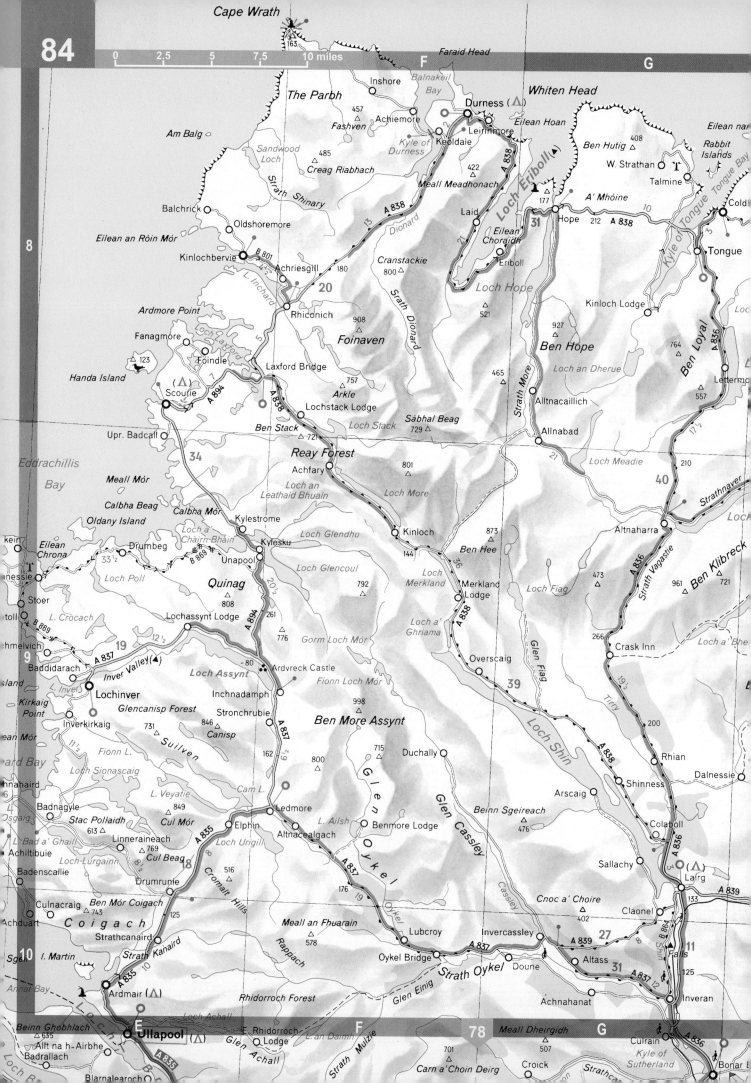

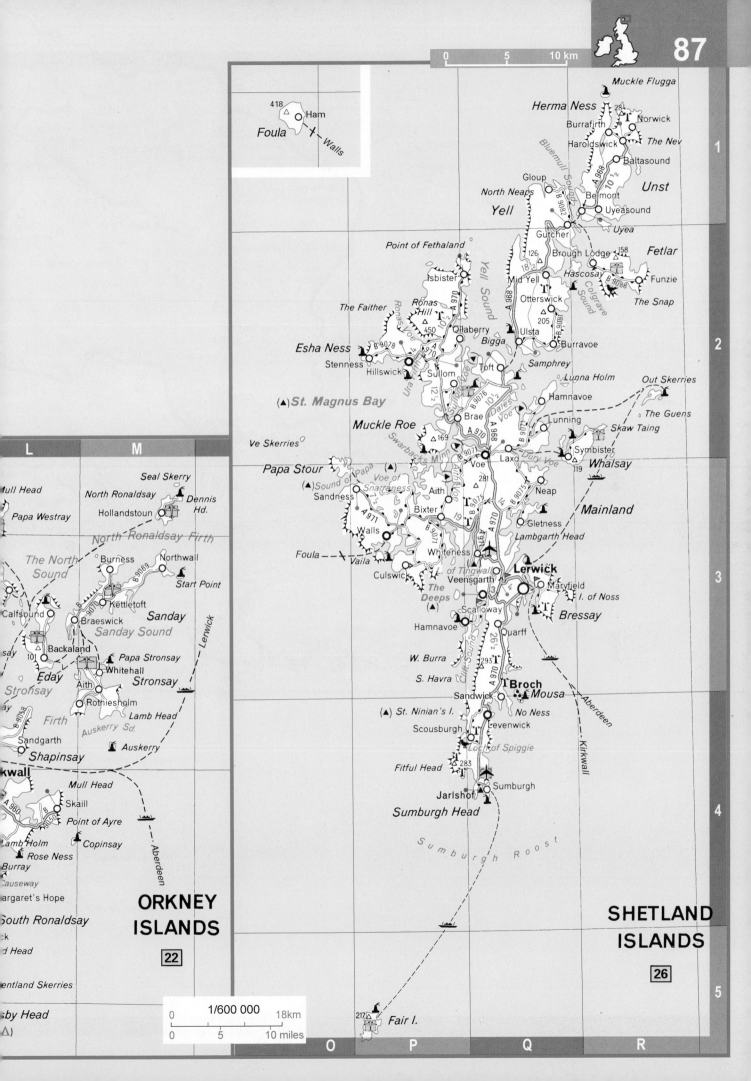

0   5   10 km

Foula
418 △
⊙ Ham
╫ Walls

Muckle Flugga
Herma Ness
Burrafirth   28½   ⊙ Norwick
Haroldswick   *The Nev*
Baltasound
Unst
Gloup
North Neaps   Belmont
Yell   ⊙ Uyeasound
⊙ Uyea
Gutcher
126   Brough Lodge   158   *Fetlar*
Point of Fethaland   18½   Hascosay   ⊙ Funzie
Isbister   Mid Yell   *The Snap*
The Faither   Ronas Hill   Otterswick
205   Ulsta
Esha Ness   450   Ollaberry   Bigga   Burravoe
Stenness   Hillswick   Sullom   Toft   Samphrey
Lunna Holm   *Out Skerries*
(▲)*St. Magnus Bay*   Hamnavoe   *The Guens*
Brae   Lunning   Skaw Taing
Muckle Roe   Symbister
Ve Skerries   Voe   Laxo   119   *Whalsay*
Papa Stour   Aith   *Dury Voe*
(▲)*Sound of*   281   Neap   *Mainland*
Sandness   *Snarraness*   Bixter   Gletness
Walls   169   Lambgarth Head
Foula   Whiteness
Vaila   Culswick   L. of Tingwall   *Lerwick*   Maryfield
Veensgarth   *I. of Noss*
The Deeps   Scalloway   *Bressay*
Hamnavoe   Quarff
W. Burra   293½
S. Havra   **Broch** *Mousa*
Sandwick
(▲)*St. Ninian's I.*   No Ness
Scousburgh   Levenwick
Loch of Spiggie
Fitful Head   283
Sumburgh
Jarlshof
Sumburgh Head

Sumburgh Roost

SHETLAND ISLANDS   26

217   *Fair I.*

L   M

Seal Skerry
Mull Head   *North Ronaldsay*   Dennis
Papa Westray   Hollandstoun   Hd.
North Ronaldsay Firth
The North Sound   Burness   Northwall
Start Point
Kettletoft
Calfsound   Braeswick   *Sanday*
101   Backaland   *Sanday Sound*
Eday   Whitehall   *Papa Stronsay*
Aith   *Stronsay*
Stronsay   Rothiesholm   *Lamb Head*
Firth   *Auskerry Sd.*
Sandgarth   △ Auskerry
Shapinsay
Mull Head
kwall   Skaill
B 960   Point of Ayre   Copinsay
Lamb Holm   *Rose Ness*
Burray
Causeway
Margaret's Hope
South Ronaldsay
d Head
ntland Skerries
by Head

ORKNEY ISLANDS   22

1/600 000   18km
0   5   10 miles

O   P   Q   R

0   2.5   5   7.5   10 miles

NGLE BAY

Canglass Point

Kells Bay

Ken

Knocknadobar
689 △

56
35   Beenmore
668 △

Ballynakilly
Upper

Castlequin

Kells

495

Doulus Head

Ring

772 △

Coomasaharn
Lake

Glencar

Bealalaw
Bridge

Bohee

Carhan House

Coomacarrea

Teeromoyle

Colly
686 △

Beginish I.

Doulus Bay

Ferta

304

Ballaghisheen
Pass

Cahersiveen /(△)
Cathair Saidhbhín

Cloon Lake

772 △

Mullaghanar

Knight's Town

Owroe Br.

7½

Valentia Island

Lissatinnig Br.

Clynacantan

Chapeltown

R 565

Portmagee Channel

498

682 △

Knocknagantee

Bray Head

Portmagee

R 565

Kilpeacan Cross Roads

Inny

Killeenleagh Br.

675 △

Tullakeel

Gearh

12

398

Teeraneragh

R 566

4

Mastergeehy /
Máistir Gaoithe

L. Namona

Derriana Lough
Cloonaghlin
Lough

Letterfinish

Ballynahow

Killurly

R 567

6

Sallahig

674

Puffin Island

R 568

Killonecaha

Ballinskelligs /
Baile an Sceilg

8½

Caherbarnagh

Sneem

St. Finan's Bay

(△) Waterville /
An Coireán

Lough Currane

of

Ken

Little Skellig

Ballybrack

Graiques

63
39

Tahilla

Abbey

410

Staigue
Stone Fort

Parknasilla

Rossr

Great Skellig

Bolus Head

Ballinskelligs Bay

499

Eagles Hill

543 △

Rossdohan
Island

Hog's Head

309

Coomakesta Pass

9   Caherdaniel

Sherky I.

Kilmakilloge
Harbour

Bu

Sheehan's Point

208

N 70

Castlecove

Derrynane

Westcove

KENMARE   RIVER

30

Scariff Island

Deenish I.

Lamb's Head

Kilcatherine Point

Gortgarriff

Ardgroom

599

Inishfarnard

R 571

Glanmore Lake

Coulagh   Bay

Ballycrovane
Harbour

Glenbeg Lough

E   Caha

684 △

Eyeries

621

B

Cod's Head

R 575

Travara Br.

Miskish

Mountains

Hungry Hill

Derr

9

Ballydonegan Bay

Allihies

Slieve

R 572

9

Curryglass

Ballynacallagh

Ballydonegan

489

Castletownbere

Bere Haven

Garnish Point

Cable Car

Firkeel

R 575

Ballynakilla

The Bull

Dursey Island

Kilmichael

5

R 572

Cahermore

15   Fair Head

Rerrin

Bere Island

Dursey Head

Crow Head

Black Ball Head

BA

Kit

Ballyroon

6½

**Muntervary or
Sheep's Head**

13

Dunmanus

Three Castle Head

Gole

Dough

Mizen Head

Barley Cove

Brow Head

A   B   C

0 2.5 5 7.5 10 miles

B

10

Loop Head

Dreenagh

Kerry Head

Glenderry

(△) B

Ballyheig

The Seven Hogs or Magharee Islands

Illauntannig

Rough Point

Brandon Point   Fahamore

Kilshannig

Brandon Head

Brandon Bay

Tralee Bay

Brandon / Cé Bhréanainn

Castlegregory (△)

Brandon Creek

Brandon Mountain

Ballyquin ( ) Lough Gill

Strand   Killmey

R 560

Ballydavid Head

Tiduff

△951

Cloghane

Stradbally

Aughacasla

Derrymo

Feohanagh

Kilcummin

Smerwick

Smerwick Harbour

Feohanagh

Ballyduff

Beenoskee

△825

Gamp

Sybil Head

Ballydavid

Ballinloghig

D I N G L E

(▲) L. Slat

82

Ballyferriter   Murreagh

Kilmalkedar

△623

Conor Pass

594

Lougher

N 86

Caherconree

S

Baile an Fheirtearaigh

Gallarus Oratory

456   616

Owenascaul

50 31

Clogher Head

Ballynana

(△) 5

Owenmore

Anascaul

Aughils

Inishtooskert

Ballineanig

R 559

Dingle / Daingean Uí Chúis

Inch

Dunquin   Ventry   Milltown

N 86

R 561

Blasket Islands / (▲)

Dún Chaoin

516△ Mount Eagle

Dingle Harb.

4½

Na Blascaodaí   Dunmore Head

Beehive Huts

Lispole / Lios Póil

Castle

Harb

Great Blasket Island

R 559

Ventry Harbour

Doonmanagh Castle

Inch

Tearaght I.

Slea Head

Parkmore Pt.

Bull's Head   Minard Head

Cromane   Knockaun

Inishnabro

Illaunstookagh   Tullig

Inishvickillane

D I N G L E   B A Y   (▲)

L. Yganavan

Rossbeigh Creek   Caragh Br.   Car

Kells Bay

Kerry (▲)

14½   R   (△)

Glenbeigh

Lough Caragh

Canglass Point

56 35

Beenmore

668△

△493

Ballynakilly Upper

Knocknadobar

495

Shan

Castlequin

689 △

Ring

Kells

Coomasaharn Lake

Glencar

Doulus Head

Ferta

6½

Coomacarrea

772 △

Bealalaw Bridge

Lough

Doulus Bay

Carhan House

Teeromoyle

686

Beginish I.

Colly △   304

Ballaghisheen Pass

Boheesh

Knight's Town

Ca3

Knight's Town

Cahersiveen / (△)

Cathair Saidhbhín

Kerry Way

Cloon Lake

Valentia Island

R 565

Owroe Br.

7½

G

Clynacantan

Cha

88

B △498

Lissatinnig Br.

772△   250

Bray Head

A

R 565

Portmagee

398

Kilpeacan Cross Roads

Killeenleagh Br.

Knocknagantee

682

675△

Teeranearagh

Mastergeehy / Máistir Gaoithe

E   R

G

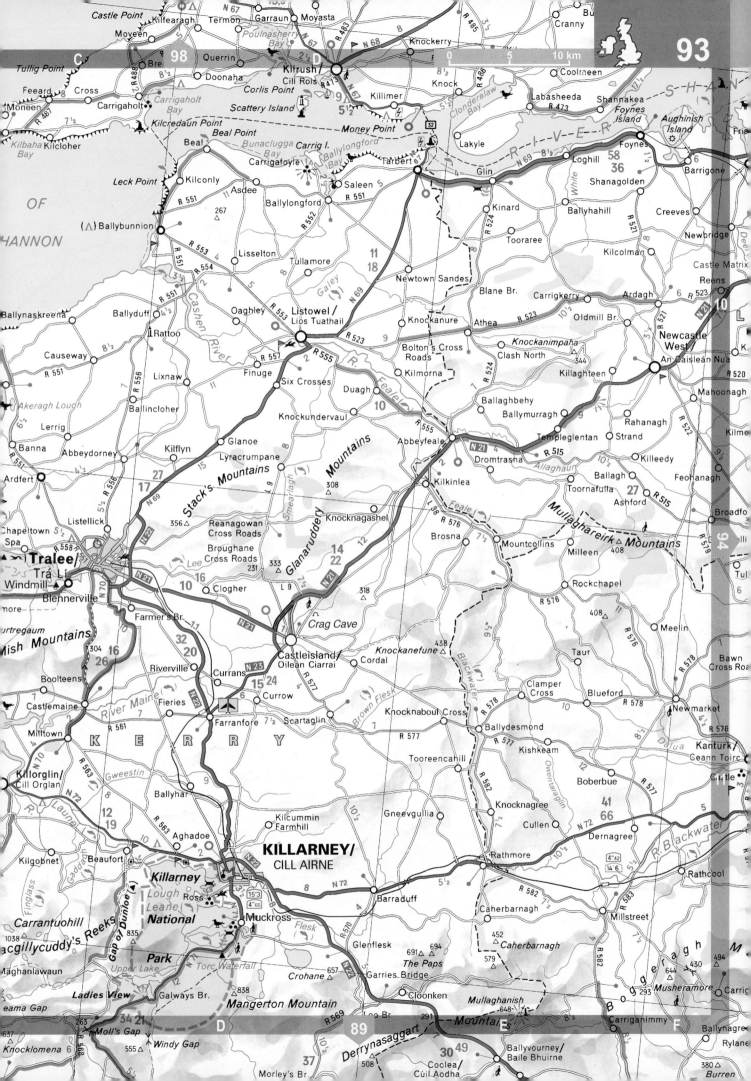

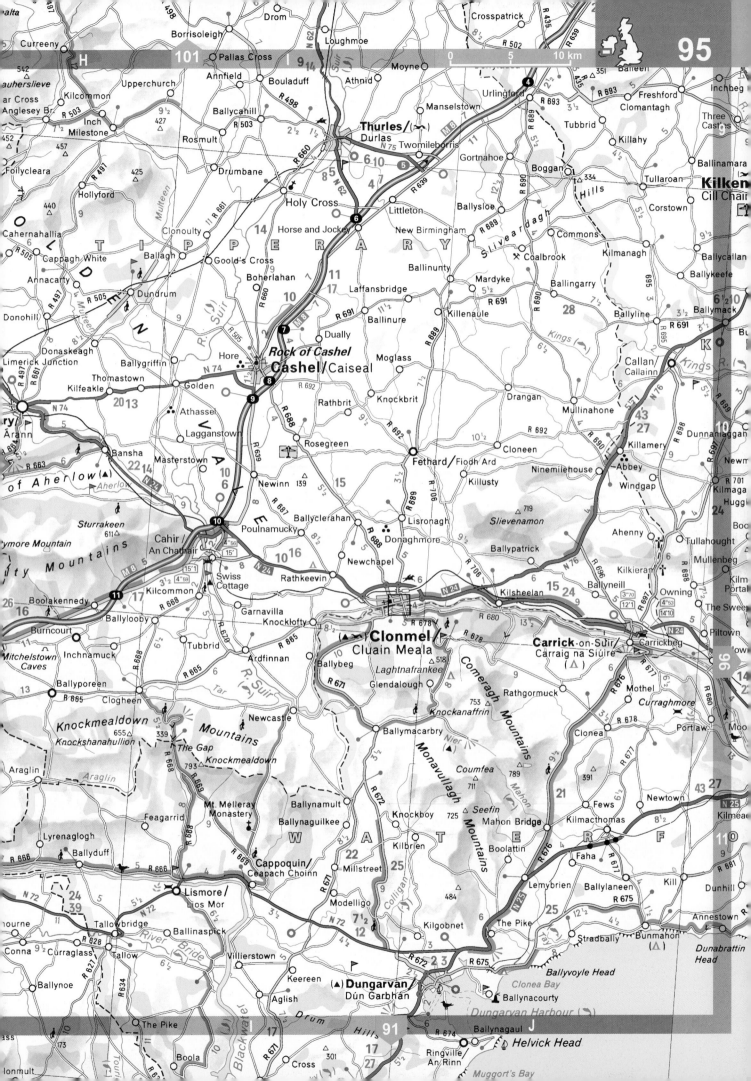

Croaghnakeela Island
Carna
Mace Head
Ard
L. Skannive
Kylesalia
Rosmuck
Kinvarra
Kilkieran/
Cill Chiaráin
Camus Bay
Bealadangan
R 340
C
St. Maodara's Island
Ardmore
Lettercallow
Lettermore Island
Lettermore
Glenicmurrin
Lough For
R 374
R 336
D
Mweenish Island
Inishbarra
Casheen Bay
Teeranea
Gorumna
Carraroe/
An Cheathrú Rua
Costelloe/Casla
R 343
Rossaveel
Lough
Ugga
Lettermullan/
Leitir Meallán
Island
Keeraunnagark
Golam Head
Ballynahown
Invera
Indrea

North Sound

GALWA

8

Rock Island
Onaght
Brannock Islands
Kilmurvy
Dún Aonghasa
Oghil Church
Kilronan/
Cill Rónáin
Oatquarter
Castle
Gregory's Sound
Inishmore/
Inis Mór
Killeany
ARAN ISLANDS/
Oileáin Árainn
Inishmaan/
Inis Meáin
Foul Sound
Inisheer/
Inis Oírr
(△)
Fardurris Point
South Sound

TIC

Doolin

O'Brien's Tower
Cliffs of Moher
Cliffs of Moher Visitor Centre
R 478
Derreen
Hags Head
Liscannor
(△) Lahinch
An Leacht

Liscannor Bay

9

Mal Bay
Rinneen
N 67

AN

Spanish Point
Spanish Point
R 482
R 474
Letter
Caherrush Point
Quilty
Milltown M
Sráid na Cat
Mutton Island
6
Kilmurry
Mullagh
29
47
Carrowmore Point
R 483
Cahermurphy
White Strand
Creegh
Killard
Creegh
Donegal Point
N 67
Doonbeg
Mountrivers Bridge
Leitrim
Corbally
Bealaha
R 484
Kilmihil
Moore Bay
(△) Kilkee/
Cill Chaoi
8½
13,5
N 67
Garraun
Moyasta
Moanmore
Cooraclare
Castle Point
Kilfearagh
Termon
N 68
Knockerry
R 485
Moveen
Poulnasherry Bay
R 483
Tullig Point
Breaghva
Querrin
Kilrush
Cill Ro
R 473
R 488
R 487
Doonaha
Corlis Point
Knock
Feeard
Cross
Carrigaholt
Carrigaholt Bay
Scattery Island
Killimer
Clondera
Bridge
Moneen
Kilbaha
Kilcredaun Point
Killmer
Money Point
32

0   2.5   5   7.5   10 miles

Croaghaun
△667   Doogort
Achill Head   R 319   Doagh
Keel   River   Inishbiggle   Castlehill
B   Keem Strand   5   110   Bunacurry   Annagh
yteoge Head   Keem Strand   Island   C
Cathedral Rocks ▲   Cashel   Salia   Claggan
(▲) **ACHILL ISLAND**   △464   4   Achill
Dooega Head   Knockmore   2   Achill Sound / Gob an Choire
Dooega / Dumha Éige   △340   Belfarsad   R 319   6
Bills Rocks ○   Derreen   Corraun   36
Ashleam Bay   △ Corraun Hill   An
521   Glassillaun
Cloghmore   Peninsula   Dooghbe
An Chloich Mhóir
Achillbeg Island
Bolinglanna

Clare Island   • Ballytoohy
C L E W   B
△
461

Old Head
△ ⚐   Kilsa
Roonagh Quay   Louisburgh   8
Emlagh Point   4½

Formoyle   Mulla
Roonah Lough   Carrownisky
Inishturk   Bridge ▲   L
Silver   (⚐)   R 335
Caher Island   Strand   Killadoon   Cregganbaun
(▲) M U R R
Kinnadoohy

Inishbofin   Doo Lough
Pass
Tonakeera Point
Mweelrea   76
Inishshark   Crump Island   Doo
817 △   Lough
Bofin   Rinvyle Point   Ardnagreevagh   Mountains
Rinvyle Castle   Rinvyle (△)   700 △   Delp
Cashleen   Salrock   Killary Harbour   6
High Island   356 △   12   Gowlaun   600 △   Lough   4½   Leena
Cleggan Bay   Tully Cross   Garraun   Fee   N 59   624
Ballynakill Harbour   6   Dawros   Kylemore Abbey   2½   △
Aughrus More   Cleggan /   Dawros   Maumturk Mo
Claddaghduff   An Cloigeann   Letterfrack   Kylemore   R 344   667
Omey Island   Moyard   Lough   Benbaun   10   Bealanabrac
Streamstown   Connemara   728 △   7
Kingstown   Sky Road   National Park   (▲)   Benbreen
Talbot Island   294   The Twelve Pins   710 △   Lough
Clifden /   △   Benbreen   Bencorr   Inagh   Finnisglin
Errislannan   An Clochán   Owenglin   692   C O N N E M A R
Cascade   Derrylea   N 59
Mannin   Derryclare Lou
Bay   Ballynahinch   Recess   De
Doonloughan   Ballinaboy   Lake   5½   Ballinafad   Sraith Salach
R 341   Toombeola   R 342   Cashel / An Caiseal
Ballyconneely   R 341
Callow   R 340
Slyne Head   Errisbeg   Bunnahown
Ballyconneely   300 △   Gowla
Bay   Roundstone   Derryrush
Inishnee   354 △
Bertraghboy Bay
Lough   Glinsk / Glinsce
Bola   Kilkie
Moyrus   L. Skannive   Kylesalia
Croaghnakeela Island   Mace   Bay
Head   Carna   Kilkieran /
Ard   Cill Chiaráin
St. Macdara's Island ⚓   R 340
Ardmore   Lettermo
Mweenish Island   Lettercallow   Island
A   98   B   C
Inishbarra   Teeranea
Casheen Bay

0   2.5   5   7.5   10 miles

B

A T L A N T

Benwee

Kid Island

Erris Head

Broad Haven

Rinroe Point

Eagle Island

Aghadoon

138
Knocknalina

Corclogh   4

Annagh Head

6

Belmullet /
Béal an Mhuirthead

Inver

R 313

Inishglora

R 313

An Geata Mór   4½

R 314

Ba
Bar

Corraun Point

Drumreagh

Trawmore
Bay

Bunnahowen /
Bun na hAbhn

7

Mullet Peninsula

7½

Elly Bay

12

7½

R 313

Doolough Point

Srah

Inishkea North

Tristia   7

Inishkea South

Aghleam

105
6½

Dooyork

6½

Geesala /
Gaoth Saile

Fallmore

Blacksod
Point

Black Rock

Duvillaun More

Duvillaun Beg

Blacksod
Bay

Tullaghan
Bay

Doohooma

Shrana

Saddle Head

Ridge Point

Fahy Lough

Doona

N 59

Slievemore

671

Valley

Ballyc

Doogort   2

Croaghaun
667

Achill Head

Dooagh

R 319   Keel   River

Keel Lough

Inishbiggle

Castlehill

Be

Bunacurry

Annagh
Island

Moyteoge Head

Keem Strand

Cathedral Rocks

Cashel

Sal̃a

Claggan

A

B

C

(▲) **ACHILL ISLAND**
Dooega Head

464

Knockmore

Dooega /Dumha Éige   340

Achill

R 319   6

39

4

112

C   O   C   E   A   N

Stags of Broad Haven

Portacloy
232
owteige /
ú Thaidhg   Porturlin
Port Durlainne   305 Glinsk
ross Port   340
llatomish   Annie Brady   Belderrig
             Bridge   Béal Deirg   Ceide
nalower   Glenamoy /   Fields
             Gleann na Múaidhe   Maumakeogh
Bellanaboy Bridge   379
                                          Ballycastle
                          Benmore
                          351
owmore Lake   31
             331
         Slieve Fyagh   Sheskin
                                                    Creevagh
Attavally   Corvoley
Bangor   Kilcon
          Largan 8½   Doobehy   Belville
Owenmore
                  Bellacorick   Eskeragh
Br.   42 26
aghaunmore R.   N 59   Crossmolina /
            Slieve Car   R 312   Crois Mhaoilíona
                                           Deel
            720   Deel Bridge
                                                    Rake Street
            Nephin Beg
            628   Keenagh   Castlehill
         Bunaveela   Errew
         Lough   387   Lahardaun
hduggaun 628   804   Cuilkillew   Nephin
ennamong Beg   Derreen   Glen
712   Birreencorragh   Ballynagoraher
581   Srahmore   Bofeenaun
                                                    Levally
                                                    Lough
                                                    Pontoon

Belderg
Harbour   Downpatrick Head
                                    Creevagh Head
Muingnabo 7   R 314   Bunatrahir
                         Bay
                                 Gortmore   Rathlackan
            R 314   Kilcummin
            Way   Killogeary
                        5½   Carrowmore   6
                        R 314   Lackan
            Western   17   Rathfran   Bay
                        4   Killala Bay
                                 Killala
                        Owenny   Moyne
            Cloonaghmore   Rathoma
                                        Rosserk
                        R 315   6   Castleconor
            Muing Lough Dahybaun
                                 Knockanillaun   N 59 Crockets Town
                                        N 59
                        6½   (▲) Ballina /
                                        Béal an Átha
                        R 315   Garrycloonagh
                        Deel   9½   LOUGH
                                       Newtown
                                       Cloghans   Corroy
                                              Mount Falcon
                        R 315   Brackwanshagh
                                       Knockmore
                        R 315 CONN   E   25 40

Lenadoon Point
                        Easky (△)
          Rathlee   R 297
                                    N 59
          Kilglass   R 297   Dromo
                        Drinaghan   53
          Inishcrone   Owenbeg
                   R 298   Culleens
                   N 59 Corbally
                              Slieve Gamph or the Ox Mountai
                        Bunnyconnellan   329
                        R 294
                                    Largan   20
                                    Bellanagraugh Br.
                        333   Mullany's Cross
                   Attymass   Kilmacteige   Arinagh
                        Corlee   Aclare   Toorle
                   Church Village   F   Banada
                   Cullin
                   Carrowmore   Curraghbau
                        Foxford   Killasse   Ower

0   2.5   5   7.5   10 miles

West Town

East To

Tory

Bloody Foreland Head

R 257

316 △   Meenacl

Brinlack
Bun na Leaca

Gweedor

*Gola Island /
Gabhla*

Derrybeg

Tie

Middletown

*Owey Island /
Llaighe*

Bunbeg /
An Bun Beag

R 258

3   Gweedo
Gaoth D

*Inishfree
Bay*

R 257

Dore

Clady

*Cruit
Island*

Kincasslagh

DONEGAL
AIRPORT

R 259

Crolly /
Croithlí

Torneady Point

*Rosses
Bay*

The

Annagary

Loughanure

519

*Aran or
Aranmore Island /
Árainn Mhór*

228 △   Leabgarrow

Burtonport
Ailt an Chorráin

Anure

Meencor

Ballintra

Rosses
(△)

Meela

Owenato

*Rutland
Island*

R 259

(△)

*Lough
Croangar*

390

Inishfree Upper

Dungloe /
An Clochán Liath

Crohy Head

Maghery

Meenatotan

R 252

Derrydruel

R 25

Gweebarra

Meenacross

384 △

Roaninish

Bay

*Trawenagh
Bay*

17
27

Doocharry
An Dúchoraidh

Gweeb

Dooey Point

Derrylough

Ballynacarrick

Ba

Dunmore Head

(△) Portnoo

Lettermacaward /
Leitir Mhic an Bhaird

Dawros Head

Clooney

Narin

Gweebarra
Bridge

335

Aghla

Rossbeg

Maas

Kilclooney

N 56

R 250

D

*Loughros More
Bay*

R 261

*L.
Machugh*

Glenties

R 253

Stracashel

Ta

Loughros Point

Glendorragha

Crannogeboy

Owenea

N 56   6

Kilrean

Slievetooey

443 △

Maghera

Laconnell

Ardara

R 262

Glen Head

Olencolmcille
Folk Village

374

Stravally

*Lough
Nalughraman*

50
502 △ 31

Neck of the Ballagh

521

Glen Bay

Rossan Point

Malin More

Glencolumbkille /
Gleann Choilm Cille

Crove

**Glengesh
Pass**

Meenybraddan

Tullynaha

*Malin
Bay*

Malin Beg /
Málainn Bhig

R 263

Meenaneary /
Mín na Aoire

Meentullynagarn

Meenavean

Arnicle
Glenbarr   Beinn
Bellochantuy   Saddell   Saddell Bay
Lussa Loch   Sgreadan Hill (▲)   Drumadoon Point
397   Ugadale Bay (▲)   Blackwater
Skeroblingarry   Black Bay (▲)   Drumadoon B
Kilchenzie   A 83   Peninver   Ardnacross Bay   Brown H
9½
(▲) Machrihanish Bay   ( ) (△)
Machrihanish   Campbeltown   1
6   B 843   A 83   Campbeltown Loch   Island Davaar
Drumlemble   Stewarton
352
Knocknaha   Beinn Ghuilean
Cnoc Moy   96   B 842
△ 446   9½   Conie Glen
Rubha Dùin Bhàin   Feochaig
Johnston's Point
S. Carrine
Macharioch
Southend
Mull of Kintyre   Sanda Sound   Sheep Island

Rathlin Island   Sanda Island
(▲ ♦)
nt   Church Quarter   ANTRIM
a-rede   N   O   R   T   H   2
Bridge   Sound
Rue Point
Benmore or Fair Head   C   H   A
astle   Ballycastle Bay   Murlough Bay
aff   A 2   Ulster   Way   Torr Head
arneatly   Ballyvoy   Glensheck
Knocklayd   379   △   Runabay Head   P
514   Ballypatrick Forest
403 △
hoe   16   B 92   Crockaneel
Glendun   Cushendun (△)   2
Glenaan   6½   Knocknacarry
Slieveanorra   A 2
508   Ossian's Grave
Trostan   Glenballyemon   Cushendall (△)
key   Red Bay
550   Glenariff or Waterfoot
Glenariff   Garron Point
(△)
Glenariff   Big Trosk
newtown-   Forest   377   Carnlough (△)   3
ommelin   Cargan   Park   Waterfalls   Carnlough Bay
B 64   A 43   Dungonnell Dam   △ 434
ogh   Collin Top   Glenarm
Martinstown   A 42   26
B 94   Carnageer   Gléncloy   B 97
rs   The Sheddings   381   Feystown
A 43   12   Carnalbanagh   B 148
Quarrytown   Sheddings   Ballygalley Head   3
A 42   Buckna   437   Carncastle   Ballygalley
Broughshane   Slemish Mountain   A 2   Drains Bay
11   ✶   L   A   R   N   E   13
Ballymena   5½
10   A 2   Larne (▲ △)
Y   M   E   N   A   Agnew's Hill   Isle   P
8   B 94   Monfields   Shoptown   32   Millbrook   Portm   A
Kells   B 59   A 36   20   Kilwaughter   A 8   Mullaghboy
53   11   Glynn   B 90   Millbay
Connor   Ballyboley   Maghermorne   Larne Lough   Island Magee
Forest

120 Great Britain

A B C D E F G H I J K L M N O P Q R S T U V W X Y Z

Page number / Numéro de page / Seitenzahl
Paginanummer / Numero di pagina / Número de Página

Place / Localité / Ort
Plaatsen / Località / Localidad

Achmelvich ....84 E 9

Grid coordinates / Coordonnées de carroyage
Koordinatenangabe / Verwijstekens ruitsysteem
Coordinate riferite alla quadrettatura
Coordenadas en los mapas

A

A Chill 71 A 12
A La Ronde 4 J 32
Abbas Combe 9 M 30
Abberley 27 M 27
Abbey 23 X 30
Abbey Dore 26 L 28
Abbey Town 54 K 19
Abbeydale 43 P 23
Abbeystead 48 L 22
Abbots Bromley 35 O 25
Abbots Langley 21 S 28
Abbots Leigh 18 M 29
Abbots Ripton 29 T 26
Abbotsbury 5 M 32
Abbotsford House 62 L 17
Abbotskerswell 4 J 32
Aber Banc 15 G 27
Aberaeron 24 H 27
Aberaman 17 J 28
Aberangell 33 I 25
Abercarn 18 K 29
Abercastle 14 E 28
Aberchirder 81 M 11
Abercynon 17 J 29
Aberdâr / Aberdare 17 J 28
Aberdare / Aberdâr 17 J 28
Aberdaron 32 F 25
Aberdaugleddau / Milford Haven 14 E 28
Aberdeen 75 N 12
Aberdour 68 K 15
Aberdour Bay 81 N 10
Aberdovey / Aberdyfi 33 H 26
Aberdyfi / Aberdovey 33 H 26
Aberedw 25 J 27
Abereiddy 14 E 28
Aberfeldy 73 I 14
Aberffraw 32 G 24
Aberford 43 P 22
Aberfoyle 67 G 15
Abergavenny / Y-Fenni 18 K 28
Abergele 41 J 23
Abergolech 15 H 28
Abergwaun / Fishguard 24 F 28
Abergwesyn 25 I 27
Abergwili 15 H 28
Abergwynfi 17 J 29
Abergwyngregyn 41 H 23
Abergynolwyn 33 I 26
Aberhonddu / Brecon 25 J 28
Aberkenfig 17 J 29
Aberlady 69 L 15
Aberlemno 75 L 13
Aberlour 80 K 11
Abermaw / Barmouth 33 H 25
Abermule 34 K 26
Abernethy 68 K 15
Abernyte 68 K 14
Aberpennar / Mountain Ash 17 J 28
Aberporth 15 G 27
Abersoch 32 G 25
Abersychan 18 K 28
Abertawe / Swansea 17 I 29
Aberteifi / Cardigan 15 G 27
Abertillery 18 K 28
Aberuthven 67 J 15
Aberystwyth 25 H 26
Abingdon 20 Q 28
Abinger Common 21 S 30
Abinger Hammer 21 S 30
Abington *Cambs.* 30 U 27
Abington *South Lanarkshire* 61 I 17
Aboyne 75 L 12
Abriachan 79 G 11
Abridge 21 U 29
Accrington 42 M 22
Achahoish 65 D 16
Achallader 66 F 14
Achanalt 78 F 11
Achaphubuil 72 E 13
Acharacle 71 C 13
Achargary 85 H 8
Acharn 67 H 14
Achduart 83 E 10
Achgarve 78 D 10
Achiemore 84 F 8
Achiltibuie 83 D 9
Achintee 78 D 11
Achintraid 78 D 11
Achlean 73 I 12
Achleck 64 B 14
Achmelvich 84 E 9
Achmore 78 D 11
Achnahanat 84 G 10
Achnamara 65 D 15
Achnanellan 72 E 13
Achnasheen 78 E 11
Achnashellach Forest 78 E 11
Achosnich 71 B 13
Achranich 71 C 14
Achray (Loch) 67 G 15
Achreamie 85 I 8
Achriesgill 84 F 8
Achtalean 77 B 11
Achvaich 79 H 10
Acklington 63 P 18
Ackworth 44 P 23
Acle 39 Y 26
Acomb 55 N 19
Acrise Place 13 X 30
Acton Burnell 34 L 26
Acton Scott 26 L 26
Acton Turville 19 N 29
Adbaston 35 M 25
Adderbury 28 Q 27
Adderley 34 M 25
Adderstone 63 O 17
Addingham 49 O 22
Addlestone 21 S 29
Adfa 33 J 26
Adlington 42 M 23
Adlington Hall 43 N 24
Advie 80 J 11
Adwick-le-Street 44 Q 23
Ae (Forest of) 53 J 18
Ae Village 53 J 18
Afan Argoed 17 J 29
Affric (Glen) 78 F 12
Affric Lodge 78 E 12
Afon Dyfrdwy / Dee (River) 34 K 24
Afon Dyfrdwy (River) / Dee *Wales* 41 K 23
Afon-wen 41 K 23
Agneash 46 G 21
Aikton 54 K 19
Ailort (Loch) 72 C 13
Ailsa Craig 59 E 18
Ainderby Quernhow 50 P 21
Ainort (Loch) 77 B 12
Ainsdale 42 K 23
Air Uig 82 Y 9
Aird 65 D 15
Aird (The) 79 G 11
Aird of Sleat 71 C 12
Airdrie 61 I 16
Airigh na h-Airde (Loch) 82 Z 9
Airor 72 C 12
Airth 67 I 15
Airton 49 N 21
Aith *Orkney Is.* 87 M 6
Aith *Shetland Is.* 87 P 3
Aitnoch 80 I 11
Akeld 63 N 17
Albourne 11 T 31
Albrighton 35 N 26
Albyn or Mor (Glen) 73 F 12
Alcaig 79 G 11
Alcester 27 O 27
Alconbury 29 T 26
Aldborough 39 X 25
Aldbourne 19 P 29
Aldbrough 45 T 22
Aldbrough St. John 49 O 20
Aldbury 21 S 28
Alde (River) 31 Y 27
Aldeburgh 31 Y 27
Aldenham 21 S 28
Alderbury 9 O 30
Alderholt 9 O 31
Alderley Edge 43 N 24
Alderney *Channel I.* 5
Aldershot 20 R 30
Alderton 27 N 28
Aldford 34 L 24
Aldingbourne 11 R 31
Aldridge 35 O 26
Aldringham 31 Y 27
Aldsworth 19 O 28
Aldunie 80 K 12
Aldwick 11 R 31
Alexandria 66 G 16
Alfold Crossways 11 S 30
Alford *Aberdeenshire* 75 L 12
Alford *Lincs.* 45 U 24
Alfreton 36 P 24
Alfrick 27 M 27
Alfriston 12 U 31
Aline (Loch) 65 C 14
Alkborough 44 S 22
Alkham 13 X 30
All Stretton 34 L 26
Allanaquoich 74 J 12
Allanton *North Lanarkshire* 61 I 16
Allanton *Scottish Borders* 63 N 16
Allendale Town 55 N 19
Allenheads 55 N 19
Allensmore 26 L 27
Allerford 17 J 30
Allerston 51 S 21
Allestree 36 P 25
Allhallows 22 V 29
Alligin Shuas 78 D 11
Allington *Kennet* 19 O 29
Allington *Salisbury* 9 O 30
Allnabad 84 G 8
Alloa 67 I 15
Allonby 54 J 19
Alloway 60 G 17
Allt na h-Airbhe 78 E 10
Alltan Fhèarna (Loch an) 85 H 9
Alltnacaillich 84 G 8
Almond (Glen) 67 I 14
Almondbank 68 J 14
Almondsbury 18 M 29
Alness 79 H 10
Alnmouth 63 P 17
Alnwick 63 O 17
Alpheton 30 W 27
Alphington 4 J 31
Alpraham 34 M 24
Alresford 30 X 28
Alrewas 35 O 25
Alsager 35 N 24
Alsh (Loch) 78 D 12
Alston 55 M 19
Alstonefield 35 O 24
Alswear 7 I 31
Altadnduin 85 H 9
Altandhu 83 D 9
Altarnun 3 G 32
Altass 84 G 10
Alternative Technology Centre 33 I 26
Altham 42 M 22
Althorne 22 W 29
Althorpe 44 R 23
Altnabreac Station 85 I 8
Altnacealgach 84 F 9
Altnaharra 84 G 9
Alton *Hants.* 10 R 30
Alton *Staffs.* 35 O 25
Alton Pancras 9 M 31
Alton Priors 19 O 29
Alton Towers 35 O 25
Altrincham 42 M 23
Alum Bay 10 P 31
Alva 67 I 15
Alvaston 36 P 25
Alvechurch 27 O 26
Alvediston 9 N 30
Alves 80 J 11
Alvescot 19 P 28
Alvie 73 I 12
Alvingham 45 U 23
Alwinton 63 N 17
Alyth 74 K 14
Amberley 11 S 31
Amble 63 P 18
Amblecote 27 N 26
Ambleside 48 L 20
Ambrosden 28 Q 28
Amersham 21 S 29
Amesbury 9 O 30
Amhuinnsuidhe 82 Y 10
Amisfield 53 J 18
Amlwch 40 G 22
Ammanford / Rhydaman 15 I 28
Amotherby 50 R 21
Ampleforth 50 Q 21
Amport 20 P 30
Ampthill 29 S 27
Amroth 15 G 28
Amulree 67 I 14
An Riabhachan 78 E 11
An Socach 74 J 13
An Teallach 78 E 10
Anchor 26 K 26
Ancroft 63 O 16
Ancrum 62 M 17
Andover 20 P 30
Andoversford 27 O 28
Andreas 46 G 20
Angle 14 E 28
Anglesey (Isle of) 40
Anglesey Abbey 30 U 27
Angmering 11 S 31
Annan 54 K 19
Annan (River) 61 J 18
Annat 78 D 11
Annat Bay 83 E 10
Annbank 60 G 17
Annbank Station 60 G 17
Anne Hathaway's Cottage 27 O 27
Annesley-Woodhouse 36 Q 24
Annfield Plain 56 O 19
Ansley 28 P 26
Anstey 36 Q 25
Anston 44 Q 23
Anstruther 69 L 15
Anthorn 54 K 19
Antony House 3 H 32
Appin 72 E 14
Appleby *Eden* 55 M 20
Appleby *North Lincolnshire* 44 S 23
Appleby Magna 36 P 25
Applecross 77 C 11
Appledore *Devon* 6 H 30
Appledore *Kent* 12 W 30
Appleford 20 Q 29
Appleton 20 P 28
Appleton Roebuck 44 Q 22
Appleton Wiske 50 P 20
Appletreewick 49 O 21
Aran Fawddwy 33 I 25
Arberth / Narberth 15 F 28
Arbigland 53 J 19
Arbirlot 69 M 14
Arbor Low 35 O 24
Arborfield 20 R 29
Arbroath 69 M 14
Arbury Hall 28 P 26
Arbuthnott 75 N 13
Archiestown 80 K 11
Ard (Loch) 67 G 15
Ardanaiseig 66 E 14
Ardarroch 78 D 11
Ardcharnich 78 E 10
Ardchiavaig 64 B 15
Ardchuilk 78 F 11
Ardchyle 67 G 14
Ardechive 72 E 13
Arden 66 G 15
Ardentallan 65 D 14
Ardeonaig 67 H 14
Ardersier 79 H 11
Ardery 72 C 13
Ardfern 65 D 15
Ardgartan 66 F 15
Ardgay 79 G 10
Ardgour 72 D 13
Ardhasaig 82 Z 10
Ardingly 11 T 30
Ardington 20 P 29
Ardivachar 76 X 11
Ardleigh 30 W 28
Ardley 28 Q 28
Ardlui 66 F 15
Ardlussa 65 C 15
Ardmair 84 E 10
Ardminish 58 C 16
Ardmore Point *Isle of Skye* 77 A 11
Ardnacross 71 C 14
Ardnamurchan 71 B 13
Ardnastang 72 D 13
Ardnave 64 A 16
Ardnave Point 64 B 16
Ardpatrick 59 D 16
Ardrishaig 65 D 15
Ardrossan 59 F 17
Ardshealach 71 C 13
Ardslignish 71 C 13
Ardtalla 58 B 16
Ardtalnaig 67 H 14
Ardtoe 71 C 13
Ardvasar 71 C 12
Ardverikie Forest 73 G 13
Ardvorlich 67 H 14
Ardwell 52 F 19
Argyll 65 D 15
Argyll Forest Park 66 F 15
Arichastlich 66 F 14
Arienas (Loch) 71 C 14
Arileod 71 A 14
Arinacrinachd 77 C 11
Arinagour 71 A 14
Arisaig 71 C 13
Arivruaich 82 Z 9
Arkaig (Loch) 72 E 13
Arkendale 50 P 21
Arkengarthdale 49 O 20
Arkholme 48 M 21
Arklet (Loch) 66 G 15
Arley 27 P 26
Arlingham 19 M 28
Arlington Court 7 I 30
Armadale *Highland* 85 H 8
Armadale *West Lothian* 61 I 16
Armadale Bay 71 C 12
Armitage 35 O 25
Armthorpe 44 Q 23
Arnabost 71 A 14
Arncliffe 49 N 21
Arncott 20 Q 28
Arncroach 69 L 15
Arne 9 N 31
Arnesby 28 Q 26
Arnicle 59 D 17
Arnisdale 72 D 12
Arnish 77 B 11
Arnol 82 A 8
Arnold 36 Q 25
Arnprior 67 H 15
Arnside 48 L 21
Aros 65 B 14
Arram 45 S 22
Arran (Isle of) 59 E 17
Arreton 10 Q 31
Arrochar 66 F 15
Arscaig 84 G 9
Arundel 11 S 31
Ascog 59 E 16
Ascot 21 R 29
Ascott House 29 R 28
Ascott-under-Wychwood 28 P 28
Ascrib Islands 77 A 11
Asfordby 36 R 25
Ash *Kent* 23 X 30
Ash *Surrey* 20 R 30
Ash Mill 7 I 31
Ashbourne 35 O 24
Ashburton 4 I 32
Ashbury 19 P 29
Ashby de la Zouch 36 P 25
Ashby Magna 28 Q 26
Ashcott 8 L 30
Ashdon 30 U 27
Ashford *Kent* 12 W 30
Ashford *Surrey* 21 S 29
Ashford-in-the-Water *Derbs.* 43 O 24
Ashie (Loch) 79 H 11
Ashill *Breckland* 38 W 26
Ashill *South Somerset* 8 L 31
Ashingdon 22 W 29
Ashington *Northumb* 56 P 18
Ashington *West Sussex* 11 S 31
Ashkirk 62 L 17
Ashleworth 27 N 28
Ashley *East Cambridgeshire* 30 V 27
Ashley *Newcastle-under-Lyme* 35 M 25
Ashley *Torridge* 7 I 31
Ashley Green 21 S 28
Ashmore 9 N 31
Ashover 36 P 24
Ashperton 26 M 27
Ashreigney 7 I 31
Ashtead 21 T 30
Ashton 34 L 24
Ashton-in-Makerfield 42 M 23
Ashton Keynes 19 O 29
Ashton-under-Lyne 43 N 23
Ashton-upon-Mersey 42 M 23
Ashurst 10 P 31
Ashwell *North Hertfordshire* 29 T 27
Ashwell *Rutland* 36 R 25
Ashwellthorpe 39 X 26
Askam in Furness 47 K 21
Askern 44 Q 23
Askernish 76 X 12
Askerswell 5 L 31
Askham 55 L 20
Askrigg 49 N 21
Askwith 49 O 22
Aslacton 31 X 26
Aslockton 36 R 25
Aspatria 54 K 19
Aspley Guise 29 S 27
Assynt (Loch) 84 E 9
Astley 34 L 25
Aston *Vale Royal* 44 Q 23
Aston *West Oxfordshire* 20 P 28
Aston Clinton 20 R 28
Aston Magna 27 O 27
Aston Rowant 20 R 28
Aston Tirrold 20 Q 29
Astwood Bank 27 O 27
Atcham 34 L 25
Athelhampton Hall 9 N 31
Athelney 8 L 30
Athelstaneford 69 L 16
Atherington 7 H 31
Athersley 43 P 23
Atherstone 36 P 26
Atherton 42 M 23
Atholl (Forest of) 73 H 13
Attadale 78 D 11
Attleborough *Breckland* 38 X 26
Attleborough *Nuneaton and Bedworth* 28 P 26
Attlebridge 39 X 25
Atwick 51 T 22
Atworth 19 N 29
Aucharnie 81 M 11
Auchavan 74 K 13
Auchenblae 75 M 13
Auchenbowie 67 I 15
Auchenbrack 61 I 18
Auchenbreck 65 E 16
Auchencairn 53 I 19
Auchencrosh 52 F 18
Auchencrow 63 N 16
Auchengray 61 J 16
Auchenmalg 52 F 19
Auchentiber 60 G 16

A

Auchindrean	78	E 10
Auchinleck	60	H 17
Auchleven	81	M 12
Auchlyne	67	G 14
Auchnafree	67	I 14
Auchnagallin	80	J 11
Auchnagatt	81	N 11
Aucholzie	74	K 12
Auchronie	74	L 13
Auchterarder	67	I 15
Auchteraw	73	F 12
Auchterderran	68	K 15
Auchterhouse	68	K 14
Auchtermuchty	68	K 15
Auchtertyre	78	D 12
Auckengill	86	K 8
Auckley	44	Q 23
Audenshaw	43	N 23
Audlem	34	M 25
Audley	35	N 24
Audley End	30	U 27
Aughton near Lancaster	48	L 21
Aughton near Ormskirk	42	L 23
Auldearn	79	I 11
Auldgirth	53	I 18
Auldhouse	60	H 16
Ault a' Chruinn	72	D 12
Aultbea	78	D 10
Aust	18	M 29
Austrey	35	P 26
Austwick	49	M 21
Avebury	19	O 29
Aveley	22	U 29
Avening	19	N 28
Aveton Gifford	4	I 33
Aviemore	73	I 12
Avoch	79	H 11
Avon (Glen)	74	J 12
Avon (River) R. Severn	28	Q 26
Avon (River) Wilts.	9	O 31
Avonbridge	67	I 16
Avonmouth	18	L 29
Avonwick	4	I 32
Awe (Loch)	65	E 15
Awliscombe	8	K 31
Awre	19	M 28
Axbridge	18	L 30
Axminster	8	L 31
Axmouth	5	K 31
Aylburton	18	M 28
Aylesbury	20	R 28
Aylesford	22	V 30
Aylesham	23	X 30
Aylsham	39	X 25
Aylton	26	M 27
Aymestrey	26	L 27
Aynho	28	Q 28
Ayr	60	G 17
Aysgarth	49	O 21
Ayside	48	L 21
Ayton Scarborough	51	S 21
Ayton Scottish Borders	63	N 16

B

Bà (Loch)	65	C 14
Babbacombe Bay	4	J 32
Babcary	8	M 30
Babell	41	K 23
Babworth	44	R 24
Back	83	B 9
Backaland	87	L 6
Backmuir of New Gilston	69	L 15
Backwater Reservoir	74	K 13
Backwell West Town	18	L 29
Baconsthorpe	39	X 25
Bacton Mid Suffolk	30	X 27
Bacton North Norfolk	39	Y 25
Bacup	43	N 22
Bad a' Ghaill (Loch)	84	E 9
Bad an Sgalaig (Loch)	78	D 10
Badachro	77	C 10
Badanloch (Loch)	85	H 9
Badanloch Lodge	85	H 9
Badcaul	78	D 10
Baddesley Ensor	35	P 26
Baddidarach	84	E 9
Badenoch	73	H 13
Badenscallie	83	E 9
Badenyon	74	K 12
Badlipster	86	K 8
Badluarach	78	D 10
Badminton	19	N 29
Badrallach	78	E 10
Bae Colwyn / Colwyn Bay	41	I 23
Bagh nam Faoileann	76	Y 11
Bagillt	41	K 23
Bagley	34	L 25

Bagshot	21	R 29
Bagworth	36	P 25
Bagwyllydiart	26	L 28
Baile Mòr	64	A 15
Bailiehill	54	K 18
Bainbridge	49	N 21
Bainton	51	S 22
Bakewell	35	O 24
Bala	33	J 25
Balallan	82	A 9
Balbeggie	68	J 14
Balblair	79	H 10
Balcary Point	53	I 19
Balchrick	84	E 8
Balcombe	11	T 30
Balderton	36	R 24
Baldrine	46	G 21
Baldwin	46	G 21
Balemartine	64	Z 14
Balephetrish Bay	70	Z 14
Balephuil	64	Z 14
Balephuil Bay	64	Z 14
Balerno	61	J 16
Baleshare	76	X 11
Balevulin	65	B 14
Balfour	87	L 6
Balfron	67	H 15
Balgray	69	L 14
Balintore Angus	74	K 13
Balintore Highland	79	I 10
Balivanich	76	X 11
Balk	50	Q 21
Ballabeg	46	F 21
Ballachulish	72	E 13
Ballajora	46	G 21
Ballamodha	46	G 21
Ballantrae	52	E 18
Ballasalla	46	G 21
Ballater	74	K 12
Ballaugh	46	G 21
Ballevullin	70	Z 14
Balliemore near Dunoon	65	E 15
Balliemore near Oban	65	D 14
Ballig	46	G 21
Ballingry	68	K 15
Ballinluig	74	J 14
Ballochan	75	L 12
Ballochroy	59	D 16
Ballyhaugh	71	A 14
Balmaclellan	53	H 18
Balmacara	72	D 12
Balmaha	67	G 15
Balmedie	75	N 12
Balminnoch	52	F 19
Balmoral Castle	74	K 12
Balmullo	69	L 14
Balnacra	78	D 11
Balnafoich	79	H 11
Balnaguard	74	I 14
Balnahard	64	B 14
Balnakeil Bay	84	F 8
Balnaknock	77	B 11
Balnapaling	79	H 10
Baltonsborough	8	M 30
Balvicar	65	D 15
Balvraid	72	D 12
Bamburgh Castle	63	O 17
Bamford	43	O 23
Bampton Cumbria	48	L 20
Bampton Devon	7	J 31
Bampton Oxon.	20	P 28
Banavie	72	E 13
Banbury	28	P 27
Banchory	75	M 12
Bancyfelin	15	G 28
Bandenscoth	81	M 11
Banff	81	M 10
Bangor	40	H 23
Bankend	53	J 18
Bankfoot	68	J 14
Bankhead	75	N 12
Banks	42	L 22
Bankshill	54	K 18
Banniskirk	85	J 8
Bannockburn	67	I 15
Banstead	21	T 30
Banwell	18	L 30
Bapchild	22	W 30
Bar Hill	29	U 27
Barbaraville	79	H 10
Barbon	48	M 21
Barcaldine	65	E 14
Barcombe Cross	11	U 31
Bardney	45	T 24
Bardsea	48	K 21
Bardsey	43	P 22
Bardsey Island	32	F 25

Barford	39	X 26
Barford-St. Martin	9	O 30
Barfreston	23	X 30
Bargoed	18	K 28
Bargrennan	52	G 18
Barham	23	X 30
Barking	30	X 27
Barking and Dagenham		
London Borough	21	U 29
Barkston	37	S 25
Barkway	29	U 28
Barlaston	35	N 25
Barlborough	44	Q 24
Barlestone	36	P 26
Barley North Hertfordshire	29	U 27
Barley Pendle	42	N 22
Barlow	43	P 24
Barmby on the Marsh	44	R 22
Barming	22	V 30
Barmouth / Abermaw	33	H 25
Barmouth Bay	33	H 25
Barmston	51	T 21
Barnack	37	S 26
Barnard Castle	49	O 20
Barnby Dun	44	Q 23
Barnby Moor		
East Riding of Yorks.	50	R 22
Barnby Moor Notts.	44	Q 23
Barnet London Borough	21	T 29
Barnetby-le-Wold	45	S 23
Barney	38	W 25
Barnham	30	W 26
Barnham Broom	38	X 26
Barnhill	80	J 11
Barnhills	52	E 18
Barningham	49	O 20
Barnoldswick	49	N 22
Barnsley	43	P 23
Barnstaple	7	H 30
Barnton	42	M 24
Barnwell	29	S 26
Barr	52	F 18
Barra	70	X 13
Barra (Sound of)	70	X 12
Barra Head	70	X 13
Barregarrow	46	G 21
Barrhead	60	G 16
Barrhill	52	F 18
Barri / Barry	18	K 29
Barrington	8	L 31
Barrisdale	72	D 12
Barrisdale Bay	72	D 12
Barrmill	60	G 16
Barrock	86	K 8
Barrow	30	V 27
Barrow Burn	63	N 17
Barrow Gurney	18	L 29
Barrow-in-Furness	47	K 21
Barrow-upon-Humber	45	S 22
Barrow-upon-Soar	36	Q 25
Barrowby	36	R 25
Barrowford	43	N 22
Barry Angus	69	L 14
Barry / Barri		
Vale of Glamorgan	18	K 29
Barsham	31	Y 26
Barston	27	O 26
Bartestree	26	M 27
Barton Eden	49	P 20
Barton Lancs.	42	L 22
Barton le Willows	50	R 21
Barton Mills	30	V 26
Barton-le-Clay	29	S 28
Barton-on-Sea	9	P 31
Barton-under-Needwood	35	O 25
Barton-upon-Humber	44	S 22
Barvas	82	A 8
Barwell	36	P 26
Barwick-in-Elmet	43	P 22
Baschurch	34	L 25
Bashall Eaves	42	M 22
Basildon Berks.	20	Q 29
Basildon Essex	22	V 29
Basing	20	Q 30
Basingstoke	20	Q 30
Baslow	43	P 24
Bass Rock	69	M 15
Bassenthwaite	54	K 19
Bassingham	37	S 24
Baston	37	S 25
Bastwick	39	Y 25
Batcombe	8	M 31
Bath	19	M 29
Bathampton	19	N 29
Batheaston	19	N 29
Bathgate	61	J 16
Batley	43	P 22

Battle	12	V 31
Baumber	45	T 24
Bawburgh	39	X 26
Bawdeswell	38	X 25
Bawdsey	31	Y 27
Bawtry	44	Q 23
Bayble	83	B 9
Baycliff	48	K 21
Baydon	19	P 29
Bayhead	76	X 11
Bayston Hill	34	L 25
Beachampton	28	R 27
Beachy Head	12	U 31
Beacon (The)	2	E 33
Beacon End	30	W 28
Beaconsfield	21	S 29
Beadlam	50	R 21
Beadnell Bay	63	P 17
Beaford	7	H 31
Beal	63	O 16
Beaminster	8	L 31
Beamish Hall	56	P 19
Beamsley	49	O 22
Bearsden	67	G 16
Bearsted	22	V 30
Beattock	61	J 18
Beauchief	43	P 24
Beaufort	18	K 28
Beaulieu	10	P 31
Beauly	79	G 11
Beauly Firth	79	G 11
Beaumaris	40	H 23
Beaumont	54	K 19
Beaupré Castle	17	J 29
Bebington	42	L 23
Beccles	31	Y 26
Beckfoot	54	J 19
Beckingham	44	R 23
Beckington	19	N 30
Beckley	12	V 31
Beckton	21	U 29
Bedale	50	P 21
Beddau	17	J 29
Beddgelert	33	H 24
Beddingham	11	U 31
Bedford	29	S 27
Bedgebury Pinetum	12	V 30
Bedlington	56	P 18
Bedlinog	17	K 28
Bedrule	62	M 17
Bedwas	18	K 29
Bedworth	28	P 26
Bee (Loch)	76	X 11
Beer	5	K 31
Beeston	36	Q 25
Beeswing	53	I 18
Begbroke	20	Q 28
Beguildy	26	K 26
Beinn a' Ghlò	74	I 13
Beinn a' Mheadhoin (Loch)	78	F 12
Beinn Dearg Highland	78	F 10
Beinn Dearg		
Perthshire and Kinross	73	I 13
Beinn Heasgarnich	67	G 14
Beinn Ime	66	F 15
Beith	60	G 16
Belbroughton	27	N 26
Belchford	45	T 24
Belford	63	O 17
Belhelvie	75	N 12
Bellabeg	74	K 12
Bellingham	55	N 18
Bellshill		
Berwick-upon-Tweed	63	O 17
Bellshill North Lanarkshire	60	H 16
Belmont	87	R 1
Belnacraig	74	K 12
Belnahua	65	C 15
Belper	36	P 24
Belsay	56	O 18
Belstead	31	X 27
Belstone	4	I 31
Belton Lincs.	37	S 25
Belton Norfolk	39	Y 26
Belton North Lincs.	44	R 23
Belton Rutland	36	R 26
Belvoir	36	R 25
Bembridge	10	Q 31
Bempton	51	T 21
Ben Alder	73	G 13
Ben Alder Lodge	73	G 13
Ben Armine Forest	85	H 9
Ben Armine Lodge	85	H 9
Ben Chonzie	67	I 14
Ben Cruachan	65	E 14
Ben-damph Forest	78	D 11

Ben Hope	84	G 8
Ben Klibreck	84	G 9
Ben Lawers	67	H 14
Ben Ledi	67	H 15
Ben Lomond	66	G 15
Ben Loyal	84	G 8
Ben Macdui	74	I 12
Ben More Argyll and Bute	65	B 14
Ben More Stirling	67	G 14
Ben More Assynt	84	F 9
Ben Nevis	72	E 13
Ben Starav	66	E 14
Ben Vorlich	67	H 14
Ben Wyvis	79	G 10
Benbecula	76	X 11
Benbuie	60	H 18
Benderloch Argyll and Bute	65	D 14
Benderloch Mountain	65	E 14
Bendronaig Lodge	78	E 11
Benenden	12	V 30
Benfleet	22	V 29
Benigton	37	U 25
Benllech	40	H 23
Benmore	67	G 14
Benmore Lodge	84	F 9
Benson	20	Q 29
Bentley Doncaster	44	Q 23
Bentley East Hampshire	20	R 30
Bentpath	54	K 18
Bentworth	10	Q 30
Benwick	29	T 26
Beoraid (Loch)	72	D 13
Bere Alston	3	H 32
Bere Ferrers	3	H 32
Bere Regis	9	N 31
Berkeley	18	M 28
Berkhamsted	21	S 28
Berneray near Barra	70	X 13
Berneray near North Uist	76	Y 10
Bernice	66	E 15
Bernisdale	77	B 11
Berriew	34	K 26
Berrington Hall	26	L 27
Berrow	18	K 30
Berry Head	4	J 32
Berry Hill	18	M 28
Berry Pomeroy	4	J 32
Berrynarbor	17	H 30
Bervie Bay	75	N 13
Berwick-St. John	9	N 31
Berwick-upon-Tweed	63	O 16
Berwyn	33	J 25
Bessacarr	44	Q 23
Bethel	33	H 24
Bethersden	12	W 30
Bethesda	33	H 24
Betley	35	M 24
Bettisfield	34	L 25
Bettws Cedewain	34	K 26
Bettws Evan	15	G 27
Bettws Gwerfil Goch	33	J 24
Bettyhill	85	H 8
Betws-y-Coed	33	I 24
Betws yn Rhos	41	J 23
Beulah near Cardigan	15	G 27
Beulah		
near Llandrindod-Wells	25	J 27
Beverley	45	S 22
Beverstone	19	N 29
Bewaldeth	54	K 19
Bewcastle	55	L 18
Bewdley	27	N 26
Bewholme	51	T 22
Bexhill	12	V 31
Bexley London Borough	21	U 29
Beyton	30	W 27
Bhaid-Luachraich (Loch)	78	D 10
Bhealaich (Loch a')	84	G 9
Bhraoin (Loch a')	78	E 10
Bhrollum (Loch)	82	A 10
Bibury	19	O 28
Bicester	28	Q 28
Bicker	37	T 25
Bickington	4	I 32
Bickleigh Mid Devon	7	J 31
Bickleigh South Hams	4	H 32
Bicton	34	L 25
Bicton gardens	5	K 31
Biddenden	12	V 30
Biddenham	29	S 27
Biddestone	19	N 29
Biddulph	35	N 24
Bidean nam Bian	72	E 14
Bideford	6	H 30
Bidford	27	O 27
Bielside	75	N 12
Bierton	20	R 28

Big Corlae	60	H 18
Bigbury	4	I 33
Bigbury-on-Sea	4	I 33
Biggar Barrow-in-Furness	47	K 21
Biggar South Lanarkshire	61	J 17
Biggin Hill	21	U 30
Biggleswade	29	T 27
Bignor	11	S 31
Bildeston	30	W 27
Bildsgreen	27	M 26
Bill of Portland	8	M 32
Billericay	22	V 29
Billesdon	36	R 26
Billingborough	37	S 25
Billinge	42	L 23
Billockby	39	Y 26
Billy Row	56	O 19
Bilsborrow	42	L 22
Bilsington	12	W 30
Bilsthorpe	36	Q 24
Bilston	35	N 26
Bilton	45	T 22
Binbrook	45	T 23
Binfield	20	R 29
Bingham	36	R 25
Bingley	43	O 22
Binham	38	W 25
Binns (The)	68	J 16
Binsted	10	R 30
Birchington	23	X 29
Birdham	10	R 31
Birdingbury	28	P 27
Birdwell	43	P 23
Birdworld	10	R 30
Birgham	62	N 17
Birkdale	42	K 23
Birkenhead	42	K 23
Birkin	44	Q 22
Birling Gap	12	U 31
Birmingham	27	O 26
Birnam	68	J 14
Birsay	86	K 6
Birsemore	75	L 12
Birstall	36	Q 25
Birtley Gateshead	56	P 19
Birtley Tynedale	55	N 18
Birtsmorton Court	27	N 27
Bisham	20	R 29
Bishop Auckland	56	P 20
Bishop Burton	44	S 22
Bishop Monkton	50	P 21
Bishop Sutton	18	M 29
Bishop Thornton	50	P 21
Bishop Wilton	50	R 22
Bishops Cannings	19	O 29
Bishop's Castle	26	L 26
Bishop's Caundle	9	M 31
Bishop's Cleeve	27	N 28
Bishop's Itchington	28	P 27
Bishops Lydeard	8	K 30
Bishop's Nympton	7	I 31
Bishop's Palace		
near St. David's	14	E 28
Bishop's Palace near Tenby	16	F 28
Bishop's Stortford	30	U 28
Bishop's Tachbrook	28	P 27
Bishop's Tawton	7	H 30
Bishop's Waltham	10	Q 31
Bishopsteignton	4	J 32
Bishopstocke	10	Q 31
Bishopston	15	H 29
Bishopstone Salisbury	9	O 30
Bishopstone Swindon	19	P 29
Bishopsthorpe	50	Q 22
Bishopton Darlington	56	P 20
Bishopton Renfrewshire	67	G 16
Bishton	18	L 29
Bisley	19	N 28
Bispham	42	K 22
Bix	20	R 29
Bixter	87	P 3
Blaby	36	Q 26
Black Bay	59	D 17
Black Corries	72	F 13
Black Down Hills	8	K 31
Black Isle	79	G 11
Black Mount	66	F 14
Black Mountain	25	I 28
Black Mountains	26	K 28
Black Notley	30	V 28
Black Torrington	6	H 31
Black Water Valley	78	F 11
Blackawton	4	I 32

A B C D E F G H I J K L M N O P Q R S T U V W X Y Z

Blackburn *Aberdeenshire* ...75 N 12
Blackburn *Lancs.* ...42 M 22
Blackburn *West Lothian* ...61 J 16
Blackfield ...10 P 31
Blackford *Cumbria* ...54 L 19
Blackford
 Perthshire and Kinross ...67 I 15
Blackhall ...57 Q 19
Blackhall Rocks ...57 Q 19
Blackhill *Aberdeenshire* ...81 O 11
Blackhill *Highland* ...77 A 11
Blacklunans ...74 J 13
Blackmoor Gate ...17 I 30
Blackmore ...22 U 28
Blackness Castle ...68 J 15
Blacko ...43 N 22
Blackpool ...42 K 22
Blackridge ...61 I 16
Blackthorn ...28 Q 28
Blacktoft ...44 R 22
Blackwater *Hart* ...20 R 30
Blackwater *Isle of Wight* ...10 Q 31
Blackwater (River) ...22 W 28
Blackwater Reservoir ...72 F 13
Blackwaterfoot ...59 D 17
Blackwell ...50 P 20
Blackwood ...18 K 29
Bladnoch ...52 G 19
Bladon ...20 P 28
Blaenannherch ...15 G 27
Blaenau Ffestiniog ...33 I 25
Blaenavon ...18 K 28
Blaengarw ...17 J 29
Blaengwrwach ...17 J 28
Blagdon ...18 L 30
Blaich ...72 E 13
Blaina ...18 K 28
Blair Atholl ...73 I 13
Blair Castle ...73 I 13
Blairgowrie ...68 J 14
Blairmore ...66 F 16
Blakeney *Glos.* ...18 M 28
Blakeney *Norfolk* ...38 X 25
Blakesley ...28 Q 27
Blamerino ...68 K 14
Blandford Forum ...9 N 31
Blanefield ...67 H 16
Blàr a Chaorainn ...72 E 13
Blarmachfoldach ...72 E 13
Blarnalearoch ...78 E 10
Blawith ...48 K 21
Blaxton ...44 R 23
Blaydon ...56 O 19
Bleadon ...18 L 30
Bleaklow Hill ...43 O 23
Blean ...23 X 30
Bleasby ...36 R 24
Blenheim Palace ...20 P 28
Bletchingdon ...20 Q 28
Bletchley ...28 R 27
Bletsoe ...29 S 27
Blewbury ...20 Q 29
Blickling ...39 X 25
Blickling Hall ...39 X 25
Blidworth ...36 Q 24
Blindley Heath ...21 T 30
Blisland ...3 F 32
Blisworth ...28 R 27
Blithe ...35 O 25
Blithfield Hall ...35 O 25
Blithfield Reservoir ...35 O 25
Blockley ...27 O 27
Blofield ...39 Y 26
Bloxham ...28 P 27
Blubberhouses ...49 O 22
Blue John Cavern ...43 O 23
Bluemull Sound ...87 Q 1
Blundellsands ...42 K 23
Blundeston ...39 Z 26
Blyth *Northumb.* ...56 P 18
Blyth *Notts.* ...44 Q 23
Blythburgh ...31 Y 27
Blythe Bridge ...35 N 25
Blyton ...44 R 23
Bo' Ness ...68 J 15
Boarhills ...69 L 15
Boat of Garten ...74 I 12
Boathvic ...79 G 10
Bocking Churchstreet ...30 V 28
Boddam ...81 O 11
Bodedern ...40 G 23
Bodelwyddan ...41 J 24
Bodenham ...26 L 27
Bodfari ...41 J 23
Bodfordd ...40 G 23
Bodham Street ...39 X 25
Bodiam Castle ...12 V 30

Bodicote ...28 Q 27
Bodmin ...3 F 32
Bodmin Moor ...3 G 32
Bodnant Garden ...41 I 23
Bognor Regis ...11 R 31
Bogue ...53 H 18
Boisdale ...70 X 12
Boisdale (Loch) ...70 Y 12
Boldon ...56 P 19
Bolham ...7 J 31
Bollington ...43 N 24
Bolney ...11 T 31
Bolnhurst ...29 S 27
Bolsover ...44 Q 24
Boltby ...50 Q 21
Bolton Alnwick ...63 O 17
Bolton *Bolton* ...42 M 23
Bolton Abbey ...49 O 22
Bolton-le-Sands ...48 L 21
Bolton on Swale ...50 P 20
Bolton-upon-Dearne ...44 Q 23
Bomere Heath ...34 L 25
Bonar Bridge ...79 G 10
Bonawe Quarries ...65 E 14
Bonby ...44 S 23
Boncath ...15 G 27
Bonchester Bridge ...62 M 17
Bonhill ...66 G 16
Bonnybridge ...67 I 16
Bonnyrigg ...61 K 16
Bont-faen / Cowbridge ...17 J 29
Bontgoch Elerch ...25 I 26
Bontnewydd ...32 H 24
Boosbeck ...50 R 20
Boot ...47 K 20
Bootle *Cumbria* ...47 J 21
Bootle *Merseyside* ...42 K 23
Bordogan ...32 G 24
Boreham ...22 V 28
Boreham Street ...12 V 31
Borehamwood ...21 T 29
Boreland ...54 K 18
Borgue
 Dumfries and Galloway ...53 H 19
Borgue *Highland* ...85 J 9
Borness ...53 H 19
Borough Green ...22 U 30
Boroughbridge ...50 P 21
Borreraig ...77 Z 11
Borrobol Forest ...85 H 9
Borrowash ...36 P 25
Borrowdale ...54 K 18
Borve *Barra Isle* ...70 X 13
Borve *Eilean Siar* ...70 X 13
Borve *Isle of Lewis* ...82 A 8
Borve *South Harris* ...76 Y 10
Borwick ...48 L 21
Bosbury ...26 M 27
Boscastle ...6 F 31
Boscombe ...9 O 31
Bosham ...10 R 31
Bosherston ...16 F 29
Bosley ...35 N 24
Boston ...37 T 25
Boston Spa ...50 P 22
Boswinger ...3 F 33
Botesdale ...30 W 26
Bothamsall ...44 R 24
Bothel ...54 K 19
Bothwell ...60 H 16
Botley ...10 Q 31
Bottesfor *Melton* ...36 R 25
Bottesford
 North Lincolnshire ...44 S 23
Bottisham ...30 U 27
Botwnnog ...32 G 25
Boughton ...36 Q 24
Boughton House ...29 R 26
Boughton Street ...22 W 30
Boulmer ...63 P 17
Boultham ...44 S 24
Bourn ...29 T 27
Bourne ...37 S 25
Bournemouth ...9 O 31
Bourton *North Dorset* ...9 N 30
Bourton
 Vale of White Horse ...19 P 29
Bourton-on-the-Water ...27 O 28
Bovey Tracey ...4 I 32
Bovingdon ...21 S 28
Bow ...7 I 31
Bow Street ...25 H 26
Bowden ...62 L 17
Bower *Highland* ...85 K 8

Bower *Tynedale* ...55 M 18
Bowerchalke ...9 O 30
Bowes ...49 N 20
Bowhill ...62 L 17
Bowland ...62 L 17
Bowland (Forest of) ...49 M 22
Bowmore ...58 B 16
Bowness ...48 L 20
Bowness-on-Solway ...54 K 19
Bowood House ...19 N 29
Box ...19 N 29
Box Hill ...21 T 30
Boxford *Babergh* ...30 W 27
Boxford *West Berkshire* ...20 P 29
Boxley ...22 V 30
Boxworth ...29 T 27
Boyton ...6 G 31
Bozeat ...29 R 27
Braaid ...46 G 21
Brabourne Lees ...12 W 30
Bracadale (Loch) ...77 A 12
Bracebridge Heath ...37 S 24
Brackley ...28 Q 27
Brackley Hatch ...28 Q 27
Bracknell ...20 R 29
Braco ...67 I 15
Bracora ...72 C 13
Bradan Resr (Loch) ...60 G 18
Bradenham ...20 R 29
Bradfield *Sheffield* ...43 P 23
Bradfield *West Berkshire* ...20 Q 29
Bradford *Bradford* ...43 O 22
Bradford *Taunton Deane* ...8 K 31
Bradford Abbas ...8 M 31
Bradford-on-Avon ...19 N 29
Brading ...10 Q 31
Bradninch ...7 J 31
Bradpole ...5 L 31
Bradwell ...43 O 24
Bradwell-on-Sea ...22 W 28
Bradworthy ...6 G 31
Brae ...87 P 2
Brae of Achnahaird ...83 D 9
Brae Roy Lodge ...73 F 13
Braeantra ...79 G 10
Braedownie ...74 K 13
Braehead ...61 J 16
Braemar ...74 J 12
Braemore ...85 J 9
Braeriach ...74 I 12
Braeswick ...87 L 6
Brafferton Helperby ...50 Q 21
Bragar ...82 A 8
Braglenbeg ...65 D 15
Braich y Pwll ...32 F 25
Braidwood ...61 I 16
Bràigh Mòr ...82 Y 9
Brailes ...28 P 27
Brailsford ...35 P 25
Braintree ...30 V 28
Braishfield ...10 P 30
Braithwaite ...54 K 20
Braithwell ...44 Q 23
Bramcote ...36 Q 25
Bramfield ...31 Y 27
Bramford ...31 X 27
Bramhall ...43 N 23
Bramham ...43 P 22
Bramhope ...43 P 22
Bramley
 Basingstoke and Deane ...20 Q 30
Bramley
 South Yorks. ...44 Q 23
Bramley *Surrey* ...21 S 30
Brampton *Cambs.* ...29 T 27
Brampton *Cumbria* ...55 L 19
Brampton *Eden* ...55 M 20
Brampton *Rotherham.* ...43 P 23
Brampton *Suffolk* ...31 Y 26
Brampton Bryan ...26 L 26
Brancaster ...38 V 25
Branderburgh ...80 K 10
Brandesburton ...51 T 22
Brandon *Durham* ...56 P 19
Brandon *Suffolk* ...30 V 26
Brandsby ...50 Q 21
Branscombe ...5 K 31
Bransgore ...9 O 31
Branston ...37 S 24
Brant Broughton ...37 S 24
Brassington ...35 P 24
Bratton ...19 N 30
Bratton Clovelly ...6 H 31
Bratton Fleming ...7 I 30
Braughing ...29 U 28
Braunston *Daventry* ...28 Q 27
Braunston *Rutland* ...36 R 26
Braunton ...6 H 30
Bray-on-Thames ...21 R 29

Bray Shop ...3 G 32
Braybrooke ...28 R 26
Brayford ...7 I 30
Brayton ...44 Q 22
Breaclete ...82 Z 9
Breadalbane ...67 G 14
Breage ...2 D 33
Bream ...18 M 28
Breamore House ...9 O 31
Brean ...18 K 30
Breasclete ...82 Z 9
Breaston ...36 Q 25
Brechin ...75 M 13
Breckland ...30 V 26
Brecon / Aberhonddu ...25 J 28
Brecon Beacons
 National Park ...25 J 28
Bredbury ...43 N 23
Bredgar ...22 W 30
Bredon ...27 N 27
Bredwardine ...26 L 27
Bremhill ...19 N 29
Brendon Hills ...7 J 30
Brenig Reservoir ...33 J 24
Brenish ...82 Y 9
Brent *London Borough* ...21 T 29
Brent Knoll ...18 L 30
Brent Pelham ...29 U 28
Brentwood ...22 U 29
Brenzett ...12 W 30
Brereton ...35 O 25
Bressay ...87 Q 3
Bretford ...28 P 26
Bretherton ...42 L 22
Brewham ...9 M 30
Brewlands Bridge ...74 K 13
Brewood ...35 N 25
Brick ...46 G 20
Bridestowe ...4 H 31
Bridge ...23 X 30
Bridge of Alford ...75 L 12
Bridge of Allan ...67 I 15
Bridge of Avon ...80 J 11
Bridge of Balgie ...73 H 14
Bridge of Brown ...74 J 12
Bridge of Buchat ...74 L 12
Bridge of Craigisla ...74 K 13
Bridge of Dee ...53 I 19
Bridge of Don ...75 N 12
Bridge of Dun ...75 M 13
Bridge of Dye ...75 M 13
Bridge of Earn ...68 J 14
Bridge of Ericht ...73 G 13
Bridge of Gairn ...74 K 12
Bridge of Gaur ...73 G 13
Bridge of Orchy ...66 F 14
Bridge of Weir ...60 G 16
Bridge Trafford ...42 L 24
Bridgemary ...10 Q 31
Bridgend *Aberdeenshire* ...80 L 11
Bridgend *Angus* ...75 L 13
Bridgend *Argyll and Bute* ...65 D 15
Bridgend *Islay* ...58 B 16
Bridgend
 Perthshire and Kinross ...68 J 14
Bridgend / Pen-y-bont ...17 J 29
Bridgend of Lintrathen ...74 K 13
Bridgerule ...6 G 31
Bridgham ...30 W 26
Bridgnorth ...27 M 26
Bridgwater ...8 L 30
Bridlington ...51 T 21
Brierfield ...43 N 22
Brierley ...43 P 23
Brierley Hill ...27 N 26
Brig ...44 S 23
Brigham ...54 J 20
Brighouse ...43 O 22
Brighstone ...10 P 32
Brighstone Forest ...10 P 32
Brightling ...12 V 31
Brightlingsea ...22 X 28
Brighton ...11 T 31
Brightwell ...20 Q 29
Brigsteer ...29 S 26
Brigstock ...29 S 26
Brill ...20 Q 28
Brimfield ...26 L 27
Brimham Rocks ...49 O 21
Brimington ...43 P 24
Brimpsfield ...19 N 28
Brimpton ...20 Q 29
Brinkburn Priory ...63 O 18
Brinkley ...30 V 27

Brinklow ...28 P 26
Brinkworth ...19 O 29
Brinyan ...86 L 6
Brisley ...38 W 25
Brislington ...18 M 29
Bristol ...18 M 29
Briston ...38 X 25
Briton Ferry ...17 I 29
Brittle (Loch) ...71 B 12
Brittwell Salome ...20 Q 29
Brixham ...4 J 32
Brixton ...36 Q 25
Brixworth ...28 R 27
Brize Norton ...20 P 28
Broad Bay ...83 B 9
Broad Blunsdon ...19 O 29
Broad Chalke ...9 O 30
Broad Haven ...14 E 28
Broad Hinton ...19 O 29
Broad Law ...61 J 17
Broad Oak ...12 V 31
Broadbridge Heath ...11 S 30
Broadclyst ...7 J 31
Broadford ...77 C 12
Broadlands ...10 P 31
Broadmayne ...9 M 31
Broadstairs ...23 Y 29
Broadstone ...9 O 31
Broadwas ...27 M 27
Broadway ...27 O 27
Broadwell Ho ...55 N 19
Broadwey ...8 M 32
Broadwindsor ...8 L 31
Broadwoodwidger ...6 H 31
Brochel ...77 B 11
Brockdish ...31 X 26
Brockenhurst ...10 P 31
Brockley ...18 L 29
Brockworth ...19 N 28
Brodick ...59 E 17
Brodick Bay ...59 E 17
Brodick Castle ...59 E 17
Brodie Castle ...79 I 11
Brodsworth ...44 Q 23
Brodsworth Hall ...44 Q 23
Brokenborough ...19 N 29
Brolass ...65 B 14
Bromborough ...42 L 24
Brome ...31 X 26
Bromfield ...26 L 26
Bromham *Bedford* ...29 S 27
Bromham *Kennet* ...19 N 29
Bromley *London Borough* ...21 U 29
Brompton *Kent* ...22 V 29
Brompton *near Northallerton* 50 P 20
Brompton-by-Sawdon ...51 S 21
Brompton on Swale ...49 O 20
Brompton Ralph ...7 K 30
Brompton Regis ...7 J 30
Bromsgrove ...27 N 26
Bromyard ...26 M 27
Bronllys ...26 K 27
Brook ...22 W 30
Brooke ...39 Y 26
Brookmans Park ...21 T 28
Broom (Loch) ...78 E 10
Broomfield *Chelmsford* ...22 V 28
Broomfield *Sedgemoor* ...8 K 30
Broomfleet ...44 S 22
Broomhaugh ...56 O 19
Brora ...85 I 9
Broseley ...34 M 26
Brotherton ...44 Q 22
Brotton ...57 R 20
Brough
 East Riding of Yorkshire ...44 S 22
Brough *Eden* ...49 N 20
Brough *Highland* ...86 J 8
Brough Head ...86 J 6
Brough Lodge ...87 R 2
Brough of Birsay ...86 J 6
Broughton *Cumbria* ...54 J 19
Broughton
 Flintshire / Sir y Fflint ...34 L 24
Broughton *Hants.* ...10 P 30
Broughton *Lancs.* ...42 L 22
Broughton *North Lincs.* ...44 S 23
Broughton *Northants.* ...28 R 26
Broughton *Oxon.* ...28 P 27
Broughton *Scottish Borders* .61 J 17
Broughton-in-Furness ...47 K 21
Broughton Mills ...47 K 21
Broughton Moor ...54 J 19
Broughton Poggs ...19 P 28
Brompton ...20 Q 29

Broxbourne ...21 T 28
Broxburn ...68 J 16
Bruar Lodge ...73 I 13
Bruichladdich ...58 A 16
Brundall ...39 Y 26
Brushford ...7 J 30
Bruton ...8 M 30
Brydekirk ...54 K 18
Brymbo ...34 K 24
Bryn-Henllan ...24 F 27
Brynamman ...17 I 28
Brynbuga / Usk ...18 L 28
Bryncethin ...17 J 29
Bryneglwys ...34 K 24
Brynmawr ...18 K 28
Brynna ...40 G 23
Bryngwyn ...26 K 27
Brynhoffnant ...15 G 27
Brynmawr ...18 K 28
Brynsiencyn ...32 H 24
Brynteg ...40 H 23
Bualintur ...71 B 12
Bubwith ...44 R 22
Buccleuch ...61 K 17
Buchanty ...67 I 14
Buchlyvie ...67 H 15
Buckden *Cambs.* ...29 T 27
Buckden *North Yorks.* ...49 N 21
Buckfast ...4 I 32
Buckfast Abbey ...4 I 32
Buckfastleigh ...4 I 32
Buckham ...4 I 32
Buckhaven ...68 L 15
Buckhorn Weston ...9 M 30
Buckie ...80 L 10
Buckingham ...28 R 27
Buckland *Herts.* ...29 T 28
Buckland *Oxon.* ...20 P 28
Buckland Abbey ...4 H 32
Buckland Brewer ...6 H 31
Buckland Dinham ...19 M 30
Buckland in-the-Moor ...4 I 32
Buckland Newton ...8 M 31
Buckland St. Mary ...8 K 31
Bucklebury ...20 Q 29
Bucklers Hard ...10 P 31
Buckley / Bwcle ...34 K 24
Buckminster ...36 R 25
Bucknall ...37 T 24
Bucknell ...26 L 26
Bucksburn ...75 N 12
Bucks green ...11 S 30
Bude ...6 G 31
Budleigh Salterton ...5 K 32
Bugbrooke ...28 Q 27
Bugle ...3 F 32
Bugthorpe ...50 R 21
Buildwas Abbey ...34 M 26
Builth Wells /
 Llanfair-ym-Muallt ...25 J 27
Bulford ...19 O 30
Bulkéley ...34 L 24
Bulkington ...28 P 26
Bulwell ...36 Q 24
Bulwick ...37 S 26
Bunarkaig ...72 F 13
Bunessan ...64 B 15
Bungay ...31 Y 26
Bunnahabhainn ...64 B 16
Bunny ...36 Q 25
Buntingford ...29 T 28
Burbage *Leics.* ...28 P 26
Burbage *Wilts.* ...19 O 29
Burchett's Green ...20 R 29
Bures ...30 W 28
Burford ...19 P 28
Burgess Hill ...11 T 31
Burgh-by-Sands ...54 K 19
Burgh Castle ...39 Y 26
Burgh-le-Marsh ...38 U 24
Burgh-St. Peter ...39 Y 26
Burghead ...80 J 10
Burghfield ...20 Q 29
Burghill ...26 L 27
Burghley House ...37 S 26
Burham ...22 V 30
Burley ...9 O 31
Burley-in-Wharfedale ...49 O 22
Burlton ...34 L 25
Burneside ...48 L 20
Burneston ...50 P 21
Burnfoot ...62 L 17
Burnham Market ...38 W 25
Burnham-on-Crouch ...22 W 28
Burnham-on-Sea ...18 L 30
Burnhaven ...81 O 11
Burnhope ...56 O 19
Burniston ...51 S 21

Burnley ....43 N 22
Burntisland ....68 K 15
Burrafirth ....87 R 1
Burravoe ....87 Q 2
Burray ....87 L 7
Burrelton ....68 K 14
Burringham ....44 R 23
Burrington *North Devon* ....7 I 31
Burrington *North Somerset* ..18 L 30
Burrough Green ....30 V 27
Burrow Head ....53 G 19
Burry Port /Porth Tywyn ....15 H 28
Burscough ....42 L 23
Burscough Bridge ....42 L 23
Burshill ....51 S 22
Bursledon ....10 Q 31
Burslem ....35 N 24
Burstwick ....45 T 22
Burton *Christchurch* ....9 O 31
Burton *Ellesmere*
  Port and Neston ....48 L 21
Burton *South Lakeland* ......48 L 21
Burton *Wrecsam / Wrexham* 34 L 24
Burton Agnes ....51 T 21
Burton Bradstock ....5 L 31
Burton Constable Hall ......45 T 22
Burton Fleming ....51 S 21
Burton in Lonsdale ....49 M 21
Burton Joyce ....36 Q 25
Burton Latimer ....29 R 26
Burton Leonard ....50 P 21
Burton Pidsea ....45 T 22
Burton-upon-Stather ....44 R 23
Burton-upon-Trent ....35 O 25
Burwarton ....26 M 26
Burwash ....12 V 31
Burwell *Cambs.* ....30 U 27
Burwell *Lincs.* ....45 U 24
Bury *Bury* ....42 N 23
Bury *Chichester* ....11 S 31
Bury St. Edmunds ....30 W 27
Busby ....60 H 16
Buscot ....19 P 28
Bushey ....21 S 29
Bute (Island of) ....59 E 16
Bute (Kyles of) ....59 E 16
Bute (Sound of) ....59 E 16
Butleigh ....8 L 30
Butley ....31 Y 27
Butt of Lewis ....83 B 8
Buttercrambe ....50 R 21
Buttermere ....47 K 20
Butterstone ....68 J 14
Buttington ....34 K 25
Buxted ....12 U 31
Buxton *Derbs.* ....43 O 24
Buxton *Norfolk* ....39 X 25
Bwcle / Buckley ....34 K 24
Bwlch ....26 K 28
Bwlch Oerddrws ....33 I 25
Bwlch y Ffridd ....33 J 26
Bwlch-y-Groes ....25 I 28
Bwlch-y-Sarnau ....25 J 26
Bwlchgwyn ....34 K 24
Bwlchllan ....25 H 27
Byfield ....28 Q 27
Byfleet ....21 S 30
Byland Abbey ....50 Q 21
Byrness ....62 M 18

C

Cabrach ....80 K 12
Cadair Idris ....33 I 25
Caddington ....29 S 28
Caddonfoot ....62 L 17
Cadhay ....5 K 31
Cadishead ....42 M 23
Cadnam ....10 P 31
Cadney ....44 S 23
Cadwell Park ....45 T 24
Caerau ....17 J 29
Caerdydd / Cardiff ....18 K 29
Caerffili / Caerphilly ....18 K 29
Caerfyrddin / Carmarthen ..15 H 28
Caergwrle ....34 K 24
Caerlaverock Castle ....53 J 19
Caerleon ....18 L 29
Caernarfon ....32 H 24
Caernarfon Bay ....32 G 24
Caerphilly / Caerffili ....18 K 29
Caersws ....25 J 26
Caerwent ....18 L 29
Caerwys ....41 K 23
Cailliness Point ....52 F 19
Cairn Edward Forest ....53 H 18
Cairn Gorm ....74 J 12

Cairn Table ....60 H 17
Cairn Toul ....74 I 12
Cairnborrow ....80 L 11
Cairndow ....66 F 15
Cairngaan ....52 F 20
Cairngarroch ....52 E 19
Cairnie ....80 L 11
Cairnpapple Hill ....67 J 16
Cairnryan ....52 E 19
Cairnsmore of Carsphairn ..60 H 18
Cairnsmore of Fleet ....53 G 19
Cairraig Fhada ....58 B 17
Caister-on-Sea ....39 Z 26
Caistor ....45 T 23
Calbourne ....10 P 31
Caldbeck ....54 K 19
Caldecott ....36 R 26
Calder (Loch) ....85 J 8
Calder Bridge ....47 J 20
Calder Mains ....85 J 8
Caldercruix ....61 I 16
Calderdale ....43 N 22
Caldermill ....60 H 17
Caldey Island ....15 F 29
Caldicot ....18 L 29
Caldwell ....49 O 20
Calf of Man ....46 F 21
Calfsound ....87 L 6
Calgary ....71 B 14
Calgary Bay ....71 B 14
Caliach Point ....71 B 14
Calke Abbey ....36 P 25
Callander ....67 H 15
Callater (Glen) ....74 J 13
Callington ....3 H 32
Calne ....19 N 29
Calow ....43 P 24
Calstock ....3 H 32
Calthwaite ....55 L 19
Calvay ....70 Y 12
Calver ....43 P 24
Calverton ....36 Q 24
Calvine ....73 I 13
Cam ....29 U 27
Cam Loch ....84 E 9
Camas Chil Mhalieu ....72 D 14
Camas-luinie ....78 D 12
Camasnacroise ....72 D 14
Camastianavaig ....77 B 11
Camber ....12 W 31
Camberley ....20 R 30
Camblesforth ....44 Q 22
Cambo ....56 O 18
Cambois ....56 P 18
Camborne ....2 E 33
Cambrian Mountains ....25 I 27
Cambridge ....29 U 27
Cambusbarron ....67 I 15
Cambuskenneth ....67 I 15
Camden *London Borough* ..21 T 29
Camelford ....6 F 32
Cammachmore ....75 N 12
Campbeltown ....59 D 17
Campsie Fells ....67 H 15
Camptown ....62 M 17
Campville ....35 P 25
Camrose ....24 E 28
Camusnagaul ....78 E 10
Candlesby ....37 U 24
Canewdon ....22 W 29
Canisbay ....86 K 8
Canna ....71 A 12
Cannich ....78 F 11
Cannich (Glen) ....78 F 11
Cannington ....8 K 30
Cannock ....35 N 25
Canonbie ....54 L 18
Canons Ashby ....28 Q 27
Canterbury ....23 X 30
Cantley ....39 Y 26
Canvey Island ....22 V 29
Caol ....72 E 13
Caolas a' Mhòrain ....76 Y 10
Caoles ....70 Z 14
Caolis ....70 X 13
Caolisport (Loch) ....65 D 16
Cape Cornwall ....2 C 33
Cape Wrath ....84 E 8
Capel ....11 T 30
Capel Curig ....33 I 24
Capel Garmon ....33 I 24
Capel Le Ferne ....13 X 30
Capel St. Mary ....31 X 27
Capel-y-Ffin ....26 K 28
Capesthorne Hall ....43 N 24
Capheaton ....56 O 18
Cappercleuch ....61 K 17

Caputh ....68 J 14
Cara Island ....58 C 17
Carbis Bay ....2 D 33
Carbost *Minginish* ....77 A 12
Carbost *Trotternish* ....77 B 11
Cardenden ....68 K 15
Cardiff / Caerdydd ....18 K 29
Cardigan / Aberteifi ....15 G 27
Cardigan Bay ....24 G 26
Cardington ....34 L 26
Cardinham ....3 G 32
Cardrona ....61 K 17
Cardross ....66 G 16
Cardurnock ....54 K 19
Carew ....15 F 28
Carfraemill ....62 L 16
Cargill ....68 J 14
Carhampton ....7 J 30
Carie ....73 H 13
Carinish ....76 Y 11
Carisbrooke ....10 Q 31
Cark ....48 L 21
Carlbt ....37 S 25
Carleen ....2 D 33
Carleton ....49 N 22
Carlisle ....55 L 19
Carlops ....61 J 16
Carloway ....82 Z 9
Carlton *Bedford* ....29 S 27
Carlton *Hambleton* ....50 Q 20
Carlton
  Hinckley and Bosworth ..36 P 26
Carlton *North Yorks.* ....44 Q 22
Carlton *Notts.* ....36 Q 25
Carlton Colville ....31 Z 26
Carlton in Lindrick ....44 Q 23
Carlton-on-Trent ....36 R 24
Carluke ....61 I 16
Carmarthen / Caerfyrddin ..15 H 28
Carmel Head ....40 G 22
Carmunnock ....60 H 16
Carmyllie ....69 L 14
Carn Ban ....60 H 16
Carn Coire na h-Easgainn ..73 H 12
Carn Eige ....78 E 12
Carn Glas-choire ....79 I 11
Carn Mairg ....73 H 14
Carnaby ....51 T 21
Carnach ....78 E 12
Carnassarie Castle ....65 D 15
Carnedd Llewelyn ....33 I 24
Carnforth ....48 L 21
Carno ....33 J 26
Carnock ....68 J 15
Carnoustie ....69 L 14
Carnwath ....61 J 16
Carradale ....59 D 17
Carradale Bay ....59 D 17
Carrbridge ....79 I 12
Carrick ....66 F 15
Carrick Roads ....2 E 33
Carron ....80 K 11
Carron (Loch) ....77 C 11
Carron Bridge ....67 H 15
Carrshield ....55 N 19
Carrutherstown ....54 J 18
Carsaig ....65 C 15
Carse of Gowrie ....68 K 14
Carseriggan ....52 G 19
Carsethorn ....53 J 19
Carsluith ....53 G 19
Carsphairn ....53 H 18
Carstairs ....61 I 16
Carterton ....19 P 28
Carterway Heads ....56 O 19
Carthew ....3 F 32
Carthorpe ....50 P 21
Cartmel ....48 L 21
Carville ....56 P 19
Cas-Gwent / Chepstow ......18 M 29
Cashlie ....67 G 14
Casnewydd / Newport ....18 L 29
Cassington ....20 P 28
Cassley (Glen) ....84 F 9
Castell-Nedd / Neath ....17 I 29
Castell Newydd Emlyn /
  Newcastle Emlyn ....15 G 27
Castell-y-Rhingyll ....15 H 28
Castle Acre ....38 W 25
Castle Ashby ....28 R 27
Castle Bolton ....49 O 21
Castle Bytham ....37 S 25
Castle Campbell ....67 I 15
Castle Cary ....8 M 30
Castle Combe ....19 N 29
Castle Donington ....36 P 25
Castle Douglas ....53 I 19

Castle Drogo ....4 I 31
Castle Eaton ....19 O 29
Castle Fraser ....75 M 12
Castle frome ....26 M 27
Castle Hedingham ....30 V 28
Castle Howard ....50 R 21
Castle Kennedy ....52 F 19
Castle Lachlan ....65 E 15
Castle Loch ....52 F 19
Castle Rising ....38 V 25
Castlebay ....70 X 13
Castleford ....43 P 22
Castlemartin ....16 E 29
Castlerigg ....54 K 20
Castleton
  Casnewydd / Newport .....18 K 29
Castleton *Derbs.* ....43 O 23
Castleton *North Yorks.* ......50 R 20
Castletown *Highland* ....85 J 8
Castletown *Isle of Man* ....46 G 21
Caston ....38 W 26
Catacol ....59 E 16
Catacol Bay ....59 D 16
Caterham ....21 T 30
Catfield ....39 Y 25
Catlodge ....73 H 12
Caton ....48 L 21
Catrine ....60 H 17
Catterall ....42 L 22
Catterick ....50 P 20
Catterick Garrison ....49 O 20
Catterline ....75 N 13
Cattistock ....8 M 31
Catton *Broadland* ....39 X 26
Catton *Tynedale* ....55 N 19
Cauldcleuch Head ....62 L 18
Cauldon ....35 O 24
Caulkerbush ....53 I 19
Cautley ....49 M 20
Cava ....86 K 7
Cavendish ....30 V 27
Caversfield ....28 Q 28
Caversham ....20 R 29
Cawdor ....79 I 11
Cawood ....44 Q 22
Caxton ....29 T 27
Caynham ....26 M 26
Caythorpe ....37 S 24
Cayton ....51 S 21
Ceall (Loch nan) ....71 C 13
Cefn Bryn ....15 H 29
Cefn-Coed-y-cymmer ....17 J 28
Cefn-mawr ....34 K 25
Cefn-y-Pant ....15 G 28
Ceinewydd / New Quay .....24 G 27
Ceiriog (Vale of) ....34 K 25
Cemaes ....40 G 22
Cemaes Head ....15 F 27
Cemmaes ....33 I 26
Cemmaes road ....33 I 26
Cenarth ....15 G 27
Ceres ....69 L 15
Cerne Abbas ....8 M 31
Cerrigydrudion ....33 J 24
Chacewater ....2 E 33
Chacombe ....28 Q 27
Chadderton ....43 N 23
Chaddesden ....36 P 25
Chadlington ....28 P 28
Chadwell St. Mary ....22 V 29
Chagford ....4 I 31
Chailey ....11 T 31
Chàirn Bhain (Loch a') ......84 E 9
Chalfont St. Giles ....21 S 29
Chalfont St. Peter ....21 S 29
Chalford ....19 N 28
Chalgrove ....20 Q 29
Challacombe ....7 I 30
Challoch ....52 G 19
Challock ....22 W 30
Chambercombe Manor ......17 H 30
Chandler's Ford ....10 P 31
Channel Islands 5
Chapel Brampton ....28 R 27
Chapel-en-le-Frith ....43 O 24
Chapel Haddlesey ....44 Q 22
Chapel le Dale ....49 M 21
Chapel St. Leonards ....45 V 24
Chapel Stile ....48 K 20
Chapelhall ....61 I 16
Chapelknowe ....54 K 18
Chapeltown *Moray* ....74 K 12
Chapeltown *Sheffield* ....43 P 23
Chapmanslade ....19 N 30
Chard ....8 L 31

Chardstock ....8 L 31
Charfield ....19 M 29
Charing ....22 W 30
Charlbury ....28 P 28
Charlecote *Park* ....27 P 27
Charleston *Manor* ....12 U 31
Charlestown *Highland* ......78 C 10
Charlestown *Restormel* .....3 F 33
Charlton ....19 N 29
Charlton Horethorne ....8 M 30
Charlton Kings ....27 N 28
Charlton Marshall ....9 N 31
Charlton Musgrove ....9 M 30
Charlton on Otmoor ....20 Q 28
Charlwood ....11 T 30
Charminster ....8 M 31
Charmouth ....5 L 31
Charney Basset ....20 P 29
Charsfield ....31 X 27
Chartham ....23 X 30
Chartridge ....21 S 28
Chartwell ....21 U 30
Chastleton ....27 P 28
Chatburn ....42 M 22
Chatham ....22 V 29
Chatsworth House ....43 P 24
Chatteris ....29 U 26
Chatto ....62 M 17
Chatton ....63 O 17
Chawleigh ....7 I 31
Cheadle *Gtr. Mches.* ....43 N 23
Cheadle *Staffs.* ....35 O 25
Checkendon ....20 Q 29
Cheddar ....18 L 30
Cheddar Gorge ....18 L 30
Cheddington ....21 S 28
Cheddleton ....35 N 24
Chedington ....8 L 31
Chedworth ....19 O 28
Cheese Bay ....76 Y 11
Chelford ....42 N 24
Chellaston ....36 P 25
Chelmarsh ....27 M 26
Chelmsford ....22 V 28
Cheltenham ....27 N 28
Chelveston ....29 S 27
Chelwood Gate ....11 U 30
Chepstow / Cas-Gwent ......18 L 29
Cherhill ....19 O 29
Cherington *Cotswold* ....19 N 28
Cherington
  Stratford-on-Avon ....27 P 27
Cheriton ....10 Q 30
Cheriton Bishop ....4 I 31
Cheriton Fitzpaine ....7 J 31
Cherry Burton ....44 S 22
Chertsey ....21 S 29
Cherwell (River) ....28 Q 28
Cheselbourne ....9 M 31
Chesham ....21 S 28
Chesham Bois ....21 S 28
Cheshunt ....21 T 28
Chesil Beach ....8 M 32
Cheslyn Hay ....35 N 26
Chester ....34 L 24
Chester-le-Street ....56 P 19
Chesterfield ....43 P 24
Chesters ....62 M 17
Chesters Fort ....55 N 18
Chesterton *Cambridge* .....29 U 27
Chesterton *Cherwell* ....28 Q 28
Cheswardine ....35 M 25
Cheswick ....63 O 16
Cheviot (The) ....63 N 17
Cheviot Hills (The) ....62 M 17
Chew Magna ....18 M 29
Chew Stoke ....18 M 29
Chewton Mendip ....18 M 30
Chicheley ....29 R 27
Chichester ....10 R 31
Chickerell ....5 M 32
Chicklade ....9 N 30
Chiddingfold ....11 S 30
Chiddingly ....12 U 31
Chiddingstone ....22 U 30
Chideock ....5 L 31
Chieveley ....20 Q 29
Chigwell ....21 U 29
Chilcompton ....18 M 30
Child Okeford ....9 N 31
Childrey ....20 P 29
Child's Ercall ....34 M 25
Chilham ....22 W 30
Chillaton ....4 H 32
Chillingham ....63 O 17
Chilmark ....9 N 30
Chiltern Hills ....20 R 29
Chilton *Sedgefield* ....56 P 20

Chilton
  Vale of White Horse ....20 Q 29
Chilton Folia ....20 P 29
Chippenham
  East Cambridgeshire ......30 V 27
Chippenham
  North Wiltshire ....19 N 29
Chipping ....42 M 22
Chipping Campden ....27 O 27
Chipping Norton ....28 P 28
Chipping Ongar ....22 U 28
Chipping Sodbury ....19 M 29
Chipping Warden ....28 Q 27
Chirbury ....34 K 26
Chirk ....34 K 25
Chirk Castle ....34 K 25
Chirmorie ....52 F 18
Chirnside ....63 N 16
Chirton ....19 O 30
Chiselborough ....19 O 29
Chislet ....23 X 30
Chiswell Green ....21 S 28
Chitterne ....19 N 30
Chittlehamholt ....7 I 31
Chittlehampton ....7 I 30
Chobham ....21 S 29
Choire (Loch) ....84 H 9
Cholderton ....9 O 30
Cholesbury ....21 S 28
Chollerton ....55 N 18
Cholsey ....20 Q 29
Chon (Loch) ....67 G 15
Chopwell ....56 O 19
Chorley ....42 M 23
Chorleywood ....21 S 29
Christchurch *Christchurch* ..9 O 31
Christchurch *Fenland* ....38 U 26
Christian Malford ....19 N 29
Christleton ....34 L 24
Christmas Common ....20 R 29
Christow ....4 J 32
Chroisg (Loch a') ....78 E 11
Chudleigh ....4 J 32
Chulmleigh ....7 I 31
Church ....42 M 22
Church Crookham ....20 R 30
Church Eaton ....35 N 25
Church Enstone ....28 P 28
Church Fenton ....44 Q 22
Church Knowle ....9 N 32
Church Leigh ....35 O 25
Church Lench ....27 O 27
Church Minshull ....34 M 24
Church Stoke ....34 K 26
Church Stretton ....34 L 26
Churcham ....19 M 28
Churchdown ....27 N 28
Churchill *North Somerset* ..18 L 29
Churchill *Oxon.* ....27 P 28
Churchingford ....8 K 31
Churnet ....35 O 24
Churnsike Lodge ....55 M 18
Churston Ferrers ....4 J 32
Churt ....10 R 30
Chwilog ....32 H 25
Cifynydd ....17 K 29
Cilcain ....34 K 24
Cilcennin ....25 H 27
Cilgerran ....15 G 27
Cilmery ....25 J 27
Cilrhedyn ....15 G 28
Cilybebyll ....17 I 28
Cilycwn ....25 I 27
Cinderford ....18 M 28
Cirencester ....19 O 28
City of London
  London Borough ....21 T 29
Clachaig ....66 E 16
Clachan *Argyl* ....66 F 15
Clachan *Kintyre* ....59 D 16
Clachan Mór ....70 Z 14
Clachan of Campsie ....67 H 16
Clachan of Glendaruel ......65 E 15
Clachtoll ....83 E 9
Clackavoid ....74 J 13
Clackmannan ....67 I 15
Clacton-on-Sea ....23 X 28
Claggan Bay ....58 B 16
Claggan ....71 C 14
Claidh (Loch) ....82 A 10
Claigan ....77 A 11
Clandon Park ....21 S 30
Clanfield ....10 Q 31
Claonel ....84 G 9
Clapham *Beds.* ....29 S 27
Clapham *North Yorks.* ....49 M 21
Clapton-in-Gordano ....18 L 29

A B C D E F G H I J K L M N O P Q R S T U V W X Y Z

Clàr (Loch nan) 85 H 9
Clarbeston Road 24 F 28
Clare 30 V 27
Clashindarroch 80 L 11
Clashmore 79 H 10
Clashnessie 84 E 9
Clatt 80 L 12
Clatteringshaws (Loch) 53 H 18
Clauchlands Point 59 E 17
Clavering 29 U 28
Claverley 27 N 26
Claverton Manor 19 N 29
Clawdd-newydd 33 J 24
Clawton 6 G 31
Claxton *Ryedale* 50 R 21
Claxton *South Norfolk* 39 Y 26
Clay Cross 36 P 24
Claydon 31 X 27
Claydon House 28 R 28
Claypole 36 R 24
Clayton 11 T 31
Clayton-le-Moors 42 M 22
Clayton West 43 P 23
Cleadale 71 B 13
Cleadon 57 P 19
Cleat 70 X 12
Cleator Moor 47 J 20
Cleckheaton 43 O 22
Cleedownton 26 M 26
Cleehill 26 M 26
Cleethorpes 45 T 23
Cleeve Abbey 7 J 30
Cleeve Prior 27 O 27
Clehonger 26 L 27
Cleigh 65 D 14
Clenchwarton 38 V 25
Clent 27 N 26
Cleobury Mortimer 26 M 26
Cleobury North 26 M 26
Clephanton 79 I 11
Clevedon 18 L 29
Clevedon-Court 18 L 29
Cleveland Hills 50 Q 20
Cleveleys 42 K 22
Cley Next the Sea 38 X 25
Cliburn 55 M 20
Cliffe *Edway* 22 V 29
Cliffe *Selby* 44 R 22
Clifton
   City of Nottingham 36 Q 25
Clifton *Eden* 55 L 20
Clifton *Rugby* 28 Q 26
Clifton Hampden 20 Q 29
Clifton-upon-Teme 27 M 27
Clipston 28 R 26
Clisham 82 Z 10
Clitheroe 42 M 22
Clive 34 L 25
Cliveden House 21 R 29
Clocaenog 33 J 24
Clocaenog Forest 33 J 24
Clola 81 O 11
Clophill 29 S 27
Clopton 29 S 26
Closeburn 53 I 18
Clotton 34 L 24
Clouds Hill 9 N 31
Cloughton 51 S 20
Clova 74 K 13
Clova (Glen) 74 K 13
Clove Lodge
Clovelly 6 G 31
Clovenfords 62 L 17
Clovulin 72 E 13
Clowne 44 Q 24
Cluanie Loch 72 E 12
Cluanie Lodge 72 E 12
Clumber Park 44 Q 24
Clun 26 K 26
Clunbury 26 L 26
Clunes Forest 72 F 13
Clungunford 26 L 26
Clunie 68 J 14
Clutton 18 M 30
Clwydian Range 34 K 24
Clydach 17 I 28
Clyde (Firth of) 59 F 17
Clyde (River) 61 J 17
Clydebank 60 G 16
Clydesdale 61 I 16
Clyffe Pypard 19 O 29
Clynnog-Fawr 32 G 24
Clyro 26 K 27
Clyst Honiton 4 J 31
Clyst Hydon 7 J 31
Clytha 18 L 28
Clywedog Resr. 25 J 26

Coalburn 61 I 17
Coaley 19 N 28
Coalville 36 P 25
Coast 78 D 10
Coatbridge 60 H 16
Coates 19 N 28
Cobham 21 S 30
Cock Bridge 74 K 12
Cockayne 50 Q 20
Cockburnspath 69 M 16
Cockenzie and Port Seton 69 L 16
Cockerham 48 L 22
Cockermouth 54 J 20
Cockfield *Babergh* 30 W 27
Cockfield *Teesdale* 56 O 20
Cocking 10 R 31
Cockleford 19 N 28
Cockshutt 34 L 25
Coddington 36 R 24
Codford St. Mary 9 N 30
Codicote 21 T 28
Codnor 36 P 24
Codsall 35 N 26
Coe (Glen) 72 F 14
Coed y Brenin Forest 33 I 25
Coedpoeth 34 K 24
Coggeshall 30 W 28
Coigach 84 E 10
Coignafearn 73 H 12
Coignafearn Forest 73 H 12
Coille Mhorgil 72 E 12
Colaboll 84 G 9
Colbost 77 A 11
Colby *Eden* 55 M 20
Colby *Isle of Man* 46 F 21
Colchester 30 W 28
Cold Ash 20 Q 29
Cold Ashby 28 Q 26
Cold Ashton 19 M 29
Cold Fell 55 M 19
Cold Norton 22 W 28
Coldbackie 84 G 8
Colden Common 10 Q 31
Coldingham 63 N 16
Coldstream 63 N 17
Colebrooke 7 I 31
Coleford *Glos.* 18 M 28
Coleford *Somerset* 18 M 30
Colemere 34 L 25
Coleorton 36 P 25
Coleshill
   North Warwickshire 27 O 26
Coleshill
   Vale of White Horse 19 P 29
Colgrave Sound 87 R 2
Colkirk 38 W 25
Coll *Argyll and Bute* 71 A 14
Coll *Eilean Siar* 83 B 9
Colliery Row 56 P 19
Collieston 81 O 11
Collingbourne Ducis 19 P 30
Collingbourne Kingston 19 P 30
Collingham *Notts.* 36 R 24
Collingham *West Yorks.* 50 P 22
Collington 26 M 27
Collyweston 37 S 26
Colmonell 52 F 18
Coln (River) 19 O 28
Colnabaichin 74 K 12
Colne 43 N 22
Colne (River) 22 X 28
Colonsay 64 B 15
Colpy 81 M 11
Colsterworth 37 S 25
Coltishall 39 Y 25
Colwall Stone 27 M 27
Colwinston 17 J 29
Colwyn Bay / Bae Colwyn 41 I 23
Colyton 5 K 31
Combe Florey 8 K 30
Combe Martin 17 H 30
Combe-St. Nicholas 8 L 31
Combeinteignhead 4 J 32
Comberton 29 U 27
Combwich 8 K 30
Come-to-Good 2 E 33
Compton *Berks.* 20 Q 29
Compton *Guildford* 21 S 30
Compton *West Sussex* 10 R 31
Compton Abdale 19 O 28
Compton Basset 19 O 29
Compton Castle 4 J 32
Compton Dando 18 M 29
Compton Wynyates 28 P 27
Comrie 67 I 14
Cona Glen 72 D 13

Conchra 65 E 15
Condicote 27 O 28
Condover 34 L 26
Congleton 35 N 24
Congresbury 18 L 29
Coningsby 37 T 24
Conington 29 T 26
Conisbrough 44 Q 23
Coniston 48 K 20
Connah's Quay 42 K 24
Connel 65 D 14
Connel Park 60 H 17
Conon Bridge 79 G 11
Contin 79 G 11
Convinth (Glen) 79 G 11
Conway Falls 33 I 24
Conwy 41 I 23
Conwy (River) 33 I 24
Conwy (Vale of) 33 I 24
Cooden Beach 12 V 31
Cookham 21 R 29
Coolham 11 S 31
Coombe Bissett 9 O 30
Copdock 31 X 27
Copford 30 W 28
Copley 56 O 20
Copmanthorpe 50 Q 22
Copplestone 7 I 31
Coppull 42 M 23
Copthorne 11 T 30
Coquet (River) 63 N 17
Corbridge 55 N 19
Corby 28 R 26
Corby Glen 37 S 25
Corfe Castle 9 N 32
Corfe Mullen 9 N 31
Corgarff Castle 74 K 12
Corhampton 10 Q 31
Cornforth 56 P 19
Cornhill 81 L 11
Cornhill-on-Tweed 63 N 17
Cornwood 4 I 32
Cornworthy 4 J 32
Corpach 72 E 13
Corpusty 39 X 25
Corran 72 E 13
Corrany 46 G 21
Corrie 59 E 17
Corrie Common 54 K 18
Corrimony 78 F 11
Corringham *Thurrock* 22 V 29
Corringham *West Lindsey* 44 R 23
Corris 33 I 26
Corry 77 C 12
Corryvreckan (Gulf of) 65 C 15
Corscombe 8 L 31
Corsham 19 N 29
Corsham Court 19 N 29
Corsley Heath 19 N 30
Corsock 53 I 18
Corstopitum 55 N 19
Corton 9 N 30
Corwen 33 J 25
Cosby 36 Q 26
Cosham 10 Q 31
Costessey 39 X 26
Cot-town 81 N 11
Cotehill 55 L 19
Cotgrave 36 Q 25
Cotham 36 R 24
Cotherstone 49 O 20
Cothi River 25 H 28
Coton 29 U 27
Cotswold Wildlife Park 19 O 28
Cottenham 29 U 27
Cottered 29 T 28
Cottesmore 37 S 25
Cottingham
   East Riding of Yorks. 45 S 22
Cottingham *Northants.* 28 R 26
Cottisford 28 Q 28
Cottonshopeburn Foot 62 M 18
Coulags 78 D 11
Coulport 66 F 15
Coulter 61 J 17
Coundon 56 P 20
Countesthorpe 36 Q 26
Coupar Angus 68 K 14
Coustoun 66 E 16
Cove *Argyll and Bute* 66 F 15
Cove *Highland* 78 C 10
Cove Bay 75 N 12
Coventry 28 P 26
Coverack 2 E 33
Cow Honeybourne 27 O 27

Cowal 65 E 15
Cowan Bridge 48 M 21
Cowbit 37 T 25
Cowbridge / Bont-faen 17 J 29
Cowdenbeath 68 J 15
Cowdray House 10 R 31
Cowes *Isle of Wight* 10 Q 31
Cowfold 11 T 31
Cowie 67 I 15
Cowling 43 N 22
Cowplain 10 Q 31
Coxheath 22 V 30
Coxhoe 56 P 19
Coxwold 50 Q 21
Coylton 60 G 17
Coylumbridge 74 I 12
Crackington Haven 6 G 31
Crafthole 3 H 32
Craggan 66 F 15
Cragside Gardens 63 O 18
Crai 25 J 28
Craig 78 E 11
Craig Lodge 65 E 16
Craig-y-nos 17 I 28
Craigdarroch 60 H 18
Craigellachie 80 K 11
Craigencallie 53 G 18
Craigendoran 66 F 16
Craigens 58 B 16
Craighead 69 M 15
Craighouse 58 C 16
Craigie 60 G 17
Craigievar Castle 75 L 12
Craigmalloch 53 G 18
Craignish (Loch) 65 D 15
Craignure 65 C 14
Craigrothie 69 L 15
Craigton 74 K 14
Craik 62 K 17
Crail 69 M 15
Crailing 62 M 17
Crailinghall 62 M 17
Crakaig 85 I 9
Cramlington 56 P 18
Cramond 68 K 16
Cranborne 9 O 31
Cranbrook 12 V 30
Crane Moor 43 P 23
Cranford St. John 29 S 26
Cranleigh 11 S 30
Cranmore 18 M 30
Cranshaws 62 M 16
Cranstal 46 G 20
Cranwell 37 S 24
Cranworth 38 W 26
Crask Inn 84 G 9
Craster 63 P 17
Crathes Castle 75 M 12
Crathie 74 K 12
Crathorne 50 Q 20
Craven Arms 26 L 26
Crawcrock 56 O 19
Crawford 61 J 17
Crawfordjohn 61 I 17
Crawick 61 I 17
Crawley *Hants.* 10 P 30
Crawley *West Sussex* 11 T 30
Crawley Down 11 T 30
Creag Meagaidh 73 G 13
Creagan 65 E 14
Creagorry 76 Y 11
Creake South 38 W 25
Credenhill 26 L 27
Crediton 7 J 31
Creech St. Michael 8 K 30
Creetown 53 G 19
Creggans 66 E 15
Creran (Loch) 65 D 14
Cressage 34 M 26
Cresswell *Castle Morpeth* 56 P 18
Cresswell *Pembrokeshire /
   Sir Benfro* 15 F 28
Creswell 44 Q 24
Crewe 35 M 24
Crewkerne 8 L 31
Cribyn 15 H 27
Criccieth 33 H 25
Crich 36 P 24
Crichton 62 L 16
Crick 28 Q 26
Crickadarn 25 K 27
Cricket St. Thomas 8 L 31
Crickhowell 26 K 28
Cricklade 19 O 29
Crickley Hill 19 N 28
Crieff 67 I 14

Crimond 81 O 11
Crimplesham 38 V 26
Crinan 65 D 15
Crinan (Loch) 65 D 15
Cringleford 39 X 26
Croachy 79 H 12
Crocketford 53 I 18
Crockham Hill 21 U 30
Croes-goch 14 E 28
Croesyceiliog 18 L 29
Croft *Herefordshire* 26 L 27
Croft *Richmondshire* 50 P 20
Croft-on-Tees 50 P 20
Crofty 15 H 29
Croggan 65 C 14
Croglin 55 M 19
Croick 79 G 10
Croig 71 B 14
Cromalt Hills 84 E 9
Cromar 74 L 12
Cromarty 79 H 10
Cromarty Bay 79 H 10
Cromarty Firth 79 H 11
Cromer 39 X 25
Cromford 35 P 24
Cromore 82 A 9
Cromra 73 G 13
Crondall 20 R 30
Cronk (The) 46 G 21
Crook *South Lakeland* 48 L 20
Crook *Wear Valley* 56 O 19
Crook of Devon 68 J 15
Crookham 63 N 17
Crookham Village 20 R 30
Crooklands 48 L 21
Cropredy 28 Q 27
Cropston 36 Q 25
Cropwell Bishop 36 R 25
Crosby *Allerdale* 54 J 19
Crosby *Isle of Man* 46 G 21
Crosby *Sefton* 42 K 23
Crosby Ravensworth 48 M 20
Croscombe 18 M 30
Cross 83 B 8
Cross Fell 55 M 19
Cross Hands 15 H 28
Cross Inn 25 H 27
Crossaig 59 D 16
Crossapol 64 Z 14
Crossbost 82 A 9
Crossford 61 I 16
Crossgates 68 J 15
Crossgill 48 L 21
Crosshill *Fife* 68 K 15
Crosshill *South Ayrshire* 60 G 17
Crosshouse 60 G 17
Crosskeys 18 K 29
Crosskirk 85 J 8
Crossmichael 53 I 19
Crossraguel Abbey 60 F 18
Crossways 9 N 31
Croston 42 L 23
Croughton 28 Q 28
Crow Hill 26 M 28
Crowborough 12 U 30
Crowcombe 8 K 30
Crowhurst 12 V 31
Crowland 37 T 25
Crowle *Doncaster* 44 R 23
Crowle *Wychavon* 27 N 27
Crowlin Island 77 C 11
Crowmarsh Gifford 20 Q 29
Crowthorne 20 R 29
Croxley Green 21 S 29
Croxton 30 W 26
Croxton Kerrial 36 R 25
Croy 79 H 11
Croyde 6 H 30
Croydon *London Borough* 21 T 29
Cruden Bay 81 O 11
Crudwell 19 N 28
Crug-y-bar 25 I 27
Cruliwig 82 Z 9
Crymmych 15 G 28
Crynant 17 I 28
Cuaig 77 C 11
Cubbington 28 P 27
Cubert 2 E 32
Cuckfield 11 T 30
Cucklington 9 M 30
Cuckney 44 Q 24
Cuddington *Aylesbury* 20 R 28
Cuddington *Vale Royal* 42 M 24

Cudworth 43 P 23
Cuffley 21 T 28
Cuhxham 20 Q 29
Cuilcudden 79 H 11
Cuillin Sound 71 B 12
Cuillins (The) 77 B 12
Culbokie 79 G 11
Culdrose 2 E 33
Culgaith 55 M 20
Culkein 83 D 9
Cullen 80 L 10
Cullen Bay 80 L 10
Cullingworth 43 O 22
Cullipool 65 D 15
Culloch 67 I 14
Cullompton 7 J 31
Culmington 26 L 26
Culmstock 8 K 31
Culnacraig 84 E 10
Culrain 79 G 10
Culross 68 J 15
Culshabbin 52 G 19
Culswic 87 P 3
Culter Fell 61 J 17
Cults 75 N 12
Culzean Castle 59 F 17
Cumbernauld 67 I 16
Cumbrian Moutains 48 K 20
Cuminestown 81 N 11
Cummersdale 54 L 19
Cummertrees 54 J 19
Cumnock 60 H 17
Cumnor 20 P 28
Cumwhitton 55 L 19
Cunninghamhead 60 G 17
Cupar 69 K 15
Curbridge 20 P 28
Curdridge 10 Q 31
Currie 61 K 16
Curry Rivel 8 L 30
Cutcloy 53 G 19
Cutnall green 27 N 27
Cuxton 22 V 29
Cwm 18 K 28
Cwm Bychan 33 H 25
Cwm Taf 17 J 28
Cwmafan 17 I 29
Cwmaman 17 J 28
Cwmbach *Carmarthenshire /
   Sir Gaerfyrddin* 15 G 28
Cwmbach *Powys / Powys* 25 J 27
Cwmbach *Rhondda, Cynon, Taf /
   Rhondda, Cynon, Taff* 17 J 29
Cwmbrân 18 L 29
Cwmcarn 18 K 29
Cwmcoy 15 G 27
Cwmllynfell 17 I 28
Cwmystwyth 25 I 26
Cwnduad 15 G 28
Cwnfelin Boeth 15 G 28
Cwrt-Newydd 15 H 27
Cydweli / Kidwelly 15 H 28
Cyffylliog 33 J 24
Cymmer 17 J 29
Cymyran Bay 40 G 23
Cynwyl Elfed 15 G 28

D

Dacre *Eden* 55 L 20
Dacre *Harrogate* 49 O 21
Daglingworth 19 N 28
Dailly 60 F 18
Daimh (Loch an) 73 G 14
Dairsie or Osnaburgh 69 L 14
Dalavich 65 E 15
Dalbeattie 53 I 19
Dalbeg 73 H 12
Dalblair 60 H 17
Dalby 46 F 21
Dalchalloch 73 H 13
Dalchruin 67 H 15
Dale 14 E 28
Dale Head 48 L 20
Dalgonar 60 H 18
Dalham 30 V 27
Dalhavaig 85 I 8
Daliburgh 76 X 12
Dalkeith 61 K 16
Dallas 80 J 11
Dalleagles 60 H 17
Dallington *Northampton* 28 R 27
Dallington *Rother* 12 V 31
Dalmally 66 F 14
Dalmellington 60 H 18
Dalmeny 68 J 16
Dalmigavie 73 H 12
Dalnabreck 71 C 13

Dalnaspidal Lodge ....73 H 13
Dalnavaid ....74 J 13
Dalnavie ....79 H 10
Dalness ....72 F 14
Dalry
  Dumfries and Galloway ....53 H 18
Dalry North Ayrshire ....60 F 16
Dalrymple ....60 G 17
Dalston ....54 L 19
Dalswinton ....53 I 18
Dalton
  Dumfries and Galloway ....54 J 18
Dalton North Yorks. ....50 P 21
Dalton in Furness ....47 K 21
Damerham ....9 O 31
Damh (Loch) ....78 D 11
Dan-yr-Ogof ....17 I 28
Danbury ....22 V 28
Danby ....50 R 20
Dane ....35 N 24
Danehill ....11 U 30
Darenth ....22 U 29
Darfield ....43 P 23
Darlington ....50 P 20
Darowen ....33 I 26
Darras Hall ....56 O 18
Darrington ....44 Q 22
Darsham ....31 Y 27
Dartford ....22 U 29
Dartford Tunnel ....22 U 29
Dartington ....4 I 32
Dartmeet ....4 I 32
Dartmoor National Park ....4 I 32
Dartmouth ....4 J 32
Darton ....43 P 23
Darvel ....60 H 17
Darwen ....42 M 22
Datchet ....21 S 29
Datchworth ....29 T 28
Dava ....80 J 11
Daventry ....28 Q 27
Davidstow ....6 G 32
Davington ....61 K 18
Daviot ....79 H 11
Dawley ....34 M 26
Dawlish ....4 J 32
Deal ....23 Y 30
Dean ....54 J 20
Dean Forest Park ....18 M 28
Deanich Lodge ....78 F 10
Deanston ....67 H 15
Dearham ....54 J 19
Debden ....30 U 28
Deben (River) ....31 X 27
Debenham ....31 X 27
Deddington ....28 Q 28
Dedham ....30 W 28
Dee / Afon Dyfrdwy (River)
  Wales ....41 K 23
Dee (River) Scotland ....75 N 12
Dee (River) / Afon Dyfrdwy .34 K 24
Deene ....29 S 26
Deepcut ....21 R 30
Deepdale ....49 M 21
Deeping-St. James ....37 T 25
Deeping St. Nicholas ....37 T 25
Deeps (The) ....87 P 3
Defford ....27 N 27
Deiniolen ....33 H 24
Delabole ....6 F 32
Delamere ....34 M 24
Delamere Forest ....42 L 24
Dell ....83 B 8
Dellifure ....80 J 11
Delnadamph Lodge ....74 K 12
Delph ....43 N 23
Denbigh / Dinbych ....33 J 24
Denby Dale ....43 P 23
Denchworth ....20 P 29
Denham ....21 S 29
Denholm ....62 L 17
Denmead ....10 Q 31
Dennington ....31 Y 27
Denny ....67 I 15
Dent ....49 M 21
Denton South Kesteven ......36 R 25
Denton Stockport ....43 N 23
Denver ....38 V 26
Derby ....36 P 25
Deri ....18 K 28
Dersingham ....38 V 25
Dervaig ....71 B 14
Derwent (River) R. Ouse ....44 R 22
Derwent (River) R. Trent ...36 P 25
Derwent (River) R. Tyne ....56 O 19
Derwent Dale ....43 O 23
Derwent Reservoir Derbs. ..43 O 23

Derwent Reservoir
  Northumb. ....56 N 19
Derwent Water ....54 K 20
Desborough ....28 R 26
Desford ....36 Q 26
Detling ....22 V 30
Devauden ....18 L 28
Deveron (River) ....81 M 11
Devil's Beef Tub ....61 J 17
Devil's Bridge / Pontarfynach 25 I 26
Devil's Elbow ....74 J 13
Devil's Punch Bowl ....10 R 30
Devizes ....19 O 29
Devonport ....3 H 32
Dewsbury ....43 P 22
Dherue (Loch an) ....84 G 8
Dial Post ....11 S 31
Dickleburgh ....31 X 26
Didcot ....20 Q 29
Diddlebury ....26 L 26
Digby ....37 S 24
Dilhorne ....35 N 25
Dilton Marsh ....19 N 30
Dilwyn ....26 L 27
Dinas ....24 F 27
Dinas Dinlle ....32 G 24
Dinas Head ....24 F 27
Dinas-Mawddwy ....33 I 25
Dinas Powys ....18 K 29
Dinbych / Denbigh ....33 J 24
Dinbych-y-pysgod / Tenby ....15 F 28
Dingwall ....79 G 11
Dinnet ....74 L 12
Dinnington
  Newcastle upon Tyne ......56 O 18
Dinnington Rotherham ....44 Q 23
Dinsdale ....50 P 20
Dinton ....9 O 30
Diptford ....4 I 32
Dirleton ....69 L 15
Dishforth ....50 P 21
Diss ....31 X 26
Disserth ....25 J 27
Distington ....53 J 20
Ditcheat ....8 M 30
Ditchingham ....31 Y 26
Ditchling Park ....28 P 28
Ditchling ....11 T 31
Ditton Priors ....26 M 26
Doc Penfro /
  Pembroke Dock ....16 F 28
Docherty (Glen) ....78 E 11
Dochgarroch ....79 H 11
Docking ....38 V 25
Dockray ....54 L 20
Dodburn ....62 L 17
Doddington Cambs. ....29 U 26
Doddington Kent ....22 W 30
Doddington Lincs. ....44 S 24
Doddington Northumb. ....63 O 17
Dodington ....19 M 29
Dodman Point ....3 F 33
Dodworth ....43 P 23
Doirlinn ....71 C 13
Dolanog ....33 J 25
Dolbenmaen ....33 H 25
Dolfor ....26 K 26
Dolgarrog ....33 I 24
Dolgellau ....33 I 25
Dolgoch Falls ....33 I 26
Dollar ....67 I 15
Dolphinholme ....48 L 22
Dolton ....7 H 31
Don (River) R. Ouse ....44 Q 23
Don (River) R. Spey ....74 K 12
Doncaster ....44 Q 23
Donhead-St. Andrew ....9 N 30
Donhead-St. Mary ....9 N 30
Donington ....37 T 25
Donington-on-Bain ....45 T 24
Donington Park Circuit ......36 P 25
Donisthorpe ....36 P 25
Donnington Berks. ....20 Q 29
Donnington Salop ....35 M 25
Donyatt ....8 L 31
Doon (Loch) ....60 G 18
Dorback Lodge ....74 J 12
Dorchester Dorset ....8 M 31
Dorchester Oxon. ....20 Q 29
Dordon ....35 P 26
Dore ....43 P 24
Dores ....79 H 11
Dorking ....21 T 30
Dormansland ....11 U 30
Dormanstown ....57 Q 20
Dornie ....78 D 12
Dornoch ....79 H 10

Dornoch Firth ....79 H 10
Dornock ....54 K 19
Dorrington ....34 L 26
Dorstone ....26 K 27
Dorusduain ....78 D 12
Douchary (Glen) ....78 F 10
Dougarie ....59 D 17
Douglas Isle of Man ....46 G 21
Douglas
  South Lanarkshire ....61 I 17
Douglastown ....74 L 14
Dounby ....86 K 6
Doune Highland ....84 G 10
Doune Stirling ....67 H 15
Dove (River) ....35 O 24
Dove Cottage ....48 K 20
Dove Holes ....43 O 24
Dovedale ....35 O 24
Dover ....13 X 30
Dovercourt ....31 X 28
Doveridge ....35 O 25
Dovey / Dyfi (River) ....33 I 26
Dowally ....74 J 14
Dowdeswell ....27 N 28
Dowlish Wake ....8 L 31
Down Ampney ....19 O 28
Downderry ....3 G 32
Downham ....30 U 26
Downham Market ....38 V 26
Downies ....75 N 12
Downton ....9 O 31
Dowsby ....37 S 25
Doynton ....19 M 29
Drakes Broughton ....27 N 27
Draughton ....49 O 22
Drax ....44 R 22
Draycott ....36 P 25
Draycott-in-the-Clay ....35 O 25
Draycott-in-the-Moors ....35 N 25
Drayton Norfolk ....39 X 25
Drayton Oxon. ....20 Q 29
Drayton-St. Leonard ....20 Q 29
Drefach near Carmarthen ...15 H 28
Drefach
  near Newcastle-Emlyn ....15 G 27
Dreghorn ....60 G 17
Drem ....69 L 15
Drenewydd / Newtown ....26 K 26
Dreswick Point ....46 G 21
Driffield ....19 O 28
Drigg ....47 J 20
Drighlington ....43 P 22
Drimnin ....71 C 14
Drinnishadder ....76 Z 10
Drissaig ....65 E 15
Droitwich ....27 N 27
Dronfield ....43 P 24
Drongan ....60 G 17
Droxford ....10 Q 31
Druidibeg (Loch) ....76 Y 12
Druim a' Chliabhain (Loch) .85 H 8
Druimindarroch ....71 C 13
Drum Castle ....75 M 12
Drumbeg ....84 E 9
Drumblade ....81 L 11
Drumburgh ....54 K 19
Drumchardine ....79 G 11
Drumclog ....60 H 17
Drumelzier ....61 J 17
Drumfearn ....71 C 12
Drumlanrig Castle ....61 I 18
Drumlemble ....58 C 17
Drumlithie ....75 M 13
Drummond Castle ....67 I 14
Drummore ....52 F 19
Drummossie Muir ....79 H 11
Drumnadrochit ....79 G 11
Drumrunie ....84 E 9
Drumsallie ....72 D 13
Drumtochty Forest ....75 M 13
Druridge Bay ....63 P 18
Drybrook ....18 M 28
Dryburgh Abbey ....62 M 17
Drygarn Fawr ....25 J 27
Drymen ....67 G 15
Drynoch ....77 B 12
Duchally ....84 F 9
Ducklington ....20 P 28
Duddington ....37 S 26
Duddo ....63 N 16
Dudley Dudley ....27 N 26
Dudley North Tyneside ......56 P 18
Duff House ....81 M 11
Duffield ....36 P 25
Dufftown ....80 K 11
Duffus ....80 J 10
Dufton ....55 M 20

Duggleby ....51 S 21
Duich (Loch) ....78 D 12
Duirinish ....77 C 12
Duke's Pass ....67 G 15
Dukinfield ....43 N 23
Dullingham ....30 V 27
Dulnain Bridge ....80 J 12
Duloe ....3 G 32
Dulverton ....7 J 30
Dumbarton ....67 G 16
Dumbleton ....27 O 27
Dumfries ....53 J 18
Dun Carloway Broch ....82 Z 9
Dunan ....66 F 16
Dunbar ....69 M 15
Dunbeath ....85 J 9
Dunblane ....67 I 15
Duncansby Head ....86 K 8
Dunchurch ....28 Q 26
Duncow ....53 J 18
Duncton ....11 S 31
Dundee ....69 K 14
Dundonald ....60 G 17
Dundrennan ....53 I 19
Dundry ....18 M 29
Dunecht ....75 M 12
Dunfermline ....68 J 15
Dungeness ....13 W 31
Dunholme ....44 S 24
Dunino ....69 L 15
Dunipace ....67 I 15
Dunkeld ....68 J 14
Dunkery Beacon ....7 J 30
Dunkeswell ....8 K 31
Dunkirk ....19 N 29
Dunley ....27 N 27
Dunlop ....60 G 16
Dunmaglass Lodge ....79 H 12
Dunnet ....85 J 8
Dunnet Bay ....85 J 8
Dunnet Head ....86 J 7
Dunning ....68 J 15
Dunnington ....50 R 22
Dunnockshaw ....42 N 22
Dunnottar Castle ....75 N 13
Dunoon ....66 F 16
Dunragit ....52 F 19
Dunrobin Castle ....85 I 10
Duns ....62 M 16
Duns Tew ....28 P 28
Dunscore ....53 I 18
Dunsfold ....11 S 30
Dunsford ....4 I 31
Dunsop Bridge ....49 M 22
Dunstable ....29 S 28
Dunstaffnage Castel ....65 D 14
Dunstanburgh Castle ....63 P 17
Dunster ....17 J 30
Dunstone ....37 S 24
Dunsyre ....61 J 16
Duntelchaig (Loch) ....79 H 11
Dunton bassett ....28 Q 26
Dunure ....59 F 17
Dunvegan ....77 A 11
Dunvegan (Loch) ....77 A 11
Dunvegan Castle ....77 A 11
Dunvegan Head ....76 Z 11
Dunwich ....31 Y 27
Durdle Door ....9 N 32
Durham ....56 P 19
Durisdeer ....61 I 18
Durleigh ....17 J 30
Durlston Head ....9 O 32
Durness ....84 F 8
Durrington ....19 O 30
Dursley ....19 M 28
Dury Voe ....87 Q 2
Duston ....28 R 27
Duthil ....79 I 12
Duxford ....29 U 27
Dyce ....75 N 12
Dyfi / Dovey (River) ....33 I 26
Dyke ....80 I 11
Dykehead ....74 K 13
Dykends ....74 K 13
Dymchurch ....13 W 30
Dymock ....27 M 28
Dyrham ....19 M 29
Dyserth ....41 J 23

E

Eaglescliffe ....50 P 20
Eaglesfield ....54 K 18
Eaglesham ....60 H 16
Eakring ....36 R 24
Ealing London Borough ......21 T 29
Earba (Lochan na h-) ....73 G 13

Earby ....49 N 22
Eardisley ....26 K 27
Earl Shilton ....36 Q 26
Earl Soham ....31 X 27
Earl Stonham ....31 X 27
Earley Winnersh ....20 R 29
Earlish ....77 A 11
Earls Barton ....28 R 27
Earls Colne ....30 W 28
Earlsferry ....69 L 15
Earlston ....62 L 17
Earn (Loch) ....67 H 14
Earn (River) ....67 J 14
Earsdon ....56 P 18
Earsham ....31 Y 26
Eartham ....11 S 31
Easdale ....65 D 15
Easebourne ....10 R 31
Easington Easington ....57 P 19
Easington
  East Riding of Yorkshire ..45 U 23
Easington
  Redcar and Cleveland .....50 R 20
Easington
  South Oxfordshire ....20 Q 28
Easington Lane ....56 P 19
Easingwold ....50 Q 21
Eassie and Nevay ....68 K 14
East Aberthaw ....17 J 29
East Barkwith ....45 T 24
East Bergholt ....30 X 28
East Brent ....18 L 30
East Budleigh ....5 K 32
East Butterwick ....44 R 23
East-Challow ....20 P 29
East Chinnock ....8 L 31
East-Coker ....8 M 31
East Cowes ....10 Q 31
East Cowton ....50 P 20
East Dereham ....38 W 25
East Ferry ....44 R 23
East Glen (River) ....37 S 25
East Grafton ....19 P 29
East Grinstead ....11 T 30
East Hagbourne ....20 Q 29
East-Halton ....45 T 23
East Hanney ....20 P 29
East Hardwick ....44 Q 23
East Harling ....30 W 26
East Haven ....69 L 14
East Hendred ....20 P 29
East Hoathly ....12 U 31
East Horsley ....21 S 30
East Huntspill ....18 L 30
East Ilsley ....20 Q 29
East Keswick ....50 P 22
East Kilbride Eilean Siar ..70 X 12
East Kilbride
  South Lanarkshire ....60 H 16
East-Knoyle ....9 N 30
East Knoyle ....9 N 30
East Lambrook ....8 L 31
East Leake ....36 Q 25
East Linton ....69 M 16
East Loch Roag ....82 Z 9
East Loch Tarbet ....77 Z 10
East Looe ....3 G 32
East Lulworth ....9 N 32
East Malling ....22 V 30
East Markham ....44 R 24
East Meon ....10 Q 31
East Mersea ....22 W 28
East Midlands Airport ....36 Q 25
East Moor ....35 P 24
East Norton ....36 R 26
East-Poringland ....39 Y 26
East Portlemouth ....4 I 33
East Rhidorroch Lodge ....78 F 10
East-Rudham ....38 W 25
East-Saltoun ....62 L 16
East Tisted ....10 R 30
East Wemyss ....68 K 15
East-Winch ....38 V 25
East Wittering ....10 R 31
East Witton ....49 O 21
East-Woodhay ....20 P 29
East-Wretham ....30 W 26
Eastbourne ....12 U 31
Eastchurch ....22 W 29
Eastdean ....18 M 29
Easter-Compton ....18 M 29
Easter Ross ....79 G 10
Eastergate ....11 S 31
Eastfield ....51 S 21
Eastgate ....55 N 19
Eastham ....42 L 24
Eastington ....19 N 28

Eastleach ....19 O 28
Eastleigh ....10 P 31
Eastoft ....44 R 23
Easton Carlisle ....55 L 18
Easton Dorset ....8 M 32
Easton Norfolk ....39 X 26
Easton-Grey ....19 N 29
Easton-in-Gordano ....18 L 29
Easton-Royal ....19 O 29
Eastriggs ....54 K 19
Eastrington ....44 R 22
Eastry ....23 X 30
Eastville ....37 U 24
Eastwood ....36 Q 25
Eaton ....34 M 24
Eaton Bray ....29 S 28
Eaton Socon ....29 T 27
Ebbw Vale / Glyn Ebwy ......18 K 28
Ebchester ....56 O 19
Ebrington ....27 O 27
Eccles ....62 M 17
Ecchinswell ....20 Q 29
Ecclefechan ....54 K 18
Eccles ....42 M 23
Eccleshall ....35 N 25
Echt ....75 M 12
Eckford ....62 M 17
Eckington Derbs. ....43 P 24
Eckington Worc. ....27 N 27
Edale ....43 O 23
Eday ....87 L 6
Eddleston ....61 K 16
Edderton ....79 H 10
Eddrachillis Bay ....84 E 9
Eden (River) ....55 M 19
Eden Project ....3 F 32
Edenbridge ....21 U 30
Edentaggart ....66 F 15
Edenthorpe ....44 Q 23
Edgefield ....39 X 25
Edgmond ....35 M 25
Edgton ....26 L 26
Edinbane ....77 A 11
Edinburgh ....68 K 16
Edington ....19 N 30
Edith Weston ....37 S 26
Edlesborough ....29 S 28
Edlingham ....63 O 17
Edmondsley ....56 P 19
Edmundbyers ....56 O 19
Edwalton ....36 Q 25
Edwinstowe ....36 Q 24
Edzell ....75 M 13
Efailnewydd ....32 G 25
Egerton ....23 W 30
Eggerness Point ....53 G 19
Eggleston ....56 N 20
Egham ....21 S 29
Egilsay ....87 L 6
Eglingham ....63 O 17
Egloskerry ....6 G 32
Eglwys Brewis ....17 J 29
Eglwysfach ....33 I 26
Eglwyswrw ....15 F 27
Egremont ....47 J 20
Egton ....50 R 20
Eigg ....71 B 13
Eight Ash Green ....30 W 28
Eil ....73 I 12
Eil (Loch) ....72 E 13
Eilde Mór (Loch) ....72 F 13
Eilean a' Chalmain ....64 A 15
Eilean Beag ....77 C 11
Eilean Chathastail ....71 B 13
Eilean Donan Castle ....78 D 12
Eilean Flodigarry ....77 B 10
Eilean Mhuire ....82 A 10
Eilean Mòr ....77 C 11
Eilean Mullagrach ....83 D 9
Eilean na Bà ....77 C 11
Eilean nan Each ....71 B 13
Eilean Trodday ....77 B 10
Eileanach Lodge ....79 G 10
Eilt (Loch) ....72 D 13
Eishken ....82 A 9
Eishort (Loch) ....77 C 12
Elan Valley ....25 J 27
Elan Village ....25 J 27
Elcho ....68 J 14
Elgin ....80 K 11
Elgol ....71 B 12
Elham ....23 X 30
Elie ....69 L 15
Eling ....10 P 31
Elkesley ....44 R 24
Elkstone ....19 N 28

A
B
C
D
E
F
G
H
I
J
K
L
M
N
O
P
Q
R
S
T
U
V
W
X
Y
Z

Elland .... 43 O 22
Ellastone .... 35 O 25
Ellen's Green .... 11 S 30
Ellerbeck .... 50 P 20
Ellerton .... 44 R 22
Ellesmere .... 34 L 25
Ellesmere Port .... 42 L 24
Ellingham .... 31 Y 26
Ellington .... 56 P 18
Ellon .... 81 N 11
Elloughton .... 44 S 22
Elmdon .... 29 U 27
Elmley Castle .... 27 N 27
Elmore .... 19 N 28
Elmstead Market .... 30 W 28
Elmswell .... 30 W 27
Elphin .... 84 E 9
Elrick .... 75 N 12
Elrig .... 52 G 19
Elsdon .... 55 N 18
Elsenham .... 30 U 28
Elsham .... 45 S 23
Elsrickle .... 61 J 16
Elstead .... 21 R 30
Elstree .... 21 T 29
Elswick .... 42 L 22
Eltisley .... 29 T 27
Elton .... 37 S 26
Elveden .... 30 W 26
Elvington .... 50 R 22
Elwick .... 57 Q 19
Elworth .... 35 M 24
Ely .... 30 U 26
Emberton .... 28 R 27
Embleton Allerdale .... 54 K 20
Embleton Alnwick .... 63 P 17
Embo .... 79 I 10
Embsay .... 49 O 22
Emneth .... 37 U 26
Empingham .... 37 S 25
Emsworth .... 10 R 31
Enaclete .... 82 Z 9
Enard Bay .... 83 D 9
Enderby .... 36 Q 26
Endmoor .... 48 L 21
Endon .... 35 N 24
Enfield London Borough .... 21 T 29
Enford .... 19 O 30
Englefield Green .... 21 S 29
English Bicknor .... 18 M 28
Englishcombe .... 19 M 29
Enham Alamein .... 20 P 30
Enmore .... 8 K 30
Ensay .... 71 B 14
Enstone .... 28 P 28
Enterkinfoot .... 61 I 18
Enville .... 27 N 26
Eochar .... 76 X 11
Eoligarry .... 70 X 12
Eoropie .... 83 B 8
Eorsa .... 65 B 14
Eport (Loch) .... 76 Y 11
Epping .... 21 U 28
Epping Forest .... 21 U 29
Epsom .... 21 T 30
Epworth .... 44 R 23
Erddig .... 34 K 24
Eredine .... 65 E 15
Eredine Forest .... 65 D 15
Eriboll .... 84 F 8
Eriboll (Loch) .... 84 F 8
Ericht (Loch) .... 73 G 13
Ericstane .... 61 J 17
Eridge Green .... 12 U 30
Eriska .... 65 D 14
Eriskay .... 70 Y 12
Erisort (Loch) .... 82 A 9
Eriswell .... 30 V 26
Erlestoke .... 19 N 30
Ermington .... 4 I 32
Erpingham .... 39 X 25
Erraid .... 64 A 15
Errochty (Loch) .... 73 H 13
Errogie .... 79 G 12
Errol .... 68 K 14
Ersary .... 70 X 13
Erskine Bridge .... 67 G 16
Ervie .... 52 E 19
Erwood .... 25 K 27
Esh Winning .... 56 O 19
Esha Ness .... 87 P 2
Esher .... 21 S 29
Esk (Glen) .... 75 L 13
Esk (River) .... 54 K 18
Eskdale .... 54 K 18
Eskdalemuir .... 61 K 18
Essendon .... 21 T 28

Essich .... 79 H 11
Eston .... 57 Q 20
Etal .... 63 N 17
Etchilhampton .... 19 O 29
Etchingham .... 12 V 30
Etherow (River) .... 43 N 23
Etherow Park .... 43 N 23
Etive (Glen) .... 72 F 14
Etive (Loch) .... 65 E 14
Eton .... 21 S 29
Ettington .... 27 P 27
Ettrick .... 61 K 17
Ettrick Forest .... 62 K 17
Ettrick Pen .... 61 K 17
Etwall .... 35 P 25
Euston .... 30 W 26
Euxton .... 42 L 22
Evanton .... 79 G 11
Evelix .... 79 H 10
Evenlode .... 27 O 28
Evenwood .... 56 O 20
Everingham .... 44 R 22
Everleigh .... 19 O 30
Evershot .... 8 M 31
Eversley .... 20 R 29
Everton .... 44 R 23
Evesham .... 27 O 27
Evesham (Vale of) .... 27 O 27
Ewe (Isle of) .... 78 D 10
Ewell .... 21 T 29
Ewelme .... 20 Q 29
Ewenny .... 17 J 29
Ewes .... 54 L 18
Ewhurst .... 11 S 30
Exbourne .... 7 I 31
Exe (River) .... 7 J 31
Exebridge .... 7 J 30
Exeter .... 4 J 31
Exford .... 7 J 30
Exminster .... 4 J 31
Exmoor National Park .... 7 I 30
Exmouth .... 4 J 32
Exton .... 7 J 31
Eyam .... 43 O 24
Eye Cambs. .... 37 T 26
Eye Suffolk .... 31 X 27
Eye Peninsula .... 83 B 9
Eyemouth .... 63 N 16
Eynort .... 77 A 12
Eynort (Loch) Highland .... 77 A 12
Eynort (Loch) Western Isles 76 Y 12
Eynsford .... 22 U 29
Eynsham .... 20 P 28
Eyre Point .... 77 B 12
Eythorne .... 23 X 30

F
Fada (Loch) .... 76 Y 11
Failsworth .... 43 N 23
Fair Isle .... 87 P 5
Fair Oak .... 10 Q 31
Fairbourne .... 33 H 25
Fairburn .... 44 Q 22
Fairford .... 19 O 28
Fairlie .... 59 F 16
Fairlight .... 12 V 31
Fakenham .... 38 W 25
Fala .... 62 L 16
Faldingworth .... 45 S 23
Falfield .... 18 M 29
Falkirk .... 67 I 16
Falkland .... 68 K 15
Fallin .... 67 I 15
Falmer .... 11 T 31
Falmouth .... 2 E 33
Falstone .... 55 M 18
Fanagmore .... 84 E 8
Fangfoss .... 50 R 22
Fannich (Loch) .... 78 E 11
Fannich Lodge .... 78 F 11
Fara .... 86 K 7
Fareham .... 10 Q 31
Faringdon .... 19 P 29
Farlam .... 55 L 19
Farleigh-Hungerford .... 19 N 30
Farley .... 9 O 30
Farley Mount .... 10 P 30
Farlow .... 26 M 26
Farmborough .... 18 M 29
Farmers .... 25 I 27
Farmtown .... 80 L 11
Farnborough Hants. .... 20 R 30
Farnborough Warw. .... 28 P 27
Farnborough
   West Berkshire .... 20 P 29

Farndon Chester .... 34 L 24
Farndon
   Newark and Sherwood .... 36 R 24
Farne Islands .... 63 P 17
Farnell .... 75 M 13
Farnham Dorset .... 9 N 31
Farnham Surrey .... 20 R 30
Farnham Royal .... 21 S 29
Farningham .... 22 U 29
Farnley .... 49 O 22
Farnsfield .... 36 Q 24
Farnworth .... 42 M 23
Farr .... 85 H 8
Farrington Gurney .... 18 M 30
Farway .... 5 K 31
Fasnakyle .... 78 F 12
Fasnakyle Forest .... 78 F 11
Fasque .... 75 M 13
Fassfern .... 72 E 13
Fauldhouse .... 61 I 16
Faversham .... 22 W 30
Fawley .... 10 P 31
Fazeley .... 35 O 26
Fearby .... 49 O 21
Fearn Lodge .... 79 H 10
Fearnan .... 67 H 14
Fearnmore .... 77 C 11
Featherstone Staffs. .... 35 N 26
Featherstone West Yorks. ... 43 P 22
Feelindre .... 15 F 27
Feering .... 30 W 28
Feetham .... 49 N 20
Felbridge .... 11 T 30
Felindre Carmarthenshire /
   Sir Gaerfyrddin .... 25 I 28
Felindre Powys .... 26 K 26
Felinfach .... 25 K 28
Felinheli .... 33 H 24
Felixkirk .... 50 Q 21
Felixstowe .... 31 Y 28
Felling .... 56 P 19
Felmingham .... 39 Y 25
Felpham .... 11 S 31
Felsham .... 30 W 27
Felsted .... 30 V 28
Feltham .... 21 S 29
Felthorpe .... 39 X 25
Felton .... 63 O 18
Feltwell .... 30 V 26
Fence .... 42 N 22
Feniton .... 8 K 31
Fenny Bentley .... 35 O 24
Fenstanton .... 29 T 27
Fenton Stoke-on-Trent .... 35 N 25
Fenton West Lindsey .... 44 R 24
Fenwick
   Berwick-upon-Tweed .... 63 O 17
Fenwick East Ayrshire .... 60 G 17
Feochaig .... 59 D 17
Feochan (Loch) .... 65 D 14
Feock .... 2 E 33
Feolin Ferry .... 58 B 16
Fern .... 74 L 13
Ferndown .... 9 O 31
Ferness .... 79 I 11
Fernhurst .... 11 R 30
Ferryden .... 75 M 13
Ferryhill .... 56 P 19
Ferryside .... 15 G 28
Fersit .... 73 F 13
Feshie (Glen) .... 73 I 12
Feshiebridge .... 73 I 12
Fetcham .... 21 S 30
Fetlar .... 87 R 2
Fetterangus .... 81 N 11
Fettercairn .... 75 M 13
Fewston .... 49 O 22
Ffestiniog .... 33 I 25
Ffestiniog (Vale of) .... 33 H 25
Fflint / Flint .... 42 K 24
Fforest Fawr .... 17 J 28
Ffostrasol .... 15 G 27
Fiaray .... 70 X 12
Fiddleton .... 61 L 18
Fifield .... 27 P 28
Filby .... 39 Y 26
Filey .... 51 T 21
Fillongley .... 27 P 26
Filton .... 18 M 29
Finchampstead .... 20 R 29
Finchingfield .... 30 V 28
Findhorn .... 80 J 11
Findhorn (River) .... 73 H 12
Findhorn Bay .... 80 J 11
Findo Gask .... 68 J 14
Findochty .... 80 L 10
Findon .... 11 S 31

Finedon .... 29 S 26
Fingest .... 20 R 29
Fingland .... 60 I 17
Finiskaig .... 72 D 13
Finmere .... 28 Q 28
Finniegill .... 61 K 18
Finningley .... 44 R 23
Finsbay .... 76 Z 10
Finstock .... 20 P 28
Finstown .... 86 K 6
Fintry Aberdeenshire .... 81 M 11
Fintry Stirling .... 67 H 15
Fionn Loch .... 78 D 10
Fionn Loch Mór .... 84 F 9
Fionnphort .... 64 A 15
Fishbourne Chichester .... 10 R 31
Fishbourne Isle of Wight .... 10 Q 31
Fishburn .... 56 P 19
Fisherfield Forest .... 78 D 10
Fisherford .... 81 M 11
Fishguard / Abergwaun .... 24 F 28
Fishnish Bay .... 65 B 14
Fishtoft .... 37 U 25
Fiskavaig .... 77 A 12
Fiskerton .... 44 S 24
Fittleworth .... 11 S 31
Fiunary .... 71 C 14
Fivehead .... 8 L 30
Flackwell Heath .... 21 R 29
Fladbury .... 27 N 27
Fladda-Chùain .... 77 A 10
Flagg .... 35 O 24
Flamborough .... 51 T 21
Flamborough Head .... 51 T 21
Flamingo Park .... 50 R 21
Flamstead .... 21 S 28
Flash .... 35 O 24
Flashader .... 77 A 11
Flatford Mill .... 30 X 28
Flax Bourton .... 18 L 29
Flaxton .... 50 R 21
Fleckney .... 36 Q 26
Fleet .... 20 R 30
Fleet (Islands of) .... 53 H 19
Fleet (Loch) .... 79 H 10
Fleet Hargate .... 37 U 25
Fleetwood .... 48 K 22
Flimby .... 53 J 19
Flint / Fflint .... 42 K 24
Flintham .... 36 R 24
Flitton .... 29 S 27
Flitwick .... 29 S 27
Flixton .... 31 Y 26
Flodday near Hellisay .... 70 X 13
Flodday near Sandray .... 70 X 13
Flodden Field .... 63 N 17
Flodigarry .... 77 B 11
Flookburgh .... 48 L 21
Floors Castle .... 62 M 17
Flotta .... 86 K 7
Flowerdale Forest .... 78 D 11
Flyford Flavell .... 27 N 27
Fochabers .... 80 K 11
Foggathorpe .... 44 R 22
Foinaven .... 84 F 8
Foindle .... 84 E 8
Folkestone .... 13 X 30
Folkingham .... 37 S 25
Folly Gate .... 7 H 31
Fontmell Magna .... 9 N 31
Ford Argyll and Bute .... 65 D 15
Ford Arun .... 11 S 31
Ford
   Berwick-upon-Tweed .... 63 N 17
Ford
   Buckinghamshire .... 20 R 28
Ford Cotswold .... 27 O 28
Ford
   Shrewsbury and Atcham ..34 L 25
Forde Abbey .... 8 L 31
Forden .... 34 K 26
Fordham .... 30 V 27
Fordingbridge .... 9 O 31
Fordoun .... 75 M 13
Fordwich .... 23 X 30
Fordyce .... 80 L 11
Foreland .... 10 Q 31
Foreland Point .... 17 I 30
Foremark Reservoir .... 36 P 25
Forest Lodge .... 74 I 13
Forest Row .... 11 U 30
Forestburn Gate .... 63 O 18
Forfar .... 74 L 14
Forgandenny .... 68 J 14
Formby .... 42 K 23
Formby Point .... 42 K 23
Fornham All Saints .... 30 W 27

Forres .... 80 J 11
Forrest Lodge .... 53 H 18
Forse .... 85 K 9
Forsinard .... 85 I 8
Fort Augustus .... 73 F 12
Fort George .... 79 H 11
Fort Victoria .... 10 P 31
Fort William .... 72 E 13
Forter .... 74 K 13
Forteviot .... 68 J 14
Forth .... 61 I 16
Forth (Firth of) .... 68 K 15
Forth (River) .... 67 G 15
Forth Bridges .... 68 J 15
Fortingall .... 73 H 14
Forton .... 35 M 25
Fortrose .... 79 H 11
Fortuneswell .... 8 M 32
Fosdyke .... 37 T 25
Foss .... 73 I 13
Foston .... 36 R 25
Foston on the Wolds .... 51 T 22
Fotherby .... 45 T 23
Fotheringhay .... 29 S 26
Foulden .... 63 N 16
Foulness Point .... 22 W 29
Foulridge .... 43 N 22
Foulsham .... 38 X 25
Fountainhall .... 62 L 16
Fountains Abbey .... 50 P 21
Four Crosses .... 34 K 25
Four Elms .... 21 U 30
Four Marks .... 10 Q 30
Fovant .... 9 O 30
Foveran .... 81 N 12
Fowey .... 3 G 32
Fowlmere .... 29 U 27
Fownhope .... 26 M 27
Foxdale .... 46 G 21
Foxholes .... 51 S 21
Foxton .... 28 R 26
Foxup .... 49 N 21
Foyers .... 73 G 12
Fraddon .... 3 F 32
Framfield .... 12 U 31
Framlingham .... 31 Y 27
Frampton-on-Severn .... 19 M 28
Framwellgate Moor .... 56 P 19
Frant .... 12 U 30
Fraserburgh .... 81 O 10
Fraserburgh Bay .... 81 O 10
Freckenham .... 30 V 27
Freckleton .... 42 L 22
Freeland .... 20 P 28
Freethorpe .... 39 Y 26
Freevater Forest .... 79 F 10
Freiston .... 37 U 25
Fremington .... 7 H 30
Frensham .... 10 R 30
Freshwater .... 10 P 31
Freshwater Bay .... 10 P 31
Freshwater East .... 16 F 29
Freshwater West .... 14 E 29
Fressingfield .... 31 X 26
Freswick .... 86 K 8
Freuchie .... 68 K 15
Freuchie (Loch) .... 67 I 14
Friday Bridge .... 37 U 26
Fridaythorpe .... 51 S 21
Frimley .... 21 R 30
Fringford .... 28 Q 28
Frinton-on-Sea .... 31 X 28
Friockheim .... 75 M 14
Frisa (Loch) .... 71 B 14
Friskney .... 37 U 24
Frithville .... 37 T 24
Frittenden .... 12 V 30
Frittwell .... 28 Q 28
Frizington .... 47 J 20
Frocester .... 19 N 28
Frodsham .... 42 L 24
Froggatt .... 43 P 24
Frome .... 19 N 30
Frosterley .... 56 O 19
Froxfield .... 20 P 29
Fuday .... 70 X 12
Fuiay .... 70 X 13
Fulbourn .... 30 U 27
Fulford .... 62 L 16
Fulking .... 11 T 31
Fuller Street .... 22 V 28
Fulwood .... 42 M 22
Funtington .... 10 R 31
Funzie .... 87 R 2
Furness Abbey .... 47 K 21
Furness Fells .... 48 K 20
Fyfield .... 22 U 28
Fyvie .... 81 M 11

G
Gaddesby .... 36 R 25
Gaick Lodge .... 73 H 13
Gainford .... 49 O 20
Gainsborough .... 44 R 23
Gairloch .... 78 C 10
Gairlochy .... 72 F 13
Gairsay .... 87 L 6
Gaitsgill .... 54 L 19
Galashiels .... 62 L 17
Galgate .... 48 L 22
Gallan Head .... 82 Y 9
Gallanach .... 65 D 14
Galloway Forest Park .... 52 G 18
Galltair .... 72 D 12
Galmisdale .... 71 B 13
Galmpton .... 4 J 32
Galson .... 82 A 8
Galston .... 60 G 17
Gamblesby .... 55 M 19
Gamlingay .... 29 T 27
Gamston .... 44 R 24
Ganavan .... 65 D 14
Ganton .... 51 S 21
Garboldisham .... 30 W 26
Gardenstown .... 81 N 10
Garelochhead .... 66 F 15
Garenin .... 82 Z 9
Garforth .... 43 P 22
Gargrave .... 49 N 22
Gargunnock .... 67 H 15
Garioch .... 81 M 12
Garlieston .... 53 G 19
Garlogie .... 75 M 12
Garmony .... 65 C 14
Garmouth .... 80 K 11
Garrabost .... 83 B 9
Garragie Lodge .... 73 G 12
Garraron .... 65 D 15
Garreg .... 33 H 25
Garrigill .... 55 M 19
Garros .... 77 B 11
Garrow .... 67 I 14
Garry (Glen) Highland .... 72 E 12
Garry (Glen)
   Perthshire and Kinross ... 73 H 13
Garry (Loch) .... 72 F 12
Garsington .... 20 Q 28
Garten (Loch) .... 74 I 12
Gartocharn .... 66 G 16
Garth .... 25 J 27
Garthorpe .... 44 R 23
Gartmore .... 67 G 15
Garton-on-The-Wolds .... 51 S 21
Garvald .... 69 M 16
Garvamore .... 73 G 12
Garve .... 79 F 11
Garvellachs .... 65 C 15
Garvestone .... 38 W 26
Garvock .... 66 F 16
Garway .... 26 L 28
Garynahine .... 82 Z 9
Gatehouse of Fleet .... 53 H 19
Gateshead .... 56 P 19
Gateside .... 68 K 15
Gatley .... 42 N 23
Gatwick Airport .... 11 T 30
Gaulden Manor .... 8 K 30
Gavard .... 64 B 15
Gaydon .... 28 P 27
Gayton King's Lynn
   and West Norfolk .... 38 V 25
Gayton Stafford .... 35 N 25
Gaywood .... 38 V 25
Geary .... 77 A 11
Geddington .... 29 R 26
Gedney Drove End .... 37 U 25
Gedney Hill .... 37 T 25
Gelligaer .... 18 K 28
Gelston .... 53 I 19
Georgeham .... 6 H 30
Georth .... 86 K 6
Gerrards Cross .... 21 S 29
Gestingthorpe .... 30 V 27
Gigha (Sound of) .... 58 C 17
Gigha Island .... 58 C 16
Gighay .... 70 Y 12
Gilberdyke .... 44 R 22
Gilcrux .... 54 J 19
Gildersome .... 43 P 22
Gilfach Goch .... 17 J 29
Gillamour .... 50 R 21
Gilling East .... 50 Q 21

Great Britain 127

Gilling West 49 O 20
Gillingham *Dorset* 9 N 30
Gillingham *Kent* 22 V 29
Gillingham *South Norfolk* 31 Y 26
Gills 86 K 8
Gilmerton 67 I 14
Gilmorton 28 Q 26
Gilston 62 L 16
Gilwern 18 K 28
Girthon 53 H 19
Girton 29 U 27
Girvan 59 F 18
Gisburn 49 N 22
Gisland 55 M 19
Gittisham 8 K 31
Gladestry 26 K 27
Glaisdale 50 R 20
Glamis 74 K 14
Glamis Castle 74 L 14
Glanaman 17 I 28
Glandwr 15 G 28
Glanton 63 O 17
Glas-allt-Shiel 74 K 13
Glas-leac Mór 83 D 9
Glas Maol 74 J 13
Glasbury 26 K 27
Glascarnoch (Loch) 78 F 10
Glascwm 26 K 27
Glasdrum 72 E 14
Glasgow 60 H 16
Glasphein 76 Z 11
Glaspwll 33 I 26
Glass (Loch) 79 G 10
Glassburn 78 F 11
Glasserton 52 G 19
Glassford 60 H 16
Glasshouses 49 O 21
Glasson 48 L 22
Glassonby 55 M 19
Glastonbury 8 L 30
Gleadless 43 P 23
Gleann Beag 78 F 10
Gleann Mór 79 G 10
Gleaston 48 K 21
Glecknabae 59 E 16
Glemsford 30 V 27
Glen auldyn 46 G 21
Glen Brittle Forest 77 B 12
Glen Finglas Reservoir 67 G 15
Glen More Forest Park 74 I 12
Glen Shee 74 J 13
Glen Trool Lodge 52 G 18
Glenbarr 59 C 17
Glenborrodale 71 C 13
Glenbranter 66 E 15
Glenbrittle House 77 B 12
Glenbuchat Castle 74 K 12
Glenbuck 60 I 17
Glencaple 53 J 18
Glencarse 68 K 14
Glencoe 72 E 13
Glencoul (Loch) 84 F 9
Glendoebeg 73 G 12
Glendurgan Garden 2 E 33
Glenegedale 58 B 16
Glenelg 72 D 12
Glenelg Bay 72 D 12
Glenfarg 68 J 15
Glenfeshie Lodge 73 I 12
Glenfiddich Lodge 80 K 11
Glenfield 36 Q 26
Glenfinnan 72 D 13
Glenforsa Airport 65 C 14
Glenfyne Lodge 66 F 15
Glengorm 71 B 14
Glengoulandie 73 H 14
Glengrasco 77 B 11
Glenkens (The) 53 H 18
Glenkin die 74 L 12
Glenkirk 61 J 17
Glenlivet 80 J 11
Glenluce 52 F 19
Glenmassan 66 E 15
Glenmaye 46 F 21
Glenmore 71 C 13
Glenprosen Village 74 K 13
Glenridding 48 L 20
Glenrothes 68 K 15
Glenside 82 A 9
Glenstriven 66 E 16
Glentham 44 S 23
Glentress 61 K 17
Glentrool Village 52 G 18
Glentworth 44 S 23
Glenuachdarach 77 B 11
Glenuig 71 C 13
Glespin 61 I 17
Gletness 87 Q 3
Glinton 37 T 26
Glossop 43 O 23
Gloucester 27 N 28
Gloup 87 Q 1
Glusburn 49 O 22
Glutt Lodge 85 I 9
Glympton 28 P 28
Glyn Ceiriog 34 K 25
Glyn-Ebwy / Ebbw Vale 18 K 28
Glyn-neath 17 J 28
Glyncorrwg 17 J 28
Glynde 11 U 31
Glyndebourne 11 U 31
Glyndyfrdwy 34 K 25
Gnosall 35 N 25
Goadby 36 R 26
Goat Fell 59 E 17
Goathland 50 R 20
Gobowen 34 K 25
Godalming 21 S 30
Godmanchester 29 T 27
Godmanstone 8 M 31
Godshill 10 Q 32
Godstone 21 T 30
Goil (Loch) 66 F 15
Golborne 42 M 23
Goldcliff 18 L 29
Goldhanger 22 W 28
Goldthorpe 44 Q 23
Golspie 85 I 10
Gomersal 43 O 22
Gometra 64 B 14
Gomshall 21 S 30
Gooderstone 38 V 26
Goodleigh 7 I 30
Goodrich 26 M 28
Goodrington 4 J 32
Goodwick 24 F 27
Goodwood House 10 R 31
Goole 44 R 22
Goonhavern 2 E 32
Goostrey 42 M 24
Gordon 62 M 16
Gordonbush 85 I 9
Gordonstown 80 L 11
Gorebridge 61 K 16
Goring 20 Q 29
Gorm Loch Mór 84 F 9
Gorran Haven 3 F 33
Gorseinon 15 H 29
Gorsleston-on-Sea 39 Z 26
Gortantaoid 64 B 16
Gosberton 37 T 25
Gosfield 30 V 28
Gosforth *Cumbria* 47 J 20
Gosforth
Newcastle upon Tyne 56 P 18
Gosport 10 Q 31
Goswick 63 O 16
Gotham 36 Q 25
Gott Bay 70 Z 14
Goudhurst 12 V 30
Gourdon 75 N 13
Gourock 66 F 16
Gowerton 15 H 29
Goxhill 45 T 22
Graemsay 86 K 7
Grafton Underwood 29 S 26
Grain 22 W 29
Grainthorpe 45 U 23
Granby 36 R 25
Grandtully 74 I 14
Grange-over-Sands 48 L 21
Grangemouth 67 I 15
Grantchester 29 U 27
Grantham 37 S 25
Grantown-on-Spey 80 J 12
Grantshouse 62 N 16
Grasby 45 S 23
Grasmere 48 K 20
Grassington 49 O 21
Grateley 9 P 30
Graveley 29 T 27
Gravesend 22 V 29
Gravir 82 A 9
Grayrigg 48 M 20
Grays Thurrock 22 V 29
Grayshott 10 R 30
Grayswood 11 R 30
Greasbrough 43 P 23
Great Addington 29 S 26
Great Altcar 42 K 23
Great Amwell 21 T 28
Great Asby 49 M 20
Great Ayton 50 Q 20
Great Baddow 22 V 28
Great Bardfield 30 V 28
Great Barford 29 S 27
Great Barr 35 O 26
Great Barrow 34 L 24
Great Barugh 50 R 21
Great Bedwyn 19 P 29
Great Bentley 31 X 28
Great Bernera 82 Z 9
Great Bircham 38 V 25
Great-Bollright 28 P 28
Great Bookham 21 S 30
Great Bourton 28 Q 27
Great Bowden 28 R 26
Great Brickhill 29 R 28
Great Bridgeford 35 N 25
Great Bromley 30 X 28
Great Broughton 50 Q 20
Great-Budworth 42 M 24
Great Burdon 50 P 20
Great Chalfield 19 N 29
Great Chesterford 30 U 27
Great Chishill 29 U 27
Great Clifton 53 J 20
Great Coates 45 T 23
Great-Comberton 27 N 27
Great Cornard 30 W 27
Great Cubley 35 O 25
Great Cumbrae Island 59 F 16
Great-Dalby 36 R 25
Great Doddington 28 R 27
Great Driffield 51 S 21
Great-Dunham 38 W 25
Great Dunmow 30 V 28
Great Easton *Essex* 30 U 28
Great Easton *Leics.* 28 R 26
Great Eccleston 42 L 22
Great Ellingham 38 W 26
Great Finborough 30 W 27
Great Glen 36 Q 26
Great Gonerby 37 S 25
Great Gransden 29 T 27
Great Harrowden 28 R 27
Great Harwood 42 M 22
Great Hockham 30 W 26
Great Horkesley 30 W 28
Great Horwood 28 R 28
Great Houghton 43 P 23
Great Langton 50 P 20
Great-Limber 45 T 23
Great Livermere 30 W 27
Great Lumley 56 P 19
Great Malvern 27 N 27
Great Marton 42 K 22
Great Massingham 38 W 25
Great Milton 20 Q 28
Great Missenden 21 R 28
Great Mitton 42 M 22
Great Musgrave 49 M 20
Great Oakley 31 X 28
Great Ormes Head 41 I 22
Great Orton 54 K 19
Great Ouse (River) 38 V 25
Great Ouseburn 50 Q 21
Great Ponton 37 S 25
Great Ryburgh 38 W 25
Great Salkeld 55 L 19
Great Sampford 30 V 28
Great Shefford 20 P 29
Great Shelford 29 U 27
Great Smeaton 50 P 20
Great Somerford 19 N 29
Great Stainton 56 P 20
Great Strickland 55 L 20
Great Torrington 6 H 31
Great Tosson 63 O 18
Great Totham 22 W 28
Great Urswick 48 K 21
Great Wakering 22 W 29
Great Waltham 22 V 28
Great Whernside 49 O 21
Great Whittington 56 O 18
Great Witley 27 M 27
Great Wolford 27 P 27
Great Wyrley 35 N 26
Great Yarmouth 39 Z 26
Great Yeldham 30 V 27
Greatford 37 S 25
Greatham *Cleveland* 57 Q 20
Greatham *Hants.* 10 R 30
Greatstone-on-Sea 12 W 31
Green Hammerton 50 Q 21
Greenfield
Flintshire / Sir y Fflint 41 K 23
Greenfield *Highland* 72 F 12
Greenhaugh 55 N 18
Greenhead 55 M 19
Greenholm 60 H 17
Greenhow Hill 49 O 21
Greenlaw 62 M 16
Greenloaning 67 I 15
Greenock 66 F 16
Greenodd 48 K 21
Greens Norton 28 Q 27
Greenside 56 O 19
Greenwich
London Borough 21 U 29
Grendon 28 R 27
Grendon Underwood 28 Q 28
Gresford 34 L 24
Greshornish 77 A 11
Greshornish (Loch) 77 A 11
Gress 83 B 9
Gretna 54 K 19
Gretton 37 R 26
Greys Court 20 R 29
Greysouthen 54 J 20
Greystoke 55 L 19
Griffithstown 18 K 28
Griminish 76 X 11
Grimley 27 N 27
Grimoldby 45 U 23
Grimsay 76 Y 11
Grimsby 45 T 23
Gringley on the Hill 44 R 23
Grinshill 34 L 25
Grinton 49 O 20
Gristhorpe 51 T 21
Grittleton 19 N 29
Groby 36 Q 26
Grogport 59 D 17
Groombridge 12 U 30
Grosebay 76 Z 10
Grosmont *Monmouthshire /*
Sir Fynwy 26 L 28
Grosmont *Scarborough* 50 R 20
Grove 20 P 29
Gruinard Bay 78 D 10
Gruinard Island 78 D 10
Gruinart 58 B 16
Gruinart (Loch) 64 B 16
Grunavat (Loch) 82 Z 9
Grundisburgh 31 X 27
Gualachulain 66 E 14
Guardbridge 69 L 14
Guernsey *Channel I.* 5
Guesting 12 V 31
Guildford 21 S 30
Guildtown 68 J 14
Guilsborough 28 Q 26
Guisborough 50 Q 20
Guiseley 43 O 22
Guist 38 W 25
Gullane 69 L 15
Gunna 70 Z 14
Gunnerside 49 N 20
Gunnerton 55 N 18
Gunness 44 R 23
Gunnislake 3 H 32
Gunthorpe 36 R 25
Gurnard 10 Q 31
Gurness Broch 86 K 6
Gurnos 17 I 28
Gussage All Saints 9 O 31
Gutcher 87 Q 1
Guthrie 75 L 14
Guyhirn 37 U 26
Gwalchmai 40 G 23
Gwaun-Cae-Gurwen 17 I 28
Gwbert-on-Sea 15 F 27
Gweek 2 E 33
Gwennap 2 E 33
Gwithian 2 D 33
Gwyddelwern 33 J 24
Gwyddgrug 15 H 28
Gwydir Castle 33 I 24
Gwytherin 33 I 24

H

Habost 83 B 8
Hackney *London Borough* 21 T 29
Haddenham *Bucks.* 20 R 28
Haddenham *Cambs.* 29 U 26
Haddington 69 L 16
Haddiscoe 39 Y 26
Haddo House 81 N 11
Haddon Hall 35 P 24
Hadfield 43 O 23
Hadleigh *Essex* 22 V 29
Hadleigh *Suffolk* 30 W 27
Hadley 34 M 25
Hadlow 22 V 30
Hadnall 34 L 25
Hadrian's Wall 55 M 18
Haggbeck 55 L 18
Hagley 27 N 26
Hagworthingham 45 U 24
Hailsham 12 U 31
Hainford 39 X 25
Hainton 45 T 23
Halam 36 R 24
Halberton 7 J 31
Hale 42 M 23
Hales 39 Y 26
Halesowen 27 N 26
Halesworth 31 Y 26
Halford 27 P 27
Halifax 43 O 22
Halistra 77 A 11
Halkirk 85 J 8
Hall 60 G 16
Halland 12 U 31
Hallaton 36 R 26
Halling 22 V 29
Hallington 55 N 18
Halloughton 36 R 24
Hallow 27 N 27
Hallsands 4 J 33
Halsall 42 L 23
Halse 8 K 30
Halsetown 2 D 33
Halstead 30 V 28
Halstock 8 M 31
Haltham 37 T 24
Halton *Aylesbury Vale* 20 R 28
Halton *Lancaster* 48 L 21
Halton Gill 49 N 21
Haltwhistle 55 M 19
Halwell 4 I 32
Halwill Junction 6 H 31
Hamble 10 Q 31
Hambleden 20 R 29
Hambledon *Hants.* 10 Q 31
Hambledon *Surrey* 11 S 30
Hambleton *Lancs.* 42 L 22
Hambleton *North Yorks.* 44 Q 22
Hambleton Hills (The) 50 Q 21
Hambridge 8 L 31
Hamilton 60 H 16
Hammersmith and Fulham
London Borough 21 T 29
Hamnavoe *near Brae* 87 Q 2
Hamnavoe *near Scallway* 87 P 3
Hampreston 9 O 31
Hampstead Norris 20 Q 29
Hampsthwaite 50 P 21
Hampton Court 21 S 29
Hampton in Arden 27 O 26
Hamstead Marshall 20 P 29
Hamsterley 56 O 19
Hamstreet 12 W 30
Hamworthy 9 N 31
Handa Island 84 E 8
Handbridge 34 L 24
Handbury 27 N 27
Handcross 11 T 30
Handforth 43 N 23
Handley 34 L 24
Handsworth 43 P 23
Hanham 18 M 29
Hanley 35 N 24
Hanley Swan 27 N 27
Hanningfield 22 V 28
Hannington 19 O 29
Hanslope 28 R 27
Happisburgh 39 Y 25
Hapton 42 N 22
Harberton 4 I 32
Harbertonford 4 I 32
Harbledown 23 X 30
Harborough Magna 28 Q 26
Harbottle 63 N 17
Harbury 28 P 27
Harby 36 R 25
Hardham 11 S 31
Hardwick 44 Q 24
Hardwick Hall 36 Q 24
Hardwicke 19 N 28
Hardy Monument 5 M 31
Hardy's Cottage 9 M 31
Hare Street 29 U 28
Haresfield 19 N 28
Harewood House 50 P 22
Hargrave 29 S 27
Hargrave Green 30 V 27
Haringey *London Borough* 21 T 29
Harlaxton 36 R 25
Harlech 33 H 25
Harleston 31 X 26
Harlestone 28 R 27
Harley 34 M 26
Harlington 29 S 28
Harlosh 77 A 11
Harlow 21 U 28
Harlow Hill 56 O 18
Harmston 37 S 24
Haroldswick 87 R 1
Harpenden 21 S 28
Harpley 38 V 25
Harport (Loch) 77 A 12
Harray (Loch of) 86 K 6
Harrietfield 67 J 14
Harrington *Allerdale* 53 J 20
Harrington *Kettering* 28 R 26
Harringworth 37 S 26
Harris *Highland* 71 A 13
Harris *Western Isles* 82 Y 10
Harris (Sound of) 76 Y 10
Harrogate 50 P 22
Harrow *London Borough* 21 S 29
Harston 29 U 27
Hartburn 56 O 18
Hartest 30 W 27
Hartfield 11 U 30
Harthill *North Lanarkshire* 61 I 16
Harthill *Rotherham* 44 Q 24
Harting 10 R 31
Hartington 35 O 24
Hartland 6 G 31
Hartland Quay 6 G 31
Hartlebury 27 N 26
Hartlepool 57 Q 19
Hartley 22 U 29
Hartley Wintney 20 R 30
Hartpury 27 N 28
Hartshill 36 P 26
Hartwell 20 R 28
Hartwell 28 R 27
Harvington 27 O 27
Harwell 20 Q 29
Harwich 31 X 28
Harwood Dale 51 S 20
Harworth 44 Q 23
Hascosay 87 R 2
Haselbury Plucknett 8 L 31
Hasland 43 P 24
Haslemere 11 R 30
Haslingden 42 N 22
Haslingfield 29 U 27
Haslington 35 M 24
Hassocks 11 T 31
Haster 86 K 8
Hastings 12 V 31
Hatch Court 8 L 31
Hatfield
County of Herefordshire 26 M 27
Hatfield *Herts.* 21 T 28
Hatfield *South Yorks.* 44 Q 23
Hatfield Broad Oak 22 U 28
Hatfield Heath 22 U 28
Hatfield Peverel 22 V 28
Hatfield Woodhouse 44 R 23
Hatherleigh 7 H 31
Hathern 36 Q 25
Hathersage 43 P 24
Hatton *Aberdeenshire* 81 O 11
Hatton *Derbs.* 35 O 25
Hatton of Fintray 75 N 12
Haugh of Urr 53 I 19
Haughton 35 N 25
Haunn 71 B 14
Havant 10 R 31
Havenstreet 10 Q 31
Haverfordwest / Hwlffordd 16 F 28
Haverhill 30 V 27
Haverigg 47 K 21
Havering *London Borough* 22 U 29
Haverthwaite 48 K 21
Hawarden 34 K 24
Hawes 49 N 21
Hawick 62 L 17
Hawkchurch 8 L 31
Hawkedon 30 V 27
Hawkesbury Upton 19 M 29
Hawkhurst 12 V 30
Hawkridge 7 J 30
Hawkshead 48 L 20
Hawkwell 22 V 29
Hawley 20 R 30
Hawling 27 O 28
Haworth 43 O 22
Hawsker 51 S 20
Haxby 50 Q 21
Haxey 44 R 23
Hay-on-Wye 26 K 27
Haydock 42 M 23
Haydon Bridge 55 N 19
Haydon Wick 19 O 29
Hayfield 43 O 23

A B C D E F G H I J K L M N O P Q R S T U V W X Y Z

Hayle ... 2 D 33
Hayling Island ... 10 R 31
Hayscastle ... 14 E 28
Hayton ... 50 R 22
Haywards Heath ... 11 T 31
Hazel Grove ... 43 N 23
Hazelbank ... 61 I 16
Hazelbury Bryan ... 9 M 31
Hazlemere ... 21 R 29
Heacham ... 38 V 25
Headcorn ... 22 V 30
Headington ... 20 Q 28
Headless Cross ... 27 O 27
Headley ... 10 R 30
Heads of Ayr ... 60 F 17
Healey ... 49 O 21
Healing ... 45 T 23
Heanor ... 36 P 24
Heast ... 71 C 12
Heath End ... 20 Q 29
Heath Hayes ... 35 O 25
Heather ... 36 P 25
Heathfield *Renfrewshire* ... 60 F 16
Heathfield *Wealden* ... 12 U 31
Heathrow Airport ... 21 S 29
Hebburn ... 56 P 19
Hebden Bridge ... 43 N 22
Hebrides (Sea of the) ... 76 Z 12
Heckfield ... 20 R 29
Heckington ... 37 T 25
Heddon on the Wall ... 56 O 19
Hedge End ... 10 Q 31
Hednesford ... 35 O 25
Hedon ... 45 T 22
Heighington *Durham* ... 56 P 20
Heighington *Lincs.* ... 44 S 24
Heights of Kinlochewe ... 78 E 11
Helensburgh ... 66 F 15
Helford ... 2 E 33
Hellifield ... 49 N 22
Hellingly ... 12 U 31
Hellisay ... 70 X 12
Hell's Mouth
  or Porth Neigwl ... 32 G 25
Helmdon ... 28 Q 27
Helmsdale ... 85 J 9
Helmsley ... 50 Q 21
Helpringham ... 37 T 25
Helpston ... 37 S 26
Helsby ... 42 L 24
Helston ... 2 E 33
Helton ... 55 L 20
Helvellyn ... 48 K 20
Hemel Hempstead ... 21 S 28
Hemingbrough ... 44 R 22
Hemingford Grey ... 29 T 27
Hemington ... 19 M 30
Hempnall ... 39 X 26
Hempton ... 38 W 25
Hemsby ... 39 Z 25
Hemswell ... 44 S 23
Hemsworth ... 43 P 23
Hemyock ... 8 K 31
Hendy ... 15 H 28
Henfield ... 11 T 31
Hengoed ... 18 K 29
Henham ... 30 U 28
Henley ... 27 O 27
Henley-on-Thames ... 20 R 29
Henllan ... 33 J 24
Henllys ... 18 K 29
Henlow ... 29 T 27
Hennock ... 4 J 32
Henshaw ... 55 M 19
Henstead ... 31 Y 26
Henstridge ... 9 M 31
Heol Senni ... 25 J 28
Hepple ... 63 N 18
Heptonstall ... 43 N 22
Herbrandston ... 14 E 28
Hereford ... 26 L 27
Heriot ... 62 L 16
Herm *Channel I.* ... 5
Herma Ness ... 87 R 1
Hermitage ... 20 Q 29
Hermitage Castle ... 62 L 18
Herne Bay ... 23 X 29
Herriard ... 20 Q 30
Herrington ... 56 P 19
Herstmonceux ... 12 U 31
Hertford ... 21 T 28
Hesket Newmarket ... 54 K 19
Hesketh Bank ... 42 L 22
Hesleden ... 57 Q 19
Hessenford ... 3 G 32
Hessle ... 45 S 22
Hest Bank ... 48 L 21

Heswall ... 42 K 24
Hethersgill ... 55 L 19
Hethpool ... 63 N 17
Heveningham ... 31 Y 27
Hever ... 21 U 30
Heversham ... 48 L 21
Hevingham ... 39 X 25
Hewelsfield ... 18 M 28
Hexham ... 55 N 19
Heybridge ... 22 W 28
Heysham ... 48 L 21
Heyshott ... 11 R 31
Heytesbury ... 9 N 30
Heythrop ... 28 P 28
Heywood ... 43 N 23
Hibaldstow ... 44 S 23
Hickling ... 36 R 25
Hickling Green ... 39 Y 25
Hidcote Manor Garden ... 27 O 27
High Bentham ... 49 M 21
High Bickington ... 7 I 31
High Birkwith ... 49 N 21
High Easter ... 22 V 28
High Ercall ... 34 M 25
High Etherley ... 56 O 20
High Force (The) ... 55 N 20
High Halden ... 12 W 30
High Halstow ... 22 V 29
High Ham ... 8 L 30
High Hesket ... 55 L 19
High Newton *Alnwick* ... 63 P 17
High Newton
  South Lakeland ... 48 L 21
High Offley ... 35 N 25
High Ongar ... 22 U 28
High Peak ... 43 O 23
High Willhays ... 4 I 31
High Wycombe ... 20 R 29
Higham *Kent* ... 22 V 29
Higham *Lancs.* ... 42 N 22
Higham
  North East Derbyshire ... 36 P 24
Higham *Suffolk* ... 30 V 27
Higham Ferrers ... 29 S 27
Higham on the Hill ... 36 P 26
Highampton ... 18 L 30
Highbridge ... 18 L 30
Highclere ... 20 P 29
Highcliffe ... 9 O 31
Higher Penwortham ... 42 L 22
Highland Wildlife Park ... 73 I 12
Highley ... 27 M 26
Highmoor Cross ... 20 R 29
Highnam ... 27 N 28
Hightae ... 54 J 18
Hightown *Congleton* ... 35 N 24
Hightown *Sefton* ... 42 K 23
Highworth ... 19 O 29
Hilborough ... 38 W 26
Hildenborough ... 22 U 30
Hilderstone ... 35 N 25
Hilgay ... 38 V 26
Hill ... 18 M 29
Hill of Fearn ... 79 I 10
Hill of Tarvit ... 69 L 15
Hillhead ... 52 G 19
Hillingdon
  London Borough ... 21 S 29
Hillington ... 38 V 25
Hillside ... 75 M 13
Hillswick ... 87 P 2
Hilmarton ... 19 O 29
Hilperton ... 19 N 30
Hilpsford Point ... 47 K 21
Hilton *Aberdeenshire* ... 81 N 11
Hilton *Eden* ... 55 M 20
Hilton *Huntingdonshire* ... 29 T 27
Hilton *North Dorset* ... 9 M 31
Hilton *South Derbyshire* ... 35 P 25
Hilton of Cadboll ... 79 I 10
Himbleton ... 27 N 27
Hinchingbrooke House ... 29 T 27
Hinckley ... 36 P 26
Hinderwell ... 57 Q 19
Hindhead ... 10 R 30
Hindley ... 42 M 23
Hindolveston ... 38 X 25
Hindon ... 9 N 30
Hingham ... 38 W 26
Hinstock ... 34 M 25
Hintlesham ... 31 X 27
Hinton-Blewett ... 18 M 30
Hirst Courtney ... 44 Q 22
Hirwaun ... 17 J 28
Histon ... 29 U 27
Hitcham ... 30 W 27
Hitchin ... 29 T 28

Hockering ... 38 X 25
Hockerton ... 36 R 24
Hockley ... 22 V 29
Hockley Heath ... 27 O 26
Hockliffe ... 29 S 28
Hoddesdon ... 21 T 28
Hodnet ... 34 M 25
Hodthorpe ... 44 Q 24
Hogsthorpe ... 45 U 24
Holbeach ... 37 U 25
Holbeach-St. Johns ... 37 T 25
Holbeach-St. Matthew ... 37 U 25
Holbeck ... 44 Q 24
Holbrook ... 31 X 28
Holbury ... 10 P 31
Holcombe ... 18 M 30
Holcombe Rogus ... 7 J 31
Holdenby ... 28 R 27
Holford ... 8 K 30
Holkam Hall ... 38 W 25
Hollandstoun ... 87 M 5
Hollesley ... 31 Y 27
Hollesley Bay ... 31 Y 27
Hollingbourne ... 22 V 30
Hollingworth ... 43 O 23
Hollybush ... 60 G 17
Hollym ... 45 U 22
Holmbridge ... 43 O 23
Holme *Huntingdonshire* ... 29 T 26
Holme *South Lakeland* ... 48 L 21
Holme-next-the-Sea ... 38 V 25
Holme
  upon Spalding-Moor ... 44 R 22
Holmer Green ... 21 R 29
Holmes Chapel ... 35 M 24
Holmesfield ... 43 P 24
Holmfirth ... 43 O 23
Holmhead ... 60 H 17
Holmpton ... 45 U 22
Holnest ... 8 M 31
Holsworthy ... 6 G 31
Holt *Dorset* ... 9 O 31
Holt *Norfolk* ... 38 X 25
Holt *Wilts.* ... 19 N 29
Holt *Wrexham* ... 34 L 24
Holt Heath ... 27 N 27
Holton *Lincs.* ... 45 T 24
Holton *Norfolk* ... 31 Y 26
Holton *South Somerset* ... 8 M 30
Holton Heath ... 9 N 31
Holton-le-Clay ... 45 T 23
Holwick ... 55 N 20
Holy Island *Anglesey* ... 40 F 23
Holy Island *North Ayrshire* ... 59 E 17
Holy Island *Northumb.* ... 63 O 16
Holybourne ... 10 R 30
Holyhead / Caergybi ... 40 G 23
Holystone ... 63 N 18
Holywell ... 2 E 32
Holywell / Treffynnon ... 41 K 23
Holywell Bay ... 2 E 32
Holywood ... 53 J 18
Honing ... 39 Y 25
Honiton ... 8 K 31
Hoo St. Werburgh ... 22 V 29
Hook
  Basingstoke and Deane ... 20 R 30
Hook
  East Riding of Yorkshire ... 44 R 22
Hook Norton ... 28 P 28
Hooke ... 8 M 31
Hope *Derbs.* ... 43 O 23
Hope *Flintshire* ... 34 K 24
Hope *Highland* ... 84 G 8
Hope *South Shropshire* ... 34 L 26
Hope (Loch) ... 84 G 8
Hope Bowdler ... 26 L 26
Hope under Dinmore ... 26 L 27
Hopeman ... 80 J 10
Hopetoun House ... 68 J 16
Hopton ... 39 Z 26
Horam ... 12 U 31
Horbury ... 43 P 23
Horden ... 57 Q 19
Hordley ... 34 L 25
Horeb ... 15 G 27
Horley ... 21 T 30
Hornby ... 48 M 21
Horncastle ... 45 T 24
Hornchurch ... 22 U 29
Horncliffe ... 63 N 16
Horning ... 39 Y 25
Horninglow ... 35 P 25
Horn's Cross ... 6 H 31
Hornsea ... 51 T 22
Hornton ... 28 P 27
Horrabridge ... 4 H 32

Horseheath ... 30 V 27
Horsehouse ... 49 O 21
Horsell ... 21 S 30
Horsford ... 39 X 25
Horsforth ... 43 P 22
Horsham ... 11 T 30
Horsham St. Faith ... 39 X 25
Horsington *East Lindsey* ... 37 T 24
Horsington
  South Somerset ... 9 M 30
Horsley *Stroud* ... 19 N 28
Horsley *Tynedale* ... 56 O 19
Horsmonden ... 12 V 30
Horstead ... 39 Y 25
Horsted Keynes ... 11 T 30
Horton *Abertawe /
  Swansea* ... 15 H 29
Horton *East Dorset* ... 9 O 31
Horton *South Somerset* ... 8 L 31
Horton Court ... 19 M 29
Horton-in-Ribblesdale ... 49 N 21
Horwich ... 42 M 23
Hoton ... 36 Q 25
Hott ... 55 M 18
Houghton ... 10 P 30
Houghton Hall ... 38 V 25
Houghton House ... 29 S 27
Houghton-le-Spring ... 56 P 19
Houghton-on-the-Hill ... 36 R 26
Hougton ... 55 L 19
Hounslow
  London Borough ... 21 S 29
Hourn (Loch) ... 72 D 12
Housesteads Fort ... 55 N 18
Houston ... 60 G 16
Houstry ... 85 J 9
Hove ... 11 T 31
Hoveton ... 39 Y 25
Hovingham ... 50 R 21
How Caple ... 26 M 28
Howden ... 44 R 22
Howe of the Mearns ... 75 M 13
Howick ... 63 P 17
Howmore ... 76 X 12
Hownam ... 62 M 17
Howwood ... 60 G 16
Hoxa (Sound of) ... 86 K 7
Hoxne ... 31 X 26
Hoy ... 86 J 7
Hoylake ... 41 K 22
Hoyland Nether ... 43 P 23
Huby ... 50 Q 21
Hucknall ... 36 Q 24
Huddersfield ... 43 O 23
Huggate ... 51 S 22
Hugh Town *I. of Scilly* ... 2
Hughenden ... 20 R 29
Hughley ... 34 M 26
Huish Champflower ... 7 J 30
Huish Episcopi ... 8 L 30
Hull (River) ... 45 S 22
Hulland ... 35 P 24
Hullavington ... 19 N 29
Hullbridge ... 22 V 29
Humber (River) ... 45 T 23
Humber Bridge ... 44 S 22
Humberston ... 45 T 23
Humbleton ... 45 T 22
Hume Castle ... 62 M 17
Humshaugh ... 55 N 18
Hundleton ... 16 F 28
Hundred House ... 26 K 27
Hungerford ... 20 P 29
Hunmanby ... 51 T 21
Hunstanton ... 38 V 25
Hunter's Inn ... 17 I 30
Hunter's Quay ... 66 F 16
Huntingdon ... 29 T 26
Huntingtower Castle ... 68 J 14
Huntly ... 80 L 11
Huntspill ... 18 L 30
Hunwick ... 56 O 19
Hurlford ... 60 G 17
Hurn ... 9 O 31
Hursley ... 10 P 30
Hurst Green ... 12 V 30
Hurstbourne Priors ... 20 P 30
Hurstbourne Tarrant ... 20 P 30
Hurstpierpoint ... 11 T 31
Hurworth-on-Tees ... 50 P 20
Hury ... 55 N 20
Husbands Bosworth ... 28 Q 26
Huthwaite ... 36 Q 24
Huttoft ... 45 U 24
Hutton *Scottish Borders* ... 63 N 16

Hutton *South Ribble* ... 42 L 22
Hutton Cranswick ... 51 S 22
Hutton Rudby ... 50 Q 20
Huxley ... 34 L 24
Huyton ... 42 L 23
Hwlfford / Haverfordwest ... 16 F 28
Hyde ... 43 N 23
Hynish ... 64 Z 14
Hynish Bay ... 64 Z 14
Hythe *Hants.* ... 10 P 31
Hythe *Kent* ... 13 X 30

I
Ibsley ... 9 O 31
Ibstock ... 36 P 25
Ickleford ... 29 T 28
Icklingham ... 30 V 27
Ickworth House ... 30 V 27
Iddesleigh ... 7 H 31
Ideford ... 4 J 32
Iden ... 12 W 31
Iden Green ... 12 V 30
Idmiston ... 9 O 30
Idrigill Point ... 77 A 12
Ightham ... 22 U 30
Ightham Mote ... 22 U 30
Ilchester ... 8 L 30
Ilderton ... 63 O 17
Ilfracombe ... 17 H 30
Ilkeston ... 36 Q 25
Ilkley ... 49 O 22
Illogan ... 2 E 33
Ilmington ... 27 O 27
Ilminster ... 8 L 31
Ilsington ... 4 I 32
Ilton ... 8 L 31
Immingham ... 45 T 23
Immingham Dock ... 45 T 23
Ince Blundell ... 42 K 23
Ince-in-Makerfield ... 42 M 23
Inch Kenneth ... 64 B 14
Inchard (Loch) ... 84 E 8
Inchbare ... 75 M 13
Inchgrundle ... 74 L 13
Inchkeith ... 68 K 15
Inchlaggan ... 72 E 12
Inchmarnock ... 59 E 16
Inchnadamph ... 84 F 9
Inchture ... 68 K 14
Indaal (Loch) ... 58 A 16
Inerval ... 58 B 17
Ingatestone ... 22 V 28
Ingbirchworth ... 43 P 23
Ingham ... 30 W 27
Ingleby Barwick ... 50 Q 20
Ingleton *Durham* ... 56 O 20
Ingleton *North Yorks.* ... 49 M 21
Inglewhite ... 42 L 22
Inglewood Forest ... 55 L 19
Ingoldmells ... 38 V 24
Ingoldsby ... 37 S 25
Ingram ... 63 O 17
Ings ... 48 L 20
Inkpen ... 20 P 29
Innellan ... 59 F 16
Inner Hebrides ... 70 Y 14
Inner Sound ... 77 C 11
Innerleithen ... 61 K 17
Innerpeffray ... 67 I 14
Innerwick ... 69 M 16
Insch ... 81 M 11
Insh ... 73 I 12
Inshore ... 84 F 8
Instow ... 6 H 30
Inver *Highland* ... 79 I 10
Inver *Perth and Kinross* ... 68 J 14
Inver (Loch) ... 84 E 9
Inver Bay ... 79 I 10
Inver Mallie ... 72 E 13
Inver Valley ... 84 E 9
Inverailligin ... 78 D 11
Inverallochy ... 81 O 10
Inveran ... 84 G 10
Inveraray ... 66 E 15
Inverarity ... 69 L 14
Inverarnan ... 66 F 15
Inverbeg ... 66 F 15
Inverbervie ... 75 N 13
Invercassley ... 84 G 10
Invercauld House ... 74 J 12
Inverchapel ... 66 F 15
Invercreran ... 72 E 14
Inverdruie ... 73 I 12
Inverewe Gardens ... 78 C 10
Inverey ... 74 J 12
Inverfarigaig ... 79 G 12

Invergarry ... 72 F 12
Invergeldie ... 67 H 14
Invergordon ... 79 H 10
Invergowrie ... 68 K 14
Inverie ... 72 C 12
Inverinan ... 65 E 15
Inverinate ... 78 D 12
Inverkeithing ... 68 J 15
Inverkeithny ... 81 M 11
Inverkip ... 66 F 16
Inverkirkaig ... 84 E 9
Inverliever Forest ... 65 D 15
Inverlochlarig ... 67 G 15
Invermoriston ... 73 G 12
Inverness ... 79 H 11
Inversanda ... 72 D 13
Inversnaid Hotel ... 66 F 15
Inveruglas ... 66 F 15
Inverurie ... 81 M 12
Invervar ... 73 H 14
Inwardleigh ... 7 H 31
Iona ... 64 A 15
Ipplepen ... 4 J 32
Ipstones ... 35 O 24
Ipswich ... 31 X 27
Irby *East Lindsey* ... 37 U 24
Irby *Wirral* ... 42 K 23
Irchester ... 29 S 27
Ireby ... 54 K 19
Ireleth ... 47 K 21
Irlam ... 42 M 23
Iron Acton ... 18 M 29
Ironbridge ... 34 M 26
Irthington ... 55 L 19
Irthlingborough ... 29 S 27
Irvine ... 60 F 17
Irwell (River) ... 42 N 23
Isbyty Ystwyth ... 25 I 27
Isla (Glen) ... 74 K 13
Islay (Sound of) ... 64 B 16
Isle of Whithorn ... 53 G 19
Isleham ... 30 V 26
Isleornsay ... 71 C 12
Isleworth ... 21 S 29
Islington *London Borough* ... 21 T 29
Islip ... 20 Q 28
Islivig ... 82 Y 9
Itchingfield ... 11 S 30
Ithon (River) ... 25 K 27
Itteringham ... 39 X 25
Iver ... 21 S 29
Iver Heath ... 21 S 29
Ivinghoe ... 21 S 28
Ivybridge ... 4 I 32
Ivychurch ... 12 W 30
Iwade ... 22 W 29
Iwerne Minster ... 9 N 31
Ixworth ... 30 W 27

J
Jacobstow ... 6 G 31
Jacobstowe ... 7 H 31
Jameston ... 15 F 29
Jamestown
  Dumfries and Galloway ... 61 K 18
Jamestown
  West Dunbartonshire ... 66 G 16
Janetstown ... 85 J 9
Jarrow ... 56 P 19
Jaywick ... 23 X 28
Jedburgh ... 62 M 17
Jedburgh Abbey ... 62 M 17
Jeffreyston ... 15 F 28
Jemimaville ... 79 H 11
Jersey *Channel I.* ... 5
Jevington ... 12 U 31
John Muir ... 69 M 15
John o' Groats ... 86 K 8
Johnshaven ... 75 N 13
Johnston ... 16 F 28
Johnstone ... 60 G 16
Johnstonebridge ... 54 J 18
Jura (Isle of) ... 58 B 16
Jura (Sound of) ... 65 C 16
Jura Forest ... 65 B 16
Jura Ho ... 58 B 16
Jurby West ... 46 G 20

K
Kainakill ... 77 C 11
Kames ... 65 E 16
Katrine (Loch) ... 67 G 15
Kea ... 2 E 33
Keal ... 37 U 24
Keal (Loch na) ... 65 B 14
Kearsley ... 42 M 23
Keasden ... 49 M 21

Kebock Head ......82 A 9
Kedington ......30 V 27
Kedleston Hall ......36 P 25
Keelby ......45 T 23
Keevil ......19 N 30
Kegworth ......36 Q 25
Keig ......75 M 12
Keighley ......43 O 22
Keillmore ......65 C 16
Keinton Mandeville ......8 M 30
Keir Mill ......53 I 18
Keiss ......86 K 8
Keith ......80 L 11
Keld ......49 N 20
Kellas Angus ......69 L 14
Kellas Moray ......80 J 11
Kelleth ......49 M 20
Kellie Castle ......69 L 15
Kellington ......44 Q 22
Kelloe ......56 P 19
Kelly Bray ......3 H 32
Kelmarsh ......28 R 26
Kelsall ......34 L 24
Kelso ......62 M 17
Kelston ......19 M 29
Keltneyburn ......73 H 14
Kelty ......68 J 15
Kelvedon ......30 W 28
Kelvedon Hatch ......22 U 29
Kemble ......19 N 28
Kemnay ......75 M 12
Kempley ......26 M 28
Kempsey ......27 N 27
Kempsford ......19 O 28
Kempston ......29 S 27
Kemsing ......22 U 30
Kendal ......48 L 21
Kenfig ......17 I 29
Kenilworth ......27 P 26
Kenknock ......67 G 14
Kenmore Highland ......77 C 11
Kenmore
   Perthshire and Kinross ......67 I 14
Kenn ......18 L 29
Kennet (River) ......19 O 29
Kennethmont ......80 L 11
Kenninghall ......30 X 26
Kennington Kent ......22 W 30
Kennington Oxon. ......20 Q 28
Kennoway ......68 K 15
Kenovay ......70 Z 14
Kensaleyre ......77 B 11
Kentallen ......72 E 13
Kentford ......30 V 27
Kentisbeare ......7 K 31
Kentmere ......48 L 20
Kenton ......4 J 32
Kents Bank ......48 L 21
Keoldale ......84 F 8
Keresley ......28 P 26
Kerrera ......65 D 14
Kerry ......26 K 26
Kersey ......30 W 27
Kershader ......82 A 9
Kershopefoot ......55 L 18
Kesgrave ......31 X 27
Kessingland ......31 Z 26
Keswick ......54 K 20
Kettering ......28 R 26
Kettleness ......50 R 20
Kettleshulme ......43 N 24
Kettletoft ......87 M 6
Kettlewell ......49 N 21
Ketton ......37 S 26
Kew ......21 T 29
Kewstoke ......18 L 29
Kexbrough ......43 P 23
Kexby ......44 R 23
Keyingham ......45 T 22
Keymer ......11 T 31
Keynsham ......18 M 29
Keyworth ......36 Q 25
Kibworth Harcourt ......36 R 26
Kidderminster ......27 N 26
Kidermorie Lodge ......79 G 10
Kidlington ......20 Q 28
Kidsgrove ......35 N 24
Kidstones ......49 N 21
Kidwelly / Cydweli ......15 H 28
Kielder ......55 M 18
Kielder Forest ......55 M 18
Kielder Reservoir ......55 M 18
Kiiphedir ......85 I 9
Kilamarsh ......44 Q 24
Kilbarchan ......60 G 16
Kilbirnie ......60 F 16
Kilbrannan Sound ......59 D 17

Kilbride ......65 D 14
Kilburn Amber Valley ......36 P 24
Kilburn Hambleton ......50 Q 21
Kilchattan ......59 E 16
Kilchenzie ......59 C 17
Kilcheran ......65 D 14
Kilchiaran ......58 A 16
Kilchoan ......71 B 13
Kilchoman ......58 A 16
Kilchrenan ......65 E 14
Kilconquhar ......69 L 15
Kilcreggan ......66 F 16
Kildale ......50 Q 20
Kildary ......79 H 10
Kildavanan ......59 E 16
Kildonan ......59 E 17
Kildonan Lodge ......85 I 9
Kildrummy ......74 L 12
Kildrummy Castle ......74 L 12
Kilfinnan ......72 F 12
Kilgetti ......15 F 28
Kilham
   Berwick-upon-Tweed ......63 N 17
Kilham
   East Riding of Yorkshire ...51 S 21
Kilkhampton ......6 G 31
Killay ......15 H 29
Killean ......59 D 17
Killearn ......67 G 15
Killen ......79 H 11
Killerton ......7 J 31
Killiechronan ......65 C 14
Killilan ......78 D 12
Killin ......67 H 14
Killinghall ......50 P 21
Killundine ......71 C 14
Kilmacolm ......60 G 16
Kilmaluag ......77 B 10
Kilmany ......69 L 14
Kilmarie ......71 B 12
Kilmarnock ......60 G 17
Kilmartin ......65 D 15
Kilmaurs ......60 G 17
Kilmelford ......65 D 15
Kilmersdon ......19 M 30
Kilmington East Devon ......8 K 31
Kilmington Salisbury ......9 N 30
Kilmorack ......79 G 11
Kilmore ......71 C 12
Kilmory Ardnamurchan ...71 B 13
Kilmory Argyll and Bute ...65 C 16
Kilmory I. Rhum ......71 A 12
Kilmory North Ayrshire ...59 E 17
Kilmuir ......77 A 11
Kilmun ......66 F 16
Kilncadzow ......61 I 16
Kilninver ......65 D 14
Kilnsey ......49 N 21
Kiloran ......64 B 15
Kilpeck ......26 L 28
Kilrenny ......69 L 15
Kilsyth ......67 H 16
Kiltarlity ......79 G 11
Kilvaxter ......77 A 11
Kilwinning ......60 F 17
Kimberley Broxtowe ......36 Q 25
Kimberley South Norfolk ...38 X 26
Kimble ......20 R 28
Kimbolton ......29 S 27
Kimmeridge ......9 N 32
Kimpton ......21 T 28
Kinbrace ......85 I 9
Kinbuck ......67 I 15
Kincardine Fife ......67 I 15
Kincardine Highland ......79 G 10
Kincardine O'Neil ......75 L 12
Kinclaven ......68 J 14
Kincraig ......73 I 12
Kineton ......28 P 27
Kinfauns ......68 J 14
Kingairloch ......72 D 14
Kingarth ......59 E 16
Kinghorn ......68 K 15
Kinglassie ......68 K 15
King's Bromley ......35 O 25
King's Cliffe ......37 S 26
King's Langley ......21 S 28
King's Lynn ......38 V 25
King's Meaburn ......55 M 20
King's Somborne ......10 P 30
King's Sutton ......28 Q 27
King's Walden ......29 T 28
Kings Worthy ......10 Q 30
Kingsbarns ......69 M 15
Kingsbridge ......4 I 33
Kingsburgh ......77 A 11

Kingsbury Episcopi ......8 L 31
Kingsclere ......20 Q 30
Kingscote ......19 N 29
Kingsdon ......8 L 30
Kingsdown ......23 Y 30
Kingsgate ......23 Y 29
Kingskerswell ......4 J 32
Kingskettle ......68 K 15
Kingsland ......26 L 27
Kingsley East Hampshire ...10 R 30
Kingsley
   Staffordshire Moorlands ...35 O 24
Kingsmuir ......74 L 14
Kingsnorth ......12 W 30
Kingsteignton ......4 J 32
Kingsthorpe ......28 R 27
Kingston Devon ......4 I 33
Kingston East Hampshire ...69 L 15
Kingston Moray ......80 K 10
Kingston
   South Cambridgeshire ...29 T 27
Kingston Bagpuize ......20 P 28
Kingston Deverill ......9 N 30
Kingston Lacy ......9 N 31
Kingston Lisle ......20 P 29
Kingston Seymour ......18 L 29
Kingston-St. Mary ......8 K 30
Kingston-upon-Hull ......45 S 22
Kingston-upon-Thames
   London Borough ......21 T 29
Kingstone ......26 L 27
Kingswear ......4 J 32
Kingswinford ......27 N 26
Kingswood ......19 M 29
Kingswood Powys ......34 K 26
Kingswood South Glos. ...18 M 29
Kington ......26 K 27
Kington Langley ......19 N 29
Kington-St. Michael ......19 N 29
Kingussie ......73 H 12
Kinkell ......75 M 12
Kinkell Bridge ......67 I 15
Kinknockie ......81 O 11
Kinlet ......27 M 26
Kinloch ......71 B 12
Kinloch Hourn ......72 D 12
Kinloch Lodge ......84 G 8
Kinloch Rannoch ......73 H 13
Kinlochard ......67 G 15
Kinlochbervie ......84 E 8
Kinlocheil ......72 E 13
Kinlochewe ......78 E 11
Kinlochleven ......72 F 13
Kinlochmoidart ......71 C 13
Kinloss ......80 J 11
Kinmuck ......75 N 12
Kinnaird ......68 K 14
Kinneff ......75 N 13
Kinnelhead ......61 J 18
Kinnerley ......34 L 25
Kinnersley ......26 L 27
Kinnesswood ......68 K 15
Kinninvie ......56 O 20
Kinross ......68 J 15
Kinrossie ......68 K 14
Kintbury ......20 P 29
Kintessack ......80 I 11
Kintore ......75 M 12
Kintra ......58 B 17
Kintyre (Peninsula) ......59 D 17
Kinver ......27 N 26
Kippax ......43 P 22
Kippen ......67 H 15
Kippford ......53 I 19
Kirby Bellars ......36 R 25
Kirby Cross ......31 X 28
Kirby Hall ......29 S 26
Kirby Misperton ......50 R 21
Kirby Muxloe ......36 Q 26
Kirby Underwood ......37 S 25
Kirdford ......11 S 30
Kirk Ella ......45 S 22
Kirk Ireton ......35 P 24
Kirk Merrington ......56 P 19
Kirk Michael ......46 G 21
Kirk Yetholm ......63 N 17
Kirkbampton ......54 K 19
Kirkbean ......53 J 19
Kirkbride ......54 K 19
Kirkbuddo ......69 L 14
Kirkburn ......51 S 22
Kirkburton ......43 O 23
Kirkby ......42 L 23
Kirkby Fleetham ......50 P 20
Kirkby-in-Ashfield ......36 Q 24

Kirkby-la-Thorpe ......37 S 25
Kirkby Lonsdale ......48 M 21
Kirkby Malham ......49 N 21
Kirkby Mallory ......36 Q 26
Kirkby Malzeard ......49 P 21
Kirkby Overblow ......50 P 22
Kirkby Stephen ......49 M 20
Kirkby Thore ......55 M 20
Kirkbymoorside ......50 R 21
Kirkcaldy ......68 K 15
Kirkcolm ......52 E 19
Kirkconnel ......60 I 17
Kirkcowan ......52 G 19
Kirkcudbright ......53 H 19
Kirkcudbright Bay ......53 H 19
Kirkfieldbank ......61 I 16
Kirkgunzeon ......53 I 19
Kirkham ......42 L 22
Kirkheaton ......56 O 18
Kirkhill ......79 G 11
Kirkhope ......61 J 18
Kirkinner ......52 G 19
Kirkintilloch ......67 H 16
Kirkland
   Dumfries and Galloway ...53 I 18
Kirkland Eden ......55 M 19
Kirklees ......43 O 23
Kirklevington ......50 P 20
Kirklington
   North Yorkshire ......50 P 21
Kirklington
   Nottinghamshire ......36 R 24
Kirklisten ......68 J 16
Kirkmaiden ......52 F 19
Kirkmichael
   Perthshire and Kinross ...74 J 13
Kirkmichael
   South Ayrshire ......60 G 17
Kirkmuirhill ......61 I 17
Kirknewton
   Berwick-upon-Tweed ...63 N 17
Kirknewton
   West Lothian ......61 J 16
Kirkoswald ......59 F 18
Kirkpatrick Durham ......53 I 18
Kirkpatrick-Fleming ......54 K 18
Kirkstone Pass ......48 L 20
Kirkton
   Dumfries and Galloway ...53 J 18
Kirkton Scottish Borders ...62 L 17
Kirkton Manor ......61 K 17
Kirkton of Culsalmond ...81 M 11
Kirkton of Durris ......75 M 12
Kirkton of Glenisla ......74 K 13
Kirkton of Kingoldrum ...74 K 13
Kirkton of Largo ......69 L 15
Kirkton of Skene ......75 N 12
Kirkton of Strathmartine ...69 K 14
Kirktown of Auchterless ...81 M 11
Kirktown of Deskford ......80 L 11
Kirkwall ......86 L 7
Kirkwhelpington ......56 N 18
Kirmington ......45 T 23
Kirmond ......45 T 23
Kirn ......66 F 16
Kirriemuir ......74 K 13
Kirtlebridge ......54 K 18
Kirtlington ......28 Q 28
Kirtomy ......85 H 8
Kirton Boston ......37 T 25
Kirton Suffolk Coastal ...31 X 27
Kirton End ......37 T 25
Kirton-in-Lindsey ......44 S 23
Kishorn (Loch) ......78 D 11
Kislingbury ......28 R 27
Kitchener Memorial ......86 J 6
Kiveton ......44 Q 23
Knaresborough ......50 P 21
Knarsdale ......55 M 19
Knebworth ......29 T 28
Kneesall ......36 R 24
Kneesworth ......29 T 27
Knighton / Trefyclawdd ...26 K 26
Knightshayes Court ......7 J 31
Kniveton ......35 O 24
Knock Argyll and Bute ...65 C 14
Knock Moray ......80 L 11
Knock Western Isles ......83 B 9
Knockandhu ......80 K 12
Knockandhu ......53 I 19
Knockie Lodge ......73 G 12
Knockin ......34 L 25
Knocknaha ......59 D 17
Knocksharry ......46 G 21
Knockvennie Smithy ......53 I 18
Knole ......22 U 30
Knossington ......36 R 25
Knottingley ......44 Q 22

Knowe ......52 G 18
Knowehead ......53 H 18
Knowesgate ......55 N 18
Knowle ......27 O 26
Knowsley ......42 L 23
Knoydart ......72 D 12
Knutsford ......42 M 24
Kyle Forest ......60 G 17
Kyle of Durness ......84 F 8
Kyle of Lochalsh ......77 C 12
Kyle of Sutherland ......79 G 10
Kyle of Tongue ......84 G 8
Kyleakin ......77 C 12
Kylerhea ......72 C 12
Kyles Scalpay ......82 Z 10
Kylestrome ......84 E 9
Kynance Cove ......2 E 34
Kyre park ......26 M 27

L

La Rocque Jersey I. 5
Laceby ......45 T 23
Lacey Green ......20 R 28
Lache ......34 L 24
Lacock ......19 N 29
Ladder Hills ......74 K 12
Ladock ......3 F 33
Ladybank ......68 K 15
Ladybower Reservoir ......43 O 23
Ladyhill ......55 N 18
Lagg ......65 C 16
Laggan Argyll and Bute ...58 B 16
Laggan near Invergarry ...72 F 12
Laggan
   near Newtonmore ......73 H 12
Laggan (Loch) ......73 G 13
Laggan Point ......58 B 16
Lagganulva ......64 B 14
Laide ......78 D 10
Lair ......78 E 11
Lairg ......84 G 9
Lake District National Park .48 K 20
Lakenheath ......30 V 26
Lamanva ......2 E 33
Lamberhurst ......12 V 30
Lambeth London Borough ...21 T 29
Lambley Gedling ......36 Q 24
Lambley Tynedale ......55 M 19
Lambourn ......20 P 29
Lamerton ......3 H 32
Lamington ......61 J 17
Lamlash ......59 E 17
Lamlash Bay ......59 E 17
Lammermuir Hills ......62 L 16
Lampeter /
   Llanbedr Pont Steffan ...15 H 27
Lamplugh ......54 J 20
Lamport ......28 R 26
Lanark ......61 I 16
Lancaster ......48 L 21
Lanchester ......56 O 19
Lancing ......11 T 31
Landmark Visitor Centre ...79 I 12
Landrake ......3 H 32
Land's End ......2 C 33
Landulph ......3 H 32
Lane End ......20 R 29
Laneast ......6 G 32
Lanercost ......55 L 19
Langar ......36 R 25
Langavat (Loch) Lewis ...82 Z 9
Langavat (Loch)
   South Harris ......76 Z 10
Langbank ......66 G 16
Langcliffe ......49 N 21
Langdale End ......51 S 21
Langdale Valley ......48 K 20
Langdon Beck ......55 N 19
Langenhoe ......30 W 28
Langford
   Mid Bedfordshire ......29 T 27
Langford
   West Oxfordshire ......19 P 28
Langford Budville ......8 K 31
Langham ......36 R 25
Langholm ......54 L 18
Langleeford ......63 N 17
Langley ......21 S 29
Langley Park ......56 O 19
Langold ......44 Q 23
Langport ......8 L 30
Langrick ......37 T 24
Langrish ......10 Q 30
Langsett ......43 O 23
Langshaw ......62 L 17
Langstrothdale
   Chase ......49 N 21

Langthwaite ......49 O 20
Langtoft ......51 S 21
Langton ......50 R 21
Langton Matravers ......9 O 32
Langwathby ......55 L 19
Lanhydrock ......3 F 32
Lanivet ......3 F 32
Lanlivery ......3 F 32
Lanreath ......3 G 32
Lanton ......62 M 17
Lapford ......7 I 31
Larachbeg ......71 C 14
Larbert ......67 I 15
Largs ......59 F 16
Larkhall ......61 I 16
Larkhill ......19 O 30
Larling ......30 W 26
Lasswade ......61 K 16
Lastingham ......50 R 21
Latchingdon ......22 W 28
Latton ......19 O 29
Lauder ......62 L 16
Lauderdale ......62 L 16
Laugharne ......15 G 28
Laughton Wealden ......12 U 31
Laughton West Lindsey ...44 R 23
Launcells ......6 G 31
Launceston ......6 G 32
Launton ......28 Q 28
Laurencekirk ......75 M 13
Laurieston ......53 H 19
Lauriston Castle ......68 K 16
Lavendon ......29 S 27
Lavenham ......30 W 27
Laverstock ......9 O 30
Laverstoke ......20 Q 30
Lawford ......30 X 28
Lawrenny ......16 F 28
Lawshall ......30 W 27
Laxay ......82 A 9
Laxey ......46 G 21
Laxey Bay ......46 G 21
Laxfield ......31 Y 27
Laxford (Loch) ......84 E 8
Laxford Bridge ......84 E 8
Laxo ......87 Q 2
Laxton
   East Riding of Yorkshire ...44 R 22
Laxton
   Newark and Sherwood ...36 R 24
Layer-de-la-Haye ......30 W 28
Layer Marney ......22 W 28
Laytham ......44 R 22
Layton ......42 K 22
Lazonby ......55 L 19
Lea Herefordshire ......26 M 28
Lea North Wiltshire ......19 N 29
Lea West Lindsey ......44 R 23
Leaden Roding ......22 U 28
Leadenham ......37 S 24
Leadgate Derwentside ...56 O 19
Leadgate Eden ......55 M 19
Leadhills ......61 I 17
Leafield ......20 P 28
Leagrave ......29 S 28
Lealholm ......50 R 20
Lealt ......65 C 15
Leargybreck ......65 C 16
Leasingham ......37 S 24
Leathaid Bhuain (Loch an) .84 F 9
Leatherhead ......21 T 30
Leathley ......49 P 22
Leavening ......50 R 21
Lebberston ......51 S 21
Lechlade ......19 O 28
Lecht Road ......74 K 12
Leckmelm ......78 E 10
Leconfield ......44 S 22
Ledbury ......27 M 27
Ledmore ......84 F 9
Ledsham ......44 Q 22
Lee ......16 H 30
Lee-on-the-Solent ......10 Q 31
Leebotwood ......34 L 26
Leeds Kent ......22 V 30
Leeds West Yorks. ......43 P 22
Leedstown ......2 D 33
Leek ......35 N 24
Leek Wootton ......27 P 27
Leeming Bar ......50 P 21
Leeswood ......34 K 24
Legbourne ......45 U 23
Legerwood ......62 M 16
Leicester ......36 Q 26
Leicester Forest East ......36 Q 26
Leigh ......42 M 23

A B C D E F G H I J K L M N O P Q R S T U V W X Y Z

Leigh *Mole Valley* .... 21 T 30
Leigh *North Wiltshire* ...... 19 O 29
Leigh *Sevenoaks* .... 22 U 30
Leigh *West Dorset* .... 8 M 31
Leigh-on-Sea .... 22 V 29
Leigh Sinton .... 27 N 27
Leighterton .... 19 N 29
Leighton Buzzard .... 29 S 28
Leim .... 58 C 17
Leintwardine .... 26 L 26
Leirinmore .... 84 F 8
Leiston .... 31 Y 27
Leith .... 68 K 16
Leitholm .... 62 M 16
Lemreway .... 82 A 9
Lendalfoot .... 52 F 18
Lenham .... 22 W 30
Lennoxtown .... 67 H 16
Leominster .... 26 L 27
Leonard Stanley .... 19 N 28
Lepe .... 10 P 31
Lephinmore .... 65 E 15
Lerwick .... 87 Q 3
Lesbury .... 63 P 17
Leslie *Aberdeenshire* .... 81 L 12
Leslie *Fife* .... 68 K 15
Lesmahagow .... 61 I 17
Leswalt .... 52 E 19
Letchworth .... 29 T 28
Letham *Angus* .... 75 L 14
Letham *Fife* .... 68 K 15
Letheringsett .... 38 X 25
Letterewe Forest .... 78 D 10
Letterfearn .... 78 D 12
Lettermore .... 84 G 8
Letters .... 78 E 10
Letterston .... 24 F 28
Leuchars .... 69 L 14
Leurbost .... 82 A 9
Leven
   East Riding of Yorks. .... 51 T 22
Leven *Fife* .... 69 K 15
Leven (Loch) .... 72 E 13
Leven (River) .... 72 F 13
Levens .... 48 L 21
Levens Hall .... 48 L 21
Levenwick .... 87 Q 4
Leverington .... 37 U 25
Leverton
   with Habblesthorpe .... 44 R 24
Levington .... 31 X 27
Levisham .... 50 R 21
Lewannick .... 3 G 32
Lewdown .... 6 H 32
Lewes .... 11 U 31
Lewis (Isle of) .... 82 Z 9
Lewis and Harris (Isle of) .... 82 Z 8
Lewisham
   London Borough .... 21 T 29
Lewknor .... 20 R 28
Leyburn .... 49 O 21
Leyland .... 42 L 22
Leysdown-on-Sea .... 22 W 29
Lezant .... 3 G 32
Lhanbryde .... 80 K 11
Lhen (The) .... 46 G 20
Liathach .... 78 D 11
Libberton .... 61 J 16
Lichfield .... 35 O 25
Liddesdale .... 55 L 18
Lidgate .... 30 V 27
Lifton .... 6 H 32
Ligger or Perran Bay .... 2 E 32
Lilbourne .... 28 Q 26
Lilleshall .... 35 M 25
Lilliesleaf .... 62 L 17
Limerhaugh .... 60 H 17
Limpsfield .... 21 U 30
Linchmere .... 10 R 30
Lincoln .... 44 S 24
Lincolnshire Wolds .... 45 T 23
Lindfield .... 11 T 30
Lindores .... 68 K 14
Lingague .... 46 F 21
Lingay *near Eriskay* .... 70 X 12
Lingay *near Pabbay* .... 70 X 13
Lingen .... 26 L 27
Lingfield .... 21 T 30
Liniclate .... 76 X 11
Linlithgow .... 67 J 16
Linn of Dee .... 74 J 13
Linn of Tummel .... 74 I 13
Linneraineach .... 84 E 9
Linney Head .... 14 E 29
Linnhe (Loch) .... 72 D 14
Linslade .... 29 R 28
Lintmill .... 80 L 10

Linton *Craven* .... 49 N 21
Linton *Herefordshire* .... 26 M 28
Linton *Scottish Borders* .... 62 M 17
Linton
   South Cambridgeshire .... 30 U 27
Linton *South Derbyshire* .... 35 P 25
Linton-on-Ouse .... 50 Q 21
Lintrathen (Loch of) .... 74 K 13
Linwood *Renfrewshire* .... 60 G 16
Linwood *West Lindsey* .... 45 T 23
Liphook .... 10 R 30
Liskeard .... 3 G 32
Lismore .... 65 D 14
Liss .... 10 R 30
Lisset .... 51 T 21
Lisvane .... 18 K 29
Litcham .... 38 W 25
Litchborough .... 28 Q 27
Litchfield .... 20 P 30
Litherland .... 42 L 23
Little-Baddow .... 22 V 28
Little-Barningham .... 39 X 25
Little Berkhamsted .... 21 T 28
Little Brington .... 28 Q 27
Little Budworth .... 34 M 24
Little Bytham .... 37 S 25
Little Chalfont .... 21 S 28
Little Clacton .... 31 X 28
Little Colonsay .... 64 B 14
Little-Coxwell .... 19 P 29
Little Cumbrae Island .... 59 F 16
Little Dewchurch .... 26 L 28
Little Galdenoch .... 52 E 19
Little Glenshee .... 67 J 14
Little Hadham .... 29 U 28
Little Hallingbury .... 22 U 28
Little Harrowden .... 28 R 27
Little Houghton .... 28 R 27
Little Loch Broom .... 78 D 10
Little Loch Roag .... 82 Z 9
Little Mill .... 18 L 28
Little-Milton .... 20 Q 28
Little Minch (The) .... 76 Z 11
Little Moreton Hall .... 35 N 24
Little Ouse (River) .... 30 V 26
Little Ouseburn .... 50 Q 21
Little-Raveley .... 29 T 26
Little Snoring .... 38 W 25
Little-Stretton .... 26 L 26
Little-Stukeley .... 29 T 26
Little Torrington .... 6 H 31
Little Urswick .... 48 K 21
Little Walsingham .... 38 W 25
Little Waltham .... 22 V 28
Little Wenlock .... 34 M 26
Littleborough .... 43 N 23
Littlebourne .... 23 X 30
Littlebury .... 30 U 27
Littlecote House .... 20 P 29
Littleferry .... 79 H 10
Littleham .... 4 J 32
Littlehampton .... 11 S 31
Littlemill .... 79 I 11
Littleport .... 30 U 26
Littlestone-on-Sea .... 12 W 31
Littleton .... 10 P 30
Littleworth .... 20 P 28
Litton Cheney .... 5 M 31
Liverpool .... 42 L 23
Liverton .... 50 R 20
Livet (Glen) .... 80 K 12
Livingston .... 61 J 16
Lizard .... 2 E 34
Lizard Peninsula .... 2 E 33
Llam .... 35 O 24
Llan .... 33 J 26
Llan-non .... 15 H 28
Llan-y-Bri .... 15 G 28
Llanaber .... 33 H 24
Llanaelhaearn .... 32 G 25
Llanarmon-yn-Ial .... 34 K 24
Llanarthne .... 24 H 28
Llanarthney .... 15 H 28
Llanasa .... 41 J 23
Llanbadarn Fawr .... 25 H 26
Llanbedr .... 33 H 25
Llanbedr Pont Steffan /
   Lampeter .... 15 H 27
Llanbedrog .... 32 G 25
Llanberis .... 33 H 24
Llanberis (Pass of) .... 33 H 24
Llanbister .... 26 K 26
Llanboidy .... 15 G 28
Llanbradach .... 18 K 29
Llanbrynmair .... 33 J 26
Llanddarog .... 15 H 28
Llanddeiniol .... 25 H 27
Llanddderfel .... 33 J 25
Llanddeusant .... 40 G 22

Llanddewi Brefi .... 25 I 27
Llanddewi Ystradenni .... 26 K 27
Llanddona .... 40 H 23
Llanddowror .... 15 G 28
Llanddulas .... 41 J 23
Llandegla .... 34 K 24
Llandeilo .... 15 I 28
Llandenny .... 18 L 28
Llandinam .... 25 J 26
Llandissilio .... 15 F 28
Llandogo .... 18 L 28
Llandovery / Llanymddyfri ... 25 I 28
Llandrindod Wells .... 25 J 27
Llandrinio .... 34 K 25
Llandudno .... 41 I 23
Llandudno Junction .... 41 I 23
Llandwrog .... 32 H 24
Llandybie .... 15 H 28
Llandyfaelog .... 15 H 28
Llandygai .... 40 H 23
Llandysul .... 15 H 27
Llanegryn .... 33 H 26
Llanelidan .... 34 K 24
Llanellen .... 18 K 28
Llanelli .... 15 H 28
Llanelltyd .... 33 I 25
Llanengan .... 32 G 25
Llanerchymedd .... 40 G 23
Llanerfyl .... 33 J 25
Llanfachraeth .... 40 G 23
Llanfaethlu .... 40 G 22
Llanfair .... 33 H 25
Llanfair-Caereinion .... 34 K 26
Llanfair-Pwllgwyngyll .... 40 H 23
Llanfair-ym-Muallt /
   Builth Wells .... 25 J 27
Llanfair-yn-Neubwll .... 40 G 23
Llanfairfechan .... 41 I 23
Llanfairynghornwy .... 40 G 22
Llanfechell .... 40 G 22
Llanferres .... 34 K 24
Llanfihangel-ar-arth .... 15 H 27
Llanfihangel Glyn Myfyr ..... 33 J 24
Llanfihangel Nant Bran ...... 25 J 28
Llanfihangel Rhyditon ...... 26 K 27
Llanfihangel-y-Creuddyn ..... 25 I 26
Llanfilo .... 26 K 28
Llanfoist .... 18 K 28
Llanfrynach .... 25 J 28
Llanfwrog .... 40 G 23
Llanfyllin .... 34 K 25
Llanfynydd *Carmarthenshire* /
   Sir Gaerfyrddin .... 15 H 28
Llanfynydd *Flintshire* /
   Sir y Fflint .... 34 K 24
Llanfyrnach .... 15 G 28
Llangadfan .... 33 J 25
Llangadog .... 25 I 28
Llangain .... 15 G 28
Llangammarch Wells .... 25 J 27
Llangarron .... 26 L 28
Llangathen .... 15 H 28
Llangedwyn .... 34 K 25
Llangefni .... 40 H 23
Llangeinor .... 17 J 29
Llangeitho .... 25 H 27
Llangeler .... 15 H 27
Llangenith .... 15 H 29
Llangennech .... 15 H 28
Llangernyw .... 33 I 24
Llangoed .... 40 H 23
Llangollen .... 34 K 25
Llangorse .... 26 K 28
Llangorwen .... 25 H 26
Llangrannog .... 15 G 27
Llangunllo .... 26 K 27
Llangunnor .... 15 H 28
Llangurig .... 25 J 26
Llangwm *Monmouthshire* /
   Sir Fynwy .... 18 L 28
Llangwm *Pembrokeshire* /
   Sir Benfro .... 16 F 28
Llangwnnadl .... 32 F 25
Llangwyryfon .... 25 H 27
Llangybi .... 15 H 27
Llangyndeyrn .... 15 H 28
Llangynidr .... 26 K 28
Llangynog *Carmarthenshire* /
   Sir Gaerfyrddin .... 15 G 28
Llangynog *Powys* .... 33 J 25
Llangynwyd .... 17 J 29
Llangywer .... 33 J 25
Llanharan .... 17 J 29
Llanharry .... 17 J 29
Llanhilleth .... 18 K 28
Llanidloes .... 25 J 26

Llanilar .... 25 H 26
Llanishen .... 18 L 28
Llanllwchaiarn .... 26 K 26
Llanllyfni .... 32 H 24
Llanmadoc .... 15 H 29
Llannefydd .... 41 J 23
Llanon .... 25 H 27
Llanpumsaint .... 15 H 28
Llanrhaeadr .... 33 J 24
Llanrhaeadr-ym-
   Mochnant .... 34 K 25
Llanrhidian .... 15 H 29
Llanrhystud .... 25 H 27
Llanrug .... 33 H 24
Llanrwst .... 33 I 24
Llansanffraid Glan Conwy .. 41 I 23
Llansannan .... 33 J 24
Llansantffraid .... 25 H 27
Llansantffraid-ym-Mechain . 34 K 25
Llansawel .... 15 H 27
Llansilin .... 34 K 25
Llansoy .... 18 L 28
Llansteffan .... 15 G 28
Llanthony .... 26 K 28
Llanthony Priory .... 26 K 28
Llantilio Crossenny .... 18 L 28
Llantrisant .... 17 J 29
Llantwit Major .... 17 J 29
Llanuwchllyn .... 33 I 25
Llanvetherine .... 18 L 28
Llanwddyn .... 33 J 25
Llanwenog .... 15 H 27
Llanwnda .... 32 H 24
Llanwnen .... 15 H 27
Llanwnog .... 25 J 26
Llanwrda .... 25 I 28
Llanwrin .... 33 I 26
Llanwrtyd Wells .... 25 J 27
Llanwyddelan .... 33 J 26
Llanybydder .... 15 H 27
Llanychaer .... 24 F 28
Llanymawddwy .... 33 J 25
Llanymddyfri / Llandovery ... 25 I 28
Llanymynech .... 34 K 25
Llanynghenedl .... 40 G 23
Llanystumdwy .... 32 H 25
Llawhaden .... 15 F 28
Llechryd .... 15 G 27
Lledrod .... 25 I 27
Lleyn Peninsula .... 32 G 25
Llithfaen .... 32 G 25
Llowes .... 26 K 27
Llston .... 15 H 29
Llwydafydd .... 24 G 27
Llwyngwril .... 33 H 25
Llwynmawr .... 34 K 25
Llyfnant Valley .... 33 I 26
Llyn Brianne .... 25 I 27
Llyn Celyn .... 33 I 25
Llyn Tegid or Bala Lake ..... 33 J 25
Llyswen .... 26 K 27
Llysworney .... 17 J 29
Llywel .... 25 J 28
Loanhead .... 61 K 16
Lochailort .... 72 D 13
Lochaline .... 65 C 14
Lochans .... 52 E 19
Locharbriggs .... 53 J 18
Lochassynt Lodge .... 84 E 9
Lochawe .... 66 E 14
Lochay (Glen) .... 67 G 14
Lochboisdale .... 70 Y 12
Lochbuie .... 65 C 14
Lochcarron .... 78 D 11
Lochdonhead .... 65 C 14
Lochdrum .... 78 F 10
Lochearnhead .... 67 H 14
Locheport .... 76 Y 11
Locherben .... 61 J 18
Lochfoot .... 53 I 18
Lochgair .... 65 D 15
Lochgarthside .... 73 G 12
Lochgelly .... 68 K 15
Lochgilphead .... 65 D 15
Lochgoilhead .... 66 F 15
Lochinver .... 84 E 9
Lochluichart .... 78 F 11
Lochmaben .... 54 J 18
Lochmaddy .... 76 Y 11
Lochore .... 68 K 15
Lochportain .... 76 Y 11
Lochranza .... 59 E 16
Lochsie (Glen) .... 74 J 13
Lochstack .... 84 F 8
Lochton *Aberdeenshire* ...... 75 M 12
Lochton *South Ayrshire* .... 52 F 18
Lochtyn / Ynys .... 15 G 27

Lochuisge .... 72 D 14
Lochwinnoch .... 60 G 16
Lochy (Loch) .... 72 F 13
Lockerbie .... 54 J 18
Lockerley .... 9 P 30
Locking .... 18 L 30
Loddington .... 28 R 26
Loddon .... 39 Y 26
Lode .... 30 U 27
Lodsworth .... 11 R 31
Lofthouse .... 49 O 21
Loftus .... 50 R 20
Logan Gardens .... 52 F 19
Loggerheads .... 35 M 25
Logie Coldstone .... 74 L 12
Logiealmond .... 67 I 14
Login .... 15 F 28
Lomond (Loch) .... 66 G 15
Londesborough .... 51 R 22
London .... 21 T 29
London Colney .... 21 T 28
Long (Loch) *Angus* .... 68 K 14
Long (Loch)
   Argyll and Bute .... 66 F 15
Long Ashton .... 18 M 29
Long Bennington .... 36 R 25
Long Bredy .... 5 M 31
Long Buckby .... 28 Q 27
Long Clawson .... 36 R 25
Long Crendon .... 20 R 28
Long Eaton .... 36 Q 25
Long Hanborough .... 20 P 28
Long Itchington .... 28 P 27
Long Lawford .... 28 Q 26
Long Man (The) .... 12 U 31
Long Marston .... 50 Q 22
Long Marton .... 55 M 20
Long Melford .... 30 W 27
Long Mountain .... 34 K 26
Long Mynd (The) .... 26 L 26
Long Preston .... 49 N 21
Long Stratton .... 31 X 26
Long Sutton *Lincs.* .... 37 U 25
Long Sutton *Somerset* .... 8 L 30
Long Wittenham .... 20 Q 29
Longay .... 77 C 12
Longbenton .... 56 P 18
Longborough .... 27 O 28
Longbridge Deverill .... 9 N 30
Longburton .... 8 M 31
Longcot .... 19 P 29
Longdon .... 35 O 25
Longfield .... 22 U 29
Longford
   Derbyshire Dales .... 35 O 25
Longford *Tewkesbury* .... 27 N 28
Longforgan .... 68 K 14
Longformacus .... 62 M 16
Longham .... 38 W 25
Longhirst .... 56 P 18
Longhorsley .... 56 O 18
Longhoughton .... 63 P 17
Longleat House .... 19 N 30
Longmanhill .... 81 M 11
Longnewton .... 50 P 20
Longney .... 19 M 28
Longniddry .... 69 L 16
Longnor .... 35 O 24
Longridge *Ribble Valley* .. 42 M 22
Longridge
   South Staffordshire ...... 35 N 25
Longridge *West Lothian* .... 61 I 16
Longside .... 81 O 11
Longstanton .... 29 U 27
Longton *South Ribble* .... 42 L 22
Longton *Stoke-on-Trent* ..... 35 N 25
Longtown *Carlisle* .... 54 L 18
Longtown *Herefordshire* .... 26 L 28
Longwick .... 20 R 28
Longworth .... 20 P 28
Lonmore .... 77 A 11
Looe .... 3 G 32
Loose .... 22 V 30
Loppington .... 34 L 25
Lorn .... 65 E 14
Lorn (Firth of) .... 65 D 14
Lossiemouth .... 80 K 10
Lostwithiel .... 3 G 32
Lothbeg .... 85 I 9
Lothersdale .... 49 N 22
Lothmore .... 85 I 9
Loudwater .... 21 R 29
Loughborough .... 36 Q 25
Loughor (River) .... 17 H 29
Loughton .... 21 U 29
Louth .... 45 U 23
Lovington .... 8 M 30

Low Bradley .... 49 O 22
Low Crosby .... 55 L 19
Low Row *Carlisle* .... 55 M 19
Low Row *Richmondshire* .... 49 N 20
Low Street .... 39 Y 25
Lowca .... 53 J 20
Lowdham .... 36 Q 24
Lower Beeding .... 11 T 30
Lower Bentham .... 49 M 21
Lower Boddington .... 28 Q 27
Lower Broadheath .... 27 N 27
Lower Cam .... 19 M 28
Lower Diabaig .... 78 C 11
Lower Dounreay .... 85 I 8
Lower Dunsforth .... 50 Q 21
Lower Halstow .... 22 W 29
Lower Hardres .... 23 X 30
Lower Heyford .... 28 Q 28
Lower Killeyan .... 58 B 17
Lower Largo .... 69 L 15
Lower Mayland .... 22 W 28
Lower Peover .... 42 M 24
Lower Upham .... 10 Q 31
Lower-Whitley .... 42 M 24
Lowestoft .... 31 Z 26
Lowgill .... 49 M 21
Lowick
   Berwick-upon-Tweed ...... 63 O 17
Lowick
   East Northamptonshire ... 29 S 26
Lowick Bridge .... 48 K 21
Lowther .... 55 L 20
Lowther Hills .... 61 J 18
Loxwood .... 11 S 30
Loyal (Loch) .... 84 G 8
Loyne (Loch) .... 72 E 12
Lùb Score .... 77 A 10
Lubcroy .... 84 F 10
Lubenham .... 28 R 26
Lubnaig (Loch) .... 67 H 15
Luccombe .... 17 J 30
Luce Bay .... 52 F 19
Lucker .... 63 O 17
Luddenden .... 43 O 22
Luddesdown .... 22 V 29
Ludford *East Lindsey* ...... 45 T 23
Ludford *South Shropshire* . 26 L 26
Ludgershall *Bucks.* .... 20 Q 28
Ludgershall *Wilts.* .... 19 P 30
Ludgvan .... 2 D 33
Ludham .... 39 Y 25
Ludlow .... 26 L 26
Lugton .... 60 G 16
Luib *Highland* .... 77 B 12
Luib *Stirling* .... 67 G 14
Luichart (Loch) .... 78 F 11
Luing .... 65 D 15
Lullington .... 35 P 25
Lulsgate Bottom .... 18 L 29
Lulworth Cove .... 9 N 32
Lumphanan .... 75 L 12
Lumsden .... 80 L 12
Lunan .... 75 M 14
Lunanhead .... 74 L 14
Luncarty .... 68 J 14
Lund .... 51 S 22
Lundie (Loch) .... 68 K 14
Lundie (Loch) .... 78 C 11
Lundin Links .... 69 L 15
Lundy .... 16 G 30
Lunning .... 87 Q 2
Lurgainn (Loch) .... 84 E 9
Lurgashall .... 11 S 30
Luskentyre .... 82 Z 10
Luss .... 66 G 15
Lusta .... 77 A 11
Lustleigh .... 4 I 32
Luston .... 26 L 27
Luthermuir .... 75 M 13
Luthrie .... 68 K 14
Luton .... 29 S 28
Luton Hoo .... 21 S 28
Lutterworth .... 28 Q 26
Luxborough .... 7 J 30
Luxulyan .... 3 F 32
Lybster .... 86 K 9
Lydbury North .... 26 L 26
Lydd .... 12 W 31
Lydd-on-Sea .... 12 W 31
Lydden .... 23 X 30
Lydeard-St. Lawrence .... 8 K 30
Lydford *Mendip* .... 8 M 30
Lydford *West Devon* .... 4 H 32
Lydham .... 26 L 26
Lydiard Millicent .... 19 O 29
Lydiard Park .... 19 O 29
Lydiate .... 42 L 23
Lydlinch .... 9 M 31

Lydney ....18 M 28
Lydstep ....15 F 29
Lyme Bay ....5 L 32
Lyme Park ....43 N 23
Lyme Regis ....5 L 31
Lyminge ....13 X 30
Lymington ....10 P 31
Lymm ....42 M 23
Lympne ....13 X 30
Lympstone ....4 J 32
Lyndhurst ....10 P 31
Lyne ....61 K 17
Lyneham *North Wiltshire* ..19 O 29
Lyneham
    West Oxfordshire ......27 P 28
Lynemouth ....56 P 18
Lyness ....86 K 7
Lynmouth ....17 I 30
Lynton ....17 I 30
Lyon (Glen) ....73 H 14
Lyonshall ....26 L 27
Lytchett Matravers ....9 N 31
Lytchett Minster ....9 N 31
Lytes Cary ....8 L 30
Lyth ....86 K 8
Lytham ....42 L 22
Lytham St. Anne's ....42 K 22
Lythe ....51 R 20

M

Maaruig ....82 Z 10
Mabie ....53 J 18
Mablethorpe ....45 U 23
Macaskin (Island) ....65 D 15
Macclesfield ....43 N 24
Macduff ....81 M 10
Machars (The) ....52 G 19
Machen ....18 K 29
Machir Bay ....58 A 16
Machrihanish ....58 C 17
Machrihanish Bay ....58 C 17
Machynlleth ....33 I 26
Madderty ....67 I 14
Maddiston ....67 I 16
Maddy (Loch) ....76 Y 11
Madeley *Staffs* ....35 M 24
Madeley
    Telford and Wrekin ...35 M 26
Madingley ....29 U 27
Madron ....2 D 33
Maenclochog ....15 F 28
Maentwrog ....33 I 25
Maerdy *Conwy* ....33 J 25
Maerdy
    Rhondda, Cynon, Taf ..17 J 28
Maes Howe ....86 K 7
Maesbrook ....34 K 25
Maesteg ....17 J 29
Maghull ....42 L 23
Magor ....18 L 29
Maiden Bradley ....9 N 30
Maiden Castle ....8 M 31
Maiden Newton ....8 M 31
Maidenhead ....20 R 29
Maidens ....59 F 17
Maidford ....28 Q 27
Maids Moreton ....28 R 27
Maidstone ....22 V 30
Maidwell ....28 R 26
Mainland *Orkney Islands* .86 J 6
Mainland *Shetland Islands* .87 R 3
Mainstone ....26 K 26
Maisemore ....27 N 28
Malborough ....4 I 33
Maldon ....22 W 28
Malham ....49 N 21
Mallaig ....71 C 12
Mallory Park Circuit .....36 P 26
Mallwyd ....33 I 25
Malmesbury ....19 N 29
Malpas ....34 L 24
Maltby ....44 Q 23
Maltby-le-Marsh ....45 U 24
Malton ....50 R 21
Malvern Wells ....27 N 27
Mamble ....26 M 26
Mamore Forest ....72 F 13
Man (Isle of) ....46 G 21
Manaccan ....2 E 33
Manaton ....4 I 32
Manchester ....43 N 23
Manderston ....62 N 16
Manea ....29 U 26
Mangersta ....82 Y 9
Mangotsfield ....18 M 29
Manish ....76 Z 10
Manningford Bruce ....19 O 30

Mannings Heath ....11 T 30
Manningtree ....31 X 28
Manorbier ....15 F 29
Mansfield ....36 Q 24
Mansfield Woodhouse ......36 Q 24
Manstone ....9 N 31
Manton ....36 R 26
Manuden ....30 U 28
Maplebeck ....36 R 24
Mapledurham ....20 Q 29
Mappleton ....45 T 22
Mappowder ....9 M 31
Mar (Forest of) ....74 J 12
Marazion ....2 D 33
March ....37 U 26
Marcham ....20 P 29
Marchington ....35 O 25
Marchwood ....10 P 31
Marden ....22 V 30
Maree (Loch) ....78 D 10
Mareham-le-Fen ....37 T 24
Maresfield ....11 U 31
Margam ....17 I 29
Margaretting ....22 V 28
Margate ....23 Y 29
Margnaheglish ....59 E 17
Marham ....38 V 26
Marholm ....37 T 26
Marian-Glas ....40 H 22
Marishader ....77 B 11
Mark *Sedgemoor* ....18 L 30
Mark *South Ayrshire* ....52 E 18
Market Bosworth ....36 P 26
Market Deeping ....37 T 25
Market Drayton ....34 M 25
Market Harborough ....28 R 26
Market Lavington ....19 O 30
Market Overton ....36 R 25
Market Rasen ....45 T 23
Market Weighton ....44 S 22
Markfield ....36 Q 25
Markinch ....68 K 15
Marks Tey ....30 W 28
Marksbury ....18 M 29
Markyate ....21 S 28
Marlborough ....19 O 29
Marldon ....4 J 32
Marlesford ....31 Y 27
Marloes ....14 E 28
Marlow ....20 R 29
Marnhull ....9 N 31
Marple ....43 N 23
Marros ....15 G 28
Marsden ....43 O 23
Marsett ....49 N 21
Marsh Gibbon ....28 Q 28
Marsham ....39 X 25
Marshaw ....48 M 22
Marshchapel ....45 U 23
Marshfield
    Casnewydd / Newport .18 K 29
Marshfield
    South Gloucestershire .19 N 29
Marshwood ....8 L 31
Marske ....49 O 20
Marske-by-the-Sea ....57 Q 20
Marstch ....20 Q 28
Marston ....37 R 25
Marston Magna ....8 M 31
Marston Moretaine ....29 S 27
Martham ....39 Y 25
Martin *New Forest* ....9 O 31
Martin *North Kesteven* ..37 T 24
Martin (Isle) ....84 E 10
Martin Mill ....23 Y 30
Martindale ....48 L 20
Martinstown ....5 M 31
Martlesham ....31 X 27
Martletwy ....15 F 28
Martley ....27 M 27
Martock ....8 L 31
Marton *Harrogate* ....50 P 21
Marton *Macclesfield* ....35 N 24
Marvig ....82 A 9
Marwell Zoological Park ...10 Q 31
Mary Arden's House ....27 O 27
Mary Tavy ....4 H 32
Marybank ....79 G 11
Maryburgh ....79 G 11
Maryculter ....75 N 12
Maryfield ....87 Q 3
Marykirk ....75 M 13
Marypark ....80 J 11
Maryport *Allerdale* .....53 J 19
Maryport
    Dumfries and Galloway .52 F 19

Marywell *Aberdeenshire* ..75 L 12
Marywell *Angus* ....69 M 14
Masham ....49 P 21
Matching Green ....22 U 28
Mathry ....14 E 28
Matlock ....36 P 24
Matlock Bath ....35 P 24
Mattersey ....44 R 23
Mattingley ....20 R 30
Mattishall ....38 X 26
Mauchline ....60 G 17
Maud ....81 N 11
Maughold ....46 H 21
Maughold Head ....46 H 21
Mawbray ....54 J 19
Mawnan ....2 E 33
Maxstoke ....27 P 26
Maxton ....62 M 17
Maybole ....60 F 17
Mayfield *East Sussex* ...12 U 30
Mayfield *Staffs* ....35 O 24
Mc Arthur's Head ....58 B 16
Meadie (Loch) ....84 G 9
Meal Bank ....48 L 20
Mealsgate ....54 K 19
Meare ....8 L 30
Measach (Falls of) ....78 E 10
Measham ....36 P 25
Meavaig ....82 Z 10
Meavy ....4 H 32
Medbourne ....28 R 26
Medmenham ....20 R 29
Medstead ....10 Q 30
Medway (River) ....22 W 29
Meidrim ....15 G 28
Meifod ....34 K 25
Meigle ....68 K 14
Meikleour ....68 J 14
Meikle Toft ....83 B 9
Melbost ....83 B 9
Melbourn ....29 U 27
Melbourne
    East Riding of Yorkshire .44 R 22
Melbourne
    South Derbyshire .....36 P 25
Melbury Osmond ....8 M 31
Meldon ....56 O 18
Melfort ....65 D 15
Melgarve ....73 G 12
Melksham ....19 N 29
Melldalloch ....65 E 16
Mellerstain ....62 M 17
Melling ....48 M 21
Mellon Charles ....78 D 10
Mellon Udrigle ....78 D 10
Mells ....19 M 30
Melmerby *Eden* ....55 M 19
Melmerby *Harrogate* .....50 P 21
Melrose ....62 L 17
Meltham ....43 O 23
Melton ....31 X 27
Melton Mowbray ....36 R 25
Melvaig ....77 C 10
Melvich ....85 I 8
Memsie ....81 N 11
Menai Bridge /
    Porthaethwy ....40 H 23
Menai Strait ....33 H 24
Mendip Hills ....18 L 30
Mendlesham ....31 X 27
Menheniot ....3 G 32
Mennock ....61 I 17
Menston ....43 O 22
Menstrie ....67 I 15
Menteith Hills ....67 H 15
Mentmore ....29 R 28
Meonstoke ....10 Q 31
Meopham ....22 V 29
Mepal ....29 U 26
Mere *Cheshire* ....42 M 24
Mere *Wilts* ....9 N 30
Mereworth ....22 V 30
Meriden ....27 P 26
Merkland Lodge ....84 F 9
Mermaid Inn ....32 H 24
Merrick ....52 G 18
Merriott ....8 L 31
Merrylaw ....62 K 18
Mersey (River) ....42 M 23
Merthyr Cynog ....25 J 27
Merthyr Tydfil ....17 J 28
Merton *Cherwell* ....20 Q 28
Merton *Devon* ....7 H 31
Merton *London Borough* ..21 T 29
Meshaw ....7 I 31
Messing ....30 W 28
Messingham ....44 S 23
Metfield ....31 Y 26

Metheringham ....37 S 24
Methil ....69 K 15
Methlick ....81 N 11
Methven ....68 J 14
Methwold ....38 V 26
Mevagissey ....3 F 33
Mexborough ....44 Q 23
Mhór (Loch) ....73 G 12
Miavaig ....82 Z 9
Michaelchurch Escley .....26 L 27
Michaelstow ....3 F 32
Micheldever ....10 Q 30
Michelham Priory ....12 U 31
Micklefield ....44 Q 22
Mickleover ....36 P 25
Mickleton *Cotswold* .....27 O 27
Mickleton *Teesdale* .....55 N 20
Mid Ardlaw ....81 N 10
Mid Calder ....61 J 16
Mid Lavant ....10 R 31
Mid Sannox ....59 E 17
Mid Yell ....87 Q 2
Midbea ....86 L 6
Middle Barton ....28 P 28
Middle Rasen ....45 S 23
Middle Tysoe ....28 P 27
Middle Wallop ....9 P 30
Middle Woodford ....9 O 30
Middleton ....54 K 18
Middleham ....49 O 21
Middlesbrough ....57 Q 20
Middlestown ....43 P 23
Middleton *Argyll and Bute* .64 Z 14
Middleton
    Berwick-upon-Tweed ..63 O 17
Middleton *Bradford* .....49 O 22
Middleton *Gtr. Mches* ...43 N 23
Middleton Cheney ....28 Q 27
Middleton-in-Teesdale ....55 N 20
Middleton-on-Sea ....11 S 31
Middleton on the Wolds ...51 S 22
Middleton St. George ....50 P 20
Middleton Tyas ....49 P 20
Middletown *Powys* ....34 K 25
Middlewich ....35 M 24
Midgeholme ....55 M 19
Midhurst ....10 R 31
Midleton ....63 N 17
Milford ....11 S 30
Milford Haven /
    Aberdaugleddau ....14 E 28
Milford-on-Sea ....9 P 31
Milland ....10 R 30
Millbrook ....3 H 32
Millhouse ....59 E 16
Millmeece ....35 N 25
Millom ....47 K 21
Millport ....59 F 16
Milltown
    Dumfries and Galloway .54 K 18
Milltown *Highland* ......78 F 11
Milltown *Moray* ....80 L 11
Milnathort ....68 J 15
Milngavie ....67 H 16
Milnrow ....43 N 23
Milnthorpe ....48 L 21
Milovaig ....76 Z 11
Milton ....79 H 10
Milton *Cambs* ....29 U 27
Milton *Carlisle* ....55 L 19
Milton *Dumfries* ....53 I 18
Milton *Highland* ....79 G 10
Milton *Stranraer* ....52 F 19
Milton Abbas ....9 N 31
Milton Abbot ....3 H 32
Milton Bryan ....29 S 28
Milton Ernest ....29 S 27
Milton Keynes ....28 R 27
Milton Libourne ....19 O 29
Milton of Campsie ....67 H 16
Milton of Cushnie ....75 L 12
Milton-on-Stour ....9 N 30
Miltonduff ....80 J 11
Miltown of Edinvillie ...80 K 11
Milverton ....8 K 30

Milwich ....35 N 25
Minard ....65 E 15
Minch (The) ....83 C 9
Minehead ....17 J 30
Minety ....19 O 29
Mingary ....76 X 12
Minginish ....77 B 12
Mingulay ....70 X 13
Minnigaff ....52 G 19
Minster *near Sheerness* .22 W 29
Minster *near Ramsgate* ..23 X 29
Minsterley ....34 L 26
Minsterworth ....19 N 28
Minterne Magna ....8 M 31
Minting ....45 T 24
Mintlaw ....81 O 11
Minto ....62 L 17
Mirfield ....43 O 22
Miserden ....19 N 28
Misson ....44 R 23
Misterton *Notts* ....44 R 23
Misterton *Somerset* ....8 L 31
Mistley ....31 X 28
Mitcheldean ....26 M 28
Mitchell ....2 E 32
Mitford ....56 O 18
Mithcham ....21 T 29
Mithian ....2 E 33
Moaness ....86 K 7
Mochdre ....41 I 23
Mochrum ....52 G 19
Modbury ....4 I 32
Moelfre ....40 H 22
Moffat ....61 J 17
Moidart ....72 C 13
Moira ....36 P 25
Mol-Chlach ....71 B 12
Mold / Yr Wyddgrug ......34 K 24
Molland ....7 I 30
Monach Islands ....76 W 11
Monadhliath Mountains ...73 H 12
Monar (Loch) ....78 E 11
Monar Lodge ....78 F 11
Monaughty Forest ....80 J 11
Moneydie ....68 J 14
Moniaive ....53 I 18
Monifieth ....69 L 14
Monikie ....69 L 14
Monk Fryston ....44 Q 22
Monkland ....26 L 27
Monkokehampton ....7 H 31
Monks Eleigh ....30 W 27
Monksilver ....7 K 30
Monkton ....60 G 17
Monmouth / Trefynwy .....18 L 28
Monreith ....52 G 19
Montacute ....8 L 31
Montgarrie ....75 L 12
Montgomery / Trefaldwyn ..34 K 26
Montrose ....75 M 13
Monyash ....35 O 24
Monymusk ....75 M 12
Monzie ....67 I 14
Moonen Bay ....76 Z 11
Moor Monkton ....50 Q 21
Moorends ....44 R 23
Moorfoot Hills ....61 K 16
Moors (The) ....52 F 19
Moortown ....45 S 23
Morar ....71 C 13
Moray Firth ....79 H 11
Morchard Bishop ....7 I 31
Morcott ....37 S 26
Morden ....9 N 31
Mordiford ....26 M 27
More (Glen) ....65 C 14
More (Loch) *near Kinloch* .84 F 9
More (Loch)
    near Westerdale ......85 J 8
Morebath ....7 J 30
Morebattle ....62 M 17
Morecambe ....48 L 21
Morecambe Bay ....48 L 21
Moresby ....53 J 20
Moreton *Epping Forest* ..22 U 28
Moreton *Purbeck* ....9 N 31
Moreton-in-Marsh ....27 O 28
Moreton-on-lugg ....26 L 27
Moreton Say ....34 M 25
Moretonhampstead ....4 I 32
Morfa Nefyn ....32 G 25
Moricambe Bay ....54 K 19
Morie (Loch) ....79 G 10
Moriston (Glen) ....72 F 12
Morland ....55 M 20
Morley ....43 P 22
Morlich (Loch) ....74 I 12

Morpeth ....56 O 18
Morriston ....17 I 29
Morte Bay ....6 H 30
Mortehoe ....16 H 30
Mortimer ....20 Q 29
Morton *near Bourne* .....37 S 25
Morton
    near Gainsborough ...44 R 23
Morton
    North East Derbyshire .36 P 24
Morton on Swale ....50 P 21
Morval ....3 G 32
Morven ....85 I 9
Morvern ....71 C 14
Morvich ....72 D 12
Morville ....34 M 26
Morwelham ....3 H 32
Morwenstow ....6 G 31
Mosborough ....43 P 24
Moss Bank ....42 L 23
Mossdale ....53 H 18
Mossend ....60 H 16
Mossley ....43 N 23
Mosstodloch ....80 K 11
Mostyn ....41 K 23
Motherwell ....61 I 16
Moulin ....74 I 13
Moulton *Forest Heath* ...30 V 27
Moulton *Lincs* ....37 T 25
Moulton *Northants* .....28 R 27
Moulton Chapel ....37 T 25
Mount Pleasant ....9 P 31
Mountain Ash /
    Aberpennar ....17 J 28
Mount's Bay ....2 D 33
Mountsorrel ....36 Q 25
Mousa ....87 Q 4
Mousehole ....2 D 33
Mouswald ....54 J 18
Mow Cop ....35 N 24
Mowtie ....75 N 13
Moy ....79 H 11
Muasdale ....59 C 17
Much Dewchurch ....26 L 27
Much Hadham ....29 U 28
Much Hoole ....42 L 22
Much Marcle ....26 M 28
Much Wenlock ....34 M 26
Muchalls ....75 N 12
Muchelney ....8 L 30
Muchrachd ....78 F 11
Muck ....71 B 13
Muckle Roe ....87 P 2
Mucklestone ....35 M 25
Muddiford ....7 H 30
Mudford ....8 M 31
Mugeary ....77 B 11
Muick (Loch) ....74 K 13
Muie ....85 H 9
Muir of Fowlis ....75 L 12
Muir of Ord ....79 G 11
Muirdrum ....69 L 14
Muirhead ....60 H 16
Muirkirk ....60 H 17
Muirshearlich ....72 E 13
Muker ....49 N 20
Mulbarton ....39 X 26
Mulben ....80 K 11
Muldoanich ....70 X 13
Mull (Isle of) ....64 B 14
Mull (Sound of) ....71 C 14
Mull of Galloway ....52 F 20
Mull of Oa ....58 A 17
Mullardoch (Loch) ....78 E 12
Mullardoch House ....78 F 11
Mullion ....2 E 33
Mumbles (The) ....15 H 29
Mumby ....45 U 24
Mundesley ....39 Y 25
Mundford ....30 V 26
Mundham ....10 R 31
Munlochy ....79 H 11
Munlochy Bay ....79 H 11
Munslow ....26 L 26
Murlaggan ....72 E 13
Murrayfield ....68 K 16
Mursley ....28 R 28
Murton *Easington* ......57 P 19
Murton *Eden* ....55 M 20
Musbury ....5 K 31
Musselburgh ....68 K 16
Muston ....51 T 21
Muthill ....67 I 15
Mwnt ....15 G 27
Mybster ....85 J 8
Myddfai ....25 I 28
Myddle ....34 L 25

A B C D E F G H I J K L M N O P Q R S T U V W X Y Z

A B C D E F G H I J K L M N O P Q R S T U V W X Y Z

Mydroilyn ....15 H 27
Mynach Falls ....25 I 26
Mynachlog-ddu ....15 F 28
Mynydd Eppynt ....25 J 27
Mynydd Mawr ....32 F 25
Mynydd Preseli ....15 F 28
Myrelandhorn ....86 K 8
Mytchett ....21 R 30
Mytholmroyd ....43 O 22

N

Na Cùiltean ....58 C 16
Naburn ....50 Q 22
Nacton ....31 X 27
Nafferton ....51 S 21
Nailsea ....18 L 29
Nailstone ....36 P 26
Nailsworth ....19 N 28
Nairn ....79 I 11
Nant (Loch) ....65 E 14
Nant-y-Moch Reservoir ..25 I 26
Nant-y-moel ....17 J 29
Nantgwynant Valley ....33 H 24
Nantwich ....34 M 24
Nantyglo ....18 K 28
Napton ....28 Q 27
Narberth / Arberth .....15 F 28
Narborough Blaby ......36 Q 26
Narborough Breckland ..38 V 25
Naseby ....28 R 26
Nash Point ....17 J 29
Nassington ....37 S 26
Nateby ....49 M 20
National Exhibition Centre ..27 O 26
National Motor Museum ..10 P 31
Naunton ....27 O 28
Navenby ....37 S 24
Naver (Loch) ....84 G 9
Nayland ....30 W 28
Naze (The) ....31 X 28
Neap ....87 Q 3
Neath / Castell-nedd ...17 I 29
Neath (River) ....17 I 28
Nebo ....33 I 24
Necton ....38 W 26
Needham Market ....31 X 27
Needingworth ....29 T 27
Needles (The) ....10 P 32
Nefyn ....32 G 25
Neidpath Castle ....61 K 17
Neilston ....60 G 16
Neist Point ....76 Z 11
Nelson
Caerffili / Caerphilly ..18 K 29
Nelson Pendle ....43 N 22
Nene (River) ....37 T 26
Nenthead ....55 M 19
Nercwys ....34 K 24
Nereabolls ....58 A 16
Ness ....83 B 8
Ness (Loch) ....73 G 12
Nesscliffe ....34 L 25
Nestley Marsh ....10 P 31
Neston ....42 K 24
Nether Broughton .....36 R 25
Nether Kellet ....48 L 21
Nether Langwith ....44 Q 24
Nether Stowey ....8 K 30
Nether Wasdale ....47 J 20
Nether Whitecleuch ...61 I 17
Netheravon ....19 O 30
Netherbrae ....81 M 11
Netherbury ....8 L 31
Netherend ....18 M 28
Netherhampton ....9 O 30
Nethermill ....54 J 18
Netherthong ....43 O 23
Netherton ....63 N 17
Nethertown ....86 K 7
Netherwitton ....56 O 18
Nethy Bridge ....74 J 12
Netley ....10 P 31
Nettlebed ....20 R 29
Nettleham ....44 S 24
Nettleton ....45 T 23
Nevern ....15 F 27
Nevis (Glen) ....72 E 13
Nevis (Loch) ....72 C 12
New Abbey ....53 J 19
New Aberdour ....81 N 11
New Alresford ....10 Q 30
New Buckenham ....31 X 26
New Byth ....81 N 11
New Clipstone ....36 Q 24
New Cumnock ....60 H 17
New Deer ....81 N 11
New Edlington ....44 Q 23

New Forest National Park ..9 P 31
New Galloway ....53 H 18
New Holland ....45 S 22
New Hythe ....22 V 30
New Leeds ....81 N 11
New Luce ....52 F 19
New Marske ....57 Q 20
New Mills ....43 O 23
New Mills Powys ....33 K 26
New Milton ....9 P 31
New Pitsligo ....81 N 11
New Quay / Ceinewydd ..24 G 27
New Rackheath ....39 Y 26
New Radnor ....26 K 27
New Romney ....12 W 31
New Rossington ....44 Q 23
New Sauchie ....67 I 15
New Scone ....68 J 14
New Silksworth ....57 P 19
New Tredegar ....18 K 28
New Waltham ....45 T 23
Newark-on-Trent ....36 R 24
Newbiggin Eden ......55 L 19
Newbiggin Teesdale ...55 N 20
Newbiggin-by-the-Sea ..56 P 18
Newbigging Angus .....69 L 14
Newbigging
South Lanarkshire ....61 J 16
Newbold Verdon ....36 P 26
Newborough
East Staffordshire ....35 O 25
Newborough
Isle of Anglesey ......32 G 24
Newbridge Caerffili /
Caerphilly ....18 K 29
Newbridge Isle of Wight ..10 P 31
Newbridge-on-Wye .....25 J 27
Newbrough ....55 N 18
Newburgh Aberdeenshire ..81 N 12
Newburgh Fife ....68 K 14
Newburgh Lancashire ..42 L 23
Newburn ....56 O 19
Newbury ....20 Q 29
Newby Bridge ....48 L 21
Newby Hall ....50 P 21
Newcastle Monmouthshire /
Sir Fynwy ....18 L 28
Newcastle
South Shropshire .....26 K 26
Newcastle Emlyn /
Castell Newydd Emlyn ..15 G 27
Newcastle-under-Lyme ..35 N 24
Newcastle-upon-Tyne ..56 P 19
Newcastle-upon-Tyne
Airport ....56 O 18
Newcastleton ....55 L 18
Newchapel ....15 G 27
Newchurch Carmarthenshire /
Sir Gaerfyrddin ....15 G 28
Newchurch Isle of Wight ..10 Q 32
Newchurch Powys ......26 K 27
Newchurch Shepway ..12 W 30
Newdigate ....11 T 30
Newent ....27 M 28
Newgale ....14 E 28
Newhall ....34 M 24
Newham Isle of Wight ..63 O 17
Newham London Borough ..21 U 29
Newhaven ....11 U 31
Newick ....11 U 31
Newington ....22 V 29
Newland ....18 M 28
Newlyn ....2 D 33
Newmachar ....75 N 12
Newmains ....61 I 16
Newmarket Isle of Lewis ..82 A 9
Newmarket Suffolk .....30 V 27
Newmill Moray ....80 L 11
Newmill Scottish Borders ..62 L 17
Newmilns ....60 G 17
Newnham Daventry ...28 Q 27
Newnham Glos. ....18 M 28
Newnham Kent ....22 W 30
Newnham Bridge ......26 M 27
Newport Essex ....30 U 28
Newport I.O.W. ....10 Q 31
Newport Pembrokes ...15 F 27
Newport Stroud ....19 M 28
Newport
Telford and Wrekin ...35 M 25
Newport /
Casnewydd Newport ..18 L 29
Newport-on-Tay ....69 L 14
Newport Pagnell ....28 R 27
Newquay ....2 E 32
Newsham ....49 O 20
Newstead ....36 Q 24

Newstead Abbey ....36 Q 24
Newton Aberdeenshire ..81 O 11
Newton Argyll and Bute ..65 E 15
Newton Babergh ......30 W 27
Newton Moray ....80 I 11
Newton Ribble Valley ..49 M 22
Newton Abbot ....4 J 32
Newton Arlosh ....54 K 19
Newton-Aycliffe ....56 P 20
Newton Ferrers ....4 H 33
Newton Flotman ....39 X 26
Newton-le-Willows ....42 M 23
Newton Longville ......28 R 28
Newton Mearns ....60 H 16
Newton-on-Rawcliffe ..50 R 21
Newton-on-Trent ......44 R 24
Newton Poppleford .....5 K 31
Newton Reigny ....55 L 19
Newton St. Cyres ....7 J 31
Newton Stewart ....52 G 19
Newton Tracey ....7 H 30
Newton Wamphray ....54 J 18
Newtongrange ....61 K 16
Newtonhill ....75 N 12
Newtonmore ....73 H 12
Newtown Cheshire ....43 N 23
Newtown Heref. ....26 M 27
Newtown Highland ....73 F 12
Newtown Isle of Man ..46 G 21
Newtown /
Drenewydd Powys ...26 K 26
Newtown Linford ......36 Q 25
Newtown St. Boswells ..62 L 17
Newtyle ....68 K 14
Neyland ....16 F 28
Nicholaston ....15 H 29
Nigg ....79 H 10
Nigg Bay ....79 H 10
Nine Ladies ....35 P 24
Ninebanks ....55 M 19
Ninfield ....12 V 31
Nisbet ....62 M 17
Nith (River) ....53 J 19
Niths ....61 I 18
Niton ....10 Q 32
Nocton ....37 S 24
Nolton ....14 E 28
Nordelph ....38 U 26
Norfolk Broads ....39 Y 25
Norham ....63 N 16
Normanby ....50 R 21
Normandy ....21 S 30
Normanton ....43 P 22
Normanton-on-the-Wolds ..36 Q 25
North Baddesley ......10 P 31
North Ballachulish ....72 E 13
North Berwick ....69 L 15
North Bovey ....4 I 32
North Bradley ....19 N 30
North Brentor ....4 H 32
North Cadbury ....8 M 30
North Cave ....44 S 22
North-Cerney ....19 O 28
North-Charlton ....63 O 17
North Cliffe ....44 R 22
North Cowton ....50 P 20
North Crawley ....29 S 27
North Creake ....38 W 25
North Curry ....8 L 30
North Dalton ....51 S 22
North Deighton ....50 P 22
North Erradale ....77 C 10
North Esk (Riv.) ....75 L 13
North Fearns ....77 B 11
North Foreland ....23 Y 29
North Frodingham .....51 T 22
North Grimston ....51 R 21
North Harris ....82 Z 10
North Hill ....3 G 32
North Hinksey ....20 Q 28
North Holmwood ......21 T 30
North Hykeham ....37 S 24
North Kelsey ....45 S 23
North Kessock ....79 H 11
North Kyme ....37 T 24
North Leigh ....20 P 28
North-Molton ....7 I 30
North Morar ....72 C 13
North Newbald ....44 S 22
North Nibley ....19 M 29
North Otterington .....50 P 21
North Petherton ....8 K 30
North Petherwin ....6 G 31
North Rigton ....50 P 22
North Ronaldsay ......87 M 5
North-Scarle ....36 R 24

North-Shian ....65 D 14
North Shields ....56 P 18
North Shore ....42 K 22
North Somercotes .....45 U 23
North Sound (The) ....87 L 6
North Stainley ....50 P 21
North Stainmore ......49 N 20
North Sunderland .....63 P 17
North Tamerton ....6 G 31
North-Tawton ....7 I 31
North Thoresby ....45 T 23
North Tidworth ....19 P 30
North Uist ....76 X 11
North Walsham ....39 Y 25
North Warnborough ...20 R 30
North Water Bridge ...75 M 13
North Weald Bassett ..22 U 28
North Wootton ....38 V 25
North York Moors
National Park ....50 R 20
Northallerton ....50 P 20
Northam ....6 H 30
Northampton ....28 R 27
Northaw ....21 T 28
Northchapel ....11 S 30
Northchurch ....21 S 28
Northfleet ....22 V 29
Northiam ....12 V 31
Northleach ....19 O 28
Northleigh ....5 K 31
Northlew ....7 H 31
Northop ....34 K 24
Northrepps ....39 Y 25
Northumberland
National Park ....63 N 18
Northwich ....42 M 24
Northwold ....38 V 26
Northwood ....34 L 25
Norton Daventry ......28 Q 27
Norton Doncaster .....44 Q 23
Norton Ryedale ....50 R 21
Norton Tewkesbury ...27 N 28
Norton Disney ....36 R 24
Norton Fitzwarren ......8 K 30
Norton in Hales ....35 M 25
Norton St. Philip ......19 N 30
Norwich ....39 X 26
Norwick ....87 R 1
Noss (Isle of) ....87 Q 3
Noss Head ....86 K 8
Nottingham ....36 Q 25
Nuffield ....20 Q 29
Nunburnholme ....51 R 22
Nuneaton ....28 P 26
Nuneham Courtenay ..20 Q 28
Nunney ....19 M 30
Nunthorpe ....50 Q 20
Nunton ....76 X 11
Nutley ....11 U 30
Nympsfield ....19 N 28

O

Oa (The) ....58 B 17
Oadby ....36 Q 26
Oakamoor ....35 O 24
Oakdale ....18 K 28
Oakengates ....35 M 25
Oakford ....7 J 31
Oakham ....36 R 25
Oakhill ....18 M 30
Oakington ....29 U 27
Oakley Aylesbury Vale ..20 Q 28
Oakley Bedfordshire ...29 S 27
Oakley Fife ....68 J 15
Oaksey ....19 N 29
Oakworth ....43 O 22
Oare Kennet ....19 O 29
Oare Swale ....22 W 30
Oare West Somerset ..17 I 30
Oathlaw ....74 L 13
Oban ....65 D 14
Occold ....31 X 27
Ochil Hills ....68 I 15
Ochiltree ....60 G 17
Ockbrook ....36 P 25
Ockle ....71 C 13
Ockley ....11 S 30
Odham ....21 R 30
Odiham ....20 R 30
Odland ....18 M 29
Odstock ....9 O 31
Offa's Dyke Path ......26 K 26
Offord Cluny ....29 T 27
Ogbourne St. Andrew ..19 O 29
Ogbourne St. George ..19 O 29
Ogil ....74 L 13
Ogle ....56 O 18

Ogmore-by-Sea ....17 J 29
Ogmore Vale ....17 J 29
Oich (Loch) ....73 F 12
Oidhche (Loch na h-) ..78 D 11
Oigh-Sgeir ....71 Z 13
Okeford Fitzpaine ......9 N 31
Okehampton ....4 H 31
Old Alresford ....10 Q 30
Old Bolingbroke ....37 U 24
Old Burghclere ....20 Q 30
Old Castleton ....55 L 18
Old Colwyn ....41 I 23
Old Dailly ....59 F 18
Old Deer ....81 N 11
Old Fletton ....37 T 26
Old Harry Rocks ....9 O 32
Old Head ....87 L 7
Old Hurst ....29 T 26
Old Hutton ....48 L 21
Old Kilpatrick ....67 G 16
Old Knebworth ....29 T 28
Old Leake ....37 U 24
Old Man of Hoy ....86 J 7
Old Man of Storr ......77 B 11
Old Radnor ....26 K 27
Old Rayne ....81 M 11
Old' Sarum ....9 O 30
Old Sodbury ....19 M 29
Old Somerby ....37 S 25
Old Warden ....29 S 27
Old Windsor ....21 S 29
Oldany Island ....84 E 9
Oldbury ....27 N 26
Oldbury on Severn ....18 M 29
Oldcotes ....44 Q 23
Oldham† ....43 N 23
Oldhamstocks ....69 M 16
Oldmeldrum ....81 N 11
Oldshoremore ....84 E 8
Olgrinmore ....85 J 8
Ollaberry ....87 P 2
Ollach ....77 B 11
Ollay (Loch) ....76 X 12
Ollerton Macclesfield ..42 M 24
Ollerton
Newark and Sherwood ..36 Q 24
Olveston ....18 M 29
Ombersley ....27 N 27
Once Brewed ....55 M 19
Onchan ....46 G 21
Onecote ....35 O 24
Onich ....72 E 13
Onllwyn ....17 I 28
Opinan ....83 D 10
Orchy (Glen) ....66 F 14
Ord ....71 C 12
Ordie ....74 L 12
Orford ....31 Y 27
Orford Ness ....31 Y 27
Orkney Islands 87
Orleton ....26 L 27
Ormesby ....50 Q 20
Ormesby St. Margaret ..39 Z 25
Ormiston ....62 L 16
Ormskirk ....42 L 23
Oronsay ....64 B 15
Orosay near Fuday ...70 X 12
Orosay near Lochboisdale ..70 X 12
Orphir ....86 K 7
Orrin (Glen) ....78 F 11
Orrin Reservoir ....78 F 11
Orsay ....58 A 16
Orsett ....22 V 29
Orston ....36 R 25
Orton ....48 M 20
Orwell ....29 T 27
Orwell (River) ....31 X 28
Osborne House ....10 Q 31
Osdale ....77 A 11
Osgaig (Loch) ....83 E 9
Osgodby ....45 S 23
Oskaig ....77 B 11
Osmington ....9 M 32
Ossett ....43 P 22
Ossington ....36 R 24
Oswaldtwistle ....42 M 22
Oswestry ....34 K 25
Otford ....22 U 30
Othery ....8 L 30
Otley Suffolk ....31 X 27
Otley West Yorks. ....49 O 22
Otterbourne ....10 P 30
Otterburn ....55 N 18
Otternish ....76 Y 10
Otterswick ....87 Q 2
Otterton ....5 K 32

Ottery St. Mary ....5 K 31
Ottringham ....45 T 22
Oulton Broad ....39 Z 26
Oulton Park Circuit ...34 M 24
Oundle ....29 S 26
Ouse (River)
English Channel .....11 T 30
Ouse (River) North Sea ..50 Q 21
Out-Rawcliffe ....42 L 22
Out Skerries ....87 R 2
Outer Hebrides ....82 Y 9
Outhgill ....49 M 20
Outwell ....38 U 26
Over ....29 U 27
Over Compton ....8 M 31
Overseal ....35 P 25
Overstrand ....39 Y 25
Overton Hants. ....20 Q 30
Overton Lancs. ....48 L 21
Overton Wrexham ....34 L 25
Overtown ....61 I 16
Ower ....10 P 31
Owermoigne ....9 N 32
Owlswick ....20 R 28
Owslebury ....10 Q 30
Owston ....36 R 26
Owston Ferry ....44 R 23
Oxburgh Hall ....38 V 26
Oxen Park ....48 K 21
Oxenhope ....43 O 22
Oxford ....20 Q 28
Oxnam ....62 M 17
Oxted ....21 T 30
Oxton
Newark and Sherwood ..36 Q 24
Oxton Scottish Borders ..62 L 16
Oxwich ....15 H 29
Oxwich Bay ....15 H 29
Oykel (Glen) ....84 F 9
Oykel Bridge ....84 F 10
Oyne ....81 M 12

P

Pabay ....77 C 12
Pabbay near Harris ...76 Y 10
Pabbay near Mingulay ..70 X 13
Pabbay (Sound of) ....76 Y 10
Packington ....36 P 25
Padbury ....28 R 28
Paddock Wood ....22 V 30
Paddockhole ....54 K 18
Padiham ....42 N 22
Padstow ....3 F 32
Pagham ....10 R 31
Paignton ....4 J 32
Pailton ....28 Q 26
Painscastle ....26 K 27
Painswick ....19 N 28
Paisley ....60 G 16
Pakefield ....31 Z 26
Palnackie ....53 I 19
Pamber End ....20 Q 30
Pandy
Monmouthshire / Sir Fynwy ..26 L 28
Pandy Powys ....33 J 26
Pangbourne ....20 Q 29
Pant ....34 K 25
Pantymenyn ....15 F 28
Papa Stour ....87 O 3
Papa Westray ....87 L 5
Papplewick ....36 Q 24
Paps of Jura ....65 B 16
Papworth Everard .....29 T 27
Parbh (The) ....84 F 8
Parbold ....42 L 23
Parc Cefn Onn ....18 K 29
Parham House ....11 S 31
Park Gate ....10 Q 31
Park of Pairc ....82 A 9
Parkeston ....31 X 28
Parkgate ....53 J 18
Parkhurst ....10 Q 31
Parnham House ....8 L 31
Parracombe ....17 I 30
Parrett (River) ....8 K 30
Parson Drove ....37 U 26
Partney ....37 U 24
Parton
Dumfries and Galloway ..53 H 18
Partridge Green ....11 T 31
Parwich ....35 O 24
Patchway ....18 M 29
Pateley Bridge ....49 O 21
Path of Condie ....68 J 15
Pathhead ....62 L 16
Patna ....60 G 17

Great Britain 133

Patrick 46 F 21
Patrington 45 T 22
Patrixbourne 23 X 30
Patterdale 48 L 20
Pattingham 35 N 26
Pattishall 28 Q 27
Paulerspury 28 R 27
Paull 45 T 22
Paulton 18 M 30
Paxton 63 N 16
Peacehaven 11 T 31
Peak District
National Park 43 O 23
Pearsie 74 K 13
Peasedown St. John 19 M 30
Peasemore 20 P 29
Peasenhall 31 Y 27
Peaslake 21 S 30
Peasmarsh 12 W 31
Peat Inn 69 L 15
Peatknowe 81 M 11
Pebmarsh 30 W 28
Pebworth 27 O 27
Peebles 61 K 17
Peel 46 F 21
Peel Fell 62 M 18
Pegswood 56 P 18
Pegwell Bay 23 Y 30
Peinchorran 77 B 12
Peldon 22 W 28
Pelton 56 P 19
Pelynt 3 G 32
Pembrey 15 H 28
Pembridge 26 L 27
Pembroke / Penfro 16 F 28
Pembroke Dock /
Doc Penfro 16 F 28
Pembrokeshire Coast
National Park 15 F 29
Pembury 12 V 30
Pen-y-bont / Bridgend 17 J 29
Pen-y-groes 32 H 24
Penalun 15 F 29
Penarth 18 K 29
Pencader 15 H 27
Pencaitland 62 L 16
Pencarrow 3 F 32
Penclawdd 15 H 29
Pencombe 26 M 27
Penderyn 17 J 28
Pendine 15 G 28
Pendine Sands 15 G 28
Pendlebury 42 N 23
Pendoylan 17 J 29
Penelewey 2 E 33
Penfro / Pembroke 16 F 28
Pengethley 26 M 28
Penhow 18 L 29
Penicuik 61 K 16
Penifiler 77 B 11
Peninver 59 D 17
Penistone 43 P 23
Penketh 42 L 23
Penkridge 35 N 25
Penley 34 L 25
Penmaen 15 H 29
Penmaenmawr 41 I 23
Penmaenpool 33 I 25
Penmark 17 J 29
Penmon 40 H 23
Pennal 33 I 26
Pennant 33 J 26
Pennerley 34 L 26
Pennines (The) 49 N 20
Pennyghael 65 B 14
Penpont 53 I 18
Penrhiwpal 15 G 27
Penrhyn 40 H 23
Penrhyn Bay 41 I 23
Penrhyndeudraeth 33 H 25
Penrith 55 L 19
Penruddock 55 L 20
Penryn 2 E 33
Pensarn 41 J 23
Penshaw 56 P 19
Penshurst 22 U 30
Pensilva 3 G 32
Pentewan 3 F 33
Pentire Point 3 F 32
Pentland Firth 86 K 7
Pentland Hills 61 J 16
Pentland Skerries 87 L 7
Pentraeth 40 H 23
Pentre-Berw 40 H 23
Pentre-Celyn 34 K 24
Pentrebeirdd 34 K 25
Penwith 2 D 33
Penybont 26 K 27
Penysarn 40 H 22
Penzance 2 D 33
Penrhyn-Coch 25 I 26
Perranaworthal 2 E 33
Perranporth 2 E 32
Perranzabuloe 2 E 33
Pershore 27 N 27
Pertenhall 29 S 27
Perth 68 J 14
Peterborough 37 T 26
Peterculter 75 N 12
Peterhead 81 O 11
Peterlee 57 P 19
Petersfield 10 R 30
Peterstone Wentlooge 18 K 29
Peterstow 26 M 28
Petham 23 X 30
Petrockstowe 7 H 31
Pett 12 V 31
Pettaugh 31 X 27
Petworth 11 S 31
Pevensey Bay 12 V 31
Pewsey 19 O 29
Pickering 50 R 21
Picklescott 34 L 26
Picton Castle 16 F 28
Piddlehinton 9 M 31
Piddletrenthide 9 M 31
Piercebridge 49 O 20
Pierowall 86 L 6
Pilgrims Hatch 22 U 29
Pillerton Hersey 28 P 27
Pillerton Priors 27 P 27
Pilley 43 P 23
Pilling 48 L 22
Pilning 18 M 29
Pilton 8 M 30
Pinchbeck 37 T 25
Pinchbeck-West 37 T 25
Pinhoe 4 J 31
Pinmore Mains 52 F 18
Pinner 21 S 29
Pinvin 27 N 27
Pinwherry 52 F 18
Pinxton 36 Q 24
Pirbright 21 S 30
Pirnmill 59 D 17
Pirton 29 T 28
Pishill 20 R 29
Pitcaple 81 M 12
Pitcombe 8 M 30
Pitcur 68 K 14
Pitlochry 74 I 13
Pitmedden 81 N 11
Pitminster 8 K 31
Pitscottie 69 L 15
Pitsford 28 R 27
Pittentrail 85 H 10
Pittenween 69 L 15
Pladda 59 E 17
Plaistow 11 S 30
Plas Newydd *Anglesey* 33 H 24
Plas Newydd
Denbighshire 34 K 25
Plean 67 I 15
Pleasington 42 M 22
Pleasley 36 Q 24
Plenmeller 55 M 19
Plockton 78 D 11
Pluckley 22 W 30
Plumbland 54 K 19
Plumpton 11 T 31
Plymouth 4 H 32
Plympton 4 H 32
Plymstock 4 H 32
Plymtree 7 J 31
Plynlimon
(Pumlumon Fawr) 25 I 26
Pocklington 50 R 22
Point Lynas 40 H 22
Point of Ayr *Flintshire* 41 K 22
Point of Ayre *Isle of Man* 46 G 20
Polbain 83 D 9
Pole of Itlaw (The) 81 M 11
Polebrook 29 S 26
Polegate 12 U 31
Polesden Lacey 21 S 30
Polesworth 35 P 26
Polkerris 3 F 32
Polloch 72 D 13
Pollock House 60 H 16
Polmont 67 I 16
Polperro 3 G 33
Polruan 3 G 33
Polwarth 62 M 16
Pondersbridge 29 T 26
Pont-ar-Gothi 15 H 28
Pontardawe 17 I 28
Pontarddulais 15 H 28
Pontarfynach /
Devil's Bridge 25 I 26
Pontargothi 15 H 28
Pontarsais 15 H 28
Pontefract 44 Q 22
Ponteland 56 O 18
Ponterwyd 25 I 26
Pontesbury 34 L 26
Pontlottyn 18 K 28
Pontlyfni 32 G 24
Pontneddfechan 17 J 28
Pontrhydfendigaid 25 I 27
Pontrhydygroes 25 I 26
Pontrilas 26 L 28
Pontsticill 17 J 28
Pontyates 15 H 28
Pontyberem 15 H 28
Pontyclun 17 J 29
Pontycymer 17 J 29
Pontypool / Pontypwl 18 K 28
Pontypridd 17 J 29
Pontypwl / Pontypool 18 K 28
Poole 9 O 31
Poole Bay 9 O 31
Poolewe 78 D 10
Pooley Bridge 55 L 20
Pooltiel (Loch) 76 Z 11
Porlock 17 J 30
Port Appin 65 D 14
Port Askaig 58 B 16
Port Bannatyne 59 E 16
Port Carlisle 54 K 19
Port Charlotte 58 A 16
Port Driseach 65 E 16
Port Ellen 58 B 17
Port Erin 46 F 21
Port-Eynon 15 H 29
Port-Eynon Point 15 H 29
Port Gaverne 3 F 32
Port Glasgow 66 F 16
Port Henderson 77 C 10
Port Isaac 3 F 32
Port Lamont 59 E 16
Port Logan 52 F 19
Port Mór 71 B 13
Port of Menteith 67 H 15
Port of Ness 83 B 8
Port Ramsay 65 D 14
Port St. Mary 46 F 21
Port Talbot 17 I 29
Port William 52 G 19
Portavadie 59 E 16
Portchester 10 Q 31
Portencross 59 F 16
Portesham 5 M 31
Portgordon 80 K 11
Portgower 85 I 9
Porth 17 J 29
Porth Neigwl
or Hell's Mouth 32 G 25
Porth Tywyn /Burry Port 15 H 28
Porthaethwy /
Menai Bridge 40 H 23
Porthcawl 17 I 29
Porthcothan 2 E 32
Porthcurno 2 D 33
Porthgwarra 2 C 33
Porthkerry 17 K 29
Porthleven 2 E 33
Porthmadog 33 H 25
Porthtowan 2 E 33
Porthyrhyd 15 H 28
Portinnisherrich 65 E 15
Portishead 18 L 29
Portknockie 80 L 10
Portland (Isle of) 8 M 32
Portlethen 75 N 12
Portmahomack 79 I 10
Portmeirion 33 H 25
Portnacroish 72 D 14
Portnaguran 83 B 9
Portnahaven 58 A 16
Portnalong 77 A 12
Portobello 68 K 16
Portreath 2 E 33
Portree 77 B 11
Portscatho 3 F 33
Portskerra 85 I 8
Portskewett 18 L 29
Portslade 11 T 31
Portslogan 52 E 19
Portsmouth 10 Q 31
Portsoy 81 L 10
Portuairk 71 B 13
Postbridge 4 I 32
Potten End 21 S 28
Potter Heigham 39 Y 25
Potter Street 21 U 28
Potterhanworth 37 S 24
Potterne 19 N 30
Potters Bar 21 T 28
Potton 29 T 27
Poughill 6 G 31
Poulshot 19 N 29
Poulton 19 O 28
Poulton-le-Fylde 42 L 22
Poundstock 6 G 31
Powburn 63 O 17
Powerstock 8 L 31
Powick 27 N 27
Powis 34 K 26
Powmill 68 J 15
Poynings 11 T 31
Poynton 43 N 23
Praa Sands 2 D 33
Prawle Point 4 I 33
Praze-an-Beeble 2 E 33
Prees 34 M 25
Preesall 48 L 22
Prendwick 63 O 17
Prescot 42 L 23
Prestatyn 41 J 22
Prestbury *Cheltenham* 27 N 28
Prestbury *Macclesfield* 43 N 24
Presteigne 26 K 27
Preston
East Riding of Yorks. 45 T 22
Preston *Kent* 23 X 30
Preston *Lancs.* 42 L 22
Preston *Rutland* 36 R 26
Preston *West Sussex* 11 S 31
Preston Candover 10 Q 30
Preston Capes 28 Q 27
Prestonpans 69 L 16
Prestwich 42 N 23
Prestwick 60 G 17
Prestwood 20 R 28
Prickwillow 30 V 26
Priest Island 83 D 10
Priest Weston 34 K 26
Princes Risborough 20 R 28
Princethorpe 28 P 26
Princetown 4 I 32
Priors Marston 28 Q 27
Probus 3 F 33
Prosen (Glen) 74 K 13
Prudhoe 56 O 19
Puckeridge 29 U 28
Pucklechurch 19 M 29
Pucks Gutter 23 X 30
Puddletown 9 M 31
Pudsey 43 P 22
Pulborough 11 S 31
Pulford 34 L 24
Pulham 9 M 31
Pulham Market 31 X 26
Punchardon 7 H 30
Puncheston 24 F 28
Purbeck (Isle of) 9 N 32
Purbrook 10 Q 31
Purton 8 L 30
Purleigh 22 V 28
Purley 20 Q 29
Purse Caundle Manor 9 M 31
Purston Jaglin 43 P 22
Purton 19 O 29
Putsborough 6 H 30
Pwllheli 32 G 25
Pyecombe 11 T 31
Pyle 17 I 29
Pylle 8 M 30

Q

Quainton 28 R 28
Quantock Hills 8 K 30
Quarff 87 Q 3
Quarr 10 Q 31
Quatt 27 M 26
Quedgeley 19 N 28
Queen Camel 8 M 30
Queen Elizabeth
Forest Park 67 G 15
Queenborough 22 W 29
Queensbury 43 O 22
Queensferry 34 K 24
Quendon 30 U 28
Quenington 19 O 28
Quinag 84 E 9
Quines's Hill 46 G 21
Quinish Point 71 B 14
Quiraing 77 B 11
Quoich (Loch) 72 E 12
Quorndon 36 Q 25
Quothquan 61 J 17

R

Raasay (Island of) 77 B 11
Raasay (Sound of) 77 B 11
Raasay Ho 77 B 11
Rachub 33 H 24
Rackenford 7 J 31
Rackwick 86 J 7
Radcliffe 42 N 23
Radcliffe-on-Trent 36 Q 25
Radlett 21 T 28
Radley 20 Q 28
Radnor Forest 26 K 27
Radstock 18 M 30
Radyr 18 K 29
Rafford 80 J 11
Raglan 18 L 28
Ragley Hall 27 O 27
Rainford 42 L 23
Rainham 22 V 29
Rainworth 36 Q 24
Rait 68 K 14
Ramasaig 76 Z 11
Rampisham 8 M 31
Rampside 47 K 21
Rampton 44 R 24
Ramsbottom 42 N 23
Ramsbury 19 P 29
Ramsey *Cambs.* 29 T 26
Ramsey *Isle of Man* 46 G 21
Ramsey Bay 46 G 21
Ramsey Island 14 D 28
Ramsey St. Mary's 29 T 26
Ramsgate 23 Y 29
Ramsgill-in-Nidderdale 49 O 21
Ranby 44 Q 24
Ranfurly 60 G 16
Rangeworthy 18 M 29
Ranish 82 A 9
Rankinston 60 G 17
Rannoch (Loch) 73 H 13
Rannoch Moor 73 F 14
Rannoch Sta 73 G 13
Ranskill 44 Q 23
Ranton 35 N 25
Ranworth 39 Y 25
Rapness 87 L 6
Rappach 84 F 10
Ratby 36 Q 26
Rathen 81 O 11
Rathmell 49 N 21
Ratho 68 J 16
Ratlinghope 34 L 26
Rattlesden 30 W 27
Rattray 68 K 14
Rattray Head 81 O 11
Raunds 29 S 26
Ravenglass 47 J 20
Ravenscar 51 S 20
Ravensthorpe 28 Q 27
Ravenstone 36 P 25
Ravenstonedale 49 M 20
Ravensworth 49 O 20
Rawcliffe 44 R 22
Rawmarsh 44 P 23
Rawtenstall 42 N 22
Rayleigh 22 V 29
Rayne 30 V 28
Read 42 M 22
Reading 20 R 29
Rearsby 36 Q 25
Reay 85 I 8
Reay Forest 84 F 9
Reculver 23 X 29
Red Wharf Bay 40 H 23
Redbourn 21 S 28
Redbourne 44 S 23
Redbridge
London Borough 21 U 29
Redcar 57 Q 20
Redcliff Bay 18 L 29
Reddding 67 I 16
Redditch 27 O 27
Redesmouth 55 N 18
Redford 69 L 14
Redhill *North Somerset* 18 L 29
Redhill
Reigate and Banstead 21 T 30
Redisham 31 Y 26
Redmarley d'Abitot 27 M 28
Redmarshall 57 P 20
Redmire 49 O 21
Redpoint 77 C 11
Redruth 2 E 33
Redwick 18 L 29
Reedham 39 Y 26
Reekie Linn 74 K 13
Reepham 45 S 24
Reeth 49 O 20
Regarby 46 G 20
Reiff 83 D 9
Reigate 21 T 30
Reighton 51 T 21
Reiss 86 K 8
Relubbus 2 D 33
Rempstone 36 Q 25
Rendcomb 19 O 28
Rendham 31 Y 27
Renfrew 60 G 16
Renish Point 76 Z 10
Renishaw 44 P 24
Rennington 63 O 17
Renton 66 G 16
Renwick 55 M 19
Repton 36 P 25
Rescobie 75 L 14
Resipole 72 C 13
Resolven 17 I 28
Resort (Loch) 82 Z 9
Restalrig 68 K 16
Reston 63 N 16
Restormel Castle 3 G 32
Retford 44 R 24
Rettendon 22 V 29
Reynoldston 15 H 29
Rhaeadr / Rhayader 25 J 27
Rhaeadr Ddu 33 I 25
Rhandirmwyn 25 I 27
Rhayader / Rhaeadr 25 J 27
Rheidol (Vale of) 25 I 26
Rhenigidale 82 Z 10
Rhian 84 G 9
Rhiconich 84 F 8
Rhigos 17 J 28
Rhilochan 85 H 9
Rhinns of Galloway (The) 52 E 19
Rhinns of Kells 53 G 18
Rhondda 17 J 29
Rhoose 17 J 29
Rhos 17 I 28
Rhoscolyn 40 G 23
Rhoscrowther 14 E 28
Rhosllanerchrugog 34 K 24
Rhosmaen 25 I 28
Rhosneigr 40 G 23
Rhossili 15 H 29
Rhostyllen 34 K 24
Rhosybol 40 G 22
Rhu 66 F 15
Rhuddlan 41 J 23
Rhum 71 A 13
Rhuthun / Ruthin 34 K 24
Rhyd-Ddu 33 H 24
Rhydaman / Ammanford 15 I 28
Rhydcymerau 15 H 27
Rhydd 27 N 27
Rhyddhywel 25 J 26
Rhydowen 15 H 27
Rhyl 41 J 23
Rhymmi / Rhymney 18 K 28
Rhymney / Rhymmi 18 K 28
Rhynie 80 L 12
Ribble (River) 49 N 22
Ribblesdale 49 N 21
Ribchester 42 M 22
Riber Castle 36 P 24
Riccall 44 Q 22
Riccarton 60 G 17
Richards Castle 26 L 27
Richborough 23 X 30
Richmond 49 O 20
Richmond-upon-Thames
London Borough 21 T 29
Rickarton 75 N 13
Rickmansworth 21 S 29
Ridgeway Cross 27 M 27
Ridgeway Path (The) 20 P 29
Ridsdale 55 N 18
Rievaulx Abbey 50 Q 21
Rigg 77 B 11
Rigside 61 I 17
Rillington 51 R 21
Rimington 49 N 22
Rimsdale (Loch) 85 H 9
Ringford 53 H 19
Ringmer 11 U 31
Ringshall 30 W 27
Ringstead
East Northamptonshire 29 S 26
Ringstead *King's Lynn
and West Norfolk* 38 V 25

A B C D E F G H I J K L M N O P Q R S T U V W X Y Z

A B C D E F G H I J K L M N O P Q R S T U V W X Y Z

Ringwood ...... 9 O 31
Ringwould ...... 23 Y 30
Rinnes (Glen) ...... 80 K 11
Rinns of Islay ...... 58 A 16
Rinns Point ...... 58 A 16
Ripe ...... 12 U 31
Ripley *Derbs.* ...... 36 P 24
Ripley *North Yorks.* ...... 50 P 21
Ripley *Surrey* ...... 21 S 30
Riplingham ...... 44 S 22
Ripon ...... 50 P 21
Rippingale ...... 37 S 25
Ripponden ...... 43 O 22
Risabus ...... 58 B 17
Risby ...... 30 V 27
Risca ...... 18 K 29
Risegate ...... 37 T 25
Riseley ...... 29 S 27
Rishton ...... 42 M 22
Risplith ...... 50 P 21
Ristol (Isle) ...... 83 D 9
Roadside of Kinneff ...... 75 N 13
Roag ...... 77 A 11
Roag (Loch) ...... 82 Z 9
Roan of Graigoch ...... 60 F 18
Roberton
Dumfries and Galloway .... 61 I 17
Roberton
Scottish Borders ...... 62 L 17
Robertsbridge ...... 12 V 31
Robin Hood's Bay ...... 51 S 20
Roby ...... 42 L 23
Rocester ...... 35 O 25
Rochdale ...... 43 N 23
Roche ...... 3 F 32
Rochester ...... 22 V 29
Rochester
Northumberland ...... 63 N 18
Rochford ...... 22 W 29
Rock ...... 3 F 32
Rockcliffe *Cumbria* ...... 54 K 19
Rockcliffe
Dumfries and Galloway .... 53 I 19
Rockfield ...... 18 L 28
Rockingham ...... 28 R 26
Rode ...... 19 N 30
Rode Heath ...... 35 N 24
Rodel ...... 76 Z 10
Rodmel ...... 11 U 31
Rodney Stoke ...... 18 L 30
Rogart ...... 85 H 9
Rogerstone ...... 18 K 29
Rogiet ...... 18 L 29
Rokeby Hall ...... 49 O 20
Rolleston *Notts.* ...... 36 R 24
Rolleston-on-Dove *Staffs.* .... 35 P 25
Rolvenden ...... 12 V 30
Romannobridge ...... 61 J 16
Romiley ...... 43 N 23
Romney Marsh ...... 12 W 30
Romsey ...... 10 P 31
Romsley ...... 27 N 26
Rona (Island of) ...... 77 C 11
Ronaldsway ...... 46 G 21
Ronas Voe ...... 87 P 2
Ronay ...... 76 Y 11
Rookhope ...... 55 N 19
Roos ...... 45 T 22
Rootpark ...... 61 I 16
Ropley ...... 10 Q 30
Ropsley ...... 37 S 25
Rora ...... 81 O 11
Rora Head ...... 86 J 7
Rosedale Abbey ...... 50 R 20
Rosehearty ...... 81 N 10
Rosemarket ...... 16 F 28
Rosemarkie ...... 79 H 11
Rosewell ...... 61 K 16
Rosgill ...... 48 L 20
Roshven ...... 71 C 13
Rosley ...... 54 K 19
Roslin ...... 61 K 16
Rosliston ...... 35 P 25
Rosneath ...... 66 F 15
Ross
Berwick-upon-Tweed ...... 63 O 17
Ross
Dumfries and Galloway .... 53 H 19
Ross of Mull ...... 64 B 15
Ross-on-Wye ...... 26 M 28
Rossall Point ...... 48 K 22
Rossett ...... 34 L 24
Rosudgeon ...... 2 D 33
Rosyth ...... 68 J 15
Rothbury ...... 63 O 18
Rothbury Forest ...... 63 O 18
Rotherfield ...... 12 U 30

Rotherham ...... 43 P 23
Rothersthorpe ...... 28 R 27
Rothes ...... 80 K 11
Rothesay ...... 59 E 16
Rothienorman ...... 81 M 11
Rothiesholm ...... 87 M 6
Rothwell *Leeds.* ...... 43 P 22
Rothwell *Northamp.* ...... 28 R 26
Rotterspury ...... 28 R 27
Rottingdean ...... 11 T 31
Roughburn ...... 73 F 13
Roughsike ...... 55 L 18
Roughton ...... 39 X 25
Rounton ...... 50 P 20
Rousay ...... 86 K 6
Routh ...... 45 S 22
Rowardennan Lodge ...... 66 G 15
Rowington ...... 27 O 27
Rowland's Castle ...... 10 R 31
Rowland's Gill ...... 56 O 19
Rownhams ...... 10 P 31
Rowsley ...... 35 P 24
Roxburgh ...... 62 M 17
Roxwell ...... 22 V 28
Roy (Glen) ...... 72 F 13
Royal Leamington Spa ...... 28 P 27
Royal Military Academy ...... 20 R 29
Royal Tunbridge Wells ...... 12 U 30
Roybridge ...... 72 F 13
Roydon *Essex* ...... 21 U 28
Roydon *Norfolk* ...... 31 X 26
Royston *Herts.* ...... 29 T 27
Royston *South Yorks.* ...... 43 P 23
Royton ...... 43 N 23
Ruabon ...... 34 K 25
Ruan High Lanes ...... 3 F 33
Ruan Minor ...... 2 E 34
Ruardean ...... 18 M 28
Rubbha na Faing ...... 58 A 16
Rubha a' Mhail ...... 64 B 16
Rubha Còigeach ...... 83 D 9
Rubha Dubh ...... 70 Z 14
Rubha Hunish ...... 77 A 10
Rubha na h-Easgainne ...... 71 B 12
Rubha Réidh ...... 77 C 10
Rubha Suisnish ...... 71 B 12
Rubh'an Dùnain ...... 71 A 12
Rudbaxton ...... 24 F 28
Ruddington ...... 36 Q 25
Rudgeway ...... 18 M 29
Rudgwick ...... 11 S 30
Rudha Ban ...... 70 Y 12
Rudston ...... 51 T 21
Rufford Old Hall ...... 42 L 23
Rufforth ...... 50 Q 22
Rugby ...... 28 Q 26
Rugeley ...... 35 O 25
Rumburgh ...... 31 Y 26
Rumney ...... 18 K 29
Runcorn ...... 42 L 23
Runswick Bay ...... 50 R 20
Runtaleave ...... 74 K 13
Runwell ...... 22 V 29
Rushall ...... 19 O 30
Rushden ...... 29 S 27
Ruskington ...... 37 S 24
Rusland ...... 48 K 21
Rusper ...... 11 T 30
Ruspidge ...... 18 M 28
Rustington ...... 11 S 31
Ruswarp ...... 51 S 20
Rutherglen ...... 60 H 16
Ruthin / Rhuthun ...... 34 K 24
Ruthven *Aberdeenshire* ...... 80 L 11
Ruthven *Angus* ...... 74 K 14
Ruthven *Highland* ...... 79 I 11
Ruthven (Loch) ...... 79 H 12
Ruthven Barracks ...... 73 H 12
Ruthwell ...... 54 J 19
Rutland Water ...... 37 S 26
Ruyton
of the Eleven Towns ...... 34 L 25
Ryal ...... 56 O 18
Ryan (Loch) ...... 52 E 19
Rycote ...... 20 Q 28
Rydal ...... 48 L 20
Ryde ...... 10 Q 31
Rye ...... 12 W 31
Ryhall ...... 37 S 25
Ryhill ...... 43 P 23
Ryhope ...... 57 P 19
Ryton ...... 56 O 19

S

Sabden ...... 42 M 22
Sacriston ...... 56 P 19

Sadberge ...... 50 P 20
Saddell ...... 59 D 17
Saddell Bay ...... 59 D 17
Sadgill ...... 48 L 20
Saffron Walden ...... 30 U 27
Saham Toney ...... 38 W 26
St. Abbs ...... 63 N 16
St. Abb's Head ...... 63 N 16
St. Agnes ...... 2 E 33
St. Albans ...... 21 T 28
St. Aldhelm's Head ...... 9 N 32
St. Andrews ...... 69 L 14
St. Ann's ...... 54 J 18
St. Ann's Head ...... 14 E 28
St. Arvans ...... 18 L 29
St. Asaph ...... 41 J 23
St. Athan ...... 17 J 29
St. Austell ...... 3 F 32
St. Bees ...... 47 J 20
St. Bees Head ...... 47 J 20
St. Blazey ...... 3 F 32
St. Boswells ...... 62 M 17
St. Breock ...... 3 F 32
St. Breward ...... 3 F 32
St. Briavels ...... 18 M 28
St. Brides ...... 14 E 28
St. Bride's Bay ...... 14 E 28
St. Brides Major ...... 17 J 29
St. Brides-Super-Ely ...... 17 K 29
St. Bridge-Wentlooge ...... 18 K 29
St. Buryan ...... 2 D 33
St. Catherine's Point ...... 10 Q 32
St. Clears / Sanclêr ...... 15 G 28
St. Cleer ...... 3 G 32
St. Columb Major ...... 3 F 32
St. Combs ...... 81 O 11
St. Cyrus ...... 75 M 13
St. David's / Tyddewi ...... 14 E 28
St. David's Head ...... 14 D 28
St. Day ...... 2 E 33
St. Dennis ...... 3 F 32
St. Dogmaels ...... 15 F 27
St. Dominick ...... 3 H 32
St. Donats ...... 17 J 29
St. Endellion ...... 3 F 32
St. Erth ...... 2 D 33
St. Ewe ...... 3 F 33
St. Fagans ...... 18 K 29
St. Fergus ...... 81 O 11
St. Fillans ...... 67 H 14
St. Florence ...... 15 F 28
St. Gennys ...... 6 G 31
St. Germans ...... 3 H 32
St. Giles ...... 7 H 31
St. Giles-on-the-Heath ...... 6 H 31
St. Govan's Head ...... 16 F 29
St. Harmon ...... 25 J 26
St. Helen Auckland ...... 56 O 20
St. Helens *I.O.W.* ...... 10 Q 31
St. Helens *Merseyside* ...... 42 L 23
St. Helier *Jersey* 5
St. Ishmael's ...... 14 E 28
St. Issey ...... 3 F 32
St. Ive ...... 3 G 32
St. Ives *Cambs.* ...... 29 T 27
St. Ives *Cornwall* ...... 2 D 33
St. John's ...... 46 G 21
St. John's Chapel ...... 55 N 19
St. John's Loch ...... 86 J 8
St. Jude ...... 46 G 20
St. Just ...... 2 C 33
St. Just in Roseland ...... 2 F 33
St. Keverne ...... 2 E 33
St. Kew ...... 3 F 32
St. Leonards *Dorset* ...... 9 O 31
St. Leonards *East Sussex* .... 12 V 31
St. Mabyn ...... 3 F 32
St. Magnus Bay ...... 87 P 2
St. Margaret's at Cliffe ...... 23 Y 30
St. Margaret's Bay ...... 23 Y 30
St. Margaret's Hope ...... 87 L 7
St. Mark's ...... 46 G 21
St. Martin's ...... 34 K 25
St. Mary in the Marsh ...... 12 W 30
St. Mary's *Orkney Islands* ... 86 L 7
St. Mary's
Perth and Kinross ...... 73 I 14
St. Mary's-Bay ...... 13 W 30
St. Mary's-Hoo ...... 22 V 29
St. Mary's Loch ...... 61 K 17
St. Mawes ...... 2 F 33
St. Mawgan ...... 3 F 32
St. Mellion ...... 3 H 32
St. Mellons ...... 18 K 29
St. Merryn ...... 3 F 32
St. Michael Penkevil ...... 2 E 33
St. Michael's Mount ...... 2 D 33

St. Michaels-on-Wyre ...... 42 L 22
St. Minver ...... 3 F 32
St. Monans ...... 69 L 15
St. Neot ...... 3 G 32
St. Neots ...... 29 T 27
St. Nicholas *Pembrokes* ... 14 E 28
St. Nicholas
Vale of Glamorgan ...... 17 K 29
St. Nicholas-at-Wade ...... 23 X 29
St. Ninian's Isle ...... 87 P 4
St. Osyth ...... 23 X 28
St. Patrick's Isle ...... 46 F 21
St. Paul's Walden ...... 29 T 28
St. Peter Port *Guernsey* ... 5
St. Peter's ...... 23 Y 29
St. Pool ...... 4 I 33
St. Stephen ...... 3 F 32
St. Teath ...... 3 F 32
St. Tudwal's Islands ...... 32 G 25
St. Tudy ...... 3 F 32
St. Vigeans ...... 69 M 14
St. Wenn ...... 3 F 32
St. Weonards ...... 26 L 28
Salcombe ...... 4 I 33
Salcombe Regis ...... 5 K 31
Sale ...... 42 N 23
Salehurst ...... 12 V 31
Salen *Argyll and Bute* ...... 65 C 14
Salen *Highland* ...... 71 C 13
Salford ...... 42 N 23
Salfords ...... 21 T 30
Salhouse ...... 39 Y 25
Saline ...... 68 J 15
Salisbury ...... 9 O 30
Salisbury Plain ...... 19 O 30
Sallachy
Ben More Assybt ...... 84 G 9
Sallachy
near Kyle of Lochalsh ... 78 D 12
Saltash ...... 3 H 32
Saltburn ...... 79 H 10
Saltburn-by-the-Sea ...... 57 R 20
Saltcoats ...... 59 F 17
Saltfleet ...... 45 U 23
Saltford ...... 18 M 29
Salthouse ...... 38 X 25
Saltney ...... 34 L 24
Salton ...... 50 R 21
Samala ...... 76 X 11
Samlesbury Old Hall ...... 42 M 22
Sampford Courtenay ...... 7 I 31
Sampford Peverell ...... 7 J 31
Sanaigmore ...... 58 A 16
Sanclêr / St. Clears ...... 15 G 28
Sancreed ...... 2 D 33
Sancton ...... 44 S 22
Sand Side ...... 47 K 21
Sanda Island ...... 59 D 18
Sanday *Highland* ...... 71 A 12
Sanday *Orkney Islands* .... 87 M 6
Sandbach ...... 35 M 24
Sandbank ...... 66 F 16
Sandbanks ...... 9 O 31
Sandend ...... 80 L 10
Sandford *Eden* ...... 49 M 20
Sandford *Mid Devon* ...... 7 J 31
Sandford *North Somerset* ... 18 L 30
Sandford
South Lanarkshire ...... 60 H 17
Sandford Orcas ...... 8 M 31
Sandgate ...... 13 X 30
Sandgreen ...... 53 H 19
Sandhaven ...... 81 N 10
Sandhead ...... 52 F 19
Sandhurst *Berks.* ...... 20 R 29
Sandhurst *Kent* ...... 12 V 30
Sandleigh ...... 20 Q 28
Sandlins ...... 31 Y 27
Sandness ...... 87 P 3
Sandon
North Hertfordshire ...... 29 T 28
Sandon *Stafford* ...... 35 N 25
Sandown ...... 10 Q 32
Sandray ...... 70 X 13
Sandridge ...... 21 T 28
Sandringham House ...... 38 V 25
Sandsend ...... 51 R 20
Sandwell ...... 27 O 26
Sandwich ...... 23 Y 30
Sandwick *Eilean Siar* ...... 76 Y 11
Sandwick *Shetland Islands* ..87 Q 4
Sandwood Loch ...... 84 E 8
Sandy ...... 29 T 27
Sandygate ...... 46 G 20
Sandyhills ...... 53 I 19

Sanna ...... 71 B 13
Sanquhar ...... 61 I 17
Santon Downham ...... 30 W 26
Santon Head ...... 46 G 21
Sapperton ...... 19 N 28
Saracen's Head ...... 37 T 25
Sarclet ...... 86 K 8
Sarisbury ...... 10 Q 31
Sark *Channel I.* 5
Sarn Meyllteyrn ...... 32 G 25
Sarre ...... 23 X 29
Satley ...... 56 O 19
Satterthwaite ...... 48 K 21
Sauchen ...... 75 M 12
Saughall ...... 42 L 24
Saughtree ...... 62 L 18
Saundersfoot ...... 15 F 28
Saunderton ...... 20 R 28
Sawbridgeworth ...... 21 U 28
Sawrey ...... 48 L 20
Sawston ...... 29 U 27
Sawtry ...... 29 T 26
Saxby ...... 36 R 25
Saxilby ...... 44 S 24
Saxlingham Nethergate ...... 39 X 26
Saxmundham ...... 31 Y 27
Saxtead Green ...... 31 X 27
Scadavay (Loch) ...... 76 Y 11
Scaddle (Glen) ...... 72 D 13
Scafell Pikes ...... 47 K 20
Scagglethorpe ...... 50 R 21
Scalasaig ...... 64 B 15
Scalby ...... 51 S 21
Scaleby ...... 55 L 19
Scalford ...... 36 R 25
Scalloway ...... 87 Q 3
Scalpay *Highland* ...... 77 C 12
Scalpay *Western Isles* ...... 77 A 10
Scamblesby ...... 45 T 24
Scampton ...... 44 S 24
Scaniport ...... 79 H 11
Scapa Flow ...... 86 K 7
Scarba ...... 65 C 15
Scarborough ...... 51 S 21
Scarcliffe ...... 44 Q 24
Scardroy ...... 78 F 11
Scarfskerry ...... 86 K 8
Scarisbrick ...... 42 L 23
Scarista ...... 76 Y 10
Scarp ...... 82 Y 9
Scavaig (Loch) ...... 71 B 12
Scawby ...... 44 S 23
Schiehallion ...... 73 H 13
Scilly (Isles of) ...... 2 B 34
Scone Palace ...... 68 J 14
Scopwick ...... 37 S 24
Scoraig ...... 83 D 10
Scorton ...... 50 P 20
Scotby ...... 55 L 19
Scotch-Corner ...... 49 P 20
Scothern ...... 45 S 24
Scotlandwell ...... 68 K 15
Scotney ...... 12 V 30
Scotstown ...... 72 D 13
Scotter ...... 44 S 23
Scotton *Harrogate* ...... 50 P 21
Scotton *Richmondshire* ...... 49 O 20
Scottow ...... 39 Y 25
Scourie ...... 84 E 8
Scousburgh ...... 87 Q 4
Scrabster ...... 85 J 8
Scraptoft ...... 36 Q 26
Scredington ...... 37 S 25
Scridain (Loch) ...... 64 B 14
Scruton ...... 50 P 21
Sculthorpe ...... 38 W 25
Scunthorpe ...... 44 S 23
Sea Palling ...... 39 Y 25
Seaford ...... 12 U 31
Seaforth (Loch) ...... 82 Z 10
Seaforth Head ...... 82 A 9
Seagrave ...... 36 Q 25
Seaham ...... 57 P 19
Seale ...... 21 R 30
Sealga (Loch na) ...... 78 D 10
Seamer *Hambleton* ...... 50 Q 20
Seamer *Scarborough* ...... 51 S 21
Seamill ...... 59 F 16
Seasalter ...... 23 X 29
Seascale ...... 47 J 20
Seaton *Allerdale* ...... 53 J 20
Seaton *East Devon* ...... 5 K 31
Seaton Carew ...... 57 Q 20
Seaton Delaval ...... 56 P 18
Seaton Delaval Hall ...... 56 P 18
Seaton Ross ...... 44 R 22
Seaton Sluice ...... 56 P 18

Seave Green ...... 50 Q 20
Seaview ...... 10 Q 31
Sebergham ...... 54 L 19
Sedbergh ...... 49 M 21
Sedgebrook ...... 36 R 25
Sedgley ...... 27 N 26
Sedlescombe ...... 12 V 31
Seend ...... 19 N 29
Seething ...... 39 Y 26
Seighford ...... 35 N 25
Seil (Isle of) ...... 65 D 15
Seilich (Loch an t-) ...... 73 H 13
Selattyn ...... 34 K 25
Selborne ...... 10 R 30
Selby ...... 44 Q 22
Selker Bay ...... 47 J 21
Selkirk ...... 62 L 17
Sellindge ...... 13 W 30
Selmeston ...... 12 U 31
Selsey ...... 10 R 31
Selston ...... 36 Q 24
Selworthy ...... 17 J 30
Semley ...... 9 N 30
Senghenydd ...... 18 K 29
Sennen ...... 2 C 33
Sennybridge ...... 25 J 28
Sessay ...... 50 Q 21
Seven Sisters
East Sussex ...... 12 U 31
Seven Sisters
Neath and Port Talbot ... 17 I 28
Sevenhampton ...... 27 O 28
Sevenoaks ...... 22 U 30
Severn (River) ...... 27 M 28
Severn Bridge ...... 18 M 29
Severn Stoke ...... 27 N 27
Sgibacleit (Loch) ...... 82 A 9
Sgiwen ...... 17 I 29
Sgurr Mór ...... 78 E 10
Shader ...... 82 A 8
Shaftesbury ...... 9 N 30
Shalbourne ...... 20 P 29
Shaldon ...... 4 J 32
Shalfleet ...... 10 P 31
Shalford ...... 21 S 30
Shandon ...... 66 F 15
Shanklin ...... 10 Q 32
Shap ...... 48 L 20
Shapinsay ...... 87 L 6
Shapwick ...... 8 L 30
Shardlow ...... 36 P 25
Shareston ...... 43 P 23
Sharnbrook ...... 29 S 27
Sharnford ...... 28 Q 26
Sharperton ...... 63 N 18
Sharpness ...... 18 M 28
Shavington ...... 34 M 24
Shaw *Gtr. Mches.* ...... 43 N 23
Shaw *West Berkshire* ...... 20 P 29
Shaw *Wilts.* ...... 19 N 29
Shawbost ...... 82 Z 9
Shawbury ...... 34 M 25
Shawford ...... 10 Q 30
Shawhead ...... 53 I 18
Shebbear ...... 6 H 31
Shebster ...... 85 I 8
Sheepwash ...... 6 H 31
Sheepy Magna ...... 36 P 26
Sheering ...... 22 U 28
Sheerness ...... 22 W 29
Sheffield ...... 43 P 23
Sheffield Park ...... 11 T 31
Shefford ...... 29 S 27
Sheldon *Birm.* ...... 19 N 29
Sheldon *Derbs.* ...... 19 N 29
Sheldon Manor ...... 19 N 29
Sheldwich ...... 22 W 30
Shell or Sealg (Loch) ...... 82 A 9
Shellingford ...... 20 P 29
Shelsley Beauchamp ...... 27 M 27
Shelton *Rushcliffe* ...... 36 R 25
Shelton *South Norfolk* ...... 31 X 26
Shelton Lock ...... 36 P 25
Shelve ...... 34 L 26
Shenley Church End ...... 28 R 27
Shenstone ...... 27 O 26
Shenval ...... 80 K 11
Shepley ...... 43 O 23
Sheppey (Isle of) ...... 22 W 29
Shepreth ...... 29 U 27
Shepshed ...... 36 Q 25
Shepton Mallet ...... 18 M 30
Sherborne *Cotswold* ...... 19 O 28
Sherborne *West Dorset* ...... 8 M 31
Sherborne St. John ...... 20 Q 30
Sherburn *Durham* ...... 56 P 19

Sherburn *Ryedale* .....51 S 21
Sherburn-in-Elmet .....44 Q 22
Shere .....21 S 30
Sherfield English .....9 P 31
Sheriff Hutton .....50 Q 21
Sheriffhales .....35 M 25
Sheringham .....39 X 25
Sherington .....28 R 27
Shernborne .....38 V 25
Sherston .....19 N 29
Sherwood Forest .....36 Q 24
Shetland Islands 87
Shevington .....42 L 23
Shiant (Sound of) .....82 A 10
Shiant Island .....82 A 10
Shiel (Glen) .....72 D 12
Shiel (Loch) .....72 D 13
Shieldaig *Loch Gairloch* .....78 C 10
Shieldaig *Loch Torridon* .....78 D 11
Shieldaig (Loch) .....78 C 11
Shieldhill .....67 I 16
Shifnal .....35 M 25
Shilbottle .....63 O 17
Shildon .....56 P 20
Shillay .....76 W 11
Shillingford .....7 J 30
Shillingstone .....9 N 31
Shillington .....29 S 28
Shilton *Rugby* .....28 P 26
Shilton *West Oxfordshire* .....19 P 28
Shimpling .....31 X 26
Shin (Loch) .....84 G 9
Shiney Row .....56 P 19
Shinfield .....20 R 29
Shipdham .....38 W 26
Shiplake .....20 R 29
Shipley *Salop* .....35 N 26
Shipley *West Yorks.* .....43 O 22
Shipston-on-Stour .....27 P 27
Shipton *Bridgnorth* .....26 M 26
Shipton *Cotswold* .....27 O 28
Shipton *Hambleton* .....50 Q 21
Shipton Moyne .....19 N 29
Shipton-under-Wychwood .....19 P 28
Shiptonthorpe .....44 R 22
Shira (Lochan) .....66 F 14
Shirebrook .....36 Q 24
Shiremoor .....56 P 18
Shirenewton .....18 L 29
Shirley *Derbyshire* .....35 O 25
Shirley *Solihull* .....27 O 26
Shoadoxhurst .....12 W 30
Shobdon .....26 L 27
Shoeburyness .....22 W 29
Shoreham .....11 T 31
Shorne .....22 V 29
Shotesham .....39 X 26
Shotley Bridge .....56 O 19
Shotley Gate .....31 X 28
Shottenden .....22 W 30
Shottermill .....10 R 30
Shotton Colliery .....57 P 19
Shotts .....61 I 16
Shouldham .....38 V 26
Shrewsbury .....34 L 25
Shrewton .....19 O 30
Shrivenham .....19 P 29
Shuna Sound .....65 D 15
Shurdington .....27 N 28
Shurrery .....85 J 8
Sibbertoft .....28 Q 26
Sibford Ferris .....28 P 27
Sible Hedingham .....30 V 28
Sibsey .....37 U 24
Sidbury .....5 K 31
Siddington .....19 O 28
Siddlington .....43 N 24
Sidford .....5 K 31
Sidinish .....76 Y 11
Sidlaw Hills .....68 K 14
Sidlesham .....10 R 31
Sidmouth .....5 K 31
Sighthill .....68 K 16
Sileby .....36 Q 25
Silecroft .....47 K 21
Silkstone .....43 P 23
Silloth .....54 J 19
Silsden .....49 O 22
Silver End .....30 V 28
Silverdale *Lancaster* .....48 L 21
Silverdale
  Newcastle-under-Lyme .....35 N 24
Silverstone .....28 Q 27
Silverstone Circuit .....28 Q 27
Silverton .....7 J 31
Simonburn .....55 N 18
Simonsbath .....7 I 30

Sinclair's Bay .....86 K 8
Sinclairston .....60 G 17
Singleton *Chichester* .....10 R 31
Singleton *Fylde* .....42 L 22
Sionascaig (Loch) .....84 E 9
Sissinghurst .....12 V 30
Sithney .....2 E 33
Sittingbourne .....22 W 29
Sixpenny Handley .....9 N 31
Skara Brae .....86 J 6
Skares .....60 H 17
Skeabost .....77 B 11
Skegness .....38 V 24
Skellingthorpe .....44 S 24
Skelmanthorpe .....43 P 23
Skelmersdale .....42 L 23
Skelmorlie .....59 F 16
Skelpick .....85 H 8
Skelton *Cleveland* .....50 R 20
Skelton *Cumbria* .....55 L 19
Skelwith Bridge .....48 K 20
Skene .....75 M 12
Skene (Loch of) .....75 M 12
Skenfrith .....26 L 28
Skeroblingarry .....59 D 17
Skerray .....85 H 8
Skervuile Lighthouse .....65 C 16
Skidby .....44 S 22
Skiddaw .....54 K 20
Skigersta .....83 B 8
Skilgate .....7 J 30
Skillington .....37 S 25
Skinburness .....54 J 19
Skipness .....59 D 16
Skipport (Loch) .....76 Y 12
Skipsea .....51 T 22
Skipton .....49 N 22
Skipton-on-Swale .....50 P 21
Skipwith .....44 R 22
Skirlaugh .....45 T 22
Skirling .....61 J 17
Skirwith .....55 M 19
Skirza .....86 K 8
Skokholm Island .....14 E 28
Skomer Island .....14 E 28
Skye (Isle of) .....77 B 12
Slaggyford .....55 M 19
Slaidburn .....49 M 22
Slaithwaite .....43 O 23
Slamannan .....67 I 16
Slapin (Loch) .....71 B 12
Slapton .....4 J 33
Sleaford .....37 S 25
Sleagill .....48 M 20
Sleat (Sound of) .....71 C 12
Sledmere .....51 S 21
Sleekburn .....56 P 18
Sleights .....51 S 20
Slickly .....86 K 8
Sligachan .....77 B 12
Sligachan (Loch) .....77 B 12
Slimbridge .....19 M 28
Slindon .....11 S 31
Slingsby .....50 R 21
Slochd .....79 I 12
Slockavullin .....65 D 15
Slough .....21 S 29
Sloy (Loch) .....66 F 15
Slumbay .....78 D 11
Slyne .....48 L 21
Smailholm .....62 M 17
Smailholm Tower .....62 M 17
Small Dole .....11 T 31
Small Hythe .....12 W 30
Smallfield .....11 T 30
Smarden .....12 W 30
Smart'Hill .....12 U 30
Smedmore .....9 N 32
Smithfield .....55 L 19
Snaefell .....46 G 21
Snainton .....51 S 21
Snaith .....44 Q 22
Snape .....31 Y 27
Snetterton Circuit .....30 W 26
Snettisham .....38 V 25
Snitterfield .....27 O 27
Snizort (Loch) .....77 A 11
Snodland .....22 V 30
Snowdon / Yr Wyddfa .....33 H 24
Snowdonia National Park .....33 I 24
Snowshill .....27 O 27
Soa .....70 Z 14
Soa Island .....64 A 15
Soar (River) .....36 Q 25
Soay .....71 B 12
Soay Sound .....71 B 12
Soham .....30 V 26

Solent (The) .....10 Q 31
Solihull .....27 O 26
Sollas .....76 X 11
Solva .....14 E 28
Solway Firth .....53 J 19
Somerby .....36 R 25
Somercotes .....36 P 24
Somerford Keynes .....19 O 29
Somersham
  Huntingdonshire .....29 U 26
Somersham *Mid Suffolk* .....31 X 27
Somerton *Norfolk* .....39 Y 25
Somerton *Oxon.* .....28 Q 28
Somerton *Somerset* .....8 L 30
Sompting .....11 S 31
Sonning Common .....20 R 29
Sopley .....9 O 31
Sorbie .....52 G 19
Sorisdale .....71 A 13
Sorn .....60 H 17
Sortat .....86 K 8
Soulby .....49 M 20
Sound (The) .....4 H 32
Sourhope .....63 N 17
South-Alloa .....67 I 15
South Balloch .....60 G 18
South Brent .....4 I 32
South Cairn .....52 E 19
South Carrine .....59 C 18
South Cave .....44 S 22
South Cerney .....19 O 28
South Charlton .....63 O 17
South Croxton .....36 R 25
South Downs .....11 R 31
South Elmsall .....44 Q 23
South Esk (River) .....75 L 13
South Ferriby .....44 S 22
South Foreland .....23 Y 30
South Glendale .....70 Y 12
South Hanningfield .....22 V 29
South Harris .....76 Z 10
South Harris Forest .....82 Z 10
South Hayling .....10 R 31
South-Heighton .....11 U 31
South Hetton .....56 P 19
South Kelsey .....45 S 23
South Killingholme .....45 T 23
South Kirkby .....44 Q 23
South Kyme .....37 T 24
South Lancing .....11 T 31
South Leverton .....44 R 24
South Lopham .....30 X 26
South-Marston .....19 O 29
South Mary Bourne .....20 P 30
South Mimms .....21 T 28
South Molton .....7 I 30
South Morar .....72 C 13
South Moreton .....20 Q 29
South Newington .....28 P 28
South-Newton .....9 O 30
South Normanton .....36 P 24
South Ockendon .....22 U 29
South Otterington .....50 P 21
South Oxhey .....21 S 29
South Petherton .....8 L 31
South Petherwin .....3 G 32
South Queensferry .....68 J 16
South Rauceby .....37 S 25
South Raynham .....38 W 25
South Ronaldsay .....87 L 7
South Shields .....56 P 19
South Shore .....42 K 22
South Stack .....40 F 23
South Stainley .....50 P 21
South Tawton .....4 I 31
South Thoresby .....45 U 24
South Uist .....70 X 12
South Walls .....86 K 7
South Warnborough .....20 R 30
South Witham .....37 S 25
South Woodham Ferrers .....22 V 29
South Wootton .....38 V 25
South Wraxall .....19 N 29
South Zeal .....4 I 31
Southam
  Stratford-on-Avon .....28 P 27
Southam *Tewkesbury* .....27 N 28
Southampton .....10 P 31
Southborough .....12 U 30
Southbourne *Dorset* .....9 O 31
Southbourne *West Sussex* .....10 R 31
Southend .....59 D 18
Southend-on-Sea .....22 W 29
Southerness .....53 J 19
Southery .....38 V 26
Southill .....29 T 27
Southminster .....22 W 29

Southport .....42 K 23
Southrop .....19 O 28
Southsea .....10 Q 31
Southwaite .....55 L 19
Southwater .....11 S 30
Southwell .....36 R 24
Southwick
  East Northamptonshire .....29 S 26
Southwick *Sunderland* .....56 P 19
Southwick *West Sussex* .....11 T 31
Southwick *Wilts.* .....19 N 30
Southwick *Widley* .....10 Q 31
Southwold .....31 Z 27
Sowerby Bridge .....43 O 22
Spalding .....37 T 25
Spaldwick .....29 S 26
Spanish Head .....46 F 21
Sparkford .....8 M 30
Spaxton .....8 K 30
Spean (Glen) .....73 F 13
Spean Bridge .....72 F 13
Speeton .....51 T 21
Speldhurst .....12 U 30
Spelsbury .....28 P 28
Spelve (Loch) .....65 C 14
Spennymoor .....56 P 19
Spey (River) .....73 G 12
Spey Bay .....80 K 10
Speymouth Forest .....80 K 11
Spilsby .....37 U 24
Spinningdale .....79 H 10
Spithead .....10 Q 31
Spittal *Dumfries*
  and Galloway .....52 G 19
Spittal *Highland* .....85 J 8
Spittal *Northumb.* .....63 O 16
Spittal *Pembrokeshire /*
  Sir Benfro .....24 F 28
Spittal of Glenshee .....74 J 13
Spixworth .....39 X 25
Spofforth .....50 P 22
Spondon .....36 P 25
Spooner Row .....39 X 26
Spott .....69 M 16
Spreyton .....7 I 31
Spridlington .....44 S 23
Springfield .....68 K 15
Springholm .....53 I 18
Sproatley .....45 T 22
Sprotbrough .....44 Q 23
Sproughton .....31 X 27
Sprouston .....62 M 17
Sprowston .....39 X 26
Spurn Head .....45 U 23
Sronlairig Lodge .....73 G 12
Sronphadruig Lodge .....73 H 13
Stack (Loch) .....84 F 8
Stack Island .....70 Y 12
Stack Rocks .....16 E 29
Staffa .....64 A 14
Staffin Bay .....77 B 11
Stafford .....35 N 25
Stagsden .....29 S 27
Staincross .....43 P 23
Staindrop .....56 O 20
Staines .....21 S 29
Stainforth *North Yorks.* .....49 N 21
Stainforth *South Yorks.* .....44 Q 23
Stainton .....55 L 20
Stainton-le-Vale .....45 T 23
Staintondale .....51 S 20
Stair *Allerdale* .....54 K 20
Stair *South Ayrshire* .....60 G 17
Staithes .....50 R 20
Stakeford .....56 P 18
Stalbridge .....9 M 31
Stalham .....39 Y 25
Stalisfield .....22 W 30
Stalling Busk .....49 N 21
Stallingborough .....45 T 23
Stalmine .....48 L 22
Stalybridge .....43 N 23
Stamford .....37 S 26
Stamford Bridge .....50 R 22
Stamfordham .....56 O 18
Stanbridge .....29 S 28
Standford-in-the-Vale .....20 P 29
Standing Stones .....82 Z 9
Standish .....42 M 23
Standlake .....20 P 28
Standon .....29 U 28
Stane .....61 I 16
Stanford .....13 X 30
Stanford-le-Hope .....22 V 29
Stanford-on-Avon .....28 Q 26
Stanghow .....50 R 20
Stanhoe .....38 W 25

Stanhope .....55 N 19
Stanion .....29 S 26
Stanley *Durham* .....56 O 19
Stanley
  Perthshire and Kinross .....68 J 14
Stanley *Wakefield* .....43 P 22
Stanmer Park .....11 T 31
Stannington .....43 P 23
Stansted Abbotts .....21 U 28
Stansted Mountfitchet .....30 U 28
Stanton .....30 W 27
Stanton Harcourt .....20 P 28
Stanton Long .....26 M 26
Stanton-upon-Hine-Heath .....34 M 25
Stanway .....27 O 28
Stanwell .....21 S 29
Stanwick .....29 S 27
Staple Fitzpaine .....8 K 31
Stapleford *Melton* .....36 R 25
Stapleford *Notts.* .....36 Q 25
Stapleford *Wilts.* .....9 O 30
Staplehurst .....22 V 30
Starcross .....4 J 32
Start Point .....4 J 33
Startforth .....49 O 20
Stathern .....36 R 25
Staughton Highway .....29 S 27
Staunton *Forest of Dean* .....27 N 28
Staunton *Monmouthshire /*
  Sir Fynwy .....18 M 28
Staveley *Cumbria* .....48 L 20
Staveley *Derbs.* .....43 P 24
Staxigoe .....86 K 8
Staxton .....51 S 21
Staylittle .....25 J 26
Staythorpe .....36 R 24
Steart .....18 K 30
Stebbing .....30 V 28
Stedham .....10 R 31
Steep .....10 R 30
Steeple .....22 W 28
Steeple Ashton .....19 N 30
Steeple Aston .....28 Q 28
Steeple Barton .....28 P 28
Steeple Bumpstead .....30 V 27
Steeple Claydon .....28 R 28
Steeple Langford .....9 O 30
Steeple Morden .....29 T 27
Steeton .....49 O 22
Stelling Minnis .....23 X 30
Stenhousemuir .....67 I 15
Stenness *Orkney Islands* .....86 K 7
Stenness *Shetland Islands* .....87 P 2
Stenton .....69 M 16
Steppingley .....29 S 27
Stevenage .....29 T 28
Stevenston .....60 F 17
Steventon .....20 Q 29
Stewartby .....29 S 27
Stewarton .....60 G 16
Stewkley .....28 R 28
Steyning .....11 T 31
Steynton .....16 E 28
Stichill .....62 M 17
Sticker .....3 F 33
Sticklepath .....4 I 31
Stickney .....37 U 24
Stiffkey .....38 W 25
Stilligarry .....76 X 12
Stillingfleet .....44 Q 22
Stillington *Hambleton* .....50 Q 21
Stillington
  Stockton-on-Tees .....56 P 20
Stilton .....29 T 26
Stirling .....67 I 15
Stithians .....2 E 33
Stob Choire Claurigh .....72 F 13
Stobo .....61 K 17
Stobs Castle .....62 L 17
Stock .....22 V 29
Stocke Talmage .....20 Q 28
Stockland .....8 K 31
Stockland Bristol .....18 K 30
Stockport .....43 N 23
Stocksbridge .....43 P 23
Stocksfield .....56 O 19
Stockton Heath .....42 M 23
Stockton-on-Tees .....50 P 20
Stockton-on-Teme .....27 M 27
Stockton on the Forest .....50 R 22
Stoer .....83 D 9
Stogumber .....7 K 30
Stogursey .....18 K 30
Stoke .....22 V 29
Stoke Albany .....28 R 26
Stoke Ash .....31 X 27
Stoke-by-Nayland .....30 W 28

Stoke Climsland .....3 H 32
Stoke Fleming .....4 J 33
Stoke Gabriel .....4 J 32
Stoke Goldington .....28 R 27
Stoke Hammond .....28 R 28
Stoke Lacy .....26 M 27
Stoke Lyne .....28 Q 28
Stoke Mandeville .....20 R 28
Stoke-on-Trent .....35 N 24
Stoke Orchard .....27 N 28
Stoke Poges .....21 S 29
Stoke-St. Mary .....8 K 31
Stoke-St. Michael .....18 M 30
Stoke St. Milborough .....26 M 26
Stoke sub Hamdon .....8 L 31
Stokeham .....44 R 24
Stokenchurch .....20 R 29
Stokenham .....4 I 33
Stokesay .....26 L 26
Stokesley .....50 Q 20
Stone *Bucks.* .....20 R 28
Stone *Staffs.* .....35 N 25
Stone Edge .....36 P 24
Stonehaugh .....55 N 18
Stonehaven .....75 N 13
Stonehenge .....9 O 30
Stonehouse *Glos.* .....19 N 28
Stonehouse
  South Lanarkshire .....61 I 16
Stoneleigh .....28 P 26
Stonesfield .....20 P 28
Stoney Cross .....9 P 31
Stoney Stanton .....36 Q 26
Stoneybridge .....76 X 12
Stoneykirk .....52 F 19
Stoneywood .....75 N 12
Stony Stratford .....28 R 27
Stornoway .....82 A 9
Storr (The) .....77 B 11
Storrington .....11 S 31
Stort (River) .....29 U 28
Stotfold .....29 T 27
Stottesdon .....26 M 26
Stoughton .....10 R 31
Stoul .....72 C 13
Stoulton .....27 N 27
Stour (River)
  English Channel .....9 N 31
Stour (River) *North Sea* .....30 V 27
Stour (River) *R. Severn* .....27 N 26
Stourbridge .....27 N 26
Stourhead House .....9 N 30
Stourport-on-Severn .....27 N 26
Stourton Caundle .....9 M 31
Stow .....62 L 16
Stow-on-the-Wold .....27 O 28
Stowbridge .....38 V 26
Stowe-by-Chartley .....35 O 25
Stowe School .....28 Q 27
Stowmarket .....30 W 27
Stowupland .....30 X 27
Straad .....59 E 16
Strachan .....75 M 12
Strachur .....66 E 15
Stradbroke .....31 X 27
Stradishall .....30 V 27
Stradsett .....38 V 26
Straiton .....60 G 18
Straloch .....74 J 13
Stranraer .....52 E 19
Strata Florida Abbey .....25 I 27
Stratfield Saye .....20 Q 29
Stratford St. Mary .....30 W 28
Stratford-upon-Avon .....27 O 27
Strath Brora .....85 H 9
Strath Dearn .....79 I 11
Strath Halladale .....85 I 8
Strath Isla .....80 K 11
Strath More .....78 F 10
Strath Mulzie .....78 F 10
Strath of Kildonan .....85 I 9
Strath Oykel .....84 F 10
Strath Skinsdale .....85 H 9
Strath Tay .....68 J 14
Strathallan .....67 I 15
Strathan .....72 E 13
Strathardle .....74 J 13
Strathaven .....60 H 16
Strathbeg (Loch of) .....81 O 11
Strathblane .....67 H 16
Strathbogie .....80 L 11
Strathbraan .....67 I 14
Strathcanaird .....84 E 10
Strathcarron .....78 D 11
Strathcoil .....65 C 14
Strathconon .....78 F 11
Strathconon Forest .....78 F 11

A
B
C
D
E
F
G
H
I
J
K
L
M
N
O
P
Q
R
S
T
U
V
W
X
Y
Z

Strathearn ....67 I 14
Stratherick ....73 G 12
Strathkinness ....69 L 14
Strathmashie ....73 H 13
Strathmiglo ....68 K 15
Strathmore ....75 M 13
Strathnairn ....79 H 11
Strathnaver ....85 H 8
Strathpeffer ....79 G 11
Strathrannoch ....79 F 10
Strathspey ....75 M 13
Strathvaich Lodge ....78 F 10
Strathy ....85 I 8
Strathy Point ....85 H 8
Strathyre ....67 H 15
Stratton Cornwall ....6 G 31
Stratton Glos. ....19 O 28
Stratton West Dorset ....5 M 31
Stratton Audley ....28 Q 28
Stratton-on-the-Fosse ....18 M 30
Stratton-St. Margaret ....19 O 29
Streatley ....20 Q 29
Street ....8 L 30
Strensall ....50 Q 21
Stretford ....42 N 23
Stretham ....30 U 26
Stretton Cheshire ....42 M 23
Stretton Staffs. ....35 N 25
Stretton-on-Dunsmore ....28 P 26
Strichen ....81 N 11
Striven (Loch) ....66 E 16
Stroma (Island of) ....86 K 7
Stromeferry ....78 D 11
Stromemore ....78 D 11
Stromness ....86 K 7
Stronachlachar ....66 G 15
Stronchreggan ....72 E 13
Stronchrubie ....84 F 9
Strone ....66 F 16
Stronmilchan ....66 F 14
Stronsay ....87 M 6
Stronsay Firth ....87 L 6
Strontian ....72 D 13
Stroud ....19 N 28
Strumble Head ....14 E 27
Stuart Castel ....79 H 11
Stuartfield ....81 N 11
Stubbington ....10 Q 31
Studland ....9 O 32
Studley Warw. ....27 O 27
Studley Wilts. ....19 N 29
Studley Royal Gardens ....50 P 21
Stuley ....76 Y 12
Sturminster Marshall ....9 N 31
Sturminster Newton ....9 N 31
Sturry ....23 X 30
Sturton-le-Steeple ....44 R 23
Suainaval (Loch) ....82 Z 9
Sudbourne ....31 Y 27
Sudbury Derbs. ....35 O 25
Sudbury Suffolk ....30 W 27
Sudbury Hall ....35 O 25
Sudeley Castle ....27 O 28
Sùil Ghorm ....71 A 13
Sulby ....46 G 21
Sulgrave ....28 Q 27
Sulhamstead ....20 Q 29
Sullom ....87 P 2
Sullom Voe ....87 P 2
Sully ....18 K 29
Sumburgh ....87 Q 4
Sumburgh Roost ....87 P 4
Summer Island ....83 D 9
Summerbridge ....49 O 21
Summercourt ....3 F 32
Sunart ....72 D 13
Sunart (Loch) ....71 C 13
Sunbury ....21 S 29
Sunderland ....57 P 19
Sunderland Bridge ....56 P 19
Sunk Island ....45 T 23
Sunningdale ....21 S 29
Sunninghill ....21 S 29
Surfleet ....37 T 25
Surlingham ....39 Y 26
Sutterton ....37 T 25
Sutton Bassetlaw ....44 R 23
Sutton Cambs. ....29 U 26
Sutton Guildford ....21 S 30
Sutton Shrops. ....34 M 25
Sutton London Borough ....21 T 29
Sutton Bank ....50 Q 21
Sutton Benger ....19 N 29
Sutton Bonington ....36 Q 25
Sutton Bridge ....37 U 25
Sutton Cheney ....36 P 26
Sutton Coldfield ....35 O 26

Sutton Courtenay ....20 Q 29
Sutton-in-Ashfield ....36 Q 24
Sutton-on-Hull ....45 T 22
Sutton-on-Sea ....45 U 24
Sutton-on-the-Forest ....50 Q 21
Sutton-on-the-Hill ....35 P 25
Sutton-on-Trent ....36 R 24
Sutton Scotney ....10 P 30
Sutton St. Edmund ....37 U 25
Sutton St. James ....37 U 25
Sutton-St. Nicholas ....26 L 27
Sutton
    under Whitestonecliffe ....50 Q 21
Sutton Valence ....22 V 30
Sutton Veny ....9 N 30
Swadlincote ....36 P 25
Swaffham ....38 W 26
Swaffham Bulbeck ....30 U 27
Swainby ....50 Q 20
Swainswick ....19 M 29
Swale (River) ....50 P 21
Swale (The) ....22 W 29
Swale Dale ....49 O 20
Swallow ....45 T 23
Swallowcliffe ....9 N 30
Swallow Falls ....33 I 24
Swallowfield ....20 R 29
Swanage ....9 O 32
Swanbridge ....18 K 29
Swanland ....44 S 22
Swanley ....22 U 29
Swannery ....5 M 32
Swanscombe ....22 U 29
Swansea / Abertawe ....17 I 29
Swanton Abbot ....39 Y 25
Swanton Morley ....38 W 25
Swanwick ....36 P 24
Swarbacks Minn ....87 P 2
Swavesey ....29 T 27
Sway ....9 P 31
Swaythling ....10 P 31
Swimbridge ....7 I 30
Swinbrook ....19 P 28
Swinderby ....36 R 24
Swindon Cheltenham ....27 N 28
Swindon Swindon ....19 O 29
Swinefleet ....44 R 22
Swineshead ....37 T 25
Swinford ....28 Q 26
Swingfield ....23 X 30
Swinton Rotherham. ....44 Q 23
Swinton Scottish Borders ....63 N 16
Swynnerton ....35 N 25
Swyre ....5 M 31
Sydenham ....20 R 28
Syderstone ....38 W 25
Sydling St. Nicholas ....8 M 31
Sykehouse ....44 Q 23
Symbister ....87 Q 2
Symington South Ayrshire ....60 G 17
Symington
    South Lanarkshire ....61 J 17
Symonds Yat ....18 M 28
Symonds Yat Rock ....18 M 28
Symondsbury ....5 L 31
Syresham ....28 Q 27
Syston ....36 Q 25
Sywell ....28 R 27

T

Tackley ....28 Q 28
Tadcaster ....44 Q 22
Taddington ....43 O 24
Tadley ....20 Q 29
Tadmarton ....28 P 27
Tadworth ....21 T 30
Taff (River) ....18 K 29
Taibach ....17 I 29
Tain ....79 H 10
Takeley ....30 U 28
Tal-y-bont Dyfed ....25 I 26
Tal-y-Bont Gwynedd ....33 H 25
Tal-y-Cafn ....41 I 23
Tal-y-Llyn Lake ....33 I 25
Talacre ....41 K 22
Talaton ....7 K 31
Talgarreg ....15 H 27
Talgarth ....26 K 28
Talke ....35 N 24
Talladale ....78 D 10
Tallaminnock ....60 G 18
Talley ....25 I 28
Talsarnau ....33 H 25
Talwrn ....40 H 23
Talybont-on-Usk Powys ....26 K 28
Talywern ....33 I 26

Tamanavay (Loch) ....82 Y 9
Tamar (River) ....6 G 31
Tamerton Foliot ....4 H 32
Tamworth ....35 O 26
Tan Hill ....49 N 20
Tan-y-pistill ....33 J 25
Tanera Beg ....83 D 9
Tanera Mór ....83 D 9
Tangley ....20 P 30
Tangmere ....11 R 31
Tannach ....86 K 8
Tannadice ....74 L 13
Tantallon Castle ....69 M 15
Taransay ....82 Y 10
Taransay (Sound of) ....82 Z 10
Tarbat Ness ....79 I 10
Tarbert Argyll and Bute ....59 D 16
Tarbert Gigha Island ....65 C 16
Tarbert Western Isles ....82 Z 10
Tarbert (Loch) ....65 C 16
Tarbet Argyll and Bute ....66 F 15
Tarbet Highland ....72 D 13
Tarbolton ....60 G 17
Tardy Gate ....42 L 22
Tarfside ....74 L 13
Tarland ....74 L 12
Tarleton ....42 L 22
Tarn (The) ....48 L 20
Tarporley ....34 M 24
Tarrant Gunville ....9 N 31
Tarrant Hinton ....9 N 31
Tarrant Keyneston ....9 N 31
Tarrington ....26 M 27
Tarskavaig ....71 C 12
Tarskavaig Point ....71 B 12
Tarves ....81 N 11
Tarvin ....34 L 24
Tathwell ....45 T 24
Tattersett ....38 W 25
Tattershall ....37 T 24
Tatton Hall ....42 M 24
Taunton ....8 K 30
Taunton Deane ....7 K 30
Taverham ....39 X 25
Tavernspite ....15 G 28
Tavistock ....4 H 32
Taw (River) ....7 I 31
Tay (Firth of) ....68 K 14
Tay (Loch) ....67 H 14
Tay Road Bridge ....69 L 14
Taynton ....27 M 28
Taynuilt ....65 E 14
Tayport ....69 L 14
Tayvallich ....65 D 15
Teacuis (Loch) ....71 C 14
Tealby ....45 T 23
Teangue ....71 C 12
Tebay ....48 M 20
Tedburn St. Mary ....4 I 31
Teddington ....27 N 28
Tees (River) ....50 P 20
Teesdale ....55 N 20
Teifi (River) ....15 G 27
Teignmouth ....4 J 32
Telford ....34 M 25
Teme (River) ....27 M 27
Templand ....54 J 18
Temple ....61 K 16
Temple Ewell ....23 X 30
Temple Grafton ....27 O 27
Temple Sowerby ....55 M 20
Templeton ....15 F 28
Tempsford ....29 T 27
Tenbury Wells ....26 M 27
Tenby / Dinbych-y-pysgod ....15 F 28
Tendring ....31 X 28
Tenterden ....12 W 30
Terling ....22 V 28
Tern Hill ....34 M 25
Terrington St. Clement ....38 U 25
Test (River) ....20 P 30
Tetbury ....19 N 29
Tetford ....45 T 24
Tetney ....45 T 23
Tetsworth ....20 Q 28
Tettenhall ....35 N 26
Tewin ....21 T 28
Tewkesbury ....27 N 28
Texa ....58 B 17
Teynham ....22 W 30
Thakeham ....11 S 31
Thame ....20 R 28
Thame (River) ....20 R 28
Thames (River) ....21 S 29
Thanet (Isle of) ....23 Y 29
Thankerton ....61 J 17
Thatcham ....20 Q 29

Thaxted ....30 V 28
Theale Berks. ....20 Q 29
Theale Somerset ....18 L 30
Theddlethorpe St. Helen ....45 U 23
Thetford ....30 W 26
Theviothead ....62 L 17
Theydon Bois ....21 U 28
Thirlestane ....62 L 16
Thirlspot ....48 K 20
Thirsk ....50 P 21
Thistleton ....37 S 25
Thixendale ....51 R 21
Thompson ....38 W 26
Thomshill ....80 K 11
Thoralby ....49 N 21
Thoresway ....45 T 23
Thorganby ....44 R 22
Thornaby-on-Tees ....50 Q 20
Thornborough ....28 R 28
Thornbury Heref. ....26 M 27
Thornbury South Glos. ....18 M 29
Thornbury Torridge ....6 H 31
Thornby ....28 Q 26
Thorncombe ....8 L 31
Thorne ....44 R 23
Thorner ....43 P 22
Thorney ....37 T 26
Thornford ....8 M 31
Thornham ....38 V 25
Thornhill
    Dumfries and Galloway ....61 I 18
Thornhill Stirling ....67 H 15
Thornton Fife ....68 K 15
Thornton Lancs. ....42 K 22
Thornton Curtis ....45 S 23
Thornton-in-Craven ....49 N 22
Thornton-le-Dale ....51 R 21
Thorntonloch ....69 M 16
Thornyhive Bay ....75 N 13
Thorpe Derbs. ....35 O 24
Thorpe Essex ....22 W 29
Thorpe-le-Soken ....31 X 28
Thorpe-on-the-Hill ....37 S 24
Thorpe Thewles ....57 P 20
Thorpeness ....31 Y 27
Thorrington ....31 X 28
Thorverton ....7 J 31
Thrapston ....29 S 26
Threapwood ....34 L 24
Three Cocks ....26 K 27
Three Crosses ....15 H 29
Threekingham ....37 S 25
Threlkeld ....54 K 20
Threlstone ....36 P 25
Throckley ....56 O 19
Thropton ....63 O 18
Throwleigh ....4 I 31
Thrumster ....86 K 8
Thruxton Circuit ....20 P 30
Thrybergn ....44 Q 23
Thundersley ....22 V 29
Thurcroft ....44 Q 23
Thurgarton ....36 R 24
Thurgoland ....43 P 23
Thurlby ....37 S 25
Thurlestone ....4 I 33
Thurlow ....30 V 27
Thurlton ....39 Y 26
Thurmaston ....36 Q 25
Thurne ....39 Y 25
Thurnham ....22 V 30
Thurnscoe ....44 Q 23
Thursby ....54 K 19
Thurso ....85 J 8
Thurstaston ....42 K 23
Thurstonfield ....54 K 19
Thurton ....39 Y 26
Thwaite ....49 N 20
Tibbermore ....68 J 14
Tibberton Glos. ....27 M 28
Tibberton Salop ....34 M 25
Tibberton Wychavon ....27 N 27
Tibshelf ....36 P 24
Ticehurst ....12 V 30
Tickhill ....44 Q 23
Ticknall ....36 P 25
Tideswell ....43 O 24
Tidworth ....19 P 30
Tigerton ....75 L 13
Tigharry ....76 X 11
Tighnabruaich ....65 E 16
Tilbury ....22 V 29
Tillathrowie ....80 L 11
Tillicoultry ....67 I 15
Tillington ....11 S 31
Tilney St. Lawrence ....38 U 25

Tilshead ....19 O 30
Tilstock ....34 L 25
Tilt (Glen) ....73 I 13
Tilton-on-the-Hill ....36 R 26
Timberscombe ....7 J 30
Timsbury ....18 M 30
Timsgarry ....82 Y 9
Tingewick ....28 Q 28
Tingwall (Loch) ....87 P 3
Tintagel ....6 F 32
Tintern Abbey ....18 L 28
Tintinhull ....8 L 31
Tintwistle ....43 O 23
Tinwald ....53 J 18
Tipton ....27 N 26
Tipton-St. john ....5 K 31
Tiptree ....22 W 28
Tirabad ....25 J 27
Tiree ....64 Z 14
Tirga Mór ....82 Z 10
Tirley ....27 N 28
Tiroran ....65 B 14
Tisbury ....9 N 30
Titchfield ....10 Q 31
Titchmarsh ....29 S 26
Tiumpan Head ....83 B 9
Tiverton Chester ....34 L 24
Tiverton Mid Devon ....7 J 31
Tobermory ....71 B 14
Toberonochy ....65 D 15
Tobson ....82 Z 9
Tockwith ....50 Q 22
Todber ....9 N 31
Toddington ....29 S 28
Todenham ....27 P 27
Todmorden ....43 N 22
Toe Head ....76 Y 10
Togston ....63 P 18
Tokavaig ....71 C 12
Toll of Birness ....81 O 11
Toller Porcorum ....8 M 31
Tollerton ....50 Q 21
Tollesbury ....22 W 28
Tolleshunt d'Arcy ....22 W 28
Tolpuddle ....9 N 31
Tolquhon Castle ....81 N 11
Tolsta Chaolais ....82 Z 9
Tolsta Head ....83 B 8
Tomatin ....79 I 11
Tombreck ....79 H 11
Tomcrasky ....72 F 12
Tomdoun ....72 E 12
Tomich ....78 F 12
Tomintoul ....74 J 12
Tomnavoulin ....80 K 12
Tomsléibhe ....65 C 14
Tonbridge ....22 U 30
Tondu ....17 J 29
Tong ....82 A 9
Tongham ....20 R 30
Tongland ....53 H 19
Tongue ....84 G 8
Tongwynlais ....18 K 29
Tonna ....17 I 28
Tonypandy ....17 J 29
Tonyrefail ....17 J 29
Topcliffe ....50 P 21
Topsham ....4 J 31
Tor Ness ....86 K 7
Torbay ....4 J 32
Torcross ....4 J 33
Torksey ....44 R 24
Torlundy ....72 E 13
Tormarton ....19 N 29
Tornapress ....78 D 11
Tornaveen ....75 M 12
Torness ....79 G 12
Torphichen ....67 J 16
Torphins ....75 M 12
Torpoint ....3 H 32
Torquay ....4 J 32
Torquhan ....62 L 16
Torridon (Loch) ....77 C 11
Torrin ....71 B 12
Torrisdale Bay ....85 H 8
Torthorwald ....53 J 18
Tortworth ....19 M 29
Torver ....48 K 20
Toscaig ....77 C 11
Totaig Loch Alsh ....78 D 12
Totaig Loch Dunvegan ....77 A 11
Totland ....10 P 31
Totley ....43 P 24
Totnes ....4 I 32
Toton ....36 Q 25
Totscore ....77 A 11

Totternhoe ....29 S 28
Totton ....10 P 31
Tournaig ....78 D 10
Tow Law ....56 O 19
Towcester ....28 R 27
Tower Hamlets
    London Borough ....21 T 29
Towie ....74 L 12
Town Yetholm ....62 N 17
Towneley Hall ....43 N 22
Townhead ....53 H 19
Townhead of Greenlaw ....53 I 19
Tradespark ....79 I 11
Trallwng / Welshpool ....34 K 26
Tranent ....69 L 16
Trapp ....25 I 28
Traquair House ....61 K 17
Trawden ....43 N 22
Trawsfynydd ....33 I 25
Trealaval (Loch) ....82 A 9
Trearddur Bay ....40 G 23
Trecastle ....25 J 28
Trecwn ....24 F 28
Tredington ....27 P 27
Treen ....2 D 33
Trefaldwyn / Montgomery ....34 K 26
Trefeglwys ....25 J 26
Treffynnon / Holywell ....41 K 23
Trefil ....18 K 28
Trefnant ....41 J 23
Trefonen ....34 K 25
Trefor ....40 G 23
Trefyclawdd / Knighton ....26 K 26
Trefynwy / Monmouth ....18 L 28
Tregaron ....25 I 27
Tregony ....3 F 33
Tregurrian ....2 E 32
Tregynon ....33 J 26
Treharris ....18 K 29
Treherbert ....17 J 28
Treig (Loch) ....73 F 13
Trelawnyd ....41 J 23
Trelech ....15 G 28
Trelech a'r Betws ....15 G 28
Trelissick Gardens ....2 E 33
Trelleck ....18 L 28
Tremadog ....33 H 25
Tremadog Bay ....32 H 25
Trenance ....2 E 32
Trengwainton Garden ....2 D 33
Trent ....8 M 31
Trent (River) ....36 R 24
Trentham ....35 N 25
Treorchy ....17 J 29
Trerice ....2 E 32
Treshnish Isles ....64 A 14
Treshnish Point ....71 A 14
Tressait ....73 I 13
Tretower ....26 K 28
Treuddyn ....34 K 24
Trevine ....14 E 28
Trevone ....3 F 32
Trevose Head ....2 E 32
Trewithen ....3 F 33
Trimdon ....56 P 19
Trimley Heath ....31 X 28
Trimsaran ....15 H 28
Tring ....21 R 28
Trispen ....2 E 33
Trochry ....67 J 14
Troedyrhiw ....17 J 28
Trollamarig (Loch) ....82 Z 10
Tromie (Glen) ....73 H 12
Troon ....60 G 17
Trossachs (The) ....67 G 15
Trotternish ....77 B 11
Troutbeck Eden ....54 L 20
Troutbeck South Lakeland ....48 L 20
Trowbridge ....19 N 30
Trudoxhill ....19 M 30
Trull ....8 K 31
Trumpington ....29 U 27
Trunch ....39 Y 25
Truro ....2 E 33
Trusthorpe ....45 U 24
Trwyn Cilan ....32 G 25
Tuath (Loch) ....64 B 14
Tuddenham Forest Heath ....30 V 27
Tuddenham
    Suffolk Coastal ....31 X 27
Tudhoe ....56 P 19
Tudweiliog ....32 G 25
Tugford ....26 M 26
Tulla (Loch) ....66 F 14
Tullibardine ....67 I 15

Tullibody ....67 I 15
Tullymurdoch ....74 K 14
Tumble ....15 H 28
Tummel (Loch) ....73 I 13
Tunstall
  East Riding of Yorkshire ...45 T 22
Tunstall Staffs. ....35 N 24
Tunstall Suffolk ....31 Y 27
Tur Langton ....36 R 26
Turnberry ....59 F 18
Turnditch ....35 P 24
Turret
  (Loch and Reservoir) ......67 I 14
Turriff ....81 M 11
Turvey ....29 S 27
Tusker Rock ....17 I 29
Tutbury ....35 O 25
Tuxford ....44 R 24
Twatt ....86 K 6
Tweed (River) ....61 J 17
Tweeddale ....61 J 17
Tweedmouth ....63 N 16
Tweedsmuir Hills ....61 J 17
Twemlow Green ....35 N 24
Twickenham ....21 S 29
Two Dales ....35 P 24
Twyford Berks. ....20 R 29
Twyford Hants. ....10 Q 30
Twyford Leics. ....36 R 25
Twynholm ....53 H 19
Twynllanan ....25 I 28
Tydd-St. Giles ....37 U 25
Tydd St. Mary ....37 U 25
Tyddewi / St. David's .....14 E 28
Tyldesley ....42 M 23
Tylorstown ....17 J 29
Tyne (River) ....56 P 19
Tynehead ....62 L 16
Tynemouth ....56 P 18
Tynewydd ....17 J 28
Tynron ....53 I 18
Tythegston ....17 J 29
Tytherington ....18 M 29
Tywardreath ....3 F 32
Tywi (River) ....25 I 27
Tywyn ....33 H 26

U

Ubiey ....18 L 30
Uckfield ....11 U 31
Uddingston ....60 H 16
Udimore ....12 V 31
Uffculme ....7 K 31
Uffington ....37 S 26
Ufford ....31 Y 27
Ugadale Bay ....59 D 17
Ugborough ....4 I 32
Ugbrooke House ....4 J 32
Ugthorpe ....50 R 20
Uig Highland ....77 A 11
Uig Western Isles ....82 Y 9
Uisg (Loch) ....65 C 14
Uiskevagh (Loch) ....76 Y 11
Ulbster ....86 K 8
Ulceby East Lindsey ......45 U 24
Ulceby North Lincolnshire ...45 T 23
Ulcombe ....22 V 30
Uldale ....54 K 19
Uley ....19 N 28
Ulgham ....56 P 18
Ullapool ....78 E 10
Ulleskelf ....44 Q 22
Ullesthorpe ....28 Q 26
Ullinish ....77 A 11
Ullock ....54 J 20
Ullswater ....48 L 20
Ulpha ....47 K 21
Ulsta ....87 Q 2
Ulva ....64 B 14
Ulverston ....48 K 21
Unapool ....84 E 9
Union Mills ....46 G 21
Unst ....87 R 1
Upavon ....19 O 30
Upchurch ....22 V 29
Uphall ....68 J 16
Uphill ....18 L 30
Upleadon ....27 M 28
Uplyme ....5 L 31
Upper Arley ....27 M 26
Upper Badcall ....84 E 9
Upper Beeding ....11 T 31
Upper Bighouse ....85 I 8
Upper Broughton ....36 R 25
Upper Chapel ....25 J 27
Upper Chute ....20 P 30

Upper Dicker ....12 U 31
Upper Hale ....20 R 30
Upper Heyford ....28 Q 28
Upper Hindhope ....62 M 17
Upper Knockando ....80 J 11
Upper Loch Torridon ......78 D 11
Upper Poppleton ....50 Q 22
Upper Sandaig ....72 D 12
Upper Tean ....35 O 25
Uppertown ....86 K 7
Uppingham ....36 R 26
Upton Dorset ....9 N 31
Upton Notts. ....36 R 24
Upton Vale of White Horse ..20 Q 29
Upton Wakefield ....44 Q 23
Upton West Somerset ......7 J 30
Upton Grey ....20 Q 30
Upton House ....28 P 27
Upton Magna ....34 M 25
Upton Noble ....9 M 30
Upton Scudamore ....19 N 30
Upton-upon-Severn ....27 N 27
Upwell ....38 U 26
Upwood ....29 T 26
Urchfont ....19 O 30
Ure (River) ....50 Q 21
Urigill (Loch) ....84 F 9
Urmston ....42 M 23
Urquhart ....80 K 11
Urquhart (Glen) ....79 G 11
Urquhart Castle ....79 G 12
Urrahag (Loch) ....82 A 8
Ushaw Moor ....56 P 19
Usk / Brynbuga ....18 L 28
Usk (River) ....18 K 28
Uttoxeter ....35 O 25
Uyea ....87 R 2
Uyeasound ....87 R 1

V

Vallay Strand ....76 X 11
Valle Crucis ....34 K 25
Valley ....40 G 23
Valtos ....82 Z 9
Vatersay ....70 X 13
Vatten ....77 A 11
Ve Skerries ....87 O 2
Venachar (Loch) ....67 H 15
Ventnor ....10 Q 32
Verham Dean ....20 P 30
Verulamium ....21 S 28
Verwood ....9 O 31
Veryan ....3 F 33
Veyatie (Loch) ....84 E 9
Vindolanda ....55 M 19
Voe ....87 Q 2
Voil (Loch) ....67 G 14
Vowchurch ....26 L 27
Vyrnwy (Lake) ....33 J 25

W

Waddesdon ....20 R 28
Waddingham ....44 S 23
Waddington Lancs. ....42 M 22
Waddington Lincs. ....37 S 24
Wadebridge ....3 F 32
Wadhurst ....12 U 30
Wag ....85 I 9
Wainfleet All Saints ....38 U 24
Wainstalls ....43 O 22
Wakefield ....43 P 22
Wakerley ....37 S 26
Wakes Colne ....30 W 28
Walberswick ....31 Y 27
Walcott ....37 T 24
Walden Head ....49 N 21
Walderslade ....22 V 29
Waldringfield ....31 X 27
Waldron ....12 U 31
Walesby ....44 R 24
Walford ....34 L 25
Walgherton ....34 M 24
Walgrave ....28 R 26
Walkden ....42 M 23
Walkeringham ....44 R 23
Walkern ....29 T 28
Wall ....35 O 26
Wallace Monument ....67 I 15
Wallasey ....42 K 23
Wallend ....22 W 29
Wallingford ....20 Q 29
Wallington House ....56 O 18
Walls ....87 P 3
Wallsend ....56 P 18
Wallyford ....69 K 16
Walney (Isle of) ....47 K 21
Walpole ....31 Y 27

Walpole St. Andrew ....38 U 25
Walpole St. Peter ....38 U 25
Walsall ....35 O 26
Walsden ....43 N 22
Walsham le Willows ....30 W 27
Walshford ....50 P 22
Walston ....61 J 16
Waltham Kent ....23 X 30
Waltham North East Lincs. ..45 T 23
Waltham Abbey ....21 U 28
Waltham Forest
  London Borough ....21 T 29
Waltham-on-the-Wolds ....36 R 25
Walton Carlisle ....55 L 19
Walton Leeds ....50 Q 22
Walton Powys ....26 K 27
Walton-East ....24 F 28
Walton-in-Gordano ....18 L 29
Walton-le-Dale ....42 M 22
Walton-on-Thames ....21 S 29
Walton-on-the-Naze ....31 X 28
Walton-Upon-Trent ....35 O 25
Walworth ....49 P 20
Wanborough ....19 O 29
Wandsworth
  London Borough ....21 T 29
Wangford ....31 Y 26
Wanlockhead ....61 I 17
Wansford
  East Riding of Yorkshire ...51 S 22
Wansford Peterborough ....37 S 26
Wanstrow ....9 M 30
Wantage ....20 P 29
Wappenham ....28 Q 27
Warboys ....29 T 26
Warbstow ....6 G 31
Warcop ....49 M 20
Wardington ....28 Q 27
Wardour Castle ....9 N 30
Ware ....21 T 28
Wareham ....9 N 31
Wargrave ....20 R 29
Wark near Coldstream ....63 N 17
Wark near Hexham ....55 N 18
Wark Forest ....55 M 18
Warkworth ....63 P 17
Warley ....27 O 26
Warlingham ....21 T 30
Warmington
  East Northamptonshire ...29 S 26
Warmington
  Stratford-on-Avon ....28 P 27
Warminster ....19 N 30
Warmsworth ....44 Q 23
Warmwell ....9 M 31
Warnborough ....20 R 30
Warnford ....10 Q 30
Warnham ....11 S 30
Warren ....43 N 24
Warren (The) ....13 X 30
Warrington ....42 M 23
Warsash ....10 Q 31
Warslow ....35 O 24
Warsop ....36 Q 24
Warter ....51 R 22
Warton Alnwick ....63 O 18
Warton near Morecambe ...48 L 21
Warton near Preston ....42 L 22
Warwick ....27 P 27
Warwick Bridge ....55 L 19
Wasbister ....86 K 6
Wasdale Head ....47 K 20
Wash (The) ....38 U 25
Washington
  Tyne and Wear ....56 P 19
Washington West Sussex ..11 S 31
Wast Water ....47 K 20
Watchet ....17 K 30
Watchfield ....19 P 29
Watchgate ....48 L 20
Water Orton ....27 O 26
Waterbeach ....30 U 27
Waterbeck ....54 K 18
Watergate Bay ....2 E 32
Waterhead ....74 L 13
Waterhouses ....35 O 24
Wateringbury ....22 V 30
Waterlooville ....10 Q 31
Waternish Point ....77 A 11
Waters Upton ....34 M 25
Waterside ....60 G 17
Waterstein ....76 Z 11
Watford Daventry ....28 Q 27
Watford Watford ....21 S 29
Wath ....50 P 21
Wath-upon-Dearne ....44 P 23
Watlington ....20 Q 29

Watten ....85 K 8
Watton Breckland ....38 W 26
Watton
  East Riding of Yorkshire ...51 S 22
Watton at Stone ....29 T 28
Waunfawr ....33 H 24
Waveney (River) ....31 Y 26
Waverton Allerdale ....54 K 19
Waverton Chester ....34 L 24
Wawne ....45 S 22
Wear (River) ....56 O 20
Weardale ....55 N 19
Weasenham St. Peter ......38 W 25
Weaver (River) ....34 M 24
Weaverthorpe ....51 S 21
Wedmore ....18 L 30
Wednesbury ....35 N 26
Wednesfield ....35 N 26
Weedon-Bec ....28 Q 27
Week St. Mary ....6 G 31
Weeley ....31 X 28
Weem ....73 I 14
Weeting ....30 V 26
Weeton ....42 L 22
Welburn ....50 R 21
Welby ....37 S 25
Welcombe ....6 G 31
Welford Daventry ....28 Q 26
Welford Stratford-on-Avon ..27 O 27
Welford West Berkshire ....20 P 29
Welham Green ....21 T 28
Well ....50 P 21
Welland ....27 N 27
Welland (River) ....37 T 25
Wellesbourne ....27 P 27
Wellingborough ....29 R 27
Wellington
  Herefordshire ....26 L 27
Wellington Salop ....34 M 25
Wellington Somerset ....8 K 31
Wellow
  Bath and North East ......19 M 30
Wellow
  Newark and Sherwood ...36 R 24
Wells ....18 M 30
Wells-next-the-Sea ....38 W 25
Wells of Ythan ....81 M 11
Welney ....38 U 26
Welsh Newton ....26 L 28
Welshampton ....34 L 25
Welshpool / Trallwng ......34 K 26
Welton Allerdale ....54 K 19
Welton Daventry ....28 Q 27
Welton West Lindsey ....44 S 24
Welton-le-Wold ....45 T 23
Welwyn ....21 T 28
Welwyn Garden City ....21 T 28
Wem ....34 L 25
Wembdon ....8 K 30
Wembley ....21 T 29
Wembury ....4 H 33
Wembworthy ....7 I 31
Wemyss Bay ....59 F 16
Wendens Ambo ....30 U 27
Wendlebury ....28 Q 28
Wendover ....20 R 28
Wendron ....2 E 33
Wenlock Edge ....26 L 26
Wennington ....48 M 21
Wensley ....49 O 21
Wensleydale ....49 O 21
Wentbridge ....44 Q 23
Wentnor ....26 L 26
Wentworth ....43 P 23
Wenvoe ....18 K 29
Weobley
  Hereford and Worcester ..26 L 27
Wereham ....38 V 26
Werrington ....6 G 32
West Alvington ....4 I 33
West Auckland ....56 O 20
West-Barns ....69 M 16
West Bay ....8 M 32
West Bergholt ....30 W 28
West-Bradenham ....38 W 26
West Bridgford ....36 Q 25
West Bromwich ....27 O 26
West-Buckland
  North Devon ....7 I 30
West-Buckland
  Taunton Deane ....8 K 31
West Butterwick ....44 R 23
West Calder ....61 J 16
West Camel ....8 M 30
West Charleton ....4 I 33
West Chevington ....63 P 18
West Chiltington ....11 S 31

West-Chinnock ....8 L 31
West Coker ....8 L 31
West Dean ....9 P 30
West-Dereham ....38 V 26
West End ....10 Q 31
West Farleigh ....22 V 30
West-Felton ....34 L 25
West-Firle ....11 U 31
West Geirinish ....76 X 11
West Grinstead ....11 T 31
West Hanningfield ....22 V 28
West Harptree ....18 M 30
West Heath ....20 R 30
West Heslerton ....51 S 21
West-Hill ....5 K 31
West Hoathly ....11 T 30
West-Huntspill ....18 L 30
West Kilbride ....59 F 16
West Kingsdown ....22 U 29
West Kirby ....41 K 22
West Langwell ....85 H 9
West Lavington ....19 O 30
West Linton ....61 J 16
West Loch Roag ....82 Z 9
West Loch Tarbert
  Argyll and Bute ....59 D 16
West Loch Tarbert
  Western Isles ....82 Z 10
West Looe ....3 G 32
West Lulworth ....9 N 32
West Lutton ....51 S 21
West Malling ....22 V 30
West Malvern ....27 M 27
West Meon ....10 Q 30
West Mersea ....22 W 28
West Moors ....9 O 31
West-Overton ....19 O 29
West Putford ....6 G 31
West-Quantoxhead ....8 K 30
West Rainton ....56 P 19
West Runton ....39 X 25
West Stafford ....9 M 31
West Strathan ....84 G 8
West Tanfield ....50 P 21
West-Tarbert ....59 D 16
West Thorney ....10 R 31
West Town ....18 L 29
West-Tytherley ....9 P 30
West Walton ....37 U 25
West Wellow ....9 P 31
West Wickam ....21 T 29
West Winch ....38 V 25
West Wittering ....10 R 31
West Witton ....49 O 21
West Woodburn ....55 N 18
West Wycombe ....20 R 29
Westbourne ....10 R 31
Westbury Cheshire ....34 L 25
Westbury Wilts. ....19 N 30
Westbury-on-Severn ....19 M 28
Westcliff ....22 W 29
Westcott ....21 S 30
Westenhanger ....13 X 30
Westerdale Highland ....85 J 8
Westerdale Scarborough ...50 R 20
Westerham ....21 U 30
Westerleigh ....19 M 29
Western Cleddau ....24 E 28
Westfield Highland ....85 J 8
Westfield Rother ....12 V 31
Westfield West Lothian ....67 I 16
Westgate-on-Sea ....23 Y 29
Westham ....12 U 31
Westhoughton ....42 M 23
Westleton ....31 Y 27
Westlinton ....11 T 31
Westmill ....29 T 28
Westnewton ....54 J 19
Weston Devon ....8 K 31
Weston
  North Hertfordshire ....29 T 28
Weston South Holland .....37 T 25
Weston
  South Northamptonshire ..28 Q 27
Weston Staffs. ....35 N 25
Weston-by-Welland ....28 R 26
Weston Favell ....28 R 27
Weston-on-the-Green ....28 Q 28
Weston-on-Trent ....36 P 25
Weston Rhyn ....34 K 25
Weston-super-Mare ....18 L 29
Weston Turville ....20 R 28
Weston-under-Lizard ....35 N 25
Weston-under-Penyard .....26 M 28
Westonbirt ....19 N 29

Westonzoyland ....8 L 30
Westray ....86 K 6
Westruther ....62 M 16
Westward ....54 K 19
Westward Ho ....6 H 30
Westwood ....19 N 30
Wetheral ....55 L 19
Wetherby ....50 P 22
Wetheringsett ....31 X 27
Wethersfield ....30 V 28
Wetwang ....51 S 21
Wey (River) ....10 R 30
Weybourne ....39 X 25
Weybridge ....21 S 29
Weyhill ....20 P 30
Weymouth ....8 M 32
Whaddon ....28 R 28
Whaley Bridge ....43 O 24
Whalley ....42 M 22
Whalsay ....87 R 2
Whalton ....56 O 18
Whaplode ....37 T 25
Whaplode Drove ....37 T 25
Wharfe (River) ....44 Q 22
Wharfedale ....49 O 22
Whatlington ....12 V 31
Whatsandwell ....36 P 24
Whauphill ....52 G 19
Whaw ....49 N 20
Wheathampstead ....21 T 28
Wheatley Notts. ....44 R 23
Wheatley Oxon. ....20 Q 28
Wheatley Hill ....56 P 19
Wheaton Aston ....35 N 25
Wheldrake ....50 R 22
Whepstead ....30 W 27
Whernside ....48 M 21
Wherwell ....10 P 30
Whickham ....56 O 19
Whimple ....7 J 31
Whipsnade ....21 S 28
Whissendine ....36 R 25
Whissonsett ....38 W 25
Whitburn South Tyneside ...57 P 19
Whitburn West Lothian ....61 I 16
Whitby ....51 S 20
Whitchurch
  Basingstoke and Deane ...20 P 30
Whitchurch
  Bath and N.E. Somerset ..18 M 29
Whitchurch Bucks. ....28 R 28
Whitchurch
  Caerdydd / Cardiff ....18 K 29
Whitchurch Devon ....4 H 32
Whitchurch
  Heref. and Worc. ....18 M 28
Whitchurch Oxon. ....20 Q 29
Whitchurch Salop ....34 L 25
White Coomb ....61 K 17
White Horse Hill ....20 P 29
White Scarcaves ....49 M 21
White Waltham ....20 R 29
Whitebridge ....73 G 12
Whitecairns ....75 N 12
Whitchurch Canonicorum ...5 L 31
Whitefield ....42 N 23
Whitehall ....87 M 6
Whitehaven ....47 J 20
Whitehill ....10 R 30
Whitehills ....81 M 10
Whitehouse
  Aberdeenshire ....75 M 12
Whitehouse
  Argyll and Bute ....59 D 16
Whitekirk ....69 M 15
Whiten Head ....84 G 8
Whiteness Sands ....79 I 10
Whiteparish ....9 P 30
Whiterashes ....81 N 12
Whitewreath ....80 K 11
Whitesand Bay Cornwall ...2 C 33
Whitesand Bay
  Pembrokes ....14 E 28
Whiteshill ....19 N 28
Whiteside ....55 M 18
Whitewell ....49 M 22
Whitewreath ....80 K 11
Whitfield Dover ....23 X 30
Whitfield
  South Northamptonshire ..28 Q 27
Whitfield Tynedale ....55 M 19
Whitgift ....44 R 22
Whithorn ....52 G 19
Whiting Bay ....59 E 17
Whitland ....15 G 28
Whitley ....20 R 29
Whitley Bay ....56 P 18

A B C D E F G H I J K L M N O P Q R S T U V W X Y Z

A B C D E F G H I J K L M N O P Q R S T U V W X Y Z

Whitley Bridge ....44 Q 22
Whitley Chapel ....55 N 19
Whitminster ....19 N 28
Whitmore ....35 N 25
Whitnash ....28 P 27
Whitsand Bay ....3 H 32
Whitstable ....23 X 29
Whitstone ....6 G 31
Whittingham ....63 O 17
Whittington *Derbs.* ....43 P 24
Whittington *King's Lynn*
   and West Norfolk ....38 V 26
Whittington *Lancaster* ....48 M 21
Whittington *Shrops.* ....34 L 25
Whittle le Woods ....42 M 22
Whittlebury ....28 R 27
Whittlesey ....37 T 26
Whittlesford ....29 U 27
Whitton *North Lincolnshire* ..44 S 22
Whitton *Powys* ....26 K 27
Whitton *Suffolk* ....31 X 27
Whittonstall ....56 O 19
Whitwell *Derbs.* ....44 Q 24
Whitwell *I.O.W.* ....10 Q 32
Whitwell-on-the-Hill ....50 R 21
Whitwick ....36 P 25
Whitworth ....43 N 23
Whixall ....34 L 25
Whygate ....55 M 18
Wiay *Highland* ....77 A 11
Wiay *Western Isles* ....76 Y 11
Wibtoft ....28 Q 26
Wick *Bro Morgannwg /*
   The Vale of Glamorgan ....17 J 29
Wick *Highland* ....86 K 8
Wick *South Glos.* ....19 M 29
Wicken *Cambs.* ....28 R 27
Wicken *Northants.* ....30 U 27
Wickenby ....45 S 24
Wickersley ....44 Q 23
Wickford ....22 V 29
Wickham ....10 Q 31
Wickham Market ....31 Y 27
Wickhambrook ....30 V 27
Wickwar ....19 M 29
Widdrington ....63 P 18
Wide Open ....56 P 18
Widecombe-in-the-Moor ..4 I 32
Wideford Hill Cairn ....86 K 7
Widemouth Bay ....6 G 31
Widford ....21 U 28
Widnes ....42 L 23
Wigan ....42 M 23
Wiggenhall
   St. Mary Magdalen ..38 V 25
Wigglesworth ....49 N 21
Wight (Isle of) ....10 P 32
Wighton ....38 W 25
Wigmore *Herefordshire* ..26 L 27
Wigmore *Medway* ....22 V 29
Wigston ....36 Q 26
Wigton ....54 K 19
Wigtown ....52 G 19

Wigtown Bay ....53 H 19
Wilberfoss ....50 R 22
Wilcot ....19 O 29
Wild Animal Kingdom ....29 S 28
Wilkhaven ....79 I 10
Wilkieston ....61 J 16
Willand ....7 J 31
Willenhall *Coventry* ....28 P 26
Willenhall *Walsall* ....35 N 26
Willerby ....45 S 22
Willersey ....27 O 27
Willingdon ....12 U 31
Willingham ....29 U 27
Willingham Forest ....45 T 23
Willington *Beds.* ....29 S 27
Willington *Derbs.* ....35 P 25
Willington *Durham* ....56 O 19
Williton ....7 K 30
Willoughby ....28 Q 27
Wilmcote ....27 O 27
Wilmington *East Essex* ..12 U 31
Wilmington *Kent* ....22 U 29
Wilmslow ....43 N 24
Wilpshire ....42 M 22
Wilsford ....37 S 25
Wilstead ....29 S 27
Wilton ....9 O 30
Wimbledon ....21 T 29
Wimblington ....29 U 26
Wimborne Minster ....9 O 31
Wimborne St. Giles ....9 O 31
Wincanton ....9 M 30
Wincham ....42 M 24
Winchburgh ....68 J 16
Winchcombe ....27 O 28
Winchelsea ....12 W 31
Winchester ....10 Q 30
Winchfield ....20 R 30
Wincle ....35 N 24
Windermere ....48 L 20
Windhill ....79 G 11
Windlesham ....21 S 29
Windrush ....19 O 28
Windrush (River) ....19 O 28
Windsor ....21 S 29
Windsor Great Park ....21 S 29
Windygates ....68 K 15
Winestead ....45 T 22
Winfarthing ....31 X 26
Winford ....18 M 29
Winforton ....26 K 27
Winfrith Newburgh ....9 N 32
Wing ....28 R 28
Wingate ....57 P 19
Wingerworth ....36 P 24
Wingfield *near Alfreton* ..36 P 24
Wingfield
   near Chesterfield ....36 P 24
Wingham ....23 X 30
Wingrave ....28 R 28
Winkfield ....21 R 29
Winkleigh ....7 I 31

Winksley ....50 P 21
Winmarleigh ....48 L 22
Winnersh ....20 R 29
Winscombe ....18 L 30
Winsford *Cheshire* ....34 M 24
Winsford *Somerset* ....7 J 30
Winsham ....8 L 31
Winshill ....35 P 25
Winslow ....28 R 28
Winster *Derbyshire Dales* ....35 P 24
Winster *South Lakeland* ....48 L 20
Winston ....49 O 20
Winstone ....19 N 28
Winterborne Kingston ....9 N 31
Winterborne Stickland ....9 N 31
Winterborne Whitechurch ..9 N 31
Winterbourne ....18 M 29
Winterbourne Abbas ....5 M 31
Winterbourne Dauntsey ....9 O 30
Winterbourne Monkton ....19 O 29
Winterbourne Stoke ....9 O 30
Winteringham ....44 S 22
Winterton ....44 S 23
Winterton-on-Sea ....39 Z 25
Winton ....49 N 20
Wintringham ....51 S 21
Winwick ....29 S 26
Wirksworth ....35 P 24
Wirral ....42 K 24
Wisbech ....37 U 25
Wisbech-St. Mary ....37 U 26
Wisborough Green ....11 S 30
Wishaw ....61 I 16
Wisley ....21 S 30
Wissey (River) ....38 V 26
Wistanstow ....26 L 26
Wistanswick ....34 M 25
Wistaston ....34 M 24
Wiston
   Dumfries and Galloway ....61 J 17
Wiston *Pembrokeshire /*
   Sir Benfro ....16 F 28
Wistow ....44 Q 22
Witchampton ....9 N 31
Witchford ....30 U 26
Witham ....22 V 28
Witham (River) ....37 T 24
Witham Friary ....9 M 30
Witheridge ....7 I 31
Withern ....45 U 24
Withernsea ....45 U 22
Withernwick ....45 T 22
Withington *Cotswold* ....19 O 28
Withington *Herefordshire* ..26 M 27
Withnell ....42 M 22
Withycombe ....4 J 32
Withypool ....7 J 30
Witley ....11 S 30
Witney ....20 P 28
Witsome ....63 N 16
Wittering ....37 S 26
Wittersham ....12 W 30
Witton le Wear ....56 O 19

Wiveliscombe ....7 K 30
Wivelsfield ....11 T 31
Wivenhoe ....30 W 28
Woburn ....29 S 28
Woburn Abbey ....29 S 28
Woburn Sands ....29 S 27
Woking ....21 S 30
Wokingham ....20 R 29
Wold Newton ....45 T 23
Woldingham ....21 T 30
Wollaston ....29 S 27
Wollaton Hall ....36 Q 25
Wolsingham ....56 O 19
Wolston ....28 P 26
Wolvercote ....20 Q 28
Wolverhampton ....35 N 26
Wolverton ....28 R 27
Wolvey ....28 P 26
Wolviston ....57 Q 20
Wombleton ....50 R 21
Wombourne ....27 N 26
Wombwell ....43 P 23
Womersley ....44 Q 22
Wonersh ....21 S 30
Wood Dalling ....39 X 25
Woodborough ....36 Q 24
Woodbridge ....31 X 27
Woodbury ....4 J 31
Woodchurch ....12 W 30
Woodcote ....20 Q 29
Woodford Halse ....28 Q 27
Woodhall Spa ....37 T 24
Woodham Ferrers ....22 V 29
Woodhouse ....43 P 23
Woodhouse Eaves ....36 Q 25
Woodingdean ....11 T 31
Woodland ....56 O 20
Woodlands ....9 O 31
Woodley ....20 R 29
Woodnesborough ....23 X 30
Woodseaves ....35 N 25
Woodsetts ....44 Q 23
Woodsford ....9 M 31
Woodstock ....20 P 28
Woodton ....39 Y 26
Woody Bay ....17 I 30
Woodville ....35 P 25
Wookey ....18 L 30
Wookey Hole ....18 L 30
Wool ....9 N 31
Woolacombe ....16 H 30
Wooler ....63 N 17
Woolfardisworthy ....6 G 31
Woolhampton ....20 Q 29
Woolpit ....30 W 27
Woolsthorpe ....36 R 25
Wooperton ....63 O 17
Woore ....35 M 25
Wootton *Bedford* ....29 S 27
Wootton *Northampton* ....28 R 27
Wootton Bassett ....19 O 29
Wootton Brige ....10 Q 31
Wootton Courtenay ....17 J 30
Wootton Rivers ....19 O 29

Wootton-Wawen ....27 O 27
Worcester ....27 N 27
Workington ....53 J 20
Worksop ....44 Q 24
Worle ....18 L 29
Wormbridge ....26 L 28
Wormingford ....30 W 28
Worminghall ....20 Q 28
Wormit ....69 L 14
Worms Head ....15 H 29
Wormsley ....26 L 27
Worplesdon ....21 S 30
Worsbrough ....43 P 23
Worsley ....42 M 23
Worsthorne ....43 N 22
Worth Matravers ....9 N 32
Worthen ....34 L 26
Worthenbury ....34 L 24
Worthing ....11 S 31
Wortley ....43 P 23
Wortwell ....31 Y 26
Wotton-under-Edge ....19 M 29
Wragby *East Lindsey* ....45 T 24
Wragby *Wakefield* ....43 P 23
Wrangle ....37 U 24
Wrawby ....44 S 23
Wray ....48 M 21
Wrea Green ....42 L 22
Wreay ....55 L 19
Wrecsam / Wrexham ....34 L 24
Wrekenton ....56 P 19
Wrentham ....31 Z 26
Wrenbury ....34 M 24
Wrestlingworth ....29 T 27
Wrexham / Wrecsam ....34 L 24
Wrington ....18 L 29
Writtle ....22 V 28
Wroot ....44 R 23
Wrotham ....22 U 30
Wroughton ....19 O 29
Wroxall ....10 Q 32
Wroxham ....39 Y 25
Wroxton ....28 P 27
Wyberton ....37 T 25
Wyche ....27 M 27
Wye ....22 W 30
Wye (River) ....26 M 28
Wykeham ....51 S 21
Wylam ....56 O 19
Wylye ....9 O 30
Wymeswold ....36 R 25
Wymondham *Leics.* ....36 R 25
Wymondham *Norfolk* ....39 X 26
Wyre ....87 L 6
Wysall ....36 Q 25
Wyvis Lodge ....79 G 10

Y

Y-Fenni / Abergavenny ..18 L 28
Y Ffor ....32 G 25
Y Llethr ....33 I 25

Y Rhiw ....32 G 25
Yafforth ....50 P 20
Yalding ....22 V 30
Yapton ....11 S 31
Yardley Gobion ....28 R 27
Yardley Hastings ....28 R 27
Yare (River) ....38 W 26
Yarm ....50 P 20
Yarmouth ....10 P 31
Yarnton ....20 Q 28
Yarrow ....62 K 17
Yate ....19 M 29
Yateley ....20 R 29
Yatton ....18 L 29
Yatton Keynell ....19 N 29
Yaxham ....38 W 26
Yaxley ....29 T 26
Yeadon ....43 O 22
Yealand Conyers ....48 L 21
Yealmpton ....4 I 32
Yelden ....29 S 27
Yell ....87 Q 1
Yelvertoft ....28 Q 26
Yelverton ....4 H 32
Yeolmbridge ....6 G 32
Yeovil ....8 M 31
Yeovilton ....8 M 30
Yesnaby ....86 J 6
Yetminster ....8 M 31
Yetts o' Muckhart ....68 J 15
Yielden ....29 S 27
Ynys / Lochtyn ....15 G 27
Ynysddu ....18 K 29
Ynyslas ....25 H 26
Ynysybwl ....17 J 29
Yockenthwaite ....49 N 21
Yockleton ....34 L 25
York ....50 Q 22
Yorkletts ....23 X 30
Yorkley ....18 M 28
Yorkshire Dales
   National Park ....49 N 21
Yorkshire Wolds ....51 S 21
Youlgreave ....35 O 24
Yoxall ....35 O 25
Yoxford ....31 Y 27
Yr Wyddfa / Snowdon ....33 H 24
Yr Wyddgrug / Mold ....34 K 24
Ysbyty Ifan ....33 I 24
Ystalyfera ....17 I 28
Ystrad-Aeron ....25 H 27
Ystrad Mynach ....18 K 29
Ystradfellte ....17 I 28
Ystradgynlais ....17 I 28
Ystradowen ....17 J 29
Ystwyth (River) ....25 H 26

Z

Zennor ....2 D 33

A B C D E F G H I J K L M N O P Q R S T U V W X Y Z

A

Aasleagh ... 105 D7
Abbert ... 106 F7
Abbey ... 100 G8
Abbeydorney ... 93 C10
Abbeyfeale ... 93 E10
Abbeylara ... 107 J6
Abbeyleix / Mainistir Laoise ... 101 J9
Abbeyshrule ... 107 J7
Abington ... 94 G10
Achill ... 104 C6
Achill Head ... 110 B6
Achill Island ... 104 B6
Achill Sound ... 104 C6
Achillbeg Island ... 104 C6
Achonry ... 112 G5
Aclare ... 112 F5
Acoose (Lough) ... 89 C11
Adamstown ... 96 L10
Adare ... 94 F10
Adrigole ... 89 C12
Aghaboe ... 101 J9
Aghabullogue ... 90 F12
Aghada ... 90 H12
Aghadiffin ... 106 F6
Aghadoe ... 89 D11
Aghadoon ... 110 B5
Aghadowey ... 118 M2
Aghagallon ... 114 N4
Aghagower ... 105 D6
Aghalane ... 113 J5
Aghalee ... 114 N4
Aghamore *Leitrim* ... 107 I6
Aghamore *Mayo* ... 105 F6
Aghamuck ... 106 H6
Aghavannagh ... 103 M9
Aghavas ... 107 I6
Aghaville ... 89 D13
Aghinlig ... 114 M4
Aghla Mountain ... 116 H3
Aghleam ... 110 B5
Aghnablaney ... 113 I4
Aghnacliff ... 107 J6
Aghnamullen ... 108 L5
Aghowle ... 96 M9
Agivey ... 118 M2
Aglish *Tipperary* ... 100 H8
Aglish *Waterford* ... 91 I11
Agnew's Hill ... 115 O3
Ahakista ... 89 D13
Ahalia (Loughs) ... 105 D7
Ahascragh ... 106 G7
Ahenny ... 95 J10
Aherla ... 90 F12
Aherlow ... 94 H10
Aherlow (Glen of) ... 95 H10
Ahoghill ... 118 M3
Aillwee Cave ... 99 E8
Ailt an Chorráin / Burtonport ... 116 G3
Aird Mhór / Ardmore ... 91 I12
Akeragh Lough ... 93 C10
Aldergrove ... 115 N4
Allaghaun ... 93 E10
Allen ... 102 L8
Allen (Bog of) ... 102 K8
Allen (Lough) ... 112 H5
Allenwood ... 102 L8
Allihies ... 88 B13
Allistragh ... 114 L4
Alloon Lower ... 106 G7
Allow ... 94 F11
Allua (Lough) ... 89 E12
Altagowlan ... 112 H5
Altan Lough ... 117 H2
Altnamackan ... 114 M5
Altnapaste ... 117 I3
An Blascaod Mór / Blasket Islands ... 92 A11
An Bun Beag / Bunbeg ... 116 H2
An Caisleán Nua / Newcastle West ... 93 E10
An Caisleán Riabhach / Castlerea ... 106 G6
An Chathair / Caher ... 95 I10
An Cheathrú Rua / Carraroe ... 98 D8
An Chloich Mhóir / Cloghmore ... 104 C6
An Clochán / Clifden ... 104 B7
An Clochán / Cloghan *Donegal* ... 117 I3
An Clochán Liath / Dungloe ... 116 G3
An Cloigeann / Cleegan ... 104 B7

An Cóbh / Cobh ... 90 H12
An Coimín / Commeen ... 117 I3
An Coireán / Waterville ... 88 B12
An Corrán / Currane ... 104 C6
An Creagán / Mount Bellew ... 106 G7
An Daingean / Dingle ... 92 B11
An Dúchoraidh / Doocharry ... 116 H3
An Fál Carrach / Falcarragh ... 117 H2
An Fhairche / Clonbur ... 105 D7
An Geata Mór ... 110 B5
An Gleann Garbh / Glengarriff ... 89 D12
An Gort / Gort ... 99 F8
An Gort Mór / Gortmore ... 105 D7
An Leacht / Lahinch ... 98 D9
An Longfort / Longford ... 107 I6
An Mám / Maam Cross ... 105 D7
An Mhala Raithní / Mulrany ... 104 C6
An Móta / Moate ... 101 I7
An Muileann gCearr / Mullingar ... 107 J7
An Nás / Naas ... 102 M8
An Ráth / Charleville ... 94 F10
An Ros / Rush ... 109 N7
An Sciobairín / Skibbereen ... 89 E13
An Seanchaisleán / Oldcastle ... 108 K6
An Spidéal / Spiddal ... 99 E8
An tAonach / Nenagh ... 100 H9
An Teampall Mór / Templemore ... 101 I9
An Tearmann / Termon ... 117 I2
An tInbhear Mór / Arklow ... 97 N9
An Tulach / Tullow ... 102 L9
An Uaimh / Navan ... 108 L7
Anascaul ... 92 B11
Anayalla ... 114 L5
Anglesborough ... 94 H10
Anglesey Bridge ... 95 H9
Annacarriga ... 99 G9
Annacarty ... 95 H10
Annaclone ... 115 N5
Annacloy ... 115 O4
Annacotty ... 94 G9
Annadorn ... 115 O5
Annagary ... 116 H2
Annagassan ... 109 M6
Annageeragh (River) ... 98 D9
Annagh Head ... 110 B5
Annagh Island ... 110 C6
Annaghdown ... 105 E7
Annaghmore Lough ... 106 H6
Annahilt ... 115 N4
Annalee ... 107 J5
Annalong ... 109 O5
Annamoe ... 103 N8
Annes Grove Gardens ... 94 G11
Annestown ... 91 K11
Annfield ... 95 I9
Annie Brady Bridge ... 111 C5
Annsborough ... 115 O5
Antrim ... 115 N3
Antrim (Glens of) ... 119 N2
Antrim Coast ... 119 O2
Antrim Mountains ... 119 N2
Anure (Lough) ... 116 H3
Araglin ... 95 H11
Árainn Mhór / Aran or Aranmore Island ... 116 G2
Aran Islands / Oileáin Árainn ... 98 C8
Archdale (Castle) ... 113 I4
Archerstown ... 108 K7
Ard ... 104 C8
Ardagh *Donegal* ... 117 J3
Ardagh *Limerick* ... 93 E10
Ardan ... 101 J8
Ardanairy ... 103 N9
Ardanew ... 108 L7
Ardara ... 116 G3
Ardattin ... 96 L9
Ardboe ... 114 M4
Ardcath ... 109 M7
Ardcloon ... 105 F7
Ardcrony ... 100 H9
Ardea ... 89 C12
Arderin ... 101 J8
Ardfert ... 93 C11
Ardfield ... 89 F13
Ardfinnan ... 95 I11
Ardgehane ... 90 F13
Ardglass ... 115 P5
Ardglass ... 90 H11

Ardgroom ... 88 C12
Ardgroom Harbour ... 88 C12
Ardkeen ... 115 P4
Ardlea ... 101 J9
Ardlougher ... 107 J5
Ardmillan ... 115 O4
Ardmoney ... 113 J5
Ardmore *Derry* ... 117 K3
Ardmore *Galway* ... 104 C8
Ardmore Point *Antrim* ... 114 N4
Ardmore Point *Craigavon* ... 114 M4
Ardmore Point *Dunganstown East* ... 103 N9
Ardmorney ... 101 J7
Ardmoy ... 106 G6
Ardnagreevagh ... 104 B7
Ardnasodan ... 105 F7
Ardpatrick ... 94 G10
Ardrahan ... 99 F8
Ardreagh ... 118 M2
Ardress House ... 114 M4
Ards Forest Park ... 117 I2
Ards Peninsula ... 115 P4
Ardscull ... 102 L8
Ardshankill ... 113 I4
Ardstraw ... 113 J3
Argideen ... 89 F13
Argory (The) ... 114 M4
Arigna ... 112 H5
Arinagh ... 112 F5
Arless ... 102 K9
Armagh ... 114 M4
Armaghbrague ... 114 M5
Armoy ... 118 N2
Arney ... 113 I5
Arra Mountains ... 100 G9
Arrow (Lough) ... 106 H5
Arryheernabin ... 117 J2
Artane ... 103 N7
Arthurstown ... 96 L11
Articlave ... 118 L2
Artigarvan ... 117 J3
Arvagh ... 107 J6
Asdee ... 93 D10
Ashbourne ... 109 M7
Ashford *Glenealy* ... 103 N8
Ashford *Limerick* ... 93 E10
Ashford Castle ... 105 E7
Ashleam Bay ... 104 B6
Ashton ... 90 F12
Askamore ... 97 M9
Askanagap ... 103 M9
Askeaton ... 94 F10
Askill ... 112 H4
Atedaun (Lough) ... 99 E9
Áth Cinn / Headford ... 105 E7
Athassel Abbey ... 95 I10
Athboy ... 108 L7
Athea ... 93 E10
Athgarvan ... 102 L8
Athlacca ... 94 G10
Athleague ... 106 H7
Athnid ... 95 I9
Athy / Baile Átha Í ... 102 L9
Atlantic Drive (The) ... 104 C6
Atorick (Lough) ... 99 G8
Attanagh ... 101 J9
Attavally ... 111 C5
Attical ... 109 N5
Attymass ... 111 E5
Attymon ... 99 G8
Aucloggen ... 105 F7
Audley's Castle ... 115 P4
Aughacasla ... 92 C11
Aughagault ... 117 I3
Aughamullan ... 114 M4
Augher ... 114 K4
Aughils ... 92 C11
Aughinish ... 99 E8
Aughinish Island ... 93 E10
Aughkeely ... 117 I3
Aughnacleagh ... 118 M3
Aughnacloy ... 114 L4
Aughnanure Castle ... 105 E7
Aughnasheelan ... 107 I5
Aughrim *Galway* ... 100 H8
Aughrim *Wicklow* ... 103 N9
Aughris ... 112 F5
Aughris Head ... 112 F5
Aughrus More ... 104 B7
Avoca ... 103 N9
Avoca (River) ... 103 N9
Avoca (Valle of) ... 103 N9
Avonbeg ... 103 M9
Avondale Forest Park ... 103 N9
Avonmore (River) ... 103 N9
Awbeg ... 94 G11

B

Baginbun Head ... 96 L11
Baile an Fheirtéaraigh / Ballyferriter ... 92 A11
Baile an Mhóta / Ballymote ... 112 G5
Baile an Róba / Ballinrobe ... 105 E7
Baile an Sceilg / Ballinskelligs ... 88 B12
Baile Átha an Rí / Athenry ... 99 F8
Baile Átha Cliath / Dublin ... 103 N8
Baile Átha Fhirdhia / Ardee ... 108 M6
Baile Átha Luain / Athlone ... 107 I8
Baile Átha Troim / Trim ... 108 L7
Baile Brigín / Balbriggan ... 109 N7
Baile Chláir / Claregalway ... 99 F7
Baile Locha Riach / Loughrea ... 99 G8
Baile Mhic Andáin / Thomastown ... 96 K10
Baile Mhistéala / Mitchelstown ... 94 H11
Baile na Finne / Fintown ... 117 H3
Baile na Lorgan / Castleblayney ... 108 L5
Baile Uí Fhiacháin / Newport ... 105 D6
Baile Uí Mhatháin / Ballymahon ... 107 I7
Baileysmill ... 115 O4
Baldoyle ... 103 N7
Balla ... 105 E6
Ballaba ... 99 F8
Ballagan Point ... 109 N5
Ballagh *Fermanagh* ... 113 J5
Ballagh *Galway* ... 106 F7
Ballagh *Limerick* ... 93 E10
Ballagh near Curraghroe ... 107 H6
Ballagh near Nahara ... 106 H7
Ballagh *Tipperary* ... 95 I10
Ballagh (Neck of the) ... 112 G3
Ballaghaderreen / Bealach an Doirín ... 106 G6
Ballaghbeama Gap ... 89 C12
Ballaghbehy ... 93 E10
Ballaghisheen Pass ... 88 C12
Ballaghkeen ... 97 M10
Ballaghmore ... 101 I9
Ballaghnatrillick ... 112 G4
Ballard ... 97 M9
Ballardiggan ... 99 F8
Balleen ... 101 J9
Ballickmoyler ... 102 K9
Balliggan ... 115 P4
Ballina ... 99 G9
Ballina / Béal an Átha ... 111 E5
Ballinabrackey ... 102 K7
Ballinabranagh ... 102 L9
Ballinaclash ... 103 N9
Ballinacor ... 103 N9
Ballinadee ... 90 G12
Ballinafad *Abanagh* ... 106 G5
Ballinafad *Galway* ... 104 C7
Ballinagar ... 101 J8
Ballinagleragh ... 113 H5
Ballinakill ... 101 K9
Ballinalack ... 107 J7
Ballinalea ... 103 N8
Ballinalee ... 107 J6
Ballinamallard ... 113 J4
Ballinamara ... 95 J9
Ballinameen ... 106 H6
Ballinamore Bridge ... 106 G7
Ballinamuck ... 107 I6
Ballinascarty ... 90 F12
Ballinaspick ... 91 I11
Ballinclashet ... 90 G12
Ballinclea ... 103 M9
Ballincloher ... 93 C10
Ballincollig ... 90 G12
Ballincrea ... 96 K11
Ballincurrig ... 90 H12
Ballindaggan ... 96 L10
Ballindarragh ... 113 J5
Ballinderry *Cookstown* ... 114 M4
Ballinderry *Terryglass* ... 100 H8
Ballinderry *Wicklow* ... 103 N9
Ballinderry Bridge ... 114 M4
Ballindine ... 105 F6
Ballindrait ... 117 J3
Ballineanig ... 92 A11
Ballineen ... 89 F12
Ballingarrane ... 94 F10

Ballingarry *Galway* ... 100 H8
Ballingarry *Limerick* ... 94 F10
Ballingarry *Tipperary* ... 95 J10
Ballingeary / Béal Átha an Ghaorthaidh ... 89 E12
Ballingurteen ... 89 E12
Ballinhassig ... 90 G12
Ballinkillin ... 96 L10
Ballinlea ... 118 M2
Ballinleeny ... 94 F10
Ballinloghig ... 92 B11
Ballinlough *Meath* ... 108 K6
Ballinlough *Roscommon* ... 106 G6
Ballinluska ... 90 H12
Ballinruan ... 99 F9
Ballinskelligs Bay ... 88 B12
Ballinspittle ... 90 G12
Ballintober ... 106 G6
Ballintogher ... 112 G5
Ballintotty ... 100 H9
Ballintoy ... 118 M2
Ballintra *Donegal* ... 112 H4
Ballintra *near Leabgarrow* ... 116 G3
Ballinunty ... 95 I10
Ballinure ... 95 I10
Ballinure (River) ... 100 H8
Ballinvarry ... 96 L10
Ballitore ... 102 L8
Ballivor ... 108 L7
Ballon ... 96 L9
Balloo Cross Roads ... 115 O4
Balloor ... 112 G4
Balloughter ... 97 M10
Balla ... 105 E6
Ballure ... 112 H4
Ballvengland ... 94 F10
Ballyagran ... 94 F10
Ballyallinan ... 94 F10
Ballyalton ... 115 P5
Ballyard ... 113 J4
Ballybannon ... 102 L9
Ballybay near Carrickmacross ... 108 L5
Ballybay near Castleblayney ... 108 L5
Ballybeg ... 95 I11
Ballyboghil ... 109 N7
Ballybogy ... 118 M2
Ballyboley Forest ... 115 O3
Ballyboy ... 101 I8
Ballybrack *Dublin* ... 103 N8
Ballybrack *Kerry* ... 88 B12
Ballybrittas ... 101 K8
Ballybrommel ... 96 L9
Ballybrood ... 94 G10
Ballybrophy ... 101 J9
Ballybryan ... 101 K7
Ballybunnion ... 93 D10
Ballycahill ... 95 I9
Ballycallan ... 95 J10
Ballycanew ... 97 N10
Ballycarney ... 97 M10
Ballycarry ... 115 O3
Ballycastle *Mayo* ... 111 D5
Ballycastle *Moyle* ... 119 N2
Ballycastle Bay ... 119 N2
Ballyclare *Newtonabbey* ... 115 N3
Ballyclare *Roscommon* ... 107 I6
Ballyclerahan ... 95 I10
Ballyclery ... 99 F8
Ballyclog ... 94 F11
Ballycommon ... 100 H9
Ballyconneely ... 104 B7
Ballyconneely Bay ... 104 B7
Ballyconnell *Cavan* ... 113 J5
Ballyconnell *Sligo* ... 112 G4
Ballycorick ... 99 E9
Ballycotton ... 91 H12
Ballycotton Bay ... 91 H12
Ballycrossaun ... 100 H8
Ballycrovane Harbour ... 88 C12
Ballycroy ... 110 C5
Ballycuirke Lough ... 99 E8
Ballycullane ... 96 L11
Ballycullen ... 103 N8
Ballycumber ... 101 I8
Ballydangan ... 100 H7
Ballydavid *Galway* ... 100 G8
Ballydavid *Kilmalkedar* ... 92 A11
Ballydavid Head ... 92 A11
Ballydavis ... 101 K8
Ballydehob ... 89 D13
Ballydesmond ... 93 E11
Ballydonegan ... 88 B13
Ballydonegan Bay ... 88 B13
Ballyduff *Dingle* ... 92 B11

Ballyduff *Kerry* ... 93 D10
Ballyduff *Waterford* ... 91 H11
Ballyduff *Wexford* ... 97 M10
Ballyeaston ... 115 O3
Ballyeighter Loughs ... 99 F9
Ballyfad ... 97 N9
Ballyfair ... 102 L8
Ballyfarnan ... 106 H7
Ballyfarnagh ... 105 F6
Ballyfasy ... 96 K10
Ballyfeard ... 90 G12
Ballyferis Point ... 115 P4
Ballyfin ... 101 J8
Ballyfinboy ... 100 H8
Ballyforan ... 106 H7
Ballyfore ... 102 K8
Ballyfoyle ... 96 K9
Ballygalley ... 119 O3
Ballygalley Head ... 119 O3
Ballygar ... 106 H7
Ballygarrett ... 97 N10
Ballygarries ... 105 E6
Ballygarvan ... 90 G12
Ballygawley *Dungannon* ... 114 K4
Ballygawley *Sligo* ... 112 G5
Ballyglass near Cornanagh ... 105 E6
Ballyglass near Kilmovee ... 106 G6
Ballygorman ... 117 K1
Ballygowan *Ards* ... 115 O4
Ballygowan Newry-Mourne ... 109 N5
Ballygriffin ... 96 L11
Ballyhack ... 96 L11
Ballyhacket ... 102 L9
Ballyhahill ... 94 G10
Ballyhahill ... 93 E10
Ballyhaise ... 107 K5
Ballyhalbert ... 115 P4
Ballyhale *Galway* ... 105 E7
Ballyhale *Kilkenny* ... 96 K10
Ballyhaunis / Béal Átha hAmhnais ... 106 F6
Ballyhean ... 105 E6
Ballyhear ... 105 E7
Ballyheelan ... 107 J6
Ballyheerin ... 117 I2
Ballyheige ... 93 C10
Ballyheige Bay ... 93 C10
Ballyhillin ... 117 J1
Ballyhoe Bridge ... 118 N2
Ballyhoe Lough ... 108 L6
Ballyhoge ... 96 M10
Ballyhooly ... 94 G11
Ballyhornan ... 115 P5
Ballyhoura Mountains ... 94 G11
Ballyhuppahane ... 101 J8
Ballyjamesduff ... 107 K6
Ballykean ... 101 K8
Ballykeel ... 95 J10
Ballykeeran ... 115 N4
Ballykeeran ... 107 I7
Ballykelly ... 118 K2
Ballykilleen ... 102 K8
Ballykinler ... 115 O5
Ballyknockan ... 103 M8
Ballylacy ... 97 N9
Ballylaghnan ... 99 G9
Ballylanders ... 94 G10
Ballylaneen ... 91 J11
Ballylesson ... 115 O4
Ballylickey ... 89 D12
Ballyliffin ... 117 J2
Ballyline ... 95 J10
Ballylintagh ... 118 L2
Ballylongford ... 93 D10
Ballylongford Bay ... 93 D10
Ballylooby ... 95 I11
Ballyloughbeg ... 118 M2
Ballylynan ... 102 K9
Ballymacarbry ... 95 I11
Ballymacaw ... 96 K11
Ballymachugh ... 107 J6
Ballymack ... 96 K10
Ballymackey ... 100 H9
Ballymackilroy ... 114 K4
Ballymacoda ... 91 I12
Ballymacrevan ... 115 N4
Ballymacurly ... 106 G7
Ballymacward ... 106 G7
Ballymadog ... 91 I12
Ballymagan ... 117 J2
Ballymagaraghy ... 118 K2
Ballymagorry ... 117 J3
Ballymakeagh ... 91 I12

A **B** **C** **D** **E** **F** **G** **H** **I** **J** **K** **L** **M** **N** **O** **P** **Q** **R** **S** **T** **U** **V** **W** **X** **Y** **Z**

Ballymakeery /
  Baile Mhic Íre ....89 E 12
Ballymakenny .... 109 M 6
Ballymartin .... 109 O 5
Ballymartle ....90 G 12
Ballymena .... 119 N 3
Ballymoe .... 106 G 6
Ballymoney *Ballymoney* ...118 M 2
Ballymoney *Limavady* ...118 K 3
Ballymore *Donegal* ....117 I 2
Ballymore *Westmeath* ....107 I 7
Ballymore Eustace ...... 103 M 8
Ballymore Lough .... 111 E 5
Ballymurphy ....96 L 10
Ballymurragh ....93 E 10
Ballymurray .... 106 H 7
Ballynabola ....96 L 10
Ballynacallagh ....88 B 13
Ballynacally ....99 E 9
Ballynacarrick .... 116 H 3
Ballynacarriga ....89 E 12
Ballynacarrigy .... 107 J 7
Ballynacarrow .... 112 G 5
Ballynaclogh .... 100 H 9
Ballynacorra ....90 H 12
Ballynacourty ....91 J 11
Ballynadrumny .... 102 L 7
Ballynafid .... 107 J 7
Ballynagaul ....91 J 11
Ballynagoraher .... 105 D 6
Ballynagore .... 101 J 7
Ballynagree ....90 F 12
Ballynaguilkee ....95 I 11
Ballynahinch .... 115 O 4
Ballynahinch Lake ...... 104 C 7
Ballynahow ....88 A 12
Ballynahown *Kilcummin* ...98 D 8
Ballynahown *Westmeath* ..101 I 7
Ballynakill *Carlow* ....96 L 9
Ballynakill *Offaly* .... 101 K 8
Ballynakill *Westmeath* ...107 I 7
Ballynakill Harbour ..... 104 B 7
Ballynakilla ....88 C 13
Ballynakilly Upper ....88 C 11
Ballynamallaght .... 117 K 3
Ballynamona ....90 G 11
Ballynamult ....92 A 11
Ballynana ....92 A 11
Ballynare .... 103 M 7
Ballynashannagh .... 117 J 2
Ballynaskeagh .... 114 N 5
Ballynaskreena ....93 C 10
Ballynastangford .... 105 E 6
Ballynastraw ....97 M 10
Ballynchatty .... 113 K 4
Ballyneaner .... 118 K 3
Ballyneety ....94 G 10
Ballyneill ....95 J 10
Ballynoe *Cork* ....90 H 11
Ballynoe *Down* .... 115 O 5
Ballynure .... 115 O 3
Ballyorgan ....94 G 11
Ballypatrick ....95 J 10
Ballypatrick Forest ..... 119 N 2
Ballyporeen ....95 H 11
Ballyquin ....92 B 11
Ballyquintin Point ...... 115 P 5
Ballyragget .... 101 J 9
Ballyrashane .... 118 M 2
Ballyreagh *Dungannon* ...114 L 4
Ballyreagh *Fermanagh* ...113 J 4
Ballyroan .... 101 K 9
Ballyroddy .... 106 H 6
Ballyroebuck ....97 M 10
Ballyronan .... 114 M 3
Ballyroney .... 115 N 5
Ballyroon ....88 C 13
Ballysadare .... 112 G 5
Ballysadare Bay .... 112 G 5
Ballyshannon *Donegal* ...112 H 4
Ballyshannon *Kildare* ...102 L 8
Ballysloe ....95 J 10
Ballysteen ....94 F 10
Ballyteige Bay ....96 L 11
Ballytoohy .... 104 C 6
Ballyvaughan ....99 E 8
Ballyvaughan Bay ....99 E 8
Ballyvester .... 115 P 4
Ballyvoge /
  Baile Uí Bhuaigh ....89 E 12
Ballyvoneen .... 106 G 7
Ballyvourney /
  Baile Bhuirne ....89 E 12
Ballyvoy .... 119 N 2
Ballyvoyle Head ....91 J 11
Ballywalter .... 115 P 4
Ballyward .... 115 N 5

Ballywilliam ....96 L 10
Balnamore .... 118 M 2
Balrath .... 108 M 7
Balrothery .... 109 N 7
Balscaddan .... 109 N 7
Baltimore ....89 D 13
Baltray .... 109 N 6
Banada .... 106 F 5
Banagher .... 101 I 8
Banagher Forest .... 118 L 3
Banbridge .... 114 N 4
Bandon River ....89 F 12
Bangor *Mayo* .... 111 C 5
Bangor *North-Down* ..... 115 O 4
Bangor Trail .... 111 C 5
Bann (River)
  Lough Neagh ....115 N 5
Bann (River) *River Slaney* ...97 M 10
Banna ....93 C 10
Banna Strand ....93 C 11
Bannow ....96 L 11
Bannow Bay ....96 L 11
Bansha ....95 H 10
Banteer ....94 F 11
Bantry / *Beanntraí* ......89 D 12
Bantry Bay ....89 C 13
Barefield ....99 F 9
Barley Cove ....88 C 13
Barna *Limerick* ....94 H 10
Barna *Offaly* .... 101 I 9
Barnacahoge .... 105 F 6
Barnaderg .... 106 F 7
Barnesmore .... 113 H 3
Barnesmore Gap .... 113 I 3
Barnmeen .... 115 N 5
Barnycarroll .... 105 F 6
Baronscourt Forest ..... 113 J 3
Barr na Trá / *Barnatra* ...110 C 5
Barra (Lough) .... 117 H 3
Barrack Village .... 101 K 9
Barraduff ....89 D 11
Barrigone ....93 E 10
Barringtonsbridge ......94 G 10
Barrow (River) .... 102 K 8
Barrow Harbour ....93 C 11
Barry .... 107 I 7
Barry's Point ....90 F 13
Batterstown .... 108 M 7
Baunskeha ....96 K 10
Bauntlieve ....99 E 9
Baurtregaum ....93 C 11
Bawn Cross Roads ......94 F 11
Bawnboy .... 113 I 5
Beagh *Galway* .... 105 F 7
Beagh *Roscommon* ...... 112 H 5
Beagh (Lough) .... 117 I 2
Beagh (Slieve) .... 113 K 4
Beal ....93 D 10
Béal an Átha / *Ballina* ...111 E 5
Béal an Átha Mhóir /
  Ballinamore .... 107 I 5
Béal an Mhuirthead /
  Belmullet .... 110 C 5
Béal Átha an Ghaorthaidh /
  Ballingeary ....89 E 12
Béal Átha na Muice /
  Swinford .... 105 F 6
Béal Átha na Sluaighe /
  Ballinasloe .... 100 H 8
Béal Átha Seanaidh /
  Ballyshannon .... 112 H 4
Béal Deirg / *Belderrig* ...111 D 5
Beal Point ....93 D 10
Béal Tairbirt / *Belturbet* ...107 J 5
Bealach Conglais /
  Baltinglass .... 102 L 9
Bealach Féich /
  Ballybofey .... 117 I 3
Bealaclugga / *New Quay* ...99 E 8
Bealad Cross Roads .....89 F 13
Bealadangan .... 105 D 5
Bealaha ....98 D 9
Bealalaw Bridge ....88 C 12
Bealanabrack .... 104 C 7
Bealin .... 107 I 7
Bealnablath ....90 F 12
Bealnamorive ....89 E 12
Beara ....89 C 12
Bearna / *Barna* ....89 D 11
Beaufort ....89 D 11
Bective .... 108 L 7
Beehive Huts ....92 A 11
Beenmore ....88 B 11
Beennaskehy ....90 G 11
Beenoskee ....92 B 11
Beg (Lough) *Antrim* .... 114 N 4
Beg (Lough) *River Bann* ...114 M 3
Beginish Island ....88 B 12

Behy ....88 C 11
Bekan .... 105 F 6
Belcarra .... 105 E 6
Belclare .... 105 F 7
Belcoo .... 113 I 5
Belderg Harbour .... 111 D 5
Belfarsad .... 104 C 6
Belfast .... 115 O 4
Belfast Lough .... 115 O 3
Belgooly ....90 G 12
Belhavel Lough .... 112 H 5
Bellacorick .... 111 D 5
Belladrihid .... 112 G 5
Bellagarvaun .... 110 C 6
Bellaghy .... 114 M 3
Bellahy .... 106 F 6
Bellameeny .... 106 H 7
Bellamont Forest ...... 108 K 5
Bellanaboy Bridge ..... 111 D 5
Bellanacargy .... 107 K 5
Bellanagare .... 106 G 6
Bellanagraugh Bridge .. 112 F 5
Bellaneck .... 113 J 5
Bellanamore .... 117 H 3
Bellanamullia .... 107 H 7
Bellananagh .... 107 J 6
Bellanode .... 114 K 5
Bellarena .... 118 L 2
Bellavary .... 105 E 6
Belleek .... 114 M 5
Belleek .... 113 H 4
Bellewstown .... 109 M 7
Belmont .... 101 I 8
Belmore Mountain ..... 113 I 5
Beltra *Croaghmoyle* .... 105 D 6
Beltra *Sligo* .... 112 G 5
Beltra Lough .... 105 D 6
Belvelly ....90 H 12
Belview Port ....96 K 11
Ben Gorm .... 104 C 7
Benbane Head .... 118 M 2
Benbaun .... 104 C 7
Benbo .... 112 H 5
Benbrack .... 113 I 5
Benbreen .... 104 C 7
Benbulben .... 112 G 4
Benburb .... 114 L 4
Bencroy or
  Gubnaveagh .... 113 I 5
Bendooragh .... 118 M 2
Benettsbridge ....96 K 10
Benmore .... 111 D 5
Benmore or Fair Head .. 119 N 2
Benneady .... 114 M 4
Benbulen .... 112 G 4
Bennacunneen .... 105 D 7
Benwee Head .... 111 C 4
Beragh .... 114 K 4
Bere Haven ....88 C 13
Bere Island ....88 C 13
Bernish Rock .... 114 M 5
Berrings ....90 F 12
Bertraghboy Bay .... 104 C 7
Bessbrook .... 114 M 5
Bettystown .... 109 N 6
Big Dog Forest .... 113 I 4
Big Island .... 100 H 8
Big Trosk .... 119 N 2
Bilboa .... 102 K 9
Bilboa (River) ....95 H 10
Billis Bridge .... 108 K 6
Bills Rocks .... 104 B 6
Binevenagh .... 118 L 2
Binn Éadair / *Howth* ... 103 N 7
Biorra / *Birr* .... 101 I 8
Birdhill ....99 G 9
Birreencorragh .... 105 D 6
Bishops Court .... 115 P 5
Black *Galway* .... 105 D 6
Black (River) *Longford* ...107 I 6
Black Ball Head ....88 B 13
Black Bull .... 103 M 7
Black Gap (The) .... 113 I 4
Black Head *Clare* ....99 E 8
Black Head *Larne* ..... 115 O 3
Black Lion .... 101 J 8
Black Rock .... 110 B 5
Blacklion .... 113 I 5
Blackpool ....94 G 10
Blackrock *Cork* ....90 G 12
Blackrock *Louth* ...... 109 M 6
Blackrock *Rathdown* ... 103 N 8
Blackskull .... 114 N 4
Blacksod Bay .... 110 B 5
Blacksod Point .... 110 B 5
Blackstairs Mountains ..96 L 10
Blackwater ....97 M 10
Blackwater (River) *Cork* ...89 F 11

Blackwater (River)
  Lough Neagh ....114 L 4
Blackwater (River)
  River Boyne .... 108 L 6
Blackwater Bridge
  Innfield .... 102 L 7
Blackwater Bridge *Tahilla* ...88 C 12
Blackwater Harbour .....97 N 10
Blackwatertown .... 114 L 4
Blanchardstown .... 103 M 7
Blane Bridge ....93 E 10
Blaney .... 113 I 4
Blarney ....90 G 12
Blasket Sound ....92 A 11
Bleach ....99 G 8
Bleach Lake ....94 F 10
Blennerville ....93 C 11
Blessington .... 103 M 8
Bloody Foreland ...... 116 H 2
Blue Ball .... 101 J 8
Blue Stack Mountains .. 113 H 3
Blueford ....93 E 11
Boa Island .... 113 I 4
Boardmills .... 115 O 4
Boderg (Lough) .... 107 I 6
Bodyke ....99 G 9
Bofeenaun .... 105 E 6
Bofin .... 104 B 7
Bofin (Lough) *Galway* .. 105 D 7
Bofin (Lough)
  Roscommon ....107 I 6
Bogay .... 117 J 2
Boggan *Meath* .... 108 L 6
Boggan *Tipperary* ......95 J 9
Boggaun .... 101 I 9
Boggeragh Mountains ..89 F 11
Bohateh ....99 G 9
Bohaun .... 105 D 6
Boheeshil ....88 C 12
Boher ....94 G 10
Boheraphuca .... 101 I 8
Boherbue ....93 E 11
Bohereen ....93 E 11
Boherlahan ....95 I 10
Bohermeen .... 108 L 7
Boherquill .... 107 J 6
Boho .... 113 I 4
Bohola .... 105 E 6
Bola (Lough) .... 104 C 7
Bolea .... 118 L 2
Boleran .... 118 L 2
Boley .... 102 L 8
Bolinglanna .... 104 C 6
Boliska Lough ....99 E 8
Bolton's Cross Roads ...93 D 10
Bolus Head ....88 A 12
Bonet .... 112 H 5
Boola ....91 I 11
Boolakennedy ....95 H 11
Boolattin ....95 J 11
Boolteens ....93 C 11
Boolyduff ....99 E 9
Boolyglass ....96 K 10
Borris ....96 L 10
Borris in Ossory ...... 101 J 9
Borrisoleigh .... 100 I 9
Boston ....99 F 8
Bottlehill ....90 G 11
Bouladuff ....95 I 9
Boviel .... 118 L 3
Bow ....99 G 9
Boyerstown .... 108 L 7
Boyle (River) .... 106 H 6
Boyne (River) .... 102 K 7
Brackagh .... 101 K 8
Brackley Lough .... 113 I 5
Bracklin .... 108 K 7
Brackloon *Mayo* ...... 106 F 6
Brackloon *Roscommon* .. 106 G 6
Bracknagh *Offaly* .... 102 K 8
Bracknagh *Roscommon* ...107 H 7
Brackwanshagh .... 111 E 5
Brandon Bay ....92 B 11
Brandon Head ....92 B 11
Brandon Hill ....96 L 10
Brannock Islands ....98 C 8
Brannockstown .... 102 L 8
Bray Head *Kerry* ....88 A 12
Bray Head *Wicklow* ... 103 N 8
Bré / *Bray* .... 103 N 8
Breaghva .... 105 E 6
Breaghwy .... 105 E 6
Bree ....96 M 10
Breenagh .... 117 I 3
Brickeens .... 105 F 6
Bricklieve Mountains .. 106 G 5
Bride *Cork* ....89 F 12

Bride *River Blackwater* ...91 I 11
Bridebridge ....90 H 11
Brideswell *Ballyellis* ...97 M 9
Brideswell *Ballynamona* .. 106 H 7
Bridge End .... 117 J 2
Bridgeland .... 103 M 9
Bridget Lough ....99 G 9
Bridgetown
  Cannock Chase ....96 M 11
Bridgetown *Clare* ......99 G 9
Bridgetown *Donegal* ... 112 H 4
Brienbridge ....99 G 9
Brittas *Limerick* ......94 G 10
Brittas *Saggart* ...... 103 M 8
Brittas Bay .... 103 N 9
Britway ....90 H 11
Broad Haven .... 110 C 5
Broad Meadow .... 109 N 7
Broadford *Clare* ....99 G 9
Broadford *Limerick* ...94 F 10
Broadway ....97 M 11
Brookeborough .... 113 J 5
Broomfield .... 108 L 5
Brosna ....93 E 11
Brosna (River) .... 101 I 8
Broughal .... 101 I 8
Broughane Cross Roads ...93 D 11
Brougher Mount .... 113 J 4
Broughshane .... 119 N 3
Brow Head ....88 C 13
Brown Flesk ....93 D 11
Brownstown ....96 K 11
Brownstown Head ......96 K 11
Bruckless .... 112 G 4
Bruff ....94 G 10
Bruree ....94 G 10
Bryansford .... 115 O 5
Buckna .... 119 N 3
Buckode .... 112 H 4
Buiríos Uí Chéin /
  Borrisokane .... 100 H 9
Bulgaden ....94 G 10
Bull (The) ....88 B 13
Bull Point .... 119 N 2
Bullaba .... 117 I 3
Bullaun ....99 G 8
Bull's Head ....92 B 11
Bun Cranncha / *Buncrana* ...117 J 2
Bun Dobhráin / *Bundoran* ...112 H 4
Bun na hAbhna /
  Bunnahowen .... 110 C 5
Bun na Leaca / *Brinlack* .. 116 H 2
Bunaclugga Bay .... 93 D 10
Bunacurry .... 110 C 6
Bunatrahir Bay .... 111 D 5
Bunaveela Lough ...... 111 D 5
Bunaw ....88 C 12
Bunbrosna .... 107 J 7
Bunclody ....96 M 10
Buncrana .... 117 J 2
Bunlahy .... 107 J 6
Bunmahon ....91 J 11
Bunnafollistran .... 105 E 7
Bunnaglass ....99 F 8
Bunnahown .... 104 C 7
Bunnanaddan .... 112 G 5
Bunny (Lough) ....99 F 8
Bunnyconnellan .... 111 E 5
Bunowen .... 105 C 6
Bunratty ....99 F 9
Burncourt ....95 H 11
Burnfoot *Birdstown* ... 117 J 2
Burnfoot *Limavady* ... 118 L 3
Burnfort ....90 G 11
Burr Point .... 115 P 4
Burren *Clare* ....99 E 8
Burren *Cork* ....90 F 12
Burren *Mayo* .... 105 E 6
Burren (The) ....99 E 8
Burren Centre Kifenora .99 E 8
Burrenfadda ....99 E 9
Burrishoole Abbey ..... 105 D 6
Burrow ....97 M 11
Burtown .... 102 L 9
Bush .... 118 M 2
Bush (The) *Dungannon* ...114 L 4
Bush (The) *Rathcor* ... 109 N 6
Bushfield .... 100 G 9
Bushmills .... 118 M 2
Butler's Bridge .... 107 J 5
Butlerstown ....90 F 13
Buttevant ....94 F 11
Butts (The) .... 101 K 9
Bweeng ....90 F 11

C

Cabragh .... 114 L 4

Cadamstown *Kildare* .. 102 L 7
Cadamstown *Offaly* ... 101 J 8
Caddy .... 114 N 3
Caggan .... 105 D 7
Caha Mountains ....89 C 12
Caha pass ....89 D 12
Caheragh ....89 E 13
Caher *Clare* ....99 G 9
Caher *Mayo* .... 105 E 7
Caher Island .... 104 B 6
Caher Roe's Den ....96 L 10
Caheradrine ....99 F 8
Caherbarnagh
  Corcaigh / Cork ....89 E 11
Caherbarnagh *Kerry* ...88 B 12
Caherconlish ....94 G 10
Caherconnel ....99 E 8
Caherconree ....92 C 11
Caherdaniel ....88 B 12
Caherea ....99 E 9
Caherlistrane .... 105 E 7
Cahermore *Cork* ......88 B 13
Cahermore *Galway* ....99 F 8
Cahermurphy ....98 D 9
Cahernahallia ....95 H 10
Cahore Point ....97 N 10
Caiseal / *Cashel* ....95 I 10
Caisleán an Bharraigh /
  Castlebar .... 105 E 6
Caisleán an Chomair /
  Castlecomer .... 101 K 9
Calafort Ros Láir /
  Rosslare Harbour .....97 M 11
Caledon .... 114 L 4
Calf Islands ....89 D 13
Callaghansmills ....99 F 9
Callainn / *Callan* ......95 J 10
Callow *Galway* .... 104 B 7
Callow *Mayo* .... 105 E 6
Callow *Roscommon* ... 106 G 6
Caltra .... 106 G 7
Caltraghlea .... 100 H 7
Calverstown .... 102 L 8
Cam Forest .... 118 L 2
Camlin (River) .... 107 I 6
Camlough .... 114 M 5
Camoge ....94 G 10
Camolin ....97 M 10
Camowen .... 113 K 4
Camp ....92 C 11
Campile ....96 L 11
Campsey .... 118 K 2
Camross .... 101 J 8
Camus Bay .... 105 D 8
Canglass Point ....88 B 12
Canningstown .... 108 K 6
Canon Island ....99 E 9
Cappagh *Dungannon* .. 114 L 4
Cappagh *Limerick* ....94 F 10
Cappagh *River* .... 100 G 8
Cappagh White ....95 H 10
Cappaghmore ....99 F 8
Cappalinnan .... 101 J 9
Cappamore ....94 G 10
Cappanacreha .... 105 D 7
Cappanrush .... 101 J 7
Cappataggle .... 100 G 8
Cappeen ....89 F 12
Car (Slieve) .... 111 D 5
Caragh (Lough) ....88 C 11
Caragh (River) ....89 C 12
Caragh Bridge ....92 C 11
Caragh Lake ....92 C 11
Carbery's Hundred Isles ...89 D 13
Carbury .... 102 L 7
Cardy .... 115 P 4
Cargan .... 119 N 3
Carhan House ....88 B 12
Cark .... 117 I 3
Cark Mountain .... 117 I 3
Carland .... 114 L 4
Carlanstown .... 108 L 6
Carlingford .... 109 N 5
Carlingford Lough ..... 109 N 5
Carn .... 113 I 4
Carna .... 104 C 8
Carnageer .... 119 O 3
Carnagh .... 119 N 2
Carnalbanagh Sheddings ...119 N 2
Carnanelly .... 114 L 3
Carnanreagh .... 118 K 3
Carnaross .... 108 L 6
Carnaween .... 112 H 3
Carncastle .... 119 O 3
Carndonagh /
  Carn Domhnach ...... 118 K 2
Carnduff .... 119 N 2

Carne .... 97 M 11
Carneatly .... 119 N 2
Carnew .... 97 M 9
Carney *Sligo* .... 112 G 4
Carney *Tipperary* .... 100 H 9
Carnlough .... 119 O 3
Carnlough Bay .... 119 O 3
Carnmore .... 99 F 8
Carnoneen .... 105 F 7
Carnowen .... 117 J 3
Carnsore Point .... 97 M 11
Carnteel .... 114 L 4
Carntogher .... 118 L 3
Carra (Lough) .... 105 E 6
Carracastle .... 106 F 6
Carragh .... 102 L 8
Carraholly .... 105 D 6
Carraig Airt / Carrigart .... 117 I 2
Carraig Mhachaire Rois /
  Carrickmacross .... 108 L 6
Carraig na Siúire /
  Carrick-on-Suir .... 95 J 10
Carran .... 99 E 8
Carrantuohill .... 89 C 11
Carrick *Wexford* .... 96 L 11
Carrick / An Charraig
  Donegal .... 112 G 4
Carrick-a-Rede
  Rope Bridge .... 118 M 2
Carrick-on-Shannon /
  Cora Droma Rúisc .... 107 H 6
Carrickaboy .... 107 K 6
Carrickashedoge .... 108 L 6
Carrickboy .... 107 I 7
Carrickfergus .... 115 O 3
Carrickhugh .... 118 K 2
Carrickmore .... 114 K 4
Carrickroe .... 114 K 4
Carrig .... 94 G 11
Carrig Island .... 93 D 10
Carrigadrohid .... 90 F 12
Carrigafoyle Castle .... 93 D 10
Carrigagulla .... 90 F 11
Carrigaholt .... 93 C 10
Carrigaholt Bay .... 93 C 10
Carrigahorig .... 100 H 8
Carrigaline .... 90 G 12
Carrigallen .... 107 J 6
Carrigan .... 107 J 6
Carrigan Head .... 112 F 4
Carriganimmy .... 89 E 12
Carrigans .... 117 J 3
Carrigatogher .... 100 H 9
Carrigfadda .... 89 E 13
Carrigglass Manor .... 107 I 6
Carriggower .... 103 N 8
Carrigkerry .... 93 E 10
Carrignavar .... 90 G 12
Carrigrohane .... 90 G 12
Carrigtohill .... 90 H 12
Carrowbehy .... 106 G 6
Carrowdore .... 115 P 4
Carrowkeel *Donegal* .... 117 J 2
Carrowkeel *Galway* .... 99 G 8
Carrowkennedy .... 105 D 6
Carrowmore *Galway* .... 99 F 8
Carrowmore *Kilmacowen* ..112 G 5
Carrowmore
  near Cloonacool .... 112 F 5
Carrowmore
  near Crossboyne .... 105 E 6
Carrowmore
  near Killasser .... 105 F 6
Carrowmore
  near Killogeary .... 111 E 5
Carrowmore Lake .... 110 C 5
Carrowmore Point .... 98 D 9
Carrowmoreknock .... 105 E 7
Carrownacon .... 105 E 6
Carrowneden .... 112 F 5
Carrownisky .... 104 C 6
Carrowntanlis .... 105 F 7
Carrowntreagh
  Roscommon .... 100 H 7
Carrowreagh *Sligo* .... 112 F 5
Carrowrory .... 107 I 7
Carry Bridge .... 113 J 5
Carrybeg .... 95 J 10
Carryduff .... 115 O 4
Casheen bay .... 98 C 8
Cashel *Donegal* .... 117 I 2
Cashel *Mayo* .... 104 C 6
Cashel
  near Glennamaddy .... 106 G 7
Cashel / An Caiseal
  Galway .... 104 C 7
Cashel (Rock of) .... 95 I 10

Cashelgarran .... 112 G 4
Cashelmore .... 117 I 2
Cashen River .... 93 D 10
Cashla .... 99 F 8
Cashla Bay .... 98 D 8
Cashleen .... 104 B 7
Casla / Costelloe .... 98 D 8
Casltepollard .... 107 K 6
Cassagh .... 96 L 10
Castle Carry .... 118 K 2
Castle Coole .... 113 J 4
Castle Gardens .... 90 F 13
Castle Haven .... 89 E 13
Castle Island .... 89 D 13
Castle Point .... 98 C 10
Castlebaldwin .... 112 G 5
Castlebar (River) .... 105 E 6
Castlebellingham .... 109 M 6
Castleblakeney .... 106 G 7
Castlebridge .... 97 M 10
Castlecaulfield .... 114 L 4
Castleconnell .... 99 G 9
Castleconor .... 111 E 5
Castlecor .... 94 F 11
Castlecove .... 88 B 12
Castlecuffe .... 101 J 8
Castledawson .... 114 M 3
Castlederg .... 113 J 3
Castledermot .... 102 L 9
Castlefinn .... 117 J 3
Castlefreke .... 89 F 13
Castlegal .... 112 G 4
Castlegar .... 99 E 8
Castlegregory .... 92 B 11
Castlehill *Ballycroy South* ..110 C 6
Castlehill
  near Rake Street .... 111 D 5
Castlejordan .... 102 K 7
Castleknock .... 103 M 7
Castlellis .... 97 M 10
Castlelyons .... 90 H 11
Castlemaine .... 93 C 11
Castlemaine Harbour .... 92 C 11
Castlemartyr .... 90 H 12
Castleplunket .... 106 G 6
Castlequin .... 88 B 12
Castlerahan .... 108 K 6
Castlerock .... 118 L 2
Castleroe .... 118 M 2
Castleshane .... 114 L 5
Castletown *Clare* .... 99 E 8
Castletown *Cork* .... 89 F 12
Castletown *Laois* .... 101 J 9
Castletown *Limerick* .... 94 F 10
Castletown *Meath* .... 108 L 6
Castletown *near Finnea* .... 107 K 6
Castletown *Westmeath* .... 107 J 7
Castletown *Wexford* .... 97 N 9
Castletown House .... 103 M 7
Castletownbere .... 88 C 13
Castletownroche .... 94 G 11
Castletownshend .... 89 E 13
Castleville .... 105 E 7
Castleward House .... 115 P 4
Castlewarren .... 96 K 9
Castlewellan .... 115 O 5
Castlewellan Forest Park .115 O 5
Cathair na Mart /
  Westport .... 105 D 6
Cathair Saidhbhín /
  Cahersiveen .... 88 B 12
Cathedral Rocks .... 104 B 6
Causeway .... 93 C 10
Causeway Head .... 118 M 2
Cavan / An Cabhán .... 107 J 6
Cavanagarvan .... 114 L 5
Cavangarden .... 112 H 4
Cé Bhréanainn / Brandon .. 92 B 11
Ceanannas / Ceanannus Mór
  (Kells) .... 108 L 6
Ceann Toirc / Kanturk .... 94 F 11
Ceapach Choinn /
  Cappoquin .... 91 I 11
Ceatharlach / Carlow .... 102 L 9
Ceathrú Thaidhg /
  Carrowteige .... 111 C 5
Cecilstown .... 94 F 11
Celbridge .... 103 M 7
Chanonrock .... 108 M 6
Chapeltown *Down* .... 115 P 5
Chapeltown
  near Portmagee .... 88 A 12
Chapeltown *near Tralee* .... 93 C 11
Charlemont .... 114 L 4
Charlestown *Craigavon* .... 114 M 4
Charlestown *Mayo* .... 106 F 6
Cheekpoint .... 96 K 11

Cherryville .... 102 L 8
Chesney's Corner .... 114 M 3
Church Ballee .... 115 P 5
Church Cross .... 89 D 13
Church Hill *Donegal* .... 117 I 3
Church Hill *Fermanagh* .... 113 I 4
Church Quarter .... 119 N 2
Church Town .... 117 J 3
Church Village .... 105 E 6
Churchstreet .... 106 G 6
Churchtown *Cookstown* .... 114 L 3
Churchtown *Cork* .... 90 H 12
Churchtown *Down* .... 115 P 4
Churchtown *Wexford* .... 96 L 11
Churchtown Point .... 114 M 3
Cill Airne / Killarney .... 89 D 11
Cill Chainnigh / Kilkenny .. 96 K 10
Cill Chaoi / Kilkee .... 98 D 9
Cill Dalua / Killaloe .... 99 G 9
Cill Dara / Kildare .... 102 L 8
Cill Mhantáin / Wicklow .... 103 N 9
Cill Mocheallóg /
  Kilmallock .... 94 G 10
Cill Orglan / Killorglin .... 93 C 11
Cill Rois / Kilrush .... 93 D 10
Cill Rónáin / Kilronan .... 98 C 8
Cionn tSáile / Kinsale .... 90 G 12
City Walls .... 96 K 11
Clabby .... 113 J 4
Cladagh .... 113 I 5
Claddagh .... 106 F 7
Claddaghduff .... 104 B 7
Clady *Antrim* .... 115 N 4
Clady *Magherafelt* .... 118 M 3
Clady *Strabane* .... 117 J 3
Clady (River) .... 116 H 2
Clady Milltown .... 114 M 5
Claggan *Donegal* .... 117 J 2
Claggan *Mayo* .... 104 C 6
Clamper Cross .... 93 E 11
Clanabogan .... 113 J 4
Clane .... 102 L 8
Clár Chlainne Mhuiris /
  Claremorris .... 105 F 6
Clara .... 103 N 9
Clara (Valle of) .... 103 N 9
Clarahill .... 101 J 8
Clare *Armagh* .... 114 M 5
Clare *Craigavon* .... 114 N 4
Clare (River) .... 105 F 7
Clare Island .... 104 B 6
Clarecastle .... 99 F 9
Clareen .... 101 I 8
Clarina .... 94 F 10
Clarinbridge .... 99 F 8
Clark's Cross Roads .... 107 J 7
Clash .... 100 H 9
Clash North .... 93 E 10
Clashmore .... 91 I 11
Claudy .... 118 K 3
Clear (Cape) .... 89 D 13
Cleggan / An Cloigeann .... 104 B 7
Cleggan Bay .... 104 B 7
Cléire (Oilean) /
  Clear Island .... 89 D 13
Cleristown .... 96 M 11
Clew Bay .... 104 C 6
Clifden Bay .... 104 B 7
Cliff .... 112 H 4
Clifferna .... 108 K 6
Cliffony .... 112 G 4
Clogga *Kilkenny* .... 96 K 11
Clogga *Wicklow* .... 97 N 9
Clogh *Ballymena* .... 119 N 3
Clogh *Kilkenny* .... 101 K 9
Clogh *Laois* .... 101 J 8
Clogh *Wexford* .... 97 M 10
Clogh Mills .... 118 N 3
Cloghan *Offaly* .... 101 I 8
Cloghan *Westmeath* .... 107 K 7
Cloghane .... 92 B 11
Cloghaneely .... 117 H 2
Clogharinka .... 102 K 7
Cloghaun .... 105 F 7
Cloghboley .... 112 G 4
Cloghbrack *Cloonbur* .... 105 D 7
Cloghbrack *Meath* .... 108 K 7
Clogheen .... 95 I 11
Clogher *Dungannon* .... 113 K 4
Clogher *Kerry* .... 93 D 11
Clogher
  near Carrownacon .... 105 E 6
Clogher *near Westport* .... 105 D 6
Clogher *Roscommon* .... 107 H 6
Clogher Head *Kerry* .... 92 A 11
Clogher Head *Louth / Lú* .. 109 N 6
Cloghera .... 99 G 9

Clogherhead .... 109 N 6
Cloghjordan .... 100 H 9
Cloghmacoo .... 108 L 6
Cloghoge .... 109 M 5
Cloghroe *Cork* .... 90 G 12
Cloghroe *Donegal* .... 117 I 3
Cloghy .... 115 P 4
Cloghy Bay .... 115 P 4
Clohamon .... 96 M 10
Clohernagh .... 96 K 11
Cloich na Coillte /
  Clonakilty .... 89 F 13
Clóirtheach / Clara .... 101 J 7
Clomantagh .... 95 J 9
Clonakenny .... 101 I 9
Clonbern .... 106 G 7
Clonbulloge .... 102 K 8
Cloncagh .... 94 F 10
Clonco Bridge .... 100 G 8
Cloncrave .... 108 K 7
Clonculen .... 107 I 7
Cloncurry .... 102 L 7
Clondalkin .... 103 M 8
Clondaw .... 97 M 10
Clonderalaw Bay .... 93 E 10
Clondulane .... 90 H 11
Clonea .... 95 J 11
Clonea Bay .... 91 J 11
Clonee .... 103 M 7
Cloneen .... 95 J 10
Clonegall .... 96 M 9
Clonelly .... 113 I 4
Clonevin .... 97 N 10
Clonfert .... 100 H 8
Clonfert Cross Roads .... 100 H 8
Clonkeevy .... 112 G 5
Clonleigh .... 117 J 3
Clonlost .... 107 K 7
Clonmacnoise .... 101 I 8
Clonmany .... 117 J 2
Clonmellon .... 108 K 7
Clonmore *Carlow* .... 103 M 9
Clonmore *Tipperary* .... 101 I 9
Clonmult .... 90 H 12
Clonony .... 101 I 8
Clonoulty .... 95 I 10
Clonroche .... 96 L 10
Clonsilla .... 103 M 7
Clontarf .... 103 N 7
Clontibret .... 114 L 5
Clontubbrid .... 101 J 9
Clonycavan .... 108 L 7
Clonygowan .... 101 K 8
Cloon Lake .... 88 C 12
Cloone .... 107 I 6
Cloone Grange .... 107 I 6
Clooncacleigha Lake .... 112 G 5
Cloonacool .... 112 F 5
Cloonagh Lough .... 106 F 6
Cloonaghlin Lough .... 88 C 12
Cloonaghmore .... 111 D 5
Cloonboo .... 105 E 7
Cloondaff .... 105 D 6
Cloondara .... 107 I 6
Clooneen .... 107 J 6
Cloonee Loughs .... 89 C 12
Cloonfad *Kiltullagh* .... 106 F 6
Cloonfad *near Old Town* .. 100 H 8
Cloonfallagh .... 105 F 6
Cloonfinish .... 105 F 6
Cloonfower .... 106 G 6
Cloonfree Lough .... 106 H 6
Cloonkeen *Kerry* .... 89 E 12
Cloonkeen *Mayo* .... 105 D 6
Cloonkeen *Roscommon* .... 106 G 6
Cloonlara .... 99 G 9
Cloonloogh .... 106 G 6
Cloonlusk .... 94 H 10
Cloonmore .... 106 F 6
Cloonoon .... 100 H 8
Cloonteen .... 94 H 10
Cloontia .... 106 G 6
Cloonusker .... 99 G 9
Cloonymorris .... 100 G 8
Cloonyquin .... 106 H 6
Cloran .... 108 L 7
Clough .... 115 O 5
Cloverhill *Cavan* .... 107 J 5
Cloverhill *Galway* .... 105 E 7
Cloyfin .... 118 M 2

Cloyne .... 90 H 12
Cluain Eois / Clones .... 113 K 5
Cluain Meala / Clonmel .... 95 I 10
Cluainín / Manorhamilton ..112 H 5
Clydagh .... 105 E 6
Clynacantan .... 88 A 12
Coachford .... 90 F 12
Coagh .... 114 M 4
Coalbrook .... 95 J 10
Coalisland .... 114 L 4
Coan .... 101 K 9
Cod's Head .... 88 B 13
Coill an Chollaigh /
  Bailieborough .... 108 L 6
Colbinstown .... 102 L 8
Coldwood .... 99 F 8
Colebrooke .... 113 J 5
Colehill .... 107 I 7
Coleraine .... 118 L 2
Colgagh .... 112 G 5
Colgagh Lough .... 112 G 5
Colligan (River) .... 95 I 11
Collin Top .... 119 N 3
Collinstown .... 107 K 7
Collon .... 109 M 6
Collooney .... 112 G 5
Colly .... 88 C 12
Colmanstown .... 106 G 7
Comber .... 115 O 4
Comeragh Mountains .... 95 J 11
Commeen .... 117 H 3
Commons .... 95 J 10
Conay Island .... 112 G 5
Cong / Conga .... 105 E 7
Conlig .... 115 O 4
Conn (Lough) .... 111 E 5
Conna .... 90 H 11
Connagh .... 100 G 9
Connemara .... 104 C 7
Connemara
  National Park .... 104 C 7
Connolly .... 99 E 9
Connonagh .... 89 E 13
Connor .... 115 N 3
Connor Pass .... 92 B 11
Convoy .... 117 I 3
Coogue .... 105 F 6
Cookstown .... 114 L 4
Coola .... 112 G 5
Coolagarry .... 106 H 7
Coolaney .... 112 G 5
Coolattin .... 97 M 9
Coolbaun .... 101 K 9
Coolbawn .... 100 H 9
Coolboy .... 97 M 9
Coolcull .... 96 L 11
Coolderry .... 101 I 8
Coole (Castle) .... 113 J 4
Coole Abbey .... 90 H 11
Coolea / Cúil Aodha .... 89 E 12
Coolearagh .... 102 L 8
Cooley Point .... 109 N 6
Coolgrange .... 96 K 10
Coolgreany .... 97 N 9
Coolkeeragh .... 117 K 2
Coolkellure .... 89 E 12
Coolmeen .... 93 E 10
Coolmore .... 112 H 4
Coolnareen .... 101 J 9
Coolrain .... 101 J 9
Coolroebeg .... 96 K 10
Coolshaghtena .... 107 H 6
Coolteige .... 106 H 6
Coomacarrea .... 88 B 12
Coomakesta Pass .... 88 B 12
Coomasaharn Lake .... 88 C 12
Coomhola .... 89 D 12
Coomhola Bridge .... 89 D 12
Coonagh .... 94 F 10
Cooraclare .... 98 D 9
Coorleagh .... 96 K 10
Coornagillagh .... 89 C 12
Cootehall .... 106 H 6
Copany .... 113 H 4
Copeland Island .... 115 P 3
Coppanagh .... 108 L 6
Cora Droma Rúisc /
  Carrick-on-Shannon .... 107 H 6
Corbally
  Castleconor West .... 111 E 5
Corbally *Clare* .... 98 D 9
Corbally *Kildare* .... 102 L 8
Corbay Upper .... 107 I 6
Corbet Milltown .... 115 N 4
Corcaigh / Cork .... 90 G 12
Corclogh .... 110 B 5
Corcomroe Abbey .... 99 E 8

Cordal .... 93 D 11
Cordarragh .... 105 D 6
Corduff .... 109 N 7
Cork Harbour .... 90 H 12
Corkey .... 119 N 2
Corkscrew Hill .... 99 E 8
Corlea .... 107 I 7
Corlee .... 105 E 5
Corlis Point .... 93 D 10
Corn Hill .... 107 I 6
Cornafulla .... 101 H 7
Cornagillagh .... 117 I 3
Cornamona .... 105 D 7
Cornanagh .... 105 E 6
Corracloona .... 113 H 4
Corrakyle .... 99 G 9
Corraleehan .... 113 I 5
Corran Cross Roads .... 114 M 5
Corrandulla .... 105 F 7
Corranny .... 113 K 5
Corraree .... 106 H 7
Corraun Hill .... 104 C 6
Corraun Peninsula .... 104 C 6
Corraun Point .... 110 B 5
Corrawaleen .... 107 I 5
Correllstown .... 107 K 7
Corrib (Lough) .... 105 E 7
Corries .... 96 L 10
Corriga .... 107 I 6
Corrigeenroe .... 106 H 5
Corrofin .... 99 E 9
Corronoher .... 94 F 10
Corroy .... 111 E 5
Corry .... 112 H 5
Corstown .... 95 J 10
Cortowm .... 108 L 6
Corvally .... 108 L 6
Corvoley .... 111 D 5
Cottoners .... 89 C 11
Coulagh Bay .... 88 B 12
Coumfea .... 95 J 11
Courtmacsherry .... 90 F 13
Courtmacsherry Bay .... 90 G 13
Courtown .... 97 N 10
Cousane Gap .... 89 E 12
Craanford .... 97 M 9
Craffield .... 103 M 9
Crag Cave .... 93 D 11
Craggaunowen
  Megalithic Centre .... 99 F 9
Craig .... 118 K 3
Craigantlet .... 115 O 4
Craigavad .... 115 O 4
Craigavon .... 114 M 4
Craignamaddy .... 114 K 3
Craigs .... 118 M 3
Crana .... 117 J 2
Cranagh .... 114 K 3
Cranfield Point .... 109 N 5
Cranford .... 117 I 2
Crannogeboy .... 116 G 3
Cranny .... 99 E 9
Cratloe .... 99 F 9
Craughwell .... 99 F 8
Crawfordsburn .... 115 O 4
Crazy Corner .... 107 K 7
Creagh .... 113 J 4
Creagh (The) .... 114 M 3
Creaghanroe .... 114 L 5
Crean's Cross Roads .... 90 F 12
Crecora .... 94 F 10
Creegh .... 98 D 9
Creeslough .... 117 I 2
Creevagh .... 111 D 5
Creevagh Head .... 111 E 5
Creeves .... 93 E 10
Creevykeel .... 112 G 4
Cregg *Clare* .... 99 E 8
Cregg *Cork* .... 89 E 13
Cregg *Galway* .... 105 E 7
Cregg *Sligo* .... 112 G 5
Creggan *Armagh* .... 108 M 5
Creggan *Dungannon* .... 114 K 4
Cregganbaun .... 104 C 6
Creggaun .... 94 F 10
Creggs .... 106 G 7
Crilly .... 114 L 4
Crindle .... 118 L 2
Crinkill .... 101 I 8
Croagh *Donegal* .... 112 G 3
Croagh *Limerick* .... 94 F 10
Croagh Patrick .... 105 C 6
Croaghaun .... 110 B 6
Croaghmoyle .... 105 D 6
Croaghnageer .... 113 I 3
Croaghnakeela Island .... 104 C 8
Croaghrimbeg .... 105 D 6

A B **C** D E F G H I J K L M N O P Q R S T U V W X Y Z

Croan (Lough) 106 H7
Croangar (Lough) 116 H3
Crockaneel 119 N2
Crockets Town 111 E5
Crockmore 113 I4
Crocknasmug 118 L2
Croghan Offaly 101 K7
Croghan Roscommon 106 H6
Croghan Mountain 103 N9
Crohane 89 D12
Crohy Head 116 G3
Crois Mhaoiliona / Crossmolina 111 E5
Croithlí / Crolly 116 H2
Cromane 92 C11
Cromoge 101 J9
Croob (Slieve) 115 N4
Crookedwood 107 K7
Crookhaven 88 C13
Crookstown Kildare 102 L8
Crookstown Moviddy 90 F12
Croom 94 F10
Croos 106 H7
Cross Cong 105 E7
Cross Waterford 91 I11
Cross (River) 105 D7
Cross Barry 90 G12
Cross Keys Cavan 107 K6
Cross Keys Meath 108 K6
Cross Keys Meath 108 M7
Cross Roads 117 I3
Crossabeg 97 M10
Crossakeel 108 K6
Crossboyne 105 E6
Crossconnell 100 H8
Crossdoney 107 J6
Crossea 107 J7
Crosserlough 107 K6
Crossgar 115 O4
Crossgare 118 L2
Crosshaven 90 H12
Crossmaglen 108 M5
Crossna 106 H5
Crossooha 99 F8
Crosspatrick Kilkenny 101 J9
Crosspatrick Wicklow 97 M9
Crosswell 106 G7
Crove 112 G3
Crow Head 88 B13
Crownarad 112 G4
Cruit Island 116 G2
Crumlin Antrim 115 N4
Crumlin Cong 105 D7
Crusheen 99 F9
Crutt 101 K9
Cúil an tSúdaire / Portarlington 101 K8
Cuilcagh 113 I5
Cuilkillew 111 E5
Cuilmore 105 F6
Culdaff 118 K2
Culdaff Bay 118 K2
Culfadda 106 G5
Culfin 104 C7
Culky 113 J5
Cullahill 101 J9
Cullane 94 G10
Cullaun 94 H10
Cullaville 108 M5
Culleens 111 F5
Cullen Cork 94 H10
Cullen Tipperary 93 E11
Cullenagh (River) 99 E9
Cullenstown near Duncormick 96 L11
Cullenstown near Newbawn 96 L10
Cullin 105 E6
Cullin (Lough) 105 E6
Cullybackey 118 M3
Cullyhanna 108 M5
Culmore 117 K2
Culnady 118 M3
Cummeragh 88 B12
Cunningburn 115 P4
Curlew Mountains 106 G6
Curracloe 97 M10
Curragh 91 I12
Curragh (The) 102 L8
Curragh Camp 102 L8
Curragh West 106 G7
Curragha 109 M7
Curraghbonaun 106 F6
Curraghboy 106 H7
Curraghmore Gardens 95 J11
Curraghroe 107 H6
Curraglass 91 H11

Currahchase Forest Park 94 F10
Curran 114 M3
Currane (Lough) 88 B12
Currans 93 D11
Curraun 105 D7
Curreel (Lough) 104 C7
Curreeny 100 H9
Currow 93 D11
Curry 105 E6
Curryglass 88 C12
Curryskeskin 118 M2
Cushendall 119 N2
Cushendun 119 N2
Cusher 114 M5
Cushina 101 K8
Cut (The) 101 K8
Cutra (Lough) 99 F8

D
Dahybaun (Lough) 111 D5
Daingean 101 K8
Dalgar 105 F7
Dalkey 103 N8
Damastown 109 N7
Damerstown 101 K9
Damhead 118 M2
Dan (Lough) 103 N8
Danesfort Kilkenny 96 K10
Danesfort Longford 107 I6
Dangan Cork 91 H12
Dangan Waterford 96 K11
Darby's Gap 97 M10
Dargle 103 N8
Darkley 114 L5
Darragh 99 E9
Dartry Mountains 112 G4
Davagh Forest Park 114 L3
Davidstown 103 M9
Dawros 104 C7
Dawros Head 116 G3
Dead 94 H10
Dealagh 98 D9
Dee 108 L6
Deel Limerick 94 F10
Deel Mayo 111 D5
Deel Westmeath 108 K7
Deel Bridge 111 D5
Deele (River) 117 I3
Deelish 89 E12
Deenish Island 88 B12
Delamont 115 O4
Delgany 103 N8
Delphi 104 C7
Delvin 108 K7
Delvin (River) 109 N7
Dennet (Burn) 117 J3
Derg 113 J3
Derg (Lough) near Donegal 113 I4
Derg (Lough) near Nenagh 100 H9
Dergalt 117 J3
Dernagree 93 E11
Derravaragh (Lough) 107 J7
Derreen near Ballynagoraher 105 D6
Derreen near Cloghmore 104 C6
Derreen near Formoyle 99 E8
Derreen near Lahinch 98 D9
Derreen Gardens 89 C12
Derreeny 88 C12
Derreeny Bridge 89 E13
Derriana Lough 88 C12
Derries 101 J8
Derry 112 G5
Derryadd 114 M4
Derryanvil 114 M4
Derrybeg 116 H2
Derryboye 115 O4
Derrybrien 99 G8
Derryclare Lough 104 C7
Derrycooly 101 I8
Derrycraff 105 D6
Derrydruel 116 G3
Derryerglinna 105 D7
Derryfadda 101 J9
Derrygolan 101 J8
Derrygonnelly 113 I4
Derrygoolin 100 G9
Derrygrogan 101 J8
Derrykeevan 114 M4
Derrykeighan 118 M2
Derrylea 104 C7
Derrylin 113 J5
Derrylough 116 G3
Derrymore 93 C11

Derrymore Island 93 C11
Derrynane 88 B12
Derrynane House 88 B12
Derrynasaggart Mountains 89 E11
Derrynawilt 113 K5
Derryneen 104 C7
Derrynoose 114 L5
Derryrush 104 C7
Derrytrasna 114 M4
Derryveagh Mountains 117 H3
Derryvohy 105 E6
Derrywode 106 G6
Dervock 118 M2
Desertmartin 114 L3
Devenish Island 113 J4
Devilsbit 101 I9
Devilsmother 105 D7
Diamond (The) Antrim 114 N4
Diamond (The) Cookstown 114 M4
Diamond (The) Omagh 113 J4
Dingle / Daingean Uí Chúis 92 B11
Dingle Bay 92 B11
Dingle Harbour 92 B11
Divis 115 N4
Doagh Newtownabbey 115 N3
Doagh Rosguill 117 I2
Doagh Beg / Dumhaigh Bhig 117 J2
Doagh Isle 117 J2
Dodder 103 M8
Doe Castle 117 I2
Dolla 100 H9
Dollingstown 114 N4
Domhnach Phádraig / Donaghpatrick 108 L6
Donabate 109 N7
Donacarney 109 N6
Donadea 102 L7
Donagh 113 J5
Donaghadee 115 P4
Donaghaguy 109 N5
Donaghey 114 L4
Donaghmore 114 L4
Donaghmore Meath 109 M7
Donard Wexford 96 L10
Donard Wicklow 103 M8
Donard (Slieve) 115 O5
Donaskeagh 95 H10
Donegal / Dún na nGall 113 H4
Donegal Airport 116 G2
Donegal Bay 112 G5
Donegal Point 98 D9
Doneraile 94 G11
Donohill 95 H10
Donore 109 M6
Donoughmore 90 F12
Doo (Lough) 99 E9
Doo Lough 104 C7
Doo Lough Pass 104 C7
Dooagh 110 B6
Doobehy 111 D5
Doocastle 106 G5
Dooega Head 104 B6
Dooey Point 116 G3
Doogary 107 J5
Dooghbeg 104 C7
Doogort 110 B5
Doohooma 110 C5
Dooish Mount 117 J3
Doolough Point 110 C5
Doon Galway 100 G7
Doon Limerick 94 H10
Doon Lough 99 F9
Doona 110 C5
Doonaha 93 D10
Doonbeg 98 D9
Doonloughan 104 B7
Doonmanagh 92 B11
Doorin Point 112 H4
Dooyork 110 C5
Dore 116 H2
Dorrusawillin 107 H5
Dough 88 C13
Douglas 90 G12
Douglas Bridge 113 J3
Doulus Bay 88 A12
Doulus Head 88 A12
Dowdallshill 109 M5
Dowling 96 K10
Downhill 118 L2
Downpatrick 115 O5
Downpatrick Head 111 D5
Downs (The) 107 K7
Dowra 113 H5

Dowth 109 M6
Drains Bay 119 O3
Drangan 95 J10
Draperstown 114 L3
Dreen 118 K3
Dreenagh 92 C10
Drimoleague 89 E13
Drinagh Cork 89 E13
Drinagh Wexford 97 M11
Drinaghan 111 E5
Dring 107 J6
Dripsey 90 F12
Dripsey (River) 90 F11
Drishaghaun 105 D7
Drishane Bridge 89 D13
Droichead Átha / Drogheda 109 M6
Droichead na Bandan / Bandon 90 F12
Drom 101 I9
Dromahair 112 H5
Dromara 115 N4
Dromcolliher 94 F10
Dromin Limerick 94 G10
Dromin Louth 109 M6
Dromina 94 F11
Dromineer 100 H9
Dromiskin 109 M6
Dromkeen 94 G10
Drommahane 90 F11
Dromod 107 I6
Dromoland Castle 99 F9
Dromore Banbridge 115 N4
Dromore Omagh 113 J4
Dromore Lake 94 F10
Dromore West 112 F5
Dromtrasna 93 E10
Drones (The) 118 M2
Drowes 112 H4
Drum Monaghan 108 K5
Drum Roscommon 101 H7
Drum Sligo 112 G5
Drum Hills 91 I11
Drum Manor Forest Park 114 L4
Drumahoe 117 K3
Drumandoora 99 F8
Drumaness 115 O4
Drumatober 100 G8
Drumbane 95 I10
Drumbeg Feddyglass 117 J3
Drumbeg Lisburn 115 O4
Drumbo 115 O4
Drumbologe 117 I3
Drumcar 109 M6
Drumcard 113 I5
Drumcliff 112 G5
Drumcliff Bay 112 G5
Drumcondra 108 M6
Drumcong 107 I5
Drumcree 108 K7
Drumcullen 114 M3
Drumduff 113 J4
Drumena Cashel 115 O5
Drumfea 96 L10
Drumfin 112 G5
Drumfree 117 J2
Drumgoft 103 M9
Drumintee 109 M5
Drumkeary 99 G8
Drumkeen 117 I3
Drumkeeran 112 H5
Drumlaheen Lough 107 I5
Drumlea 107 I5
Drumlegagh 113 J4
Drumlish 107 I6
Drumlosh 101 I7
Drummannon 114 M4
Drummin 96 L10
Drummullin 106 H6
Drumnakilly 114 L4
Drumone 108 K6
Drumquin 113 J4
Drumraney 107 I7
Drumreagh 110 B5
Drumshanbo 107 H5
Drumskinny 113 I4
Drumsna 118 L3
Duagh 93 D10
Dually 95 I10
Dublin Bay 103 N7
Duff 112 H4
Duffy 102 L7
Duleek 109 M7
Dumha Éige / Dooega 104 B6
Dún Aengus 98 C8

Dún A'Rí Forest Park 108 L6
Dún Chaoin / Dunquin 92 A11
Dún Dealgan / Dundalk 109 M5
Dún Garbhán /Dungarvan 91 J11
Dún Mánmhaí / Dunmanway 89 E12
Dún Mór / Dunmore 106 F7
Dún na nGall / Donegal 113 H4
Dunabrattin Head 91 K11
Dunadry 115 N3
Dunaff 117 J2
Dunaff Head 117 J2
Dunaghy 118 M2
Dunagree Point 118 L2
Dunamase (Rock of) 101 K8
Dunamon 106 H7
Dunany 109 N6
Dunany Point 109 N6
Dunbel 96 K10
Dunboyne 103 M7
Dunbrody Abbey 96 L11
Dunbulcaun Bay 99 F8
Duncannon 96 L11
Duncormick 96 M11
Dundalk Bay 109 M6
Dunderrow 90 G12
Dundonald 115 O4
Dundrod 115 N4
Dundrum Down 115 O5
Dundrum Dublin 103 N8
Dundrum Tipperary 95 H10
Dundrum Bay 115 O5
Dunfanaghy 117 I2
Dungannon 114 L4
Dunganstown 96 L10
Dungarvan Harbour 91 J11
Dungiven 118 L3
Dungloe / An Clochán Liath 116 G3
Dungonnell Dam 119 N3
Dungourney 90 H12
Dunguaire Castle 99 F8
Dunhill 91 K11
Duniry 100 G8
Dunkellin 99 F8
Dunkerrin 101 I9
Dunkineely 112 G4
Dunkitt 96 K11
Dunlavin 102 L8
Dunleer 109 M6
Dunlewy 117 H2
Dunloe (Gap of) 89 D11
Dunloy 118 M2
Dunluce Castle 118 M2
Dunmanus 89 D13
Dunmanus Bay 88 C13
Dunmore 109 O5
Dunmore Cave 96 K9
Dunmore East 96 L11
Dunmore Head Dunquin 92 A11
Dunmore Head near Culdaff 118 K2
Dunmore Head near Portnoo 116 G3
Dunmurry 115 N4
Dunnamaggan 96 K10
Dunnamanagh 118 L3
Dunnamore 114 L3
Dunnycove Bay 89 F13
Dunowen Head 89 F13
Dunree Head 117 J2
Dunsany 108 M7
Dunshaughlin 108 M7
Dunworly Bay 90 F13
Durlas / Thurles 95 I9
Durrow 101 J9
Durrus 89 D13
Dursey Head 88 B13
Dursey Island 88 B13
Duvillaun Beg 110 B5
Duvillaun More 110 B5
Dyan 114 L4
Dysart 107 J7
Dysert O'Dea 99 E9

E
Éadan Doire / Édenderry 102 K7
Eagle (Mount) 92 A11
Eagle Island 110 B5
Eagles Hill 88 B12
Eany 112 H3
Eanymore 112 H3
Easky 111 F5
Easky Lough 112 F5
East Ferry 90 H12

East Town 116 H2
Eddy Island 99 F8
Eden 115 O3
Ederny 113 J4
Edgeworthstown 107 J6
Edgeworthstown / Meathas Troim 107 J6
Egish (Lough) 108 L5
Eglinton 118 K2
Eglish 114 L4
Eighter 108 K6
Eleven Lane Ends 114 M5
Ellistrin 117 I3
Elly Bay 110 B5
Elphin 106 H6
Elton 94 G10
Elva (Slieve) 99 E8
Emlagh Point 104 C6
Emly 94 G10
Emmoo 106 H7
Emo 101 K8
Emo Court 101 K8
Emyvale 114 L4
Ennel (Lough) 107 J7
Ennis / Inis 99 F9
Enniscorthy / Inis Córthaidh 97 M10
Enniskean 89 F12
Enniskerry 103 N8
Enniskillen 113 J4
Ennistimon / Inis Díomáin 99 E9
Eochaill / Youghal 91 I12
Erne (Lower Lough) 113 I4
Erne (River) 107 J6
Erne (Upper Lough) 113 J5
Erra 117 I6
Errew Abbey 111 E5
Erriff (River) 105 D7
Errigal Mountain 117 H2
Erril 101 I9
Erris Head 110 B5
Errisbeg 104 C7
Errislannan 104 B7
Ervey Cross Roads 113 K5
Eshnadarragh 113 K5
Eshnadeelada 113 K5
Eske 113 H3
Eske (Lough) 113 H3
Esker 99 F8
Esker South 107 I6
Eskeragh 111 D5
Eskragh 113 K4
Eyeries 88 C12
Eyrecourt 100 H8

F
Faha 91 J11
Fahamore 92 B11
Fahan 117 J2
Fahy 100 H8
Fahy Lough 110 C5
Fair Green 99 F9
Fair Head 88 C13
Fairyhouse 108 M7
Fairymount 106 G6
Fallmore 110 B5
Fanad 117 I2
Fanad Head 117 J2
Fane River 108 M5
Fanore 99 E8
Farahy 94 G11
Fardrum 101 I7
Fardurris Point 98 D8
Farmer's Bridge 93 D11
Farnagh 101 I7
Farnaght 107 I6
Farnanes Cross Roads 90 F12
Farnoge 96 K10
Farran 90 F12
Farran Forest Park 90 F12
Farrancassidy Cross Roads 112 H4
Farranfore 93 D11
Fastnet Rock 89 D13
Faughan 118 K3
Fawney 117 K3
Fea (Lough) 114 L3
Feagarrid 95 I11
Feakle 99 F9
Feale (River) 93 D10
Fearn Hill 113 J3
Fedamore 94 G10
Fee (Lough) 104 C7
Feeagh (Lough) 105 D6
Feeard 92 C10
Feenagh 94 F10

Feeny ...118 K 3
Feevagh ...106 H 7
Fenagh ...107 I 5
Fenit ...92 C 11
Fennagh ...96 L 9
Fennor ...91 K 11
Feohanagh *Kerry* ...92 A 11
Feohanagh *Limerick* ...94 F 10
Feohanagh (River) ...101 I 8
Ferbane ...101 I 8
Fergus (River) ...99 E 9
Fern (Lough) ...117 I 2
Ferns ...97 M 10
Ferry Bridge ...94 F 10
Ferrybank ...97 N 9
Ferrycarrig ...97 M 10
Ferta ...88 B 12
Fethard ...96 L 11
Fews ...95 J 11
Feystown ...119 O 3
Fiddown ...96 K 10
Fieries ...93 D 11
Finavarra ...99 E 8
Finglas ...103 N 7
Finglass ...89 C 11
Finn (Lough) ...117 H 3
Finn (River) ...117 J 3
Finnea ...107 J 6
Finnisglin ...104 C 7
Fintona ...113 K 4
Fintragh Bay ...112 G 4
Finuge ...93 D 10
Finvoy ...118 M 2
Fiodh Ard / Fethard ...95 I 10
Fionnaithe / Finny ...105 D 7
Firkeel ...88 B 13
Fisherhill ...105 E 6
Five Corners ...115 N 3
Fivealley ...101 I 8
Fivemilebridge ...90 G 12
Fivemiletown ...113 K 4
Flagmount *Corlea* ...99 G 9
Flagmount *Kilkenny* ...96 K 10
Flat Head ...90 G 12
Flesk ...89 D 11
Florence Court ...113 I 5
Florence Court
  Forest Park ...113 I 5
Foaty Island/Fota Island ...90 H 12
Foilycleara ...95 H 10
Folk Park ...99 F 9
Fontstown ...102 L 8
Forbes (Lough) ...107 I 6
Fordstown ...108 L 6
Fore ...107 K 6
Forkill ...109 M 5
Forlorn Point ...96 M 11
Formoyle *Lonford* ...107 I 7
Formoyle *Mayo* ...104 C 6
Formoyle
  near Ballivaghan ...99 E 8
Formoyle near Inagh ...99 E 9
Formoyle (Lough) ...105 D 7
Fort Stewart ...117 J 2
Forthill ...107 I 7
Fota Island ...90 H 12
Foul Sound ...98 D 8
Foulksmills ...96 L 11
Fountain Cross ...99 E 9
Four Mile House ...106 H 6
Four Roads ...106 H 7
Fourknocks ...109 N 7
Foxford ...105 E 6
Foxhall ...105 E 7
Foyle (Lough) ...118 K 2
Foynes ...93 E 10
Foynes Island ...93 E 10
Francis' Gap ...99 G 8
Freemount ...94 F 11
Frenchpark ...106 G 6
Freshford ...95 J 9
Freynestown ...102 L 8
Frosses ...112 H 3
Frower Point ...90 G 12
Fuerty ...106 H 7
Funshin More ...99 F 8
Funshinagh (Lough) ...106 H 7
Funshion ...94 G 11
Furbogh ...99 E 8
Furnace ...105 D 7
Furnace Lough ...105 D 6
Furness ...103 M 8
Fyagh (Slieve) ...111 D 5

G
Gabriel (Mount) ...89 D 13
Gaddagh ...89 C 11

Gaillimh / Galway ...99 E 8
Gainestown ...107 K 7
Galbally *Dungannon* ...114 L 4
Galbally *Limerick* ...94 H 10
Galbally *Wexford* ...96 M 10
Galbolie ...108 K 6
Galey ...93 D 10
Gallarus Oratory ...92 A 11
Galley Head ...89 F 13
Gallion (Slieve) ...114 L 3
Galmoy ...101 J 9
Galty Mountains ...95 H 10
Galtymore Mountain ...95 H 10
Galway Bay ...98 D 8
Galways Bridge ...89 D 12
Gaoth Dobhair /
  Gweedore ...116 H 2
Gaoth Sáile / Geesala ...110 C 5
Gap (The) ...95 I 11
Gara (Lough) ...106 G 6
Garadice ...102 L 7
Garadice Lough ...107 I 5
Garbally ...100 H 8
Garinish Island ...88 C 12
Garnavilla ...95 I 10
Garnish Point ...88 B 13
Garrane ...89 E 12
Garranlahan ...106 G 6
Garraun *Clare* ...98 D 9
Garraun *Galway* ...100 G 8
Garraun (Mount) ...104 C 7
Garries Bridge ...89 D 12
Garrison ...112 H 4
Garristown ...109 M 7
Garrycloonagh ...111 E 5
Garrycullen ...96 L 11
Garryduff ...118 M 2
Garryfine ...94 F 10
Garrykennedy ...100 G 9
Garryspillane ...94 G 10
Garryvoe ...91 H 12
Gartan Lough ...117 I 3
Gartree Point ...114 N 4
Garty Lough ...107 J 6
Garvagh *Coleraine* ...118 L 3
Garvagh *Rowan* ...107 I 6
Garvaghy ...114 K 4
Garvary ...113 J 4
Gattabaun ...101 J 9
Gearagh (The) ...90 F 12
Gearha Bridge ...88 C 12
Geashill ...101 K 8
Geevagh ...112 H 5
George (Lough) ...99 F 9
Gerahies ...89 D 13
Giant's Causeway ...118 M 2
Giles Quay ...109 N 6
Gilford ...114 M 4
Gill (Lough) *near Sligo* ...112 G 5
Gill (Lough) *nearTralee* ...92 B 11
Glanaruddery Mountains ...93 D 11
Glandore ...89 E 13
Glandore Harbour ...89 E 13
Glangevlin ...113 I 5
Glanmire ...90 G 12
Glanmore Lake ...89 C 12
Glanoe ...93 D 10
Glantane ...90 F 11
Glanworth ...94 G 11
Glarryford ...118 M 3
Glasdrumman ...109 O 5
Glaslough ...114 L 5
Glasmullan ...117 J 2
Glassan ...107 I 7
Glasshouse Lake ...107 J 5
Glassillaun ...104 C 6
Glastry ...115 P 4
Gleann Cholm Cille /
  Glencolumbkille ...112 F 3
Gleann Domhain /
  Glendowan ...117 I 3
Gleann na Muaidhe /
  Glenamoy ...111 C 5
Glen ...117 I 2
Glen (River) *Cork* ...90 F 11
Glen (River) *Donegal* ...112 G 3
Glen Bay ...112 F 3
Glen Head ...112 F 3
Glen Lough *Donegal* ...117 I 2
Glen Lough *Westmeath* ...107 J 7
Glenaan ...119 N 2
Glenade ...112 H 4
Glenade Lough ...112 H 4
Glenamoy (River) ...111 D 5
Glenariff ...119 N 2

Glenariff Forest Park ...119 N 2
Glenariff or Waterfoot ...119 N 2
Glenarm ...119 O 3
Glenavy ...115 N 4
Glenballyemon ...119 N 2
Glenbeg Lough ...88 C 12
Glenbeigh ...92 C 11
Glenboy ...112 H 5
Glenbridge Lodge ...103 M 8
Glenbrohane ...94 G 10
Glenbrook ...90 G 12
Glencar ...88 C 12
Glencar Lough ...112 G 4
Glencloy ...119 O 3
Glencolmcille Folk Village ...112 F 3
Glencree ...103 N 8
Glencullen ...103 N 8
Glendalough *Brockagh* ...103 M 8
Glendalough *Waterford* ...95 J 11
Glenderry ...92 C 10
Glendorragha ...116 G 3
Glendovan Mountains ...117 H 3
Glendree ...99 F 9
Glendum ...119 N 2
Glenealy ...103 N 9
Gleneely *near Ballybofey* ...113 I 3
Gleneely *near Cardonagh* ...118 K 2
Glenelly ...114 K 3
Glenelly Valley ...114 K 3
Glenfarne ...113 I 5
Glenflesk ...89 D 11
Glengad Head ...118 K 1
Glengarriff (River) ...89 D 12
Glengarriff Harbour ...89 D 12
Glengesh Pass ...112 G 3
Glengormley ...115 O 3
Glenhead ...118 K 2
Glenhull ...114 K 3
Glenicmurrin Lough ...98 D 8
Glenmacnass ...103 M 8
Glenmalur ...103 M 9
Glenmore *Clare* ...99 E 9
Glenmore *Kilkenny* ...96 K 10
Glennagevlagh ...105 D 7
Glennamaddy ...106 G 7
Glennascaul ...99 F 8
Glenoe ...115 O 3
Glenshane Pass ...118 L 3
Glenshesk ...119 N 2
Glentaisie ...119 N 2
Glentane ...106 G 7
Glentogher ...118 K 2
Glentrasna ...105 D 7
Glenvale ...118 M 3
Glenvar / Gleann Bhairr ...117 I 2
Glenveagh National Park ...117 I 2
Glenville ...90 G 11
Glin ...93 E 10
Glin Castle ...93 E 10
Glinsce / Glinsk ...104 C 7
Glinsk *Donegal* ...117 I 2
Glinsk *Mayo* ...111 D 5
Glounthaune ...90 G 12
Glyde (River) ...108 M 6
Glynn *Carlow* ...96 L 10
Glynn *Larne* ...115 O 3
Gneevgullia ...93 E 11
Gob an Choire /
  Achill Sound ...104 C 6
Gobbins (The) ...115 O 3
Gokane Point ...89 E 13
Gola Island / Gabhla ...116 G 2
Golagh Lough ...113 H 4
Golam Head ...98 C 8
Golden ...95 I 10
Golden Vale ...95 H 10
Goleen ...88 C 13
Goold's Cross ...95 I 10
Goresbridge ...96 K 10
Gorey / Guaire ...97 N 9
Gormanston ...109 N 7
Gort an Choirce /
  Gortahork ...117 H 2
Gortaclare ...113 K 4
Gortahill ...113 I 5
Gortaleam ...106 F 7
Gortarevan ...100 H 8
Gortaroo ...91 I 12
Gortaway ...117 J 2
Gorteen ...106 G 6
Gorteen Bridge ...101 J 8
Gorteeny ...100 G 8
Gortgarriff ...88 C 12
Gortgarrigan ...112 H 5
Gortin ...113 K 3
Gortin Glen Forest Park ...113 K 3

Gortletteragh ...107 I 6
Gortmore *near Ballycastle* ...111 D 5
Gortmore *near Bangor* ...111 C 5
Gortmullan ...113 J 5
Gortnadeeve ...106 G 7
Gortnahoo ...95 J 9
Gortnasillagh ...106 G 6
Gortree ...117 J 3
Gortymadden ...100 G 8
Gorumna Island ...98 C 8
Gosford Forest Park ...114 M 5
Gougane Barra
  Forest Park ...89 D 12
Gougane Barra Lake ...89 E 12
Gouladoo ...89 C 13
Gowla ...104 C 7
Gowlaun ...104 C 7
Gowlin ...96 L 10
Gowna (Lough) ...107 J 6
Gowran ...96 K 10
Gracehill ...118 N 3
Graffy ...116 H 3
Gráig na Manach /
  Graiguenamanagh ...96 L 10
Graigue ...102 L 9
Graigue Hill ...96 L 9
Graigue More ...96 M 10
Graigues ...88 B 12
Granabeg ...103 M 8
Gránard / Granard ...107 J 6
Grand Canal ...101 I 8
Graney ...102 L 9
Graney (River) ...99 G 9
Graney (Lough) ...99 G 9
Grange *Kildare* ...102 K 7
Grange *Kilkenny* ...96 K 10
Grange *Louth* ...109 N 5
Grange *Sligo* ...112 G 4
Grange *Waterford* ...91 I 12
Grange (River) ...106 F 7
Grange Con ...102 L 9
Grangebellew ...109 M 6
Grangeford ...102 L 9
Grangegeeth ...108 M 6
Granias Gap ...117 K 2
Grannagh ...99 F 8
Gransha ...115 O 3
Granville ...114 L 4
Greagh ...107 I 6
Great Blasket Island ...92 A 11
Great Island ...90 H 12
Great Newtown Head ...96 K 11
Great Skellig ...88 A 12
Great Sugar Loaf ...103 N 8
Greatman's Bay ...98 D 8
Greenan ...103 N 9
Greenanstown ...109 N 7
Greencastle *Donegal* ...118 L 2
Greencastle
  Newry-Mourne ...109 N 5
Greencastle *Omagh* ...114 K 3
Greenfield ...105 E 7
Greenisland ...115 O 3
Greenore ...109 N 5
Greenore Point ...97 N 11
Gregans Castle ...99 E 8
Gregory's Sound ...98 D 8
Grenagh ...90 G 11
Grey Abbey ...115 P 4
Grey Point ...115 O 3
Greysteel ...118 K 2
Greystone ...114 L 4
Greystones ...103 N 8
Grianan of Aileach ...117 J 2
Grogan ...101 I 8
Groomsport ...115 P 3
Gubaveeny ...113 I 5
Gubbaroe Point ...113 I 4
Gulladoo Lough ...107 J 6
Gulladuff ...118 M 3
Gullion (Slieve) ...109 M 5
Gur (Lough) ...94 G 10
Gurteen *Cappalusk* ...99 G 7
Gurteen *Leitrim* ...112 H 5
Gusserane ...96 L 11
Gwebarra Bridge ...116 H 3
Gweebarra ...116 H 3
Gweebarra Bay ...116 G 3
Gweestin ...93 D 11
Gweestion ...105 E 6
Gyleen ...90 H 12

H
Hacketstown ...103 M 9
Hags Head ...98 D 9
Hamiltonsbawn ...114 M 4
Hand Cross Roads (The) ...99 E 9
Hannahstown ...115 N 4

Hare Island ...89 D 13
Harristown ...96 K 10
Harrow (The) ...97 M 10
Healy Pass ...89 C 12
Helen's Bay ...115 O 3
Helvick Head ...91 J 11
Herbertstown ...94 G 10
High Island ...104 B 7
Highwood ...112 H 5
Hill Street ...107 H 6
Hillsborough ...115 N 4
Hilltown *Harristown* ...96 L 11
Hilltown
  Newry and Mourne ...115 N 5
Hind ...106 H 7
Hog's Head ...88 B 12
Holeopen Bay West ...90 G 13
Hollyford ...95 H 10
Hollyfort ...97 M 9
Hollymount ...105 E 7
Hollywood ...103 M 8
Holy Cross ...95 I 10
Holy Island ...99 G 9
Holycross ...94 G 10
Holywell ...113 I 5
Holywell Hill ...117 J 2
Holywood ...115 O 4
Hook Head ...96 L 11
Hore Abbey ...95 I 10
Horn Head ...117 I 2
Horse and Jockey ...95 I 10
Horse Island ...89 D 13
Horseleap ...101 J 7
Hospital ...94 G 10
Hugginstown ...96 K 10
Hungry Hill ...88 C 12
Hurlers Cross ...99 F 9
Hurley ...109 M 7
Hyne (Lough) ...89 E 13

I
Ilen ...89 E 13
Illaunstookagh ...92 C 11
Illauntannig ...92 B 11
Illies ...117 J 2
Illnacullin ...89 D 12
Inagh ...99 E 9
Inagh (Lough) ...104 C 7
Inch *Donegal* ...117 J 2
Inch *near Whitegate* ...90 H 12
Inch *near Youghal* ...91 I 12
Inch *Tipperary* ...95 H 9
Inch *Wexford* ...97 N 9
Inch Abbey ...115 O 4
Inch Island ...117 J 2
Inchagoill ...105 E 7
Inchamore Bridge ...108 L 7
Inchbeg ...96 J 9
Inchcleraun ...107 H 7
Inchee Bridge ...89 D 12
Inchicronan Lough ...99 F 9
Inchigeelagh ...89 E 12
Inchiquin ...105 E 7
Inchiquin Lough *Clare* ...99 E 9
Inchiquin Lough *Kerry* ...89 D 12
Inchmore ...107 I 7
Inchnamuck ...95 H 11
Inchydoney Island ...90 F 13
Indreabhán / Inveran ...98 D 8
Inis / Ennis ...99 F 9
Inis Bó Finne / Inishbofin ...117 I 2
Inis Meáin / Inishmaan ...98 D 8
Inis Mór / Inishmore ...98 C 8
Inis Oírr / Inisheer ...98 D 8
Inishannon ...90 G 12
Inishbarra ...98 C 8
Inishbiggle ...110 C 6
Inishbofin ...104 B 7
Inishcarra ...90 G 12
Inishcarra Reservoir ...90 F 12
Inishcrone ...111 E 5
Inishdoorus ...105 D 7
Inishfarnard ...88 B 12
Inishfree Bay ...116 G 2
Inishfree Upper ...116 G 3
Inishglora ...110 B 5
Inishkea North ...110 B 5
Inishkea South ...110 B 5
Inishmaine Island ...105 E 7
Inishmicatreer ...105 E 7
Inishmurray ...112 G 4
Inishnabro ...92 A 11
Inishnee ...104 C 7
Inishowen ...117 J 2
Inishowen Head ...118 L 2
Inishshark ...104 B 7

Inishtooskert ...92 A 11
Inishtrahull ...118 K 1
Inishtrahull Sound ...118 K 1
Inishturk ...104 B 6
Inishvickillane ...92 A 11
Inistioge ...96 K 10
Innfield ...102 L 7
Innisfree ...112 G 5
Inniskeen ...108 M 5
Inny (River) ...107 J 6
Inver *Donegal* ...112 H 4
Inver *Mayo* ...110 C 5
Inver Bay ...112 H 4
Ireland's Eye ...103 N 7
Irish Agricultural
  Museum ...97 M 11
Irishtown ...105 F 7
Iron (Lough) ...107 J 7
Iron Mountains ...113 I 5
Irvinestown ...113 J 4
Island Lake ...106 F 6
Island Reavy (Lough) ...115 N 5
Islandmore ...115 P 4
Iveragh ...88 B 12

J
J. F. Kennedy Park ...96 L 11
Jamestown *Cloonteem* ...107 H 6
Jamestown *Laois* ...101 K 8
Japanese Gardens ...102 L 8
Jerpoint Abbey ...96 K 10
Jerrettspass ...114 M 5
Johnstown *Kildare* ...103 M 8
Johnstown *Kilkenny* ...101 J 9
Johnstown *Meath* ...108 M 7
Johnstown *near Arklow* ...103 N 9
Johnstown
  near Coolgreany ...97 N 9
Johnstown Bridge ...107 I 6
Johnstownbridge ...102 L 7
Jonesborough ...109 M 5
Joyce ...105 D 7
Julianstown ...109 N 6

K
Kanturk Castle ...94 F 11
Katesbridge ...115 N 5
Keadew ...107 H 5
Keady ...114 L 5
Keady Mountain ...118 L 2
Kealduff ...89 C 12
Kealkill ...89 D 12
Kearney ...115 P 4
Kearney Point ...115 P 4
Keeagh ...99 E 8
Keel ...110 B 6
Keel (Lough) ...117 I 2
Keel Lough ...110 B 6
Keeloges ...106 G 7
Keem Strand ...110 B 6
Keenagh *Longford* ...107 I 7
Keenagh *Mayo* ...111 D 5
Keeraunnagark ...98 D 8
Keereen ...91 I 11
Keimaneigh (The pass of) ...89 E 12
Kells *Ballymena* ...115 N 3
Kells *Kerry* ...88 B 12
Kells *Kilkenny* ...96 K 10
Kells (Ceanannus Mor) /
  Ceanannas *Meath* ...108 L 6
Kells Bay ...88 B 11
Kells Priory ...96 K 10
Kellysgrove ...100 H 8
Kenmare River ...88 B 12
Kentstown ...108 M 7
Kerry (Ring of) ...88 B 12
Kerry Head ...92 C 10
Kesh *Fermanagh* ...113 I 4
Kesh *Toomour* ...106 G 5
Keshcarrigan ...107 I 5
Key (Lough) ...106 H 5
Kid Island ...110 B 5
Kilbaha ...93 C 10
Kilbaha Bay ...93 C 10
Kilbane ...99 G 9
Kilbarry ...89 E 12
Kilbeacanty ...99 F 8
Kilbeggan ...101 J 7
Kilbeheny ...94 H 11
Kilbennan ...105 F 7
Kilberry *Bert* ...108 L 6
Kilberry *Kildare* ...102 K 8
Kilbreedy ...94 F 10
Kilbrickan ...105 D 7
Kilbricken ...101 J 9
Kilbride *near Blessington* ...103 M 8
Kilbride *near Ratoah* ...103 M 7

A B C D E F G H I J K L M N O P Q R S T U V W X Y Z

A B C D E F G H I J K L M N O P Q R S T U V W X Y Z

Kilbride *near Trim* .... 108 L 7
Kilbride *near Wicklow* .... 103 N 9
Kilbrien .... 95 J 11
Kilbrin .... 94 F 11
Kilbrittain .... 90 F 12
Kilcaimin .... 99 F 8
Kilcar .... 112 G 4
Kilcatherine Point .... 88 B 12
Kilcavan .... 101 J 8
Kilchreest .... 99 G 8
Kilclaran .... 99 G 9
Kilclief .... 115 P 5
Kilcloher .... 93 C 10
Kilclonfert .... 101 J 8
Kilclooney .... 116 G 3
Kilcock .... 102 L 7
Kilcogy .... 107 J 6
Kilcolgan .... 99 F 8
Kilcolman *Cashel* .... 90 F 12
Kilcolman
    Dunmoylan East .... 93 E 10
Kilcoltrim .... 96 L 10
Kilcomin .... 101 I 9
Kilcommon *near Caher* .... 95 I 10
Kilcommon *near Milestone* .... 95 H 9
Kilcon .... 111 E 5
Kilconly *Galway* .... 105 F 7
Kilconly *Kerry* .... 93 D 10
Kilcoo .... 115 N 5
Kilcoole .... 103 N 8
Kilcormac .... 101 I 8
Kilcotty .... 97 M 10
Kilcredan .... 91 I 12
Kilcredaun Point .... 93 C 10
Kilcrohane .... 89 C 13
Kilcrow .... 100 H 8
Kilcullen .... 102 L 8
Kilcummin *Kerry* .... 92 B 11
Kilcummin *Mayo* .... 111 E 5
Kilcummin Farmhill .... 93 D 11
Kilcurly .... 109 M 5
Kilcurry .... 109 M 5
Kildalkey .... 108 L 7
Kildangan .... 102 K 8
Kildavin .... 96 L 9
Kilderry .... 96 K 9
Kildoney Point .... 112 H 4
Kildorrery .... 94 G 11
Kildress .... 114 L 4
Kildrum .... 115 N 3
Kilfeakle .... 95 H 10
Kilfearagh .... 98 D 10
Kilfenora .... 99 E 9
Kilfinnane .... 94 G 10
Kilfinny .... 94 F 10
Kilflyn .... 93 D 10
Kilgarvan .... 89 D 12
Kilglass *Galway* .... 106 G 7
Kilglass *Sligo* .... 111 E 5
Kilglass Lough .... 107 H 6
Kilgobnet *Kerry* .... 89 C 11
Kilgobnet *Waterford* .... 91 J 11
Kilgory Lough .... 99 F 9
Kilgowan .... 102 L 8
Kiljames .... 96 K 10
Kilkea .... 102 L 9
Kilkeary .... 100 H 9
Kilkeasy .... 96 K 10
Kilkeel .... 109 N 5
Kilkeeran High Crosses .... 95 J 10
Kilkenny West .... 107 I 7
Kilkerrin .... 106 G 7
Kilkieran / Cill Chiaráin .... 104 C 8
Kilkieran Bay .... 104 C 7
Kilkiernan .... 96 K 9
Kilkinamurry .... 115 N 5
Kilkinlea .... 93 E 10
Kilkishen .... 99 F 9
Kill *Cavan* .... 108 K 5
Kill *Waterford* .... 91 J 11
Killabunane .... 89 D 12
Killaclug .... 94 H 11
Killacolla .... 94 F 10
Killadangan .... 105 D 6
Killadeas .... 113 I 4
Killadoon .... 104 C 6
Killadysert .... 99 E 9
Killafeen .... 99 F 8
Killag .... 96 M 11
Killagan Bridge .... 118 M 2
Killaghteen .... 93 E 10
Killahy .... 95 J 9
Killakee .... 103 N 8
Killala .... 111 E 5
Killala Bay .... 111 E 5

Killallon .... 108 K 6
Killaloo .... 118 K 3
Killamery .... 95 J 10
Killane .... 102 K 8
Killanena .... 99 F 9
Killann .... 96 L 10
Killard .... 98 D 9
Killard Point .... 115 P 5
Killarga .... 112 H 5
Killarney National Park .... 89 D 11
Killarone .... 105 E 7
Killary Harbour .... 104 C 7
Killashandra .... 107 J 5
Killashee .... 107 I 6
Killasser .... 105 F 6
Killavally *Mayo* .... 105 D 6
Killavally *Westmeath* .... 101 J 7
Killavil .... 106 G 5
Killavullen .... 94 G 11
Killea *Donegal* .... 117 J 3
Killea *Tipperary* .... 101 I 9
Killeagh .... 91 H 12
Killealy .... 115 N 3
Killeany .... 98 D 8
Killedmond .... 96 L 10
Killeedy .... 93 E 10
Killeen *Ardamullivan* .... 99 F 9
Killeen *Armagh* .... 114 M 5
Killeen *Dungannon* .... 114 M 4
Killeenaran .... 99 F 8
Killeeneenmore .... 99 F 8
Killeenleagh Bridge .... 88 B 12
Killeevan .... 113 K 5
Killeglan .... 106 H 7
Killeigh .... 101 J 8
Killen .... 113 J 3
Killenagh .... 97 N 10
Killenaule .... 95 I 10
Killeshil .... 101 K 8
Killeshin .... 102 K 9
Killeter .... 113 I 3
Killeter Forest .... 113 I 3
Killevy .... 109 M 5
Killevy Churches .... 109 M 5
Killilan Bridge .... 99 G 8
Killimer .... 93 D 10
Killimor .... 100 H 8
Killinaboy .... 99 E 9
Killinaspick .... 96 K 10
Killinchy .... 115 O 4
Killincooly .... 97 N 10
Killiney *Dublin* .... 103 N 8
Killiney *Kerry* .... 92 B 11
Killiney Bay .... 103 N 8
Killinick .... 97 M 11
Killinierin .... 97 N 9
Killinkere .... 108 K 6
Killinny .... 99 F 8
Killinthomas .... 102 K 8
Killinure Lough .... 107 I 7
Killiskey .... 103 N 8
Killkelly .... 105 F 6
Killmuckbridge .... 97 N 10
Killogeary .... 111 E 5
Killogeenaghan .... 101 I 7
Killonecaha .... 88 B 12
Killoran .... 100 G 8
Killoscobe .... 106 G 7
Killough .... 115 P 5
Killough .... 103 N 8
Killowen .... 109 N 5
Killucan .... 108 K 7
Killukin .... 107 H 6
Killurin .... 96 M 10
Killurly .... 88 B 12
Killusty .... 95 J 10
Killwaughter .... 115 O 3
Killyclogher .... 113 K 4
Killyclug .... 117 I 3
Killycolpy .... 114 M 4
Killygar .... 107 J 5
Killygordon .... 117 I 3
Killykeen Forest Park .... 107 J 5
Killylea .... 114 L 4
Killyleagh .... 115 P 4
Killyon .... 101 I 8
Kilmacanoge .... 103 N 8
Kilmacduagh Monastery .... 99 F 8
Kilmacoo .... 103 N 9
Kilmacow .... 96 K 11
Kilmacrenan .... 117 I 2
Kilmacteige .... 111 F 5
Kilmacthomas .... 95 J 11
Kilmactranny .... 106 H 5
Kilmacurragh .... 103 N 9
Kilmaganny .... 96 K 10
Kilmaine .... 105 E 7

Kilmainham Wood .... 108 L 6
Kilmakilloge Harbour .... 88 C 12
Kilmaley .... 99 E 9
Kilmalkedar .... 92 B 11
Kilmanagh .... 95 J 10
Kilmeadan .... 96 K 11
Kilmeage .... 102 L 8
Kilmeedy .... 94 F 10
Kilmeelickin .... 105 D 7
Kilmeena .... 105 D 6
Kilmessan .... 108 M 7
Kilmichael
    near Castletownbere .... 88 B 13
Kilmichael *near Macroom* .... 89 E 12
Kilmichael Point .... 97 N 9
Kilmihil .... 98 E 9
Kilmona .... 90 G 12
Kilmoon .... 89 D 13
Kilmore *Armagh* .... 114 M 4
Kilmore *Clare* .... 99 G 9
Kilmore *Down* .... 115 O 4
Kilmore *Mayo* .... 105 E 6
Kilmore *Roscommon* .... 107 H 6
Kilmore *Wexford* .... 96 M 11
Kilmore Quay .... 96 M 11
Kilmorna .... 93 D 10
Kilmorony .... 102 L 9
Kilmovee .... 106 F 6
Kilmurry *Cork* .... 90 F 12
Kilmurry *Limerick* .... 94 G 10
Kilmurry *near Kilkishen* .... 99 F 9
Kilmurry *near Milltown* .... 98 D 9
Kilmurry *Wicklow* .... 102 L 9
Kilmurry Mac Mahon .... 93 E 10
Kilmurvy .... 98 C 8
Kilmyshall .... 96 M 10
Kilnagross .... 107 I 6
Kilnalag .... 106 G 6
Kilnaleck .... 107 K 6
Kilnamanagh .... 97 M 10
Kilnamona .... 99 E 9
Kilntown .... 115 N 4
Kilpatrick .... 90 F 12
Kilpeacan Cross Roads .... 88 B 12
Kilpedder .... 103 N 8
Kilquigquin .... 97 M 9
Kilraghts .... 118 M 2
Kilrane .... 97 M 11
Kilrea .... 118 M 3
Kilrean .... 116 H 3
Kilreekill .... 100 G 8
Kilroghter .... 99 E 8
Kilross *Donegal* .... 117 I 3
Kilross *Tipperary* .... 94 H 10
Kilruddery .... 103 N 8
Kilsallagh *Galway* .... 106 G 7
Kilsallagh *Mayo* .... 104 C 6
Kilsallaghan .... 103 N 7
Kilsally .... 114 M 4
Kilsaran .... 109 M 6
Kilshanchoe .... 102 L 7
Kilshannig .... 92 B 11
Kilshanny .... 99 E 9
Kilsheelan .... 95 J 10
Kilskeer .... 108 L 6
Kilskeery .... 113 J 4
Kiltealy .... 96 L 10
Kilteel .... 103 M 8
Kilteely .... 94 G 10
Kiltegan .... 103 M 9
Kilternan .... 103 N 8
Kiltimagh .... 105 E 6
Kiltober .... 101 J 7
Kiltoom .... 107 H 7
Kiltormer .... 100 H 8
Kiltullagh .... 99 G 8
Kiltyclogher .... 113 H 4
Kilvine .... 105 F 7
Kilworth .... 94 H 11
Kilworth Mountains .... 94 H 11
Kinale (Lough) .... 107 J 6
Kinard .... 93 E 10
Kinawley .... 113 J 5
Kincasslagh .... 116 G 2
Kindrohid .... 117 J 2
Kindrum .... 117 I 2
Kingarrow .... 117 H 3
Kings River .... 95 J 10
Kingscourt .... 108 L 6
Kingsland .... 106 G 6
Kingsmill .... 114 M 4
Kingstown .... 104 B 7
Kinlough .... 112 H 4
Kinnadoohy .... 104 C 6
Kinnagoe Bay .... 118 K 2
Kinnegad .... 108 K 7
Kinnitty .... 101 I 8

Kinsale (Old Head of) .... 90 G 13
Kinsale Harbour .... 90 G 12
Kinsalebeg .... 91 I 12
Kinsaley .... 103 N 7
Kinvarra
    near Camus Bay .... 105 D 7
Kinvarra
    near Kinvarra Bay .... 99 F 8
Kinvarra Bay .... 99 F 8
Kippure .... 103 N 8
Kircubbin .... 115 P 4
Kirkhills .... 118 M 2
Kirkistown .... 115 P 4
Kishkeam .... 93 E 11
Kitconnell .... 100 G 8
Knappagh .... 105 D 6
Knappogue Castle .... 99 F 9
Knight's Town .... 88 B 12
Knock *Clare* .... 93 E 10
Knock *Mayo* .... 105 F 6
Knock *Tipperary* .... 101 I 9
Knockaderry .... 94 F 10
Knockadoon Head .... 91 I 12
Knockainy .... 94 G 10
Knockalla Mount .... 117 J 2
Knockalongy .... 112 F 5
Knockalough .... 99 E 9
Knockanaffrin .... 95 J 11
Knockananna .... 103 M 9
Knockanefune .... 93 E 11
Knockanevin .... 94 G 11
Knockanillaun .... 111 E 5
Knockanimpaha .... 93 E 10
Knockanure .... 93 D 10
Knockaunalour .... 90 G 12
Knockaunavoher .... 94 G 10
Knockaunnaglashy .... 92 C 11
Knockboy *near Dungarvan* .... 95 I 11
Knockboy *near Waterford* .... 96 K 11
Knockboy (Mount) .... 89 D 12
Knockbrack .... 117 I 3
Knockbrandon .... 97 M 9
Knockbride .... 108 L 6
Knockbridge .... 109 M 6
Knockbrit .... 95 I 10
Knockcloghrim .... 114 M 3
Knockcroghery .... 106 H 7
Knockdrin .... 107 K 7
Knockerry .... 98 D 10
Knockferry .... 105 E 7
Knocklayd .... 119 N 2
Knocklofty .... 95 I 10
Knocklomena .... 89 C 12
Knocklong .... 94 G 10
Knockmealdown .... 95 I 11
Knockmealdown
    Mountains .... 95 H 11
Knockmore .... 104 B 6
Knockmore (Mount) .... 104 C 6
Knockmourne .... 90 H 11
Knockmoy Abbey .... 106 F 7
Knocknaboul Cross .... 93 E 11
Knocknacarry .... 119 N 2
Knocknacree .... 102 L 9
Knocknadobar .... 88 B 12
Knocknagantee .... 88 C 12
Knocknagashel .... 93 D 11
Knocknagree .... 93 E 11
Knocknahilan .... 90 F 12
Knocknalina .... 110 C 5
Knocknalower .... 110 C 5
Knockowen .... 89 C 12
Knockraha .... 90 G 12
Knocks *Cork* .... 89 F 12
Knocks *Fermanagh* .... 113 J 5
Knocks *Laois* .... 101 J 8
Knockshanahullion .... 95 H 11
Knockskagh .... 89 F 12
Knocktopher .... 96 K 10
Knocktown .... 96 M 11
Knockundervaul .... 93 D 10
Knockvicar .... 106 H 5
Knowth .... 108 M 6
Kylemore .... 100 H 8
Kylemore Abbey .... 104 C 7
Kylemore Lough .... 104 C 7

L

Laban .... 99 F 8
Labasheeda .... 93 E 10
Lack .... 113 J 4
Lackagh .... 102 K 8
Lackan *Carlow* .... 96 K 9
Lackan *Wicklow* .... 103 M 8
Lackan bay .... 111 E 5
Lackareagh .... 89 F 12
Laconnell .... 116 G 3

Ladies View .... 89 D 12
Lady's Island Lake .... 97 M 11
Ladysbridge .... 90 H 12
Ladywell .... 96 K 10
Laffansbridge .... 95 I 10
Lag .... 117 K 2
Lagan (River) .... 115 N 4
Lagan Valley .... 115 O 4
Lagavara .... 118 M 2
Lagganstown .... 95 I 10
Laghey Corner .... 114 L 4
Laghtnafrankee .... 95 J 11
Laghy .... 113 H 4
Lahardaun .... 111 E 5
Lakyle .... 93 E 10
Lambay Island .... 109 N 7
Lambeg .... 115 N 4
Lamb's Head .... 88 B 12
Lanesborough .... 107 I 6
Laney (River) .... 89 F 12
Laracor .... 108 L 7
Laragh *Kildare* .... 102 L 7
Laragh *Monaghan* .... 108 L 5
Laragh *Wicklow* .... 103 N 8
Laragh *Mayo* .... 111 D 5
Largan *Sligo* .... 111 F 5
Largy .... 112 G 4
Largydonnell .... 112 H 4
Larkhill .... 88 C 12
Larne .... 115 O 3
Larne Lough .... 115 O 3
Lattin .... 94 H 10
Laune (River) .... 93 C 11
Lauragh .... 88 C 12
Laurelvale .... 114 M 4
Laurencetown .... 100 H 8
Lavagh .... 112 F 5
Lavagh More .... 117 H 3
Lawrencetown .... 114 N 4
Leabgarrow .... 116 G 3
League (Slieve) .... 112 F 4
League .... 89 D 13
Leamaneh Castle .... 99 E 9
Leamlara .... 90 H 12
Leamore Strand .... 103 N 8
Leane (Lough) .... 89 D 11
Leannan (River) .... 117 I 2
Leap (The)
    near Enniscorthy .... 96 M 10
Leap (The) *near New Ross* .... 96 L 10
Lecale Peninsula .... 115 O 5
Lecarrow *Leitrim* .... 112 H 5
Lecarrow *Roscommon* .... 107 H 7
Leckanarainey .... 112 H 4
Leckanvy .... 105 C 6
Leckaun .... 112 H 5
Leckavrea Mountain .... 105 D 7
Leckemy .... 118 K 2
Lee .... 93 C 11
Lee (River) .... 90 G 12
Lee Reservoir .... 90 F 12
Leek Point .... 93 C 10
Leenane .... 104 C 7
Legan or Lenamore .... 107 J 7
Leganany Dolmen .... 115 N 5
Leggah .... 107 J 6
Legoniel .... 115 O 4
Lehardan .... 117 J 2
Leighlinbridge .... 96 L 9
Leinster (Mount) .... 96 L 10
Leitir Meallāin /
    Lettermullan .... 98 C 8
Leitir Mhic an Bhaird /
    Lettermacaward .... 116 H 3
Leitrim *Banbridge* .... 115 O 5
Leitrim *Creegh* .... 98 D 9
Leitrim *Leitrim* .... 107 H 6
Leixlip .... 103 M 7
Lemanaghan .... 101 I 8
Lemybrien .... 91 J 11
Lenadoon Point .... 111 E 5
Lenan Head .... 117 J 2
Lene (Lough) .... 107 K 7
Lerrig .... 93 C 10
Leslie Hill .... 114 L 5
Letterbarra .... 112 H 3
Letterbreen .... 113 I 5
Lettercallow .... 98 C 8
Lettercraffroe Lough .... 105 D 7
Letterfinish .... 88 C 12
Letterfrack .... 104 C 7
Letterkelly .... 99 E 9
Letterkenny /
    Leitir Ceanainn .... 117 I 3
Letterleague .... 117 I 3
Lettermore .... 98 D 8
Lettermore Island .... 98 C 8

Levally .... 106 F 7
Levally Lough .... 105 E 6
Licketstown .... 96 K 11
Liffey (River) .... 102 M 8
Lifford .... 117 J 3
Light House Island .... 115 P 3
Limavady .... 118 L 3
Limerick / Luimneach .... 94 G 10
Limerick Junction .... 95 H 10
Lios Dúin Bhearna /
    Lisdoonvarna .... 99 E 8
Lios Mór / Lismore .... 91 I 11
Lios Póil / Lispole .... 92 B 11
Lios Tuathail / Listowel .... 93 D 10
Lisacul .... 106 G 6
Lisbane .... 115 O 4
Lisbellaw .... 113 J 5
Lisburn .... 115 N 4
Liscannor .... 98 D 9
Liscannor Bay .... 98 D 9
Liscarney .... 105 D 6
Liscarroll .... 94 F 11
Liscolman .... 118 M 2
Liscooly .... 117 J 3
Lisdoart .... 114 K 4
Lisdowney .... 101 J 9
Lisduff *Cavan* .... 108 K 6
Lisduff *Leitrim* .... 107 I 6
Lisduff *Offaly* .... 101 I 8
Lisgarode .... 100 H 9
Lisgoold .... 90 H 12
Lislea *Magherafelt* .... 118 M 3
Lislea *Newry-Mourne* .... 114 M 5
Lismacaffry .... 107 J 6
Lismoghry .... 117 J 3
Lismoyle .... 106 H 7
Lisnacree .... 109 N 5
Lisnageer .... 108 K 5
Lisnagleer .... 114 L 4
Lisnagry .... 94 G 9
Lisnagunogue .... 118 M 2
Lisnamuck .... 118 L 3
Lisnarrick .... 113 I 4
Lisnaskea .... 113 J 5
Lisnavagh .... 102 L 9
Lispatrick .... 90 G 13
Lisroe .... 99 E 9
Lisronagh .... 95 I 10
Lisryan .... 107 J 6
Lissadell House .... 112 G 4
Lissalway .... 106 G 6
Lissamona .... 89 D 13
Lissatinnig Bridge .... 88 C 12
Lissavaird .... 89 F 13
Lisselton .... 93 D 10
Lissinagroagh .... 112 H 5
Lissiniska .... 112 H 4
Lissycasey .... 99 E 9
Listellick .... 93 C 11
Listerlin .... 96 K 10
Listooder .... 115 O 4
Lisvarrinane .... 94 H 10
Little Bray .... 103 N 8
Little Island .... 90 G 12
Little Skellig .... 88 A 12
Littleton .... 95 I 10
Lixnaw .... 93 D 10
Loanends .... 115 N 4
Lobinstown .... 108 M 6
Loch Garman / Wexford .... 97 M 11
Loghill .... 93 E 10
Lombardstown .... 94 F 11
Londonderry .... 117 K 3
Lonehort Point .... 88 C 13
Long Island .... 89 D 13
Longford .... 101 I 8
Longhill .... 101 K 9
Longwood .... 108 L 7
Loo Bridge .... 89 D 12
Loobagh .... 94 G 10
Loop Head .... 92 C 10
Lorrha .... 100 H 8
Loskeran .... 91 J 11
Losset *Cavan* .... 107 J 6
Losset *Donegal* .... 117 I 2
Lough Bradan Forest .... 113 J 4
Lough Gowna .... 107 J 6
Lough Key Forest Park .... 106 H 6
Lough Navar Forest .... 113 I 4
Loughanavally .... 107 J 7
Loughanillaunmore .... 98 D 8
Loughanure .... 116 H 2
Loughbrickland .... 114 N 5
Lougher .... 92 C 11
Loughermore .... 118 K 3
Loughfad Hill .... 113 I 4
Loughgall .... 114 M 4

Loughglinn ...... 106 G 6
Loughguile ...... 119 N 2
Loughinisland ...... 115 O 4
Loughlinstown ...... 103 N 8
Loughmoe ...... 101 I 9
Loughmorne ...... 108 L 5
Loughros More Bay ...... 116 G 3
Loughros Point ...... 116 G 3
Loughsalt Mount ...... 117 I 2
Loughshinny ...... 109 N 7
Louisburgh ...... 104 C 6
Loup (The) ...... 114 M 3
Louth ...... 108 M 6
Lower Ballinderry ...... 114 N 4
Lower Lake ...... 103 N 8
Lowertown ...... 89 D 13
Lowerymore ...... 113 I 3
Lowtown ...... 115 N 5
Lucan ...... 103 M 7
Luggacurren ...... 101 K 9
Lugnaquillia Mountain ...... 103 M 9
Luimneach / Limerick ...... 94 G 10
Lukeswell ...... 96 K 10
Lullymore ...... 102 L 8
Lurgan *Craigavon* ...... 114 N 4
Lurgan *Frenchpark* ...... 106 G 6
Lurganboy *Donegal* ...... 117 J 2
Lurganboy *Leitrim* ...... 112 H 5
Lusk ...... 109 N 7
Lyle ...... 115 N 3
Lyracrumpane ...... 93 D 10
Lyre ...... 90 F 11
Lyrenaglogh ...... 95 H 11

M
Maas ...... 116 G 3
Mac Gregor's Corner ...... 119 N 3
Mac Laughlins Corner ...... 118 M 3
Mac Mahon's Town ...... 114 K 4
Mac Swyne's Bay ...... 112 G 4
Mace ...... 105 D 6
Mace Head ...... 104 C 8
Macgillycuddy's Reeks ...... 89 C 12
Machugh (Lough) ...... 116 G 3
Mackan ...... 113 J 5
Macnean Lower (Lough) ...... 113 I 5
Macnean Upper (Lough) ...... 113 I 5
Macosquin ...... 118 L 2
Macroom /
  Maigh Chromtha ...... 89 F 12
Maddan ...... 114 L 5
Maddockstown ...... 96 K 10
Maganey ...... 102 L 9
Magee (Island) ...... 115 O 3
Maghaberry ...... 115 N 4
Maghanlawaun ...... 89 C 12
Maghera *Clare* ...... 99 F 9
Maghera *Donegal* ...... 116 G 3
Maghera *Down* ...... 115 O 5
Maghera *Magherafelt* ...... 118 L 3
Magherabane ...... 117 J 2
Magherafelt ...... 114 M 3
Magheragall ...... 115 N 4
Magheralin ...... 114 N 4
Magheramason ...... 117 J 3
Magheramorne ...... 115 O 3
Magheraveely ...... 113 K 5
Maghery *near Dungannon* ... 114 M 4
Maghery *near Dunglow* ...... 116 G 3
Magilligan ...... 118 L 2
Magilligan Point ...... 118 L 2
Magilligan Strand ...... 118 L 2
Maguiresbridge ...... 113 J 5
Mahee Island ...... 115 P 4
Mahon ...... 95 J 11
Mahon (Lough) ...... 90 G 12
Mahoonagh ...... 93 E 10
Maigh Chromtha /
  Macroom ...... 89 F 12
Maigh Cuilinn /
  Moycullen ...... 105 E 7
Maigh Nuad / Maynooth .. 103 M 7
Maigue (River) ...... 94 F 10
Main ...... 118 N 3
Maine (River) ...... 93 C 11
Mainham ...... 102 L 8
Mainistir Fhear Mai /
  Fermoy ...... 90 H 11
Mainistir na Búille /
  Boyle ...... 106 H 6
Mainistir na Corann /
  Midleton ...... 90 H 12
Máistir Gaoithe /
  Mastergeehy ...... 88 B 12
Mal Bay ...... 98 D 9
Mala / Mallow ...... 94 G 11
Málainn Bhig / Malin Beg .. 112 F 3

Malin ...... 118 K 2
Malin Bay ...... 112 F 3
Malin Head ...... 117 J 1
Malin More ...... 112 F 3
Mallusk ...... 115 N 3
Mamore (Gap of) ...... 117 J 2
Manger ...... 112 H 4
Mangerton Mountain ...... 89 D 12
Mannin Bay ...... 104 B 7
Mannin Lake ...... 105 F 6
Manorcunningham ...... 117 J 3
Manselstown ...... 95 I 9
Mansfieldstown ...... 109 M 6
Mantua ...... 106 H 6
Manulla ...... 105 E 6
Manulla (River) ...... 105 E 6
Maothail / Mohill ...... 107 I 6
Marble Arch Caves ...... 113 I 5
Marble Hill ...... 117 I 2
Mardyke ...... 95 J 10
Markethill ...... 114 M 5
Marshalstown ...... 96 M 10
Martin ...... 90 G 12
Martinstown *Emlygrennan* ... 94 G 10
Martinstown
  Grennanstown ...... 108 L 7
Martinstown
  South Somerset ...... 119 N 3
Mask (Lough) ...... 105 D 7
Massford ...... 115 N 4
Masshill ...... 112 F 5
Masterstown ...... 95 I 10
Matehy ...... 90 G 12
Matrix (Castle) ...... 94 F 10
Mattock (River) ...... 108 M 6
Mauherslieve ...... 95 H 9
Maum ...... 105 D 7
Maumakeogh ...... 111 D 5
Maumeen Lough ...... 104 B 7
Maumtrasna ...... 105 D 7
Maumturk Mountains ...... 104 C 7
Mauricesmills ...... 99 E 9
Mayo ...... 105 E 6
Mayo (Plains of) ...... 105 E 6
Mayobridge ...... 114 N 5
Mazetown ...... 115 N 4
Mealagh ...... 89 D 12
Meanus ...... 94 G 10
Meathas Troim /
  Edgeworthstown ...... 107 J 6
Meela (Lough) ...... 116 G 3
Meelick ...... 100 H 8
Meelin ...... 93 E 11
Meenaclady ...... 116 H 2
Meenacross ...... 116 G 3
Meenanarwa ...... 117 H 3
Meenaneary /
  Mín na Aoire ...... 112 G 3
Meenatotan ...... 116 H 3
Meenavean ...... 112 F 3
Meencorwick ...... 116 H 3
Meenglass ...... 113 I 3
Meenlaragh ...... 117 H 2
Meenreagh ...... 113 I 3
Meentullynagarn ...... 112 G 3
Meenybraddan ...... 112 H 3
Meeting of the Waters ...... 103 N 9
Mellifont Abbey ...... 109 M 6
Melmore Head ...... 117 I 2
Melvin (Lough) ...... 112 H 4
Menlough ...... 106 G 7
Mew Island ...... 115 P 3
Michelstown Caves ...... 95 H 11
Middletown ...... 116 H 2
Middletown *Armagh* ...... 114 L 5
Midfield ...... 105 F 6
Mile ...... 117 J 2
Milebush ...... 115 O 3
Milehouse ...... 96 M 10
Milemill ...... 102 L 8
Milestone ...... 95 H 9
Milford *Armagh* ...... 114 L 5
Milford *Cork* ...... 94 F 10
Mill Town ...... 114 L 5
Millbay ...... 115 O 3
Millbrook *Derry* ...... 118 K 3
Millbrook *Larne* ...... 115 O 3
Millbrook *Oldcastle* ...... 108 K 6
Milleen ...... 93 E 11
Milford ...... 117 I 2
Millisle ...... 115 P 4
Millroad ...... 96 M 10
Millstreet *Cork* ...... 89 E 11
Millstreet *Waterford* ...... 91 I 11
Milltown *Armagh* ...... 114 L 5
Milltown *Ballymoney* ...... 118 M 2
Milltown *Banbridge* ...... 114 N 5

Milltown *Cavan* ...... 107 J 5
Milltown *Craigavon* ...... 114 M 4
Milltown *Dublin* ...... 103 M 8
Milltown *Kildare* ...... 102 L 8
Milltown *near Dingle* ...... 92 B 11
Milltown
  near Mount Bellew ...... 106 G 7
Milltown *near Tralee* ...... 93 C 11
Milltown *near Tuam* ...... 105 F 7
Milltown *Omagh* ...... 114 K 4
Milltown *Wexford* ...... 97 M 10
Miltownpass ...... 107 K 7
Minane Bridge ...... 90 G 12
Minard Head ...... 92 B 11
Mine Head ...... 91 J 12
Minerstown ...... 115 O 5
Minterburn ...... 114 L 4
Mizen Head ...... 88 C 13
Moanmore ...... 98 D 9
Modelligo ...... 91 I 11
Modreeny ...... 100 H 9
Mogeely ...... 90 H 12
Moglass ...... 95 I 10
Moher (Cliffs of) ...... 98 D 9
Moher Lough ...... 105 D 6
Mohil ...... 96 K 9
Móinteach Milic /
  Mountmellick ...... 101 K 8
Moira ...... 115 N 4
Moll's Gap ...... 89 D 12
Monard ...... 95 H 10
Monaseed ...... 97 M 9
Monaster ...... 94 G 10
Monasteraden ...... 106 G 6
Monasteranenagh Abbey ... 94 G 10
Monasterboice ...... 109 M 6
Monasterevin ...... 102 K 8
Monavullagh Mountains ... 95 J 11
Mondello Park ...... 102 L 8
Monea ...... 113 I 4
Moneen *Clare* ...... 93 C 10
Moneen *Galway* ...... 105 F 7
Money Point ...... 93 D 10
Moneydig ...... 118 M 3
Moneygall ...... 101 I 9
Moneyglass ...... 114 M 3
Moneygold ...... 112 G 4
Moneylahan ...... 112 G 4
Moneymore ...... 114 L 3
Moneyneany ...... 118 L 3
Moneyreagh ...... 115 O 4
Monilea ...... 107 K 7
Moniva ...... 106 F 7
Monkstown *Cork* ...... 90 G 12
Monkstown
  Newtownabbey ...... 115 O 3
Monroe ...... 107 J 7
Montpelier ...... 99 G 9
Mooncoin ...... 96 K 11
Moone ...... 102 L 9
Moord ...... 91 I 12
Moore Bay ...... 98 C 9
Moorfields ...... 115 N 3
More (Island) ...... 105 D 6
Morenane ...... 94 F 10
Morley's Bridge ...... 89 D 12
Morningstar ...... 94 G 10
Mornington ...... 109 N 6
Mosney ...... 109 N 7
Moss-Side ...... 118 M 2
Mossley ...... 115 O 3
Mothel ...... 95 J 11
Motte Stone ...... 103 N 9
Mount Falcon ...... 111 E 5
Mount Garret ...... 96 L 10
Mount Hamilton or Sperrin 114 K 3
Mount Melleray Monastery .95 I 11
Mount Norris ...... 114 M 5
Mount Nugent ...... 107 K 6
Mount Stewart Gardens ... 115 P 4
Mount Talbot ...... 106 H 7
Mount Temple ...... 107 I 7
Mount Uniacke ...... 91 H 12
Mount Usher Gardens ... 103 N 8
Mountbolus ...... 101 J 8
Mountcastle ...... 117 J 3
Mountcharles ...... 112 H 4
Mountcollins ...... 93 E 11
Mountfield ...... 114 K 4
Mounthenry ...... 105 E 7
Mountjoy *Dungannon* ...... 114 M 4
Mountjoy *Omagh* ...... 113 J 4
Mountrath ...... 101 J 8
Mountrivers Bridge ...... 98 D 9
Mountshannon ...... 100 G 9
Mourne (Lough)
  near Ballybofey ...... 113 I 3

Mourne (Lough)
  near Carrickfergus ... 115 O 3
Mourne Beg ...... 113 I 3
Mourne Mountains ...... 109 N 5
Mourne River ...... 113 J 3
Moveen ...... 98 C 10
Moville / Bun an Phobail .. 118 K 2
Mowhan ...... 114 M 5
Moy ...... 114 L 4
Moy (River) ...... 111 E 5
Moyagh ...... 117 J 3
Moyallan ...... 114 M 4
Moyard ...... 104 B 7
Moyarget ...... 118 N 2
Moyasta ...... 98 D 9
Moydow ...... 107 I 7
Moygashel ...... 114 L 4
Moyglass ...... 99 G 8
Moylough *Galway* ...... 106 G 7
Moylough *Sligo* ...... 106 F 5
Moynalty ...... 108 L 6
Moynalvy ...... 108 L 7
Moyne *Roscommon* ...... 106 G 6
Moyne *Tipperary* ...... 107 J 6
Moyne *Wicklow* ...... 103 M 9
Moyne Abbey ...... 111 E 5
Moyrus ...... 104 C 7
Moyteoge Head ...... 110 B 6
Moyvally ...... 102 L 7
Moyvore ...... 107 J 7
Moyvoughly ...... 107 I 7
Muck (Isle of) ...... 115 O 3
Muckamore ...... 115 N 3
Muckanagh Lough ...... 99 F 9
Muckish Mountain ...... 117 H 2
Mucklon ...... 102 L 7
Muckno Lake ...... 108 L 5
Muckros Head ...... 112 G 4
Muckross ...... 89 D 11
Muff ...... 117 K 2
Muggort's Bay ...... 91 J 11
Muinchille / Cootehill ...... 108 K 5
Muine Bheag /
  Bagenalstown ...... 96 L 9
Muineachán / Monaghan .. 114 L 5
Muing ...... 111 D 5
Muingnabo ...... 111 C 5
Mulhuddart ...... 103 M 7
Mulkear ...... 94 G 10
Mullach Íde / Malahide .. 103 N 7
Mullagh *Cavan* ...... 108 L 6
Mullagh *Galway* ...... 100 G 8
Mullagh *Mayo* ...... 104 C 6
Mullagh *Meath* ...... 103 M 7
Mullaghanattin ...... 88 C 12
Mullaghanish ...... 89 E 11
Mullaghareirk Mountains ... 93 E 10
Mullaghash ...... 118 K 3
Mullaghbane ...... 109 M 5
Mullaghboy ...... 115 O 3
Mullaghcarn ...... 113 K 3
Mullaghcleevaun ...... 103 M 8
Mullaghclogha ...... 114 K 3
Mullaghmore
  Cliffony North ...... 112 G 4
Mullaghmore *Magherafelt* .118 L 3
Mullaghmore Head ...... 112 G 4
Mullaghroe ...... 106 G 6
Mullan *Coleraine* ...... 118 L 2
Mullan *Figullar* ...... 114 L 4
Mullany'sCross ...... 111 F 5
Mullartown ...... 109 O 5
Mullen ...... 106 G 6
Mullenbeg ...... 96 K 10
Mullet Peninsula ...... 110 B 5
Mullinahone ...... 95 J 10
Mullinasole ...... 112 H 4
Mullinavat ...... 96 K 10
Mulroy Bay ...... 117 I 2
Multeen ...... 95 H 10
Multyfarnham ...... 107 J 7
Mungret ...... 94 F 10
Muntervary
  or Sheep's Head ...... 88 C 13
Murley ...... 113 K 4
Murlough Bay ...... 119 N 2
Murntown ...... 97 M 11
Murreagh ...... 92 A 11
Murrisk ...... 105 D 6
Murroe ...... 94 G 10
Murroogh ...... 99 E 8
Musheramore ...... 89 F 11
Mussenden Temple ...... 118 L 2
Mutton Island ...... 98 D 9
Mweelrea Mountains ...... 104 C 7
Mweenish Island ...... 104 C 8
Myshall ...... 96 L 9

N
Na Cealla Beaga /
  Killybegs ...... 112 G 4
Na Clocha Liatha /
  Greystones ...... 103 N 8
Na Dúnaibh / Downies ... 117 I 2
Na Sceirí / Skerries ...... 109 N 7
Nacorra (Lough) ...... 105 D 6
Nacung (Lough) ...... 117 H 2
Nad ...... 90 F 11
Nafooey (Lough) ...... 105 D 7
Nagles Mountains ...... 90 G 11
Nalughraman (Lough) .. 116 G 3
Naminn (Lough) ...... 117 J 2
Namona (Lough) ...... 88 B 12
Nanny ...... 108 M 7
Narin ...... 116 G 3
Narraghmore ...... 102 L 8
Narrow Water Castle ...... 109 N 5
Naul ...... 109 N 7
Neagh (Lough) ...... 114 M 4
Neale ...... 105 E 7
Nealstown ...... 101 I 9
Nenagh ...... 100 H 9
Nephin ...... 111 D 5
Nephin (Glen) ...... 105 D 6
Nephin Beg ...... 111 D 5
Nephin Beg Range ...... 111 C 5
New Birmingham ...... 95 J 10
New Buildings ...... 117 J 3
New Inn *Cavan* ...... 108 K 6
New Inn *Galway* ...... 100 G 8
New Kildimo ...... 94 F 10
New Quay / Bealaclugga .. 99 E 8
New Twopothouse Village ..94 G 11
Newbawn ...... 96 L 10
Newbliss ...... 113 K 5
Newbridge *Fingal* ...... 109 N 7
Newbridge *Limerick* ...... 94 F 10
Newbridge
  near Tuomard ...... 106 G 7
Newbridge /
  An Droichead Nua ... 102 L 8
Newcastle *Down* ...... 115 O 5
Newcastle *Dublin* ...... 103 M 8
Newcastle *Galway* ...... 99 F 7
Newcastle *Tipperary* ...... 95 I 11
Newcastle *Wicklow* ...... 103 N 8
Newcestown ...... 90 F 12
Newchapel ...... 95 I 10
Newferry ...... 114 M 3
Newgrange ...... 109 N 6
Newinn ...... 95 I 10
Newmarket *Cork* ...... 93 F 11
Newmarket *Kilkenny* ...... 96 K 10
Newmarket on Fergus ...... 99 F 9
Newmills *Donegal* ...... 117 I 3
Newmills *Dungannon* ...... 114 L 4
Newport *Tipperary* ...... 100 G 9
Newport Bay ...... 105 C 6
Newport Trench ...... 114 M 4
Newry ...... 114 M 5
Newtown *Cork* ...... 94 G 11
Newtown *Galway* ...... 99 F 8
Newtown *Kildare* ...... 102 L 7
Newtown *Laois* ...... 101 K 9
Newtown *Limerick* ...... 94 G 10
Newtown *near Knock* ...... 101 I 9
Newtown *near Nenagh* ... 100 H 9
Newtown *Offaly* ...... 100 H 8
Newtown *Roscommon* ... 100 H 7
Newtown *Tipperary* ...... 95 H 10
Newtown *Waterford* ...... 95 J 11
Newtown *Wexford* ...... 96 M 11
Newtown Cashel ...... 107 I 7
Newtown Cloghans ...... 111 E 5
Newtown-Crommelin ...... 119 N 3
Newtown Cunningham ... 117 J 3
Newtown Forbes ...... 107 I 6
Newtown Gore ...... 107 I 5
Newtown
  Mount Kennedy ...... 103 N 8
Newtown Sandes ...... 93 D 10
Newtownabbey ...... 115 O 4
Newtownards ...... 115 O 4
Newtownbreda ...... 115 O 4
Newtownbutler ...... 113 J 5
Newtownhamilton ...... 114 M 5
Newtownlow ...... 101 J 7
Newtownlynch ...... 99 E 8
Newtownshandrum ...... 94 F 10
Newtownstewart ...... 113 J 3
Nier ...... 95 J 11
Ninemilehouse ...... 95 J 10
Nobber ...... 108 L 6

Nohaval ...... 90 G 12
Nore ...... 101 J 9
Nore (River) ...... 96 K 10
North Channel ...... 119 O 2
North Ring ...... 90 F 13
North Sound ...... 98 C 8
Nose of Howth ...... 103 N 7
Noughaval *Doora* ...... 99 F 9
Noughaval *Noughaval* ...... 99 E 8
Nowen Hill ...... 89 E 12
Nuns Quarter ...... 115 O 4
Nurney *Carlow* ...... 96 L 9
Nurney *Kildare* ...... 102 L 8
Nutt's Corner ...... 115 N 4

O
Oaghley ...... 93 D 10
Oatfield ...... 99 F 9
Oatquarter ...... 98 C 8
O'Brien's Tower ...... 98 D 9
O'Flynn (Lough) ...... 106 G 6
Oghil *Clare* ...... 100 H 8
Oghil *Galway* ...... 98 C 8
Ogonnelloe ...... 99 G 9
O'Grady (Lough) ...... 99 G 9
Oileán Ciarraí /
  Castleisland ...... 93 D 11
Oilgate ...... 97 M 10
Oily ...... 112 G 4
Old Court ...... 89 E 13
Old Head *Ballymackeane* ... 90 G 13
Old Head *Louisburgh* ...... 104 C 6
Old Kilcullen ...... 102 L 8
Old Kildimo ...... 94 F 10
Old Ross ...... 96 L 10
Old Town *Donegal* ...... 117 I 3
Old Town *Laois* ...... 101 J 9
Old Town *Roscommon* ... 100 H 8
Old Town *Wexford* ...... 96 L 10
Old Twopothouse ...... 94 G 11
Oldleighlin ...... 96 K 9
Oldmill Bridge ...... 93 E 10
Oldtown *Dublin* ...... 109 N 7
Oldtown *Roscommon* ...... 101 I 7
Omagh ...... 113 K 4
Omeath ...... 109 N 5
Omey Island ...... 104 B 7
Onaght ...... 98 C 8
Oola ...... 94 H 10
Oorid Lough ...... 105 D 7
Oranmore ...... 99 F 8
Oriel (Mount) ...... 108 M 6
Oristown ...... 108 L 6
Oritor ...... 114 L 4
Ossian's Grave ...... 119 N 2
Ougther (Lough) ...... 107 J 6
Oulart ...... 97 M 10
Ovens ...... 90 G 12
Owel (Lough) ...... 107 J 7
Owenascaul ...... 92 B 11
Owenator ...... 116 H 3
Owenavorragh ...... 97 M 10
Owenbeag ...... 117 H 3
Owenbeg ...... 111 F 5
Owenbeg (River) ...... 112 G 5
Owenboliska ...... 99 E 8
Owenboy ...... 90 G 12
Owenbristy ...... 99 F 8
Owencarrow ...... 117 I 2
Owendalulleegh ...... 99 G 8
Owenea ...... 116 G 3
Owengarve *Clew Bay* ...... 105 D 6
Owengarve *River Moy* ... 106 F 5
Owenglin ...... 104 C 7
Oweniny ...... 111 D 5
Owenkillew *Glenelly* ...... 114 K 3
Owenkillew *Lough Swilly* ... 117 J 2
Owenmore Bridge ...... 105 D 6
Owennacurra ...... 90 H 12
Owenreagh Hill ...... 117 J 3
Owenriff ...... 105 D 7
Owentaraglin ...... 93 E 11
Owentocker ...... 116 H 3
Owenur (River) ...... 106 H 6
Ower ...... 105 E 7
Owing ...... 95 J 10
Owroe Bridge ...... 89 D 12
Owvane ...... 89 D 12
Oysterhaven ...... 90 G 12

P
Palace ...... 96 L 10
Palatine ...... 102 L 9
Pallas ...... 101 J 8
Pallas Cross ...... 100 I 9
Pallas Green ...... 94 G 10
Pallaskenry ...... 94 F 10

A B C D E F G H I J K L M N O P Q R S T U V W X Y Z

A – P

Paps (The) ....89 E 11
Park *Bellavary* ....105 E 6
Park *Derry* ....118 K 3
Parke's Castle ....112 H 5
Parkgate ....115 N 3
Parkmore ....99 F 8
Parkmore Point ....92 A 11
Parknasilla ....88 C 12
Parteen ....99 G 9
Partry ....105 E 6
Partry Mountains ....105 D 7
Passage ....106 H 7
Passage East ....96 L 11
Passage West ....90 G 12
Patrickswell ....94 F 10
Patterson's Spade Mill ....115 N 3
Paulstown ....96 K 9
Peake ....90 F 12
Peatlands ....114 M 4
Peterswell ....99 F 8
Pettigoe ....113 I 4
Phoenix Park ....103 M 7
Piercetown ....97 M 11
Pigeons (The) ....107 I 7
Pike ....100 H 8
Pike (The) *near Boola* ...91 I 11
Pike (The) *near Lamybrien* ..91 J 11
Pike (The) *Tipperary* ....100 H 8
Pike Corner ....108 L 7
Pike of Rush Hall ....101 J 9
Piltown ....95 K 10
Pluck ....117 J 3
Plumbridge ....113 K 3
Pollagh ....101 I 8
Pollan Bay ....117 J 2
Pollatomish ....111 C 5
Pollnalaght ....113 J 4
Pollshask ....106 G 7
Pomeroy ....114 L 4
Pontoon ....105 E 6
Port ....116 F 3
Port Ballintrae ....118 M 2
Port Durlainne / Porturlin ..111 C 5
Port Láirge / Waterford ...96 K 11
Port Laoise / Portlaoise ..101 K 8
Port Omna / Portumna ......100 H 8
Portacloy ....111 C 5
Portadown ....114 M 4
Portaferry ....115 P 4
Portaleen ....118 K 2
Portavogie ....115 P 4
Portbradden ....118 M 2
Portglenone ....118 M 3
Portland ....100 H 8
Portlaw ....96 K 11
Portmagee ....88 A 12
Portmagee Channel ....88 A 12
Portmarnock ....103 N 7
Portmuck ....115 O 3
Portnablagh ....117 I 2
Portnoo ....116 G 3
Portrane ....109 N 7
Portroe ....100 G 9
Portrush ....118 M 2
Portsalon ....117 J 2
Portstewart ....118 M 2
Poulaphouca Reservoir .....103 M 8
Poulnamucky ....95 I 10
Poulnasherry Bay ....98 D 10
Power Head ....90 H 12
Power's Cross ....100 H 8
Powerscourt Demesne ....103 N 8
Powerstown ....96 K 10
Poyntz Pass ....114 M 5
Priesthaggard ....96 L 11
Prosperous ....102 L 8
Puckaun ....100 H 9
Puffin Island ....88 A 12
Punchestown ....103 M 8

Q

Quarrytown ....119 N 3
Querrin ....93 D 10
Quigley's Point ....118 K 2
Quilty ....98 D 9
Quin ....99 F 9
Quoile ....115 O 4

R

Rabbit Islands ....89 E 13
Race End ....117 I 2
Raffrey ....115 O 4
Raghly ....112 G 4
Raghtin More ....117 J 2
Rahan ....101 J 8
Rahanagh ....93 E 10
Rahara ....106 H 7

Raharney ....108 K 7
Raheen ....96 L 10
Raigh ....105 D 7
Railyard ....101 K 9
Rake Street ....111 D 5
Ram Head ....91 I 12
Ramor (Lough) ....108 K 6
Ramore Head ....118 M 2
Rams Island ....114 N 4
Ramsgrange ....96 L 11
Randalstown ....114 N 3
Rapemills ....101 I 8
Raphoe ....117 J 3
Rasharkin ....118 M 3
Rashedoge ....117 I 3
Rath ....101 I 8
Ráth Caola / Rathkeale ....94 F 10
Ráth Droma / Rathdrum .....103 N 9
Rathangan ....102 L 8
Rathaspick ....107 J 7
Rathbrit ....95 I 10
Rathcabban ....100 H 8
Rathconrath ....107 J 7
Rathcool ....89 F 11
Rathcoole ....103 M 8
Rathcore ....109 N 6
Rathcormack *near Fermoy* ..90 H 11
Rathcormack *near Sligo* ..112 G 5
Rathcroghan ....106 H 6
Rathdangan ....103 M 9
Rathdowney ....101 J 9
Rathduff ....90 G 11
Rathedan ....96 L 9
Rathfeigh ....108 M 7
Rathfriland ....115 N 5
Rathfylane ....96 L 10
Rathgarogue ....96 L 10
Rathgormuck ....95 J 11
Rathkeevin ....95 I 10
Rathkenny ....108 M 6
Rathlackan ....111 E 5
Rathlee ....111 E 5
Rathlin Island ....119 N 2
Rathlin O'Birne Island ....112 F 4
Rathlin Sound ....119 N 2
Rathmelton ....117 J 2
Rathmines ....103 N 8
Rathmolyon ....108 L 7
Rathmore ....89 E 11
Rathmullan ....117 J 2
Rathnew ....103 N 9
Rathnure ....96 L 10
Rathoma ....111 E 5
Rathowen ....107 J 7
Rathvilla ....101 K 8
Rathvilly ....102 L 9
Ratoath ....108 M 7
Raven Point (The) ....97 M 10
Ravensdale ....109 M 5
Ray *near Dunfanaghy* .....117 H 2
Ray *near Rathmillan* .....117 J 2
Ray (River) ....117 H 2
Rea (Lough) ....99 G 8
Reaghstown ....108 M 6
Reanagower Cross Roads ....93 D 11
Reananeree /
  Rae na nDoirí ....89 E 12
Reanascreena ....89 E 13
Rear Cross ....95 H 9
Red Bay ....119 N 2
Redcastle ....118 K 2
Redcross ....103 N 9
Redgate ....97 M 10
Redhills ....107 K 5
Ree (Lough) ....107 I 7
Reelan ....117 H 3
Reen ....89 D 12
Reens ....94 F 10
Reevanagh ....96 K 9
Relaghbeg ....108 L 6
Rerrin ....88 C 13
Rhode ....101 K 7
Richhill ....114 M 4
Ridge ....96 K 9
Ridge Point ....110 C 5
Rine (River) ....99 F 9
Rineanna Point ....99 F 9
Ringabella Bay ....90 H 12
Ringarogy Island ....89 D 13
Ringaskiddy ....90 H 12
Ringboy ....115 P 4
Ringfad Point ....115 P 5
Ringsend ....118 L 2
Ringstown ....101 J 8
Ringville / An Rinn ....91 J 11
Rinmore Point ....117 I 2

Rinn (River) ....107 I 6
Rinn Lough ....107 I 6
Rinneen *Clare* ....98 D 9
Rinneen *Cork* ....89 E 13
Rinroe Point ....110 C 5
Rinville ....99 F 8
Rinvyle ....104 C 7
Rinvyle Castle ....104 B 7
Rinvyle Point ....104 B 7
River ....110 B 6
Riverchapel ....97 N 10
Riverstick ....90 G 12
Riverstown *Cork* ....90 G 12
Riverstown *Sligo* ....112 G 5
Riverstown *Tipperary* ....101 I 8
Riverville ....93 D 11
Roadford ....98 D 8
Roaninish ....116 G 3
Roaringwater Bay ....89 D 13
Robe ....105 E 6
Robert's Head ....90 H 12
Robertstown ....102 L 8
Robinstown ....108 L 7
Roche's Point ....90 H 12
Rochestown ....96 K 11
Rochfortbridge ....101 K 7
Rock (The) ....114 L 4
Rock Island ....98 C 8
Rockabill ....109 N 7
Rockchapel ....93 E 11
Rockcorry ....108 K 5
Rockhill ....94 F 10
Rockmills ....94 G 11
Rodeen ....107 H 6
Roe ....118 L 3
Roe Valley ....118 L 2
Roney Point ....97 N 10
Rooaun ....100 H 8
Roonagh Quay ....104 C 6
Roonah Lough ....104 C 6
Roosky *Leitrim* ....112 H 4
Roosky *Mayo* ....106 F 6
Roosky *Roscommon* ....107 I 6
Ropefield ....112 G 5
Ros an Mhil / Rossaveel ...98 D 8
Ros Comáin /
  Roscommon ....106 H 7
Ros Cré / Roscrea ....101 I 9
Ros Láir / Rosslare ....97 M 11
Ros Mhic Thriúin /
  New Ross ....96 L 10
Rosapenna ....117 I 2
Rosbercon ....96 L 10
Rosegreen ....95 I 10
Rosenallis ....101 J 8
Rosguill ....117 I 2
Roskeeragh Point ....112 F 4
Rosmuck ....105 D 7
Rosmult ....95 I 9
Rosnakill ....117 I 2
Ross *Lough Leane* ....89 D 11
Ross *Lough Sheelin* ......107 K 6
Ross Abbey ....105 E 7
Ross Lake ....105 E 7
Ross Port ....111 C 5
Ross West ....105 E 6
Rossan Point ....112 F 3
Rossbeg ....116 G 3
Rossbehy Creek ....92 C 11
Rossbrin ....89 D 13
Rosscahill ....105 E 7
Rosscarbery ....89 E 13
Rosscarbery Bay ....89 E 13
Rosscor ....113 H 4
Rossdohan Island ....88 C 12
Rosserk Abbey ....111 E 5
Rossgeir ....117 J 3
Rossglass ....115 O 5
Rossinver ....112 H 4
Rosslare Bay ....97 M 11
Rosslare Point ....97 M 11
Rosslea ....113 K 5
Rossmore *Cork* ....89 F 12
Rossmore *Laois* ....102 K 9
Rossmore Forest Park ......114 K 5
Rossmore Island ....88 C 12
Rossnowlagh ....112 H 4
Rosstrevor ....109 N 5
Rosturk ....105 C 6
Rough Point ....92 B 11
Roughty ....89 D 12
Roundfort ....105 E 7
Roundstone ....104 C 7

Roundwood ....103 N 8
Roury ....89 E 13
Rousky ....114 K 3
Rowallane Gardens ....115 O 4
Rower (The) ....96 L 10
Royal Canal ....107 I 7
Royaloak ....96 L 9
Ruan ....99 F 9
Rubane ....115 P 4
Rue Point ....119 N 2
Runabay Head ....119 N 2
Runnabackan ....106 H 6
Rushen (Slieve) ....113 J 5
Russborough House ....103 M 8
Rutland Island ....116 G 3
Ryefield ....108 K 6
Ryehill ....106 F 7
Rylane Cross ....90 F 12

S

Saddle Head ....110 B 5
Saggart ....103 M 8
St. Finan's Bay ....88 A 12
St. John's Lough ....107 I 5
St. John's Point ....115 P 5
St. John's Point ....112 G 4
St. Johnstown ....117 J 3
St. Macdara's Island ......104 C 8
St. Margaret's ....103 N 7
St. Mochta's House ....108 M 6
St. Mullin's ....96 L 10
Saintfield ....115 O 4
Saleen *Cork* ....90 H 12
Saleen *Kerry* ....93 D 10
Salia ....104 C 6
Sallahig ....88 B 12
Sallins ....102 M 8
Sallybrook ....90 G 12
Sally Gap ....103 N 8
Sallypark ....100 H 9
Salrock ....104 C 7
Saltee Islands ....96 M 11
Salthill ....99 E 8
Sandholes ....114 L 4
Sandyford ....103 N 8
Santry ....103 N 7
Saul ....115 O 4
Sawel Mountain ....118 K 3
Scalp Mountain ....117 J 2
Scardaun *Mayo* ....105 E 7
Scardaun *Roscommon* ......106 H 7
Scarnagh ....97 N 9
Scarriff / An Scairbh .....99 G 9
Scarriff Island ....88 B 12
Scartaglin ....93 D 11
Scarva ....114 M 5
Scattery Island ....93 D 10
Schull / Skull ....89 D 13
Scolban (Lough) ....113 H 4
Scotch Town ....114 K 3
Scotshouse ....113 K 5
Scotstown ....114 K 5
Scrabo Hill ....115 O 4
Scramoge ....107 H 6
Screeb Cross ....105 D 7
Screen ....97 M 10
Screggan ....101 J 8
Scribbagh ....113 H 4
Sculogue Gap ....96 L 10
Scur (Lough) ....107 I 5
Seaforde ....115 O 5
Seapatrick ....114 N 4
Seefin ....95 J 11
Seskinore ....113 K 4
Seskinryan ....96 L 9
Seven Heads ....89 F 13
Seven Hogs or
  Magharee Islands (The) ..92 B 11
Shalwy ....112 G 4
Shanacashel ....88 C 11
Shanagarry ....90 H 12
Shanagh ....99 F 8
Shanagolden ....93 E 10
Shanahoe ....101 J 9
Shanballard ....99 G 7
Shanbally *Cork* ....90 G 12
Shanbally *Galway* ....106 G 7
Shanballymore ....94 G 11
Shanco ....114 L 4
Shanes Castle ....114 N 3
Shankill ....103 N 8
Shanlaragh ....89 E 12
Shanlis ....108 M 6
Shannagh (Lough) ....115 N 5
Shannakea ....105 D 7
Shannawona ....105 D 7
Shannon ....99 F 9

Shannon (River) ....100 H 8
Shannon Airport ....99 F 9
Shannon Harbour ....101 I 8
Shannonbridge ....100 H 8
Shanragh ....101 K 9
Shantonagh ....108 L 5
Sharavogue ....101 I 8
Sheddings (The) ....119 N 3
Sheeanamore ....103 M 9
Sheeaun ....99 G 9
Sheeffry Hills ....105 C 6
Sheehan's Point ....88 B 12
Sheelin (Lough) ....107 K 6
Sheep Haven ....117 I 2
Sheever (Lough) ....107 K 7
Shehy Mountains ....89 D 12
Shercock ....108 L 6
Sherkin Island ....89 D 13
Sherky Island ....88 C 12
Sheskin ....111 D 5
Sheskinapoll ....117 J 3
Shillelagh ....97 M 9
Shinrone ....101 I 9
Shiven ....106 G 7
Shoptown ....115 N 3
Shot Head ....89 C 13
Shranamanragh Bridge ......110 C 5
Shrule ....105 E 7
Silent Valley ....109 O 5
Sillan (Lough) ....108 L 5
Silvermine Mountains ......100 H 9
Silvermines ....100 H 9
Silver Bridge ....108 M 5
Silver Strand ....104 B 7
Sinking ....106 F 7
Sion Mills ....113 J 3
Six Crosses ....93 D 10
Six Road Ends ....115 P 4
Six Towns (The) ....114 L 3
Sixmilebridge ....99 F 9
Sixmilecross ....114 K 4
Skannive (Lough) ....104 C 8
Skeagh ....107 J 7
Skehana ....101 K 9
Skehanagh ....106 G 7
Skerries (The) ....118 M 2
Skreen *Meath* ....108 M 7
Skreen *Sligo* ....112 F 5
Sky Road ....104 B 7
Slade ....96 L 11
Slane ....108 M 6
Slane (Hill of) ....108 M 6
Slaney (River) ....97 M 10
Slat (Lough) ....92 B 11
Slate (River) ....102 L 8
Slea Head ....92 A 11
Slemish Mountain ....119 N 3
Sliabh na Caillighe ....108 K 6
Slieve Anierin ....113 I 5
Slieve Aught Mountains ....99 G 8
Slieve Bernagh ....99 G 9
Slieve Bloom Mountains ....101 J 8
Slieve Gamph
  or the Ox Mountains .....111 F 5
Slieve Mish Mountains .....93 C 11
Slieve Miskish Mountains ..88 C 13
Slieveanorra ....119 N 2
Slievecallan ....99 E 9
Slievefelim Mountains .....94 H 9
Slievekimalta ....100 H 9
Slievekirk ....117 K 3
Slievemore *Dungannon* ....114 K 4
Slievemore *Mayo* ....110 B 5
Slievemurry ....106 G 7
Slievenamon ....95 J 10
Slieveroe ....96 K 11
Slievetooey ....116 G 3
Sligeach / Sligo ....112 G 5
Sligo Bay ....112 F 5
Sliveardagh Hills ....95 J 10
Slyne Head ....104 B 7
Smerwick ....92 A 11
Smerwick Harbour ....92 A 11
Smithborough ....114 K 5
Smithstown ....101 K 9
Snaght (Slieve)
  Derryveagh Mts. ....117 H 3
Snaght (Slieve) *Inishowen* .117 J 2
Snave ....89 D 12
Sneem ....88 C 12
Soldierstown ....115 N 4
Sord / Swords ....103 N 7
South Sound ....98 D 8
Spa ....93 C 11
Spa (The) ....115 O 4
Spanish Point *Locality* ..98 D 9
Spanish Point *Mal Bay* ...98 D 9

Speenoge ....117 J 2
Spelga Dam ....115 N 5
Sperrin Mountains ....118 K 3
Spink ....101 K 9
Spittaltown ....101 J 7
Springfield ....113 I 4
Springhill ....114 M 3
Springwell Forest ....118 L 2
Squires Hill ....115 O 4
Sraghmore ....103 N 8
Srah / An tSraith ....105 E 6
Srahduggaun ....111 C 6
Srahmore *near Bangor* ....111 C 5
Srahmore *near Newport* ...105 D 6
Srahmore *River* ....105 D 6
Sráid na Cathrach /
  Milltown Malbay ....98 D 9
Stabannan ....109 M 6
Stackallan ....108 M 6
Stack's Mountains ....93 D 11
Staffordstown ....114 M 3
Stags (The) ....89 E 13
Stags of Broad Haven ......111 C 4
Staigue Stone Fort ....88 B 12
Stamullin ....109 N 7
Staplestown ....102 L 8
Stepaside ....103 N 8
Stewartstown ....114 L 4
Stickstown ....90 F 12
Stillorgan ....103 N 8
Stone Bridge ....113 K 5
Stonyford *Kilkenny* ......96 K 10
Stonyford *Lisburn* ....115 N 4
Stormont ....115 O 4
Strabane ....117 J 3
Stracashel ....117 H 3
Stradbally *Kerry* ....92 B 11
Stradbally *Laois* ....101 K 8
Stradbally *Waterford* ....91 J 11
Stradone ....107 K 6
Stradreagh ....118 L 2
Straffan ....103 M 8
Stragar ....112 G 3
Strahart ....96 M 10
Straid *Donegal* ....117 J 2
Straid *Larne* ....115 O 3
Straid *Moyle* ....118 M 2
Straith Salach / Recess ...104 C 7
Strand ....93 E 10
Strandhill ....112 G 5
Strangford ....115 P 4
Strangford Lough ....115 P 4
Stranocum ....118 M 2
Stranorlar ....117 I 3
Stratford ....102 L 9
Stravally ....112 G 3
Streamstown ....104 B 7
Streedagh Point ....112 G 4
Streek Head ....89 C 13
Street ....107 J 6
Strokestown ....106 H 6
Stroove ....118 L 2
Struell Wells ....115 O 5
Strule ....113 J 3
Sturrakeen ....95 H 10
Suck (River) ....106 G 6
Suir (River) ....101 I 9
Summercove ....90 G 12
Summerhill ....108 L 7
Suncroft ....102 L 8
Sunderlin (Lough) ....107 I 7
Swan ....101 K 9
Swanlinbar ....113 I 5
Swan's Cross Roads ....114 K 5
Swatragh ....118 L 3
Sweep (The) ....95 J 10
Swilly (Lough) ....117 J 2
Swilly (River) ....117 J 2
Sybil Head ....92 A 11

T

Table Mountain ....103 M 8
Tacumshane ....97 M 11
Tacumshin Lake ....97 M 11
Taghmon ....96 M 11
Taghshinny ....107 I 7
Tagoat ....97 M 11
Tahilla ....88 C 12
Talbot Island ....104 B 7
Talbotstown ....102 M 9
Tallaght ....103 N 8
Tallanstown ....108 M 6
Tallow ....91 H 11
Tallowbridge ....91 H 11
Talt (Lough) ....111 F 5
Tamlaght *Fermanagh* ......113 J 5

Tamlaght *Magherafelt* ....118 M 3
Tamnamore ....114 M 4
Tandragee ....114 M 4
Tang ....107 I 7
Tangaveane ....116 H 3
Tappaghan Mount ....113 J 4
Tara (Hill of) ....108 M 7
Tarbert ....93 D 10
Tardree Forest ....115 N 3
Tarker (Lough) ....108 L 5
Tarmon ....112 H 5
Tarsaghaunmore ....111 C 5
Tassagh ....114 L 5
Taughblane ....115 N 4
Taur ....93 E 11
Tawin ....99 E 8
Tawin Island ....99 E 8
Tawny ....117 I 2
Tawnyinah ....106 F 6
Tawnylea ....112 H 5
Tay ....95 J 11
Tay (Lough) ....103 N 8
Taylor's Cross ....101 I 8
Tearaght Island ....92 A 11
Tedavnet ....114 K 5
Teelin ....112 G 4
Teemore ....113 J 5
Teeranea ....98 D 8
Teeranearagh ....88 B 12
Teerelton ....89 F 12
Teermaclane ....105 D 7
Teernakill ....105 D 7
Teeromoyle ....88 B 12
Teevurcher ....108 L 6
Temple (The) ....115 O 4
Temple of the Winds ....115 P 4
Templeboy ....112 F 5
Templederry ....100 H 9
Templeglentan ....93 E 10
Templehouse Lake ....112 G 5
Templemartin ....90 F 12
Templenoe ....89 C 12
Templeoran ....101 J 7
Templepatrick ....115 N 3
Templeshanbo ....96 L 10
Templetouhy ....101 I 9
Templetown ....96 L 11
Tempo ....113 J 4
Terenure ....103 N 8
Termon ....98 D 10
Termonbarry ....107 I 6
Termonfeckin ....109 N 6

Terryglass ....100 H 8
Tevrin ....107 K 7
Thomas Street ....106 H 7
Thomastown *Meath* ....108 L 6
Thomastown *Tipperrary* ....95 H 10
Thoor Ballylee ....99 F 8
Three Castle Head ....88 C 13
Three Castles ....96 J 9
Three Rock ....103 N 8
Tiduff ....92 B 11
Tievealehid ....116 H 2
Tievemore ....113 I 4
Tillyvoos ....112 H 4
Tiltinbane ....113 I 5
Timahoe ....102 L 8
Timoleague ....90 F 13
Timolin ....102 L 9
Tinahely ....103 M 9
Tinnahinch ....96 L 10
Tinriland ....102 L 9
Tiobraid Árann /
    Tipperary ....95 H 10
Tirnaneill ....114 L 5
Tirneevin ....99 F 8
Toames ....89 F 12
Tobar an Choire /
    Tubbercurry ....112 F 5
Tober ....101 J 7
Toberbeg ....102 M 8
Toberdoney ....118 M 2
Tobermore ....114 L 3
Tobernadarry ....105 E 7
Toberscanavan ....112 G 5
Toe Head ....89 E 13
Toem ....95 H 10
Togher *Cork* ....89 E 12
Togher *Louth* ....109 N 6
Togher *Offaly* ....101 K 8
Tolka ....103 M 7
Tollymore Forest Park ....115 O 5
Tombrack ....97 M 10
Tomdarragh ....103 N 8
Tomhaggard ....97 M 11
Tonabrocky ....99 E 8
Tonakeera Point ....104 C 7
Tonyduff ....108 K 6
Toomaghera ....99 E 8
Toomard ....106 G 7
Toombeola ....104 C 7
Toome ....114 M 3
Toomyvara ....100 H 9
Toor ....100 H 9

Tooraree ....93 E 10
Tooreencahill ....93 E 11
Toorlestraun ....112 F 5
Toormore ....89 D 13
Toormore Bay ....89 D 13
Toornafulla ....93 E 10
Toraigh /
    Tory Island ....116 H 2
Torc Waterfall ....89 D 11
Torneady Point ....116 G 2
Torr Head ....119 N 2
Tory Sound ....117 H 2
Tourig (River) ....91 I 11
Tower ....90 G 12
Trá Lí / Tralee ....93 C 11
Trá Mhór /
    Tramore ....96 K 11
Trabane Strand ....112 F 4
Tracton ....90 G 12
Trafrask ....89 D 12
Tragumna ....89 E 13
Tralee Bay ....92 C 11
Tramore Bay ....96 K 11
Tranarossan Bay ....117 I 2
Travara Bridge ....88 C 12
Trawbreaga Bay ....117 K 2
Trawenagh Bay ....116 G 3
Trawmore Bay ....110 C 5
Trean ....105 D 7
Treantagh ....117 I 2
Treehoo ....107 K 5
Treenlough ....106 G 6
Trien ....106 G 6
Trillick ....113 J 4
Tristia ....110 C 5
Trory ....113 J 4
Trostan ....119 N 2
Truskmore ....112 G 4
Trust ....100 G 7
Tuaim / Tuam ....105 F 7
Tuamgraney ....99 G 9
Tuar Mhic Éadaigh /
    Tourmakeady ....105 D 7
Tubber ....99 F 8
Tubbrid *Kilkenny* ....95 J 9
Tubbrid *Tipperary* ....95 I 11
Tulach Mhór /
    Tullamore ....101 J 8
Tulla *near Ennis* ....99 F 9
Tulla *near Gort* ....99 F 8
Tullagh Point ....117 J 2
Tullaghan ....112 G 4
Tullaghan Bay ....110 C 5

Tullaghanstown ....108 L 7
Tullagher ....96 K 10
Tullaghobegly ....117 H 2
Tullaherin ....96 K 10
Tullahought ....95 J 10
Tullakeel ....88 C 12
Tullamore ....93 D 10
Tullaroan ....95 J 10
Tullig ....92 C 11
Tullig Point ....93 C 10
Tullokyne ....105 E 7
Tully
    Lower Lough Erne ....113 I 4
Tully *near Ballyshannon* ...113 H 4
Tully *Upper Lough Erne* .....113 J 5
Tully Cross ....104 C 7
Tully National Stud ....102 L 8
Tullyallen ....109 M 6
Tullyamalra ....108 L 5
Tullycanna ....96 L 11
Tullydush ....117 J 2
Tullyhogue ....114 L 4
Tullylease ....94 F 11
Tullymacreeve ....109 M 5
Tullynaha ....112 H 3
Tullynally Castle ....107 J 6
Tullyroan ....114 M 4
Tullyvin ....108 K 5
Tulrohaun ....105 F 6
Tulsk ....106 H 6
Turlough ....105 E 6
Turloughmore ....105 F 7
Turner's Rock Tunnel ....89 D 12
Turreen ....107 I 7
Tuskar Rock ....97 N 11
Twelve Pins (The) ....104 C 7
Twomileborris ....95 I 9
Tylas ....108 M 7
Tynagh ....100 G 8
Tynan ....114 L 5
Tyrella ....115 O 5
Tyrellspass ....101 J 7

U

Uachtar Ard /
    Oughterard ....105 E 7
Uaigh / Owey Island ....116 G 2
Ugga Beg (Lough) ....98 D 8
Ulster American
    Folk Park ....113 J 4
Ulster Folk
    Museum (The) ....115 O 4

Union Hall ....89 E 13
Unshin ....112 G 5
Upper Ballinderry ....115 N 4
Upper Lake ....103 M 8
Upperchurch ....95 H 9
Upperlands ....118 M 3
Urbalreagh ....117 K 1
Urglin Glebe ....102 L 9
Urlaur ....106 F 6
Urlaur Lough ....106 F 6
Urlingford ....95 J 9

V

Valencia Island ....88 A 12
Valley ....110 C 5
Valleymount ....103 M 8
Vartry Reservoir ....103 N 8
Ventry ....92 A 11
Ventry Harbour ....92 A 11
Vicarstown ....102 K 8
Victoria Bridge ....113 J 3
Villierstown ....91 I 11
Virginia ....108 K 6
Virginia Road ....108 K 6
Vow ....118 M 3

W

Waddingtown ....96 M 11
Walshestown ....97 M 11
Walshtown ....90 H 12
Ward ....103 N 7
Ward (River) ....103 N 7
Waringsford ....115 N 4
Waringstown ....114 N 4
Warrenpoint ....109 N 5
Washing Bay ....114 M 4
Watch Ho.-Village ....96 M 9
Waterfall ....90 G 12
Waterfoot or Glenariff ....119 N 2
Waterford Harbour ....96 L 11
Watergrasshill ....90 G 11
Waterworks ....114 L 3
Wattle Bridge ....113 J 5
Welchtown ....117 I 3
Wellington Bridge ....96 L 11
Wells Cross ....114 M 4
Wesport Bay ....105 C 6
West Town ....116 H 2
Westcove ....88 B 12
Westport House ....105 D 6
Westport Quay ....105 D 6
Wexford Bay ....97 N 10

Wexford Harbour ....97 M 10
Whale Head ....117 J 2
Wheathill ....113 I 5
Whiddy Island ....89 D 12
White *Limerick* ....93 E 10
White *Louth* ....109 M 6
White Castle ....118 K 2
White Hall ....89 D 13
White Island ....113 I 4
White Park Bay ....118 M 2
White Strand ....98 D 9
Whiteabbey ....115 O 3
Whitechurch *Cork* ....90 G 12
Whitechurch *Waterford* ....91 I 11
Whitecross ....114 M 5
Whitegate ....90 H 12
Whitehall *Roscommon* .....107 I 6
Whitehall *Westmeath* ......107 K 7
Whitehead ....115 O 3
Whites Town ....109 N 6
White'sCross ....90 G 12
Whitesides Corner ....114 M 3
Wicklow Gap ....103 M 8
Wicklow Mountains ....103 N 8
Wicklow Way ....103 N 8
Wildfowl
    and Wetlands Trust ....115 O 4
Wilkinstown ....108 L 6
Willbrook ....99 E 9
Williamstown *Galway* ....106 G 6
Williamstown
    Westmeath ....107 I 7
Windgap ....95 J 10
Windmill ....102 L 7
Windy Gap *Kerry* ....89 D 12
Windy Gap *Louth* ....109 N 5
Windy Gap *Mayo* ....105 E 6
Wolfhill ....101 K 9
Womanagh ....91 I 12
Woodburn ....115 O 3
Woodcock Hill ....99 F 9
Woodenbridge ....103 N 9
Woodford (River) ....99 G 8
Woodstown ....96 L 11

Y

Yellow Furze ....108 M 6
Yganavan (Lough) ....92 C 11
Youghal ....100 H 9
Youghal Bay ....91 I 12

A B C D E F G H I J K L M N O P Q R S T U V W X Y Z

Town plans

Sights
Place of interest
Interesting place of worship:
Church - Protestant church
Roads
Motorway - Dual carriageway
Numbered junctions: complete, limited
Major thoroughfare
Unsuitable for traffic or street subject to restrictions
Pedestrian street - Tramway
Car park - Park and Ride
Tunnel
Station and railway
Funicular
Cable-car

Various signs
Tourist Information Centre
Mosque - Synagogue
Tower - Ruins
Windmill
Garden, park, wood
Cemetery

Stadium - Golf course - Racecourse
Outdoor or indoor swimming pool
View - Panorama
Monument - Fountain
Pleasure boat harbour
Lighthouse
Airport - Underground station
Coach station
Ferry services:
passengers and cars - passengers only

Main post office with poste restante - Hospital
Covered market
Gendarmerie - Police
Town Hall
University, College
Public buildings located by letter:
Museum
Theatre

Plans

Curiosités
Bâtiment intéressant
Édifice religieux intéressant : catholique - protestant
Voirie
Autoroute - Double chaussée de type autoroutier
Échangeurs numérotés : complet - partiels
Grande voie de circulation
Rue réglementée ou impraticable
Rue piétonne - Tramway
Parking - Parking Relais
Tunnel
Gare et voie ferrée
Funiculaire, voie à crémaillère
Téléphérique, télécabine

Signes divers
Information touristique
Mosquée - Synagogue
Tour - Ruines
Moulin à vent
Jardin, parc, bois
Cimetière

Stade - Golf - Hippodrome
Piscine de plein air, couverte
Vue - Panorama
Monument - Fontaine
Port de plaisance
Phare
Aéroport - Station de métro
Gare routière
Transport par bateau :
passagers et voitures, passagers seulement

Bureau principal de poste restante - Hôpital
Marché couvert
Gendarmerie - Police
Hôtel de ville
Université, grande école
Bâtiment public repéré par une lettre :
Musée
Théâtre

Stadtpläne

Sehenswürdigkeiten
Sehenswertes Gebäude
Sehenswerter Sakralbau:Katholische - Evangelische Kirche
Straßen
Autobahn - Schnellstraße
Nummerierte Voll- bzw. Teilanschlussstellen
Hauptverkehrsstraße
Gesperrte Straße oder mit Verkehrsbeschränkungen
Fußgängerzone - Straßenbahn
Parkplatz - Park-and-Ride-Plätze
Tunnel
Bahnhof und Bahnlinie
Standseilbahn
Seilschwebebahn

Sonstige Zeichen
Informationsstelle
Moschee - Synagoge
Turm - Ruine
Windmühle
Garten, Park, Wäldchen
Friedhof

Stadion - Golfplatz - Pferderennbahn
Freibad - Hallenbad
Aussicht - Rundblick
Denkmal - Brunnen
Yachthafen
Leuchtturm
Flughafen - U-Bahnstation
Autobusbahnhof
Schiffsverbindungen:
Autofähre, Personenfähre
Hauptpostamt (postlagernde Sendungen) - Krankenhaus
Markthalle
Gendarmerie - Polizei
Rathaus
Universität, Hochschule
Öffentliches Gebäude, durch einen Buchstaben
gekennzeichnet:
Museum
Theater

Plattegronden

Bezienswaardigheden
Interessant gebouw
Interessant kerkelijk gebouw: Kerk - Protestantse kerk
Wegen
Autosnelweg - Weg met gescheiden rijbanen
Knooppunt / aansluiting: volledig, gedeeltelijk
Hoofdverkeersweg
Onbegaanbare straat, beperkt toegankelijk
Voetgangersgebied - Tramlijn
Parkeerplaats - P & R
Tunnel
Station, spoorweg
Kabelspoor
Tandradbaan

Overige tekens
Informatie voor toeristen
Moskee - Synagoge
Toren - Ruïne
Windmolen
Tuin, park, bos
Begraafplaats

Stadion - Golfterrein - Renbaan
Zwembad: openlucht, overdekt
Uitzicht - Panorama
Gedenkteken, standbeeld - Fontein
Jachthaven
Vuurtoren
Luchthaven - Metrostation
Busstation
Vervoer per boot:
Passagiers en auto's - uitsluitend passagiers

Hoofdkantoor voor poste-restante - Ziekenhuis
Overdekte markt
Marechaussee / rijkswacht - Politie
Stadhuis
Universiteit, hogeschool
Openbaar gebouw, aangegeven met een letter::
Museum
Schouwburg

Piante

Curiosità
Edificio interessante
Costruzione religiosa interessante: Chiesa - Tempio
Viabilità
Autostrada - Doppia carreggiata tipo autostrada
Svincoli numerati: completo, parziale
Grande via di circolazione
Via regolamentata o impraticabile
Via pedonale - Tranvia
Parcheggio - Parcheggio Ristoro
Galleria
Stazione e ferrovia
Funicolare
Funivia, cabinovia

Simboli vari
Ufficio informazioni turistiche
Moschea - Sinagoga
Torre - Ruderi
Mulino a vento
Giardino, parco, bosco
Cimitero

Stadio - Golf - Ippodromo
Piscina: all'aperto, coperta
Vista - Panorama
Monumento - Fontana
Porto turistico
Faro
Aeroporto - Stazione della metropolitana
Autostazione
Trasporto con traghetto:
passeggeri ed autovetture - solo passeggeri

Ufficio centrale di fermo posta - Ospedale
Mercato coperto
Carabinieri - Polizia
Municipio
Università, scuola superiore
Edificio pubblico indicato con lettera:
Museo
Teatro

Planos

Curiosidades
Edificio interessante
Edificio religioso interessante: católica - protestante
Vías de circulación
Autopista - Autovía
Enlaces numerados: completo, parciales
Vía importante de circulación
Calle reglamentada o impracticable
Calle peatonal - Tranvía
Aparcamiento - Aparcamientos «P+R»
Túnel
Estación y línea férrea
Funicular, línea de cremallera
Teleférico, telecabina

Signos diversos
Oficina de Información de Turismo
Mezquita - Sinagoga
Torre - Ruinas
Molino de viento
Jardín, parque, madera
Cementerio

Estadio - Golf - Hipódromo
Piscina al aire libre, cubierta
Vista parcial - Vista panorámica
Monumento - Fuente
Puerto deportivo
Faro
Aeropuerto - Estación de metro
Estación de autobuses
Transporte por barco:
pasajeros y vehículos, pasajeros solamente

Oficina de correos - Hospital
Mercado cubierto
Policía National - Policía
Ayuntamiento
Universidad, escuela superior
Edificio público localizado con letra :
Museo
Teatro

Plans de ville
Town plans / Stadtpläne / Stadsplattegronden
Piante di città / Planos de ciudades

Shetland Islands
Orkney Islands
Hebrides
Loch Shin
Loch Ness
Spey
Dee
Aberdeen
Coll Tiree
Loch Tay
Dundee
Jura
Stirling
Perth
Islay
Glasgow
Edinburgh
Newcastle-upon-Tyne
Carlisle
Durham
Lough Neagh
Belfast
Isle of Man
York
L. Conn
L. Allen
Swale
Blackpool
Wharfe
Leeds
Kingston-upon-Hull
L. Mask
Ribble
Manchester
Trent
Galway
L. Corrib
L. Ree
Boyne
IRELAND
Liverpool
Lincoln
Lough Derg
DUBLIN
Chester
Sheffield
Suir
Barrow
Stoke-on-Trent
Nottingham
Norwich
Limerick
Derby
Leicester
Wolverhampton
Blackwater
Birmingham
Coventry
Cambridge
Killarney
Lee
Cork
Stratford
Warwick
GREAT BRITAIN
Ipswich
Cheltenham
Oxford
Colchester
Newport
LONDON
Canterbury
Reading
Cardiff
Bristol
Bath
Windsor
Dover
Exe
Winchester
Folkestone
Southampton
Brighton
Exeter
Bournemouth
Portsmouth
Plymouth
Isles of Scilly
Alderney
Guernsey
Jersey

GREAT BRITAIN
- Aberdeen 150
- Bath 150
- Birmingham............. 151
- Bournemouth 152
- Brighton and Hove 153
- Bristol 154
- Cambridge............. 155
- Canterbury............. 156
- Cardiff 157
- Chester 158
- Coventry............... 159
- Dundee............... 159
- Durham............... 160
- Edinburgh 161
- Exeter................. 162
- Glasgow 163
- Leeds 164
- Leicester 165
- Lincoln................. 165
- Liverpool 166-167
- Greater London 168-169
- London 170-171
- Manchester 172
- Newcastle-upon-Tyne ... 173
- Norwich 174
- Nottingham............. 174
- Oxford 175
- Perth 176
- Plymouth 177
- Portsmouth and Southsea 178
- Southampton 179
- Stirling.................. 180
- Stratford-upon-Avon 181
- Winchester............. 182
- Windsor................. 183
- York 184

IRELAND
- Belfast 185
- Cork 186
- Galway................. 187
- Dublin 188-189
- Killarney 190
- Limerick 191

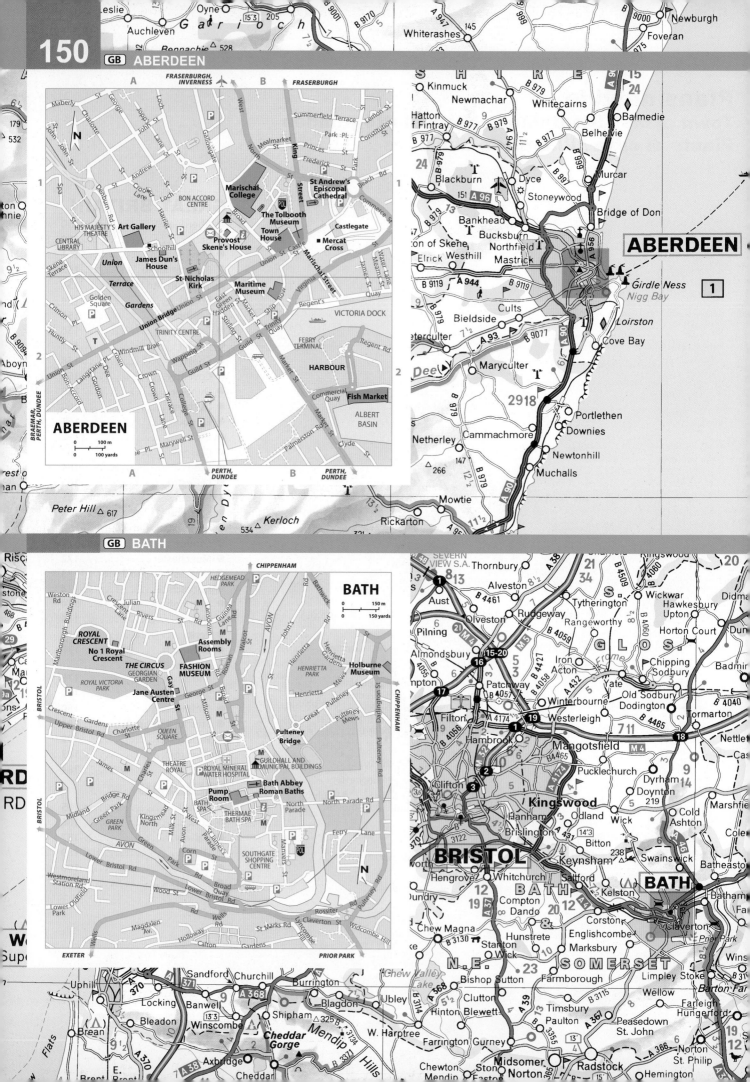

GB BATH

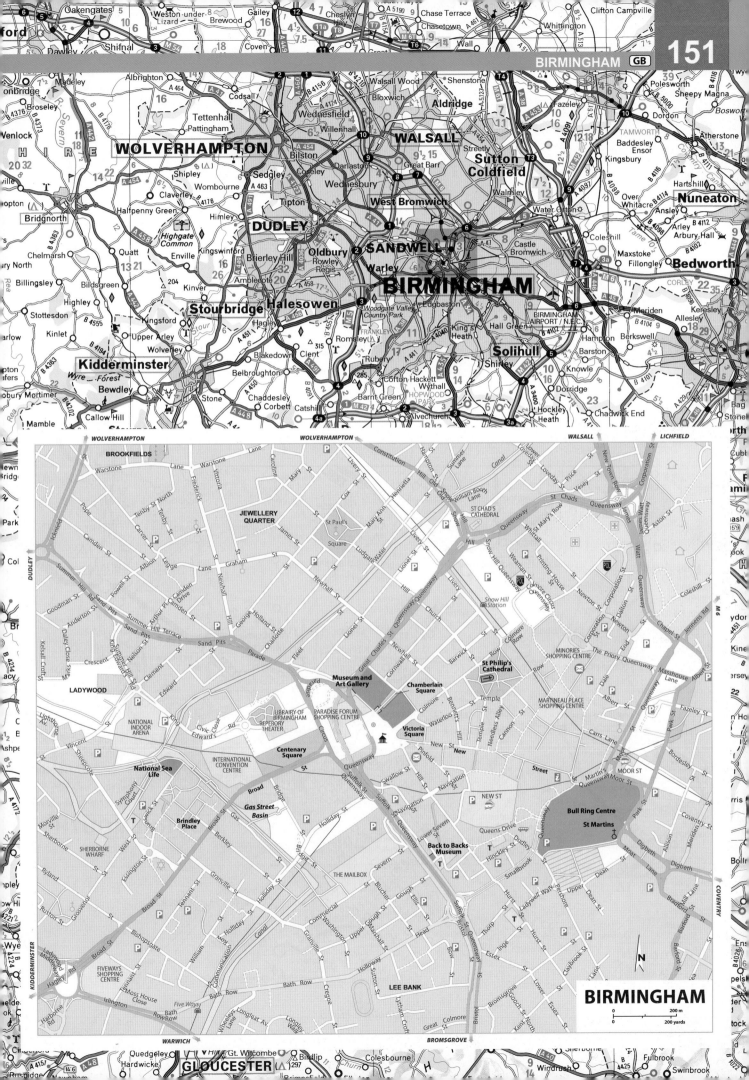

BIRMINGHAM

0   200 m
0   200 yards

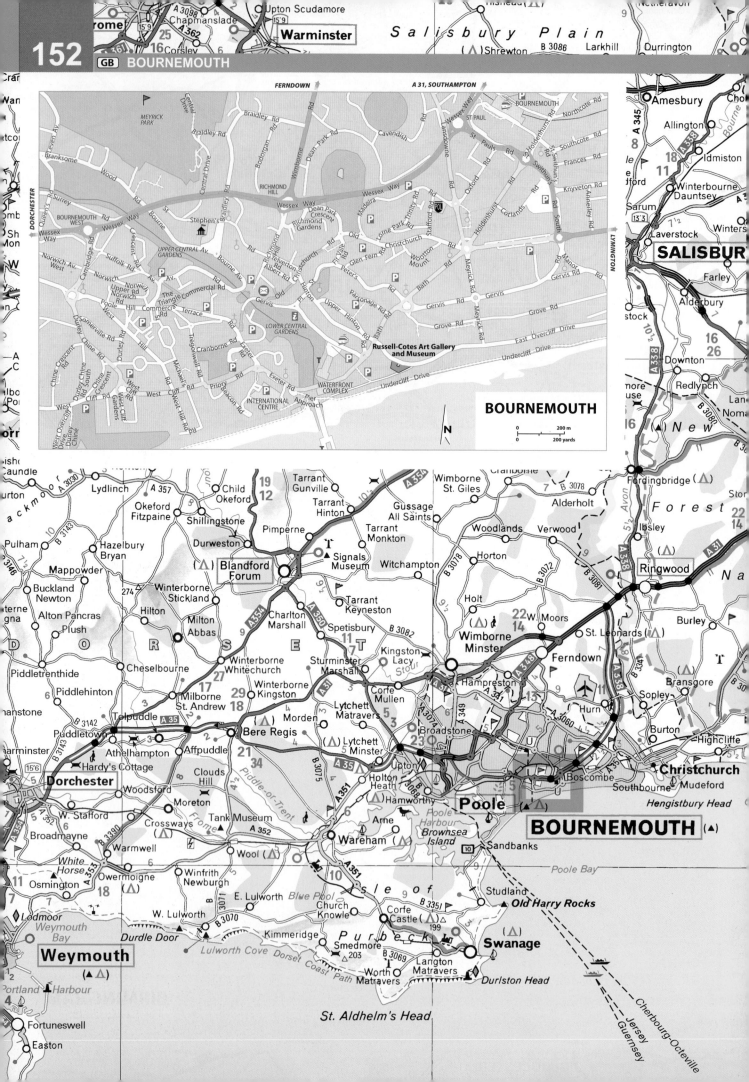

BRIGHTON AND HOVE

0 ——— 300 m
0 ——— 300 yards

N

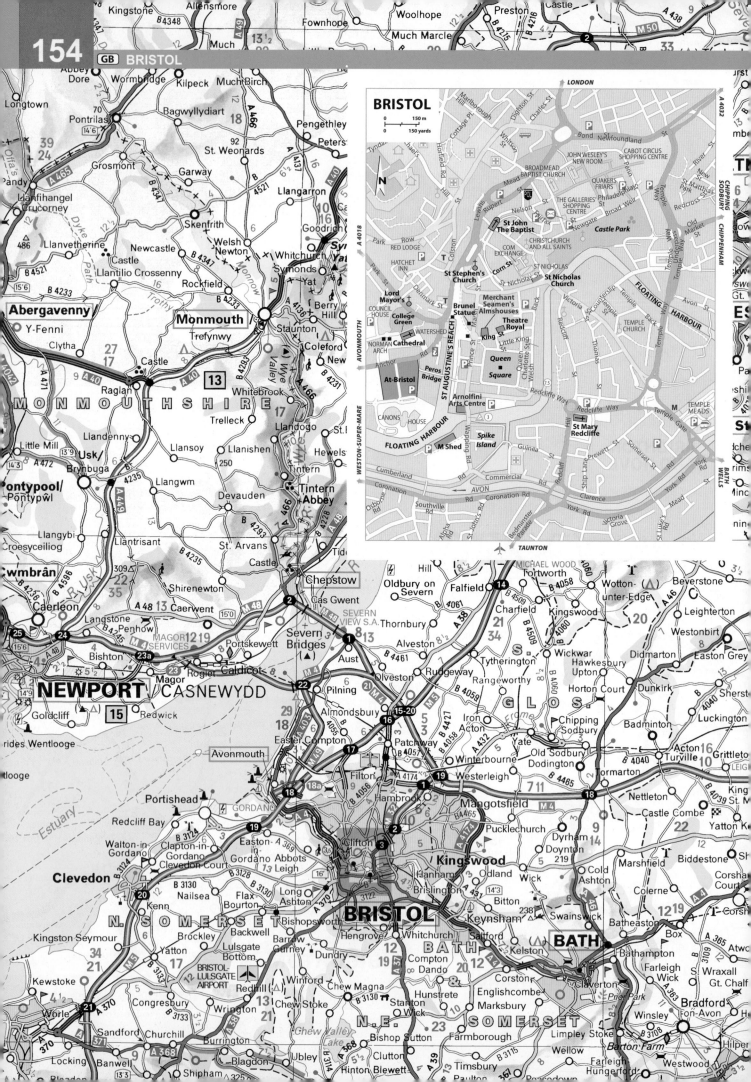

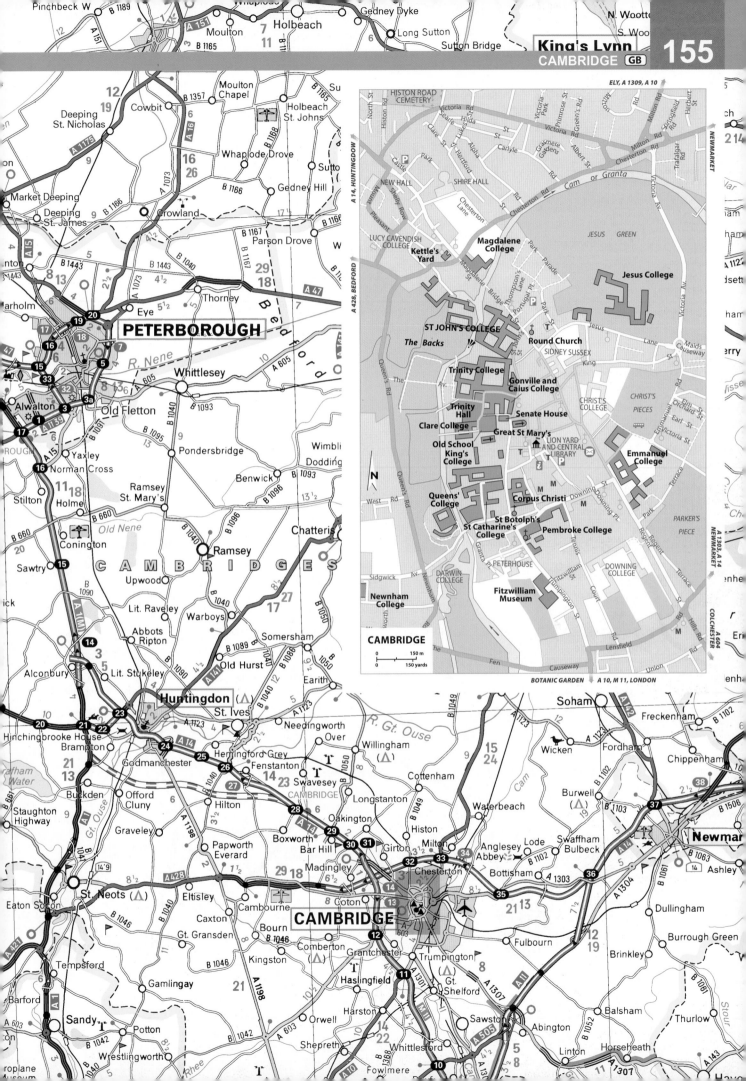

Peldon
East Mersea
St. Osyth
Clacton-on-Sea (▲)
Tolleshunt D'Arcy
Mersea Island
Cudmore Grove
Jaywick

CANTERBURY
0 — 150 m
0 — 150 yards

WHITSTABLE

Heybridge
Goldhanger
Tollesbury
R. Blackwater
Sales Point
Bradwell-on-Sea

ST DUNSTAN'S CHURCH
WEST
Mandeville
Roper Rd
North Lane
Station Rd West
St. Stephen's Rd
The Causeway
GREAT STOUR
Northgate
New Ruttington Lane
Victoria Row
Union St
Military Rd
Tourtel Rd
Old Ruttington Lane

Lower Mayland
Steeple
B 1021

Cold Norton
Latchingdon
B 1020
B 1012
B 1010
Althorne
Southminster

West Gate
Westgate Grove
Station Rd
Kirby's Lane
St. Radigunds St
St. Peters
BLACKFRIARS
St. Alphege
Lane
King's School
St George's Pl
St. Peter's
North Holmes Rd

LONDON, A2

Burnham-on-Crouch
R. Crouch
Foulness Point
Canewdon
(Λ)
Ashingdon
Rochford
B 1013

Whitehall Rd
Rheims Way
Westgate
St Peter's Lane
Black Griffin Lane
Canterbury Weavers
Hospital of Eastbridge
Beaney House of Art and Knowledge
CATHEDRAL
Christ Church Gate
Burgate
The Parade
St Augustine's College
St Augustine's Abbey
Longport

Foulness Island

Greyfriars Chapel
Canterbury Heritage Museum
Canterbury Tales
Hawk's Lane
Roman Museum
St Georges Lane

Great Wakering
Shoeburyness
A 13
A 1159
B-1017
Westcliff
-on-Sea
Thorpe
A 13
Shoebury Ness

Norman Castle
Castle St
Dane John Gardens
City Walls
Pin Hill
Old Dover Rd
WHITEFRIARS SHOPPING CENTRE
Marlowe Av
Watling
Rose Lane
Upper Bridge
Dover St
St George's Rd
Lower Chantry Lane
Upper Chantry Lane
N

SOUTHEND-ON-SEA (▲)

ASHFORD, MAIDSTONE
Memorial to Christopher Marlowe
EAST Station Rd
POL
DOVER

Isle of Grain
Grain
Wallend
R. Medway
Queenborough

Sheerness
Minster
B 2008
B 2231
Warden Point
(Λ) Eastchurch
B 2231
Leysdown-on-Sea
Isle of Sheppey
The Swale

(▲) **Margate**
Cliftonville
Foreness Point
Westgate-on-Sea
B 2051
Kingsgate
North For...

Upchurch
Iwade
Lower Halstow
Newington
Sittingbourne
A 249
B 2005

Herne Bay
Reculver
(Λ) Birchington
B 2050
A 299
A 28
I. of Thanet
St. Peter's
Broadstai...

Whitstable
Seasalter
B 2205
A 299
St Nicolas-at-Wade
Sarre
(Λ)
Minster
Abbey
A 256
A 299
Ramsgat...

Bapchild
Teynham
Oare
Faversham
(Λ)
Yorkletts
Hoath
Chislet
A 28
Pucks Gutter
Richborough
Pegwell Bay
Sandwich Bay

Bredgar
M2
B 2040
THANET WAY
Boughton Street
GATE
A 2
Blean
Sturry
Fordwich
A 291
Preston
Ash
A 257
Sandwich (Λ)

MAIDSTONE
Newnham
Doddington
Sheldwich
Harbledown
CANTERBURY
Littlebourne
Wingham
Woodnesborough
A 258
Deal (▲)
The Do...

Hollingbourne
Warren St.
Stalisfield
Selling
Shottenden
Chartham
Bridge
Patrixbourne
Eastry
Aylesham
Barfreston

Lenham
M 20
HIGH SPEED
Chilham
A 252
Petham
Lower Hardres
Barham
A 2
Ringwould
Kingsdown
St Margaret's-at-Cliffe

Egerton
Charing
A 28 Gt. Stour
N. Downs Way
A 251
Waltham
Stelling Minnis
Lydden Circuit
Lydden
Martin Mill
Whitfield
A 256
St. Margaret's Bay

Pluckley
Hothfield
Kennington
A 2070
Wye
Brook
Lyminge Forest
Elham
A 260
Swingfield
Temple Ewell
Alkham
South Foreland

Headcorn
Smarden
Bethersden
Ashford
M 20
Brabourne Lees
Lyminge
Acrise Place
B 2065
Hawkinge
A 20
B 2011
DOVER

Biddenden
Kingsnorth
(Λ)
Shadoxhurst
Sellindge
Stanford
Lydden Circuit
Swingfield
Alkham

High Halden
Woodchurch
A 28
Westenhanger
B 2067
Zoo
Lympne
B 2067
Terminal
Capel-le-Ferne (Λ)
The Warren
E. Wear Bay
Sandgate

Tenterden
Hamstreet
Bilsington
Newchurch
B 2080
B 2082
Hythe
FOLKESTONE
(▲ Λ)

Rolvenden
B 2086

SWANSEA · MERTHYR TYDFIL · CAERPHILLY · A 48 BRISTOL

THOMPSON'S PARK
Pencisely · Cardiff Rd · Pen-Hill Rd
Romilly · Pontcanna St · Cathedral Rd · Mortimer Rd
Egerton St · Glynne St · Wyndham Crescent · Talbot · Hamilton
Pembroke · Wyndham Pl · Springfield Pl
Romilly Rd · Romilly Crescent · King's · Ryder · Walk · Cathedral Rd · Sophia · Park Pl · North Rd
WELSH OFFICE · UNIVERSITY COLLEGE
Cathays · Miskin St · Richmond · Clive
TEMPLE OF PEACE · ALEXANDRA GARDENS
Bute Park · NATIONAL MUSEUM OF WALES · City Hall · Gorsedd Gardens
OLD COUNTY HALL · Law Courts
Greyfriars Rd · CAPITOL CENTRE
Cardiff Castle · Military Museums
Castle Arcade · High St Arcade · St John's Church
Cardiff Arms Park · ST DAVID'S SHOPPING CENTRE · Queen St
Central Market · TABERNACLE
Millenium Stadium · Morgan Arcade · Royal Arcade · Bute Terrace
CARDIFF CENTRAL · Tyndall St · CALLAGHAN SQUARE · Tresillian Way
SWAMINARAYANA TEMPLE · Bute East Dock
Universal St · Centre Gardens · Penarth Rd · Canal Parade · Lloyd
SEVENOAKS PARK
GRANGETOWN MUSLIM CULTURAL CENTRE · Stevenson · Overstone Court · Dumballs Rd
Embankment · CARDIFF BAY
BUTETOWN · THE RED DRAGON CENTRE
Coal Exchange · Clarence
THE SALVATION ARMY
St Cuthbert's · Wales Milennium Centre
Pierhead Building · Y Senedd
Techniquest · MERMAID QUAY
HAMADRYAD PARK · Norwegian Church · CARDIFF BAY
Windsor Esplanade · CARDIFF BAY WETLANDS RESERVE
CARDIFF BAY YACHT CLUB · QUEEN ALEXANDRA DOCK
LECKWITH WOODS

CARDIFF

0   200 m
0   200 yards

N

PENARTH · BRIGEND

CAERPHILLY
Cymmer · Senghenydd · Llanbradach · Machen · Risca · Caerleon · Langstone · Penhow · Caerwent · SEVERN VIEW S.A.
Tonyrefail · Bedwas · Rogerstone · MAGOR SERVICES · Severn Bridges · Aust
Pontypridd · Caerphilly/Caerffili · Portskewett · Pilning
Beddau · Thornhill · Parc Cefn Onn · NEWPORT CASNEWYDD · Magor · Roglet · Caldicot
Talbot Green · Llantrisant · Pentyrch · Tongwynlais · Lisvane · Castleton · Marshfield · Goldcliff · Redwick · Almondsbury
Miskin · Radyr · Llanishen · St Brides Wentlooge · Easter Compton
CARDIFF WEST · Whitchurch · St Mellons · Peterstone Wentlooge · Avonmouth · Filton
St Brides Super-Ely · St Fagans · Rumney · Portishead · GORDANO · Clifton
Pendoylan · Ely · Redcliff Bay
CARDIFF/CAERDYDD
Bonvilston · St Nicholas · Dinas Powys · Walton-in-Gordano · Clapton-in-Gordano · Clevedon Court · Abbots Leigh
Beaupre Castle · Wenvoe · Penarth · Easton-in-Gordano · Long Ashton
GLAMORGAN · Penmark · Sully · Clevedon · Kenn · Flax Bourton · BRISTOL
Brewis · St Athan · Swanbridge · N. SOMERSET · Nailsea · Bishopsworth
East Aberthaw · Rhoose · Porthkerry · BARRY/Barri · Kingston Seymour · Brockley · Backwell · Barrow Gurney · Dundry
CARDIFF AIRPORT · Flat Holm · Yatton · Lulsgate Bottom · Winford · Chew Magna
BRISTOL-LULSGATE AIRPORT · Redhill · Chew Stoke
WESTON-super-Mare · Congresbury · Wrington
Severn Estuary

CHESTER (inset map)

HOYLAKE — A 41, ELLESMERE PORT
M 56, MANCHESTER
M 53, LIVERPOOL
MANCHESTER, NANTWICH
A 5115, A 41, WHITCHURCH

Garden Lane · Bouverie St · Walpole St · Louise St · Raymond St · Chichester St · Garden Lane · St Oswalds Way · Delamere St · St George · Liverpool Rd · Walter St · Cornwall St · Talbot St · Trafford St · Victoria · Brook St · Francis St · Egerton St · Crewe St

NORTHGATE ARENA
St Oswalds Way · Hoole Way · Canal Side · Leadworks Lane · Steam Mill St · Russell St

NORTHGATE

King Charles Tower
The Walls
Kaleyards Gate
Chester Cathedral
Town Hall
FORUM SHOPPING CENTRE
EASTGATE
THE ROWS
NEWGATE
Stanley Palace
Dewa Roman Experience
WATERGATE
White Friars · Grey Friars · Black Friars
Grosvenor Museum
St John's · **St John's**
Roman Amphitheatre
Grosvenor Park
QUEEN'S PARK
BRIDGATE
Old Dee Bridge
Queen's Park
Roodee
The Walls

N

CHESTER
0 — 150 m
0 — 150 yards

QUEENSFERRY
New Crane
WATERGATE
WREXHAM — A 55, CONWY

Main map

SOUTHPORT · Birkdale · Ainsdale · Scarisbrick · Rufford · Rufford Old Hall · Burscough Bridge · Burscough · Hesketh Bank · Much Hoole

Formby · Gt. Altcar · Halsall · Ormskirk · Skelmersdale · Aughton · Lydiate · Ince Blundell · Up Holland · Hightown · Maghull · Blundellsands · Crosby · Litherland · Aintree · Kirkby · ST. HELENS · Knowsley · Bootle · New Brighton · LIVERPOOL · Roby · Huyton · Wallasey · Woolton · Hough Green · Farnworth · BIRKENHEAD · West Kirby · Irby · Thurstaston · Pensby · Port Sunlight · Widnes · Speke · Hale · Runcorn

Bebington · Bromborough · Eastham · Heswall · Thornton Hough · Parkgate · Neston · Willaston · LIVERPOOL JOHN LENNON AIRPORT · Ellesmere Port · Whitby · Backford Cross · Stoak · Elton · Frodsham · Bridge Trafford · Little Barrow · Great Barrow · Upton · CHESTER · Christleton · Waverton · Handbridge · Saughall · Sealand · Lache · Saltney · Broughton · Hawarden · Buckley/Bwcle · Ewloe · Northop Hall · Northop · Queensferry · Connah's Quay · Flint/Fflint · Mold/Yr Wyddgrug · Bagillt · Greenfield · Holywell/Treffynnon · Mostyn · Bodelwyddan

Rhyl · Prestatyn · Talacre · Point of Ayr · Llanasa · Trelawnyd · Dyserth · Rhuallt · Babell · Caerwys · Afon-wen · Halkyn · Kinmel Bay · Pensarn · Rhuddlan · Castle · St Asaph · Tremeirchion · Bodfari · Nannerch · Cilcain · Rhostyllen · Llannefydd · Trefnant · Henllan · Llandyrnog · Denbigh/Dinbych · Loggerheads · Bylchau · Llanrhaeadr · Moel Famau · Nercwys · Leeswood · Treuddyn · Ruthin/Rhuthun · Cyffylliog · Clocaenog · Pentre Celyn · Llanarmon-yn-Ial · Llanfynydd · Caergwrle · Hope · Burton · Penyffordd · Pulford · Aldford · Handley · Clawddnewydd · Llandegla · Bwlchgwyn · Brymbo · Coedpoeth · Gresford · Rossett · Holt · Farndon · Broxton · Tattenhall · Burwardsley

FLINTSHIRE · DENBIGHSHIRE · CHESHIRE WEST AND CHESTER

Brenig Resr. · Clocaenog Forest · Llanfihangel Glyn Myfyr · Bettws Gwerfil Goch · Bryneglwys · Llanelidan · Clawdd-newydd · WREXHAM/Wrecsam · Erddig · Marchwiel · Worthenbury · Malpas · Tilston

Offa's Dyke · Clywedog · Cym-y-Brain

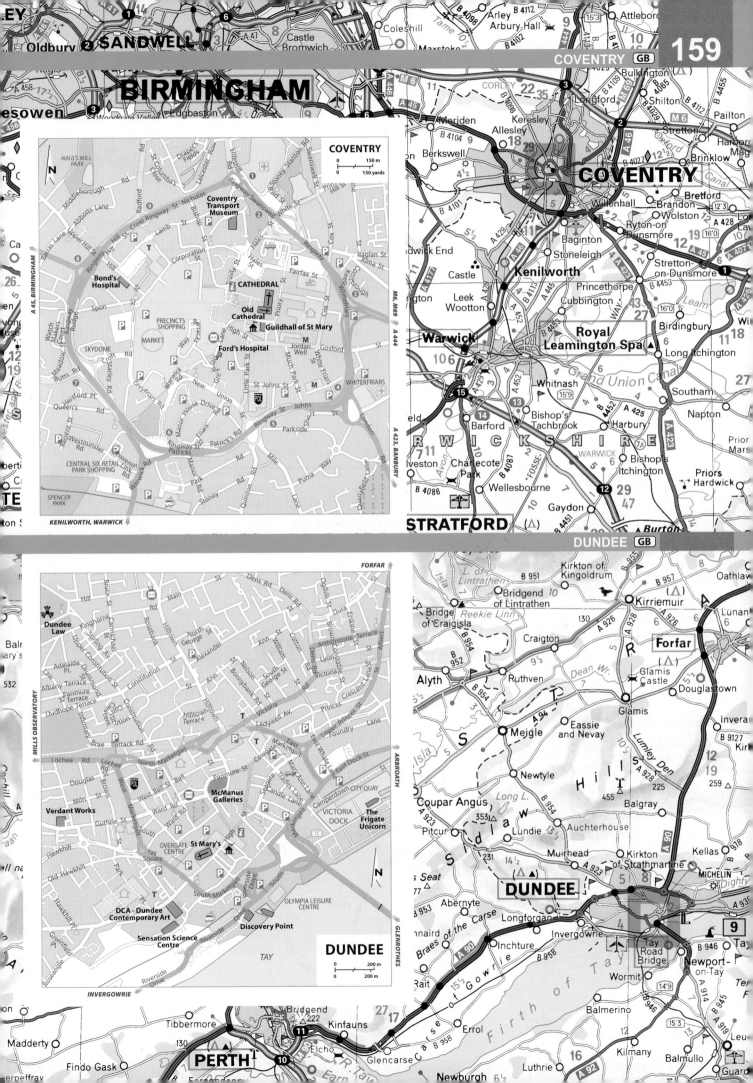

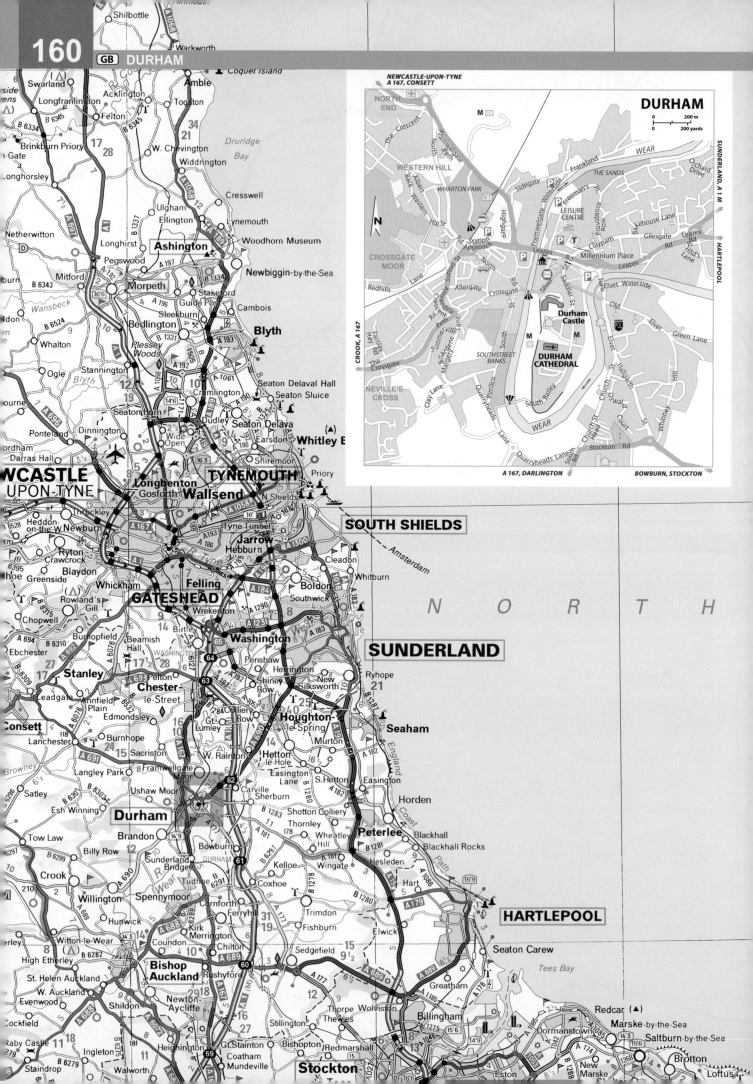

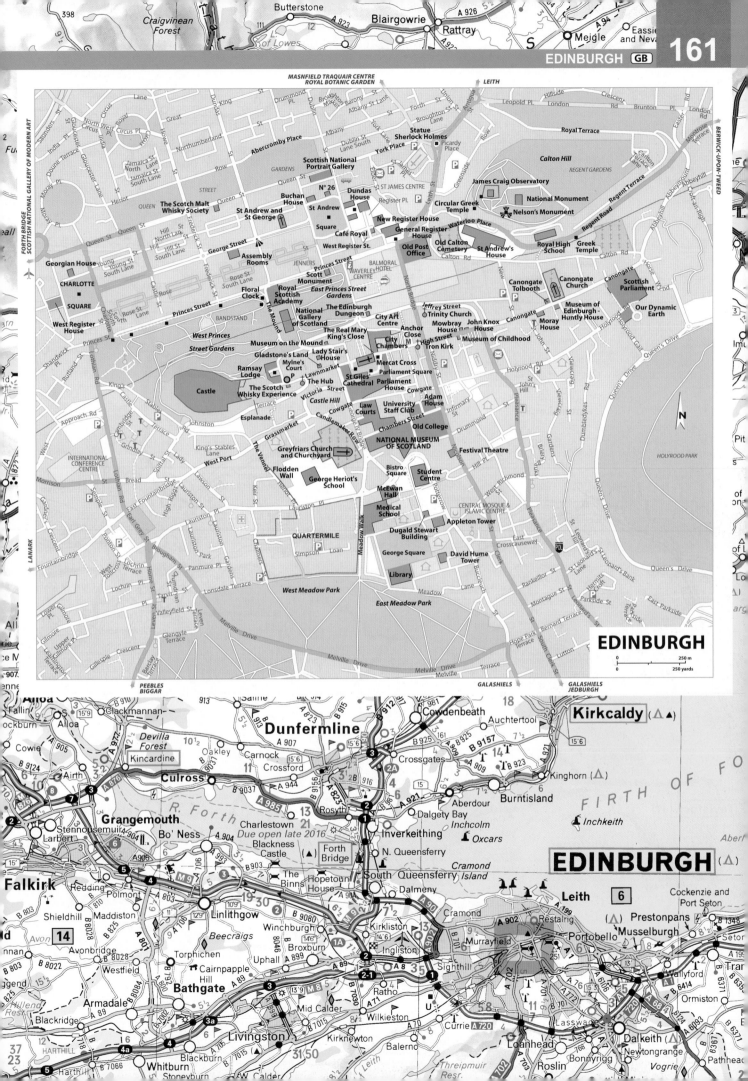

GLASGOW

0 — 450 m
0 — 450 yards

N

DUMBARTON · STIRLING · KIRKINTILLOCH

Points of interest and streets (city map):

Botanic Gardens, Hunterian Art Gallery, MACKINTOSH HOUSE, Hunterian Museum, University-Gilmorehill Building, MAIN BUILDING, WESTERN INFIRMARY, KELVIN HALL, Kelvingrove Park, Park Circus, KELVINGROVE ART GALLERY AND MUSEUM, Queen's Cross Church, Tenement House, The National Piping Centre, Beresford, CCA, Glasgow School of Art, Willow Tearoom, Sauchiehall Street, The Mitchell Library, Scottish Exhibition and Conference Center, Exhibition Centre Station, Clyde Auditorium - The "Armadillo", Glasgow Tower, Science Centre, La grue Finnieston, Daily Record Building, Willow Tea Rooms, The Lighthouse, Merchants' House, City Chambers, George Street, Gallery of Modern Art, Princes Square, Trades Hall, Buchanan Galleries, Buchanan Street Bus Station, Queen Street, Central Station, St Enoch SHOPPING CENTRE, Glasgow Cross, Tolbooth Steeple, Bridgegate Steeple, The Barras, Glasgow Green, People's Palace, Doulton Fountain, Templeton Business Centre, Scotland Street School Museum, Martyr's School, Royal Infirmary, CATHEDRAL, Necropolis, St Mungo Museum of Religious Life and Art, Provand's Lordship, King's Drive

HAMILTON MOTHERWELL · LIVINGSTON · EAST KILBRIDE

MOTHERWELL · HAMILTON · KILMARNOCK · KILMARNOCK

Regional map:

Greenock, Port Glasgow, Langbank, Bishopton, Kilmacolm, Bridge of Weir, Houston, Linwood, Ranfurly, Kilbarchan, Johnstone, PAISLEY, Barrhead, Neilston, Howwood, Lochwinnoch, Kilbirnie, Beith, Barrmill, Dunlop, Uplawmoor, Lugton, Newton Mearns, Eaglesham, Ballageich Hill, EAST KILBRIDE, Busby, Carmunnock, Blantyre, Bothwell, Uddingston, Cambuslang, Rutherglen, GLASGOW, Clydebank, Renfrew, Bearsden, Old Kilpatrick, Duntocher, Dumbarton, Erskine Bridge, Milngavie, Torrance, Kirkintilloch, Lenzie, Muirhead, Condorrat, Cumbernauld, Stepps, Coatbridge, Airdrie, Chapelhall, Holytown, Mossend, Bellshill, Newarthill, Motherwell, Wishaw, Hamilton, Larkhall, Overtown, Law, Cleland, Garfin

Kilpatrick Hills, R. Clyde, Kelvin, Creuch Hill, Strathgryfe, Muirshiel, Heathfield, Lennoxtown, Campsie, Riggend, Stand, Caldercruix, Longriggend, Slamannan

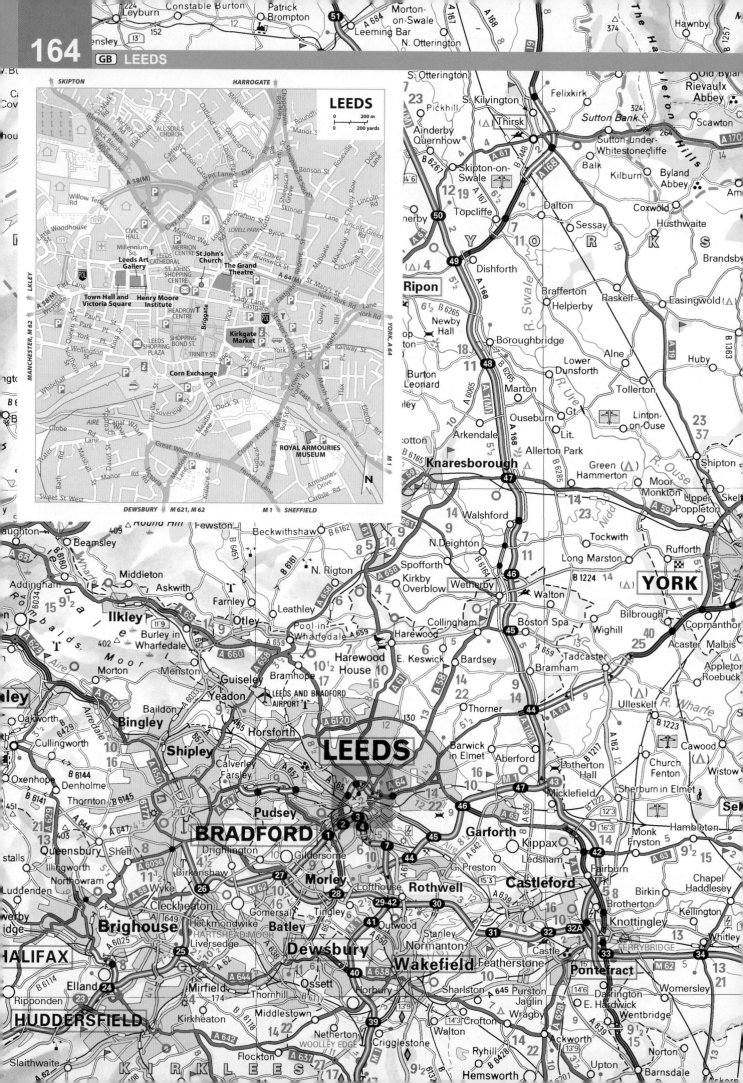

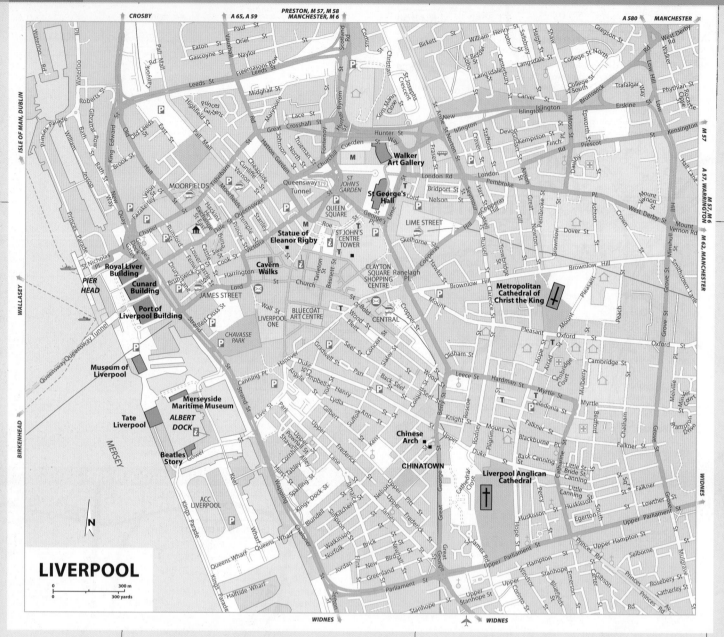

LIVERPOOL

0 — 300 m
0 — 300 yards

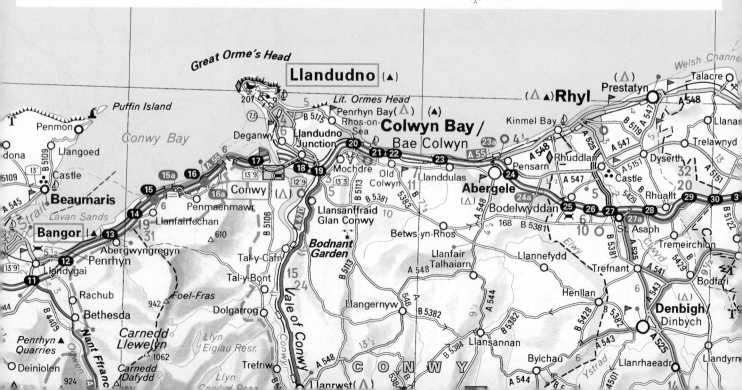

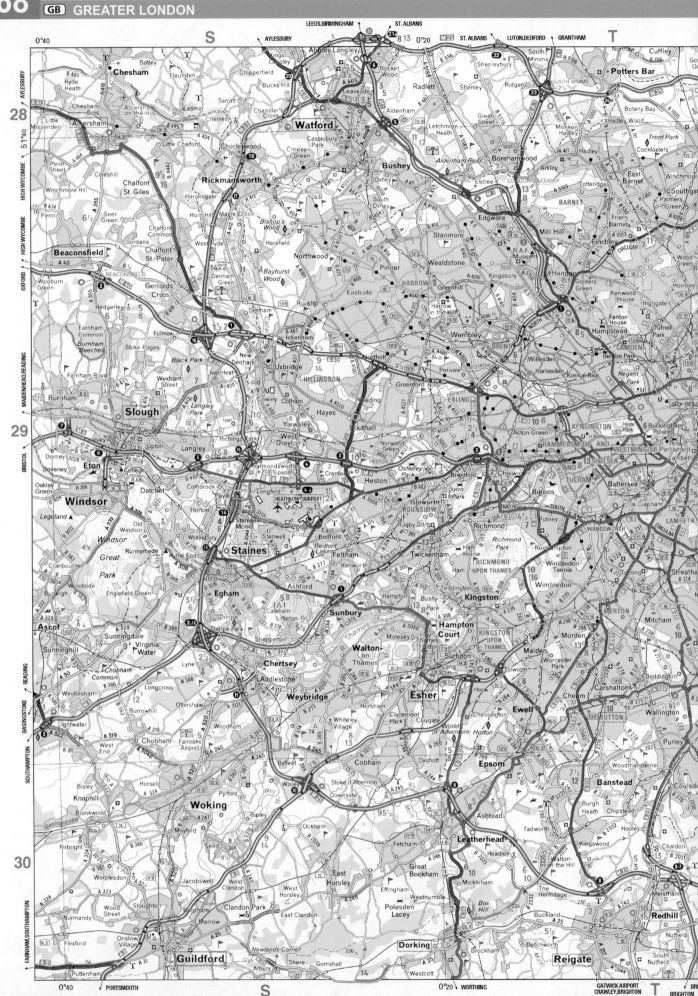

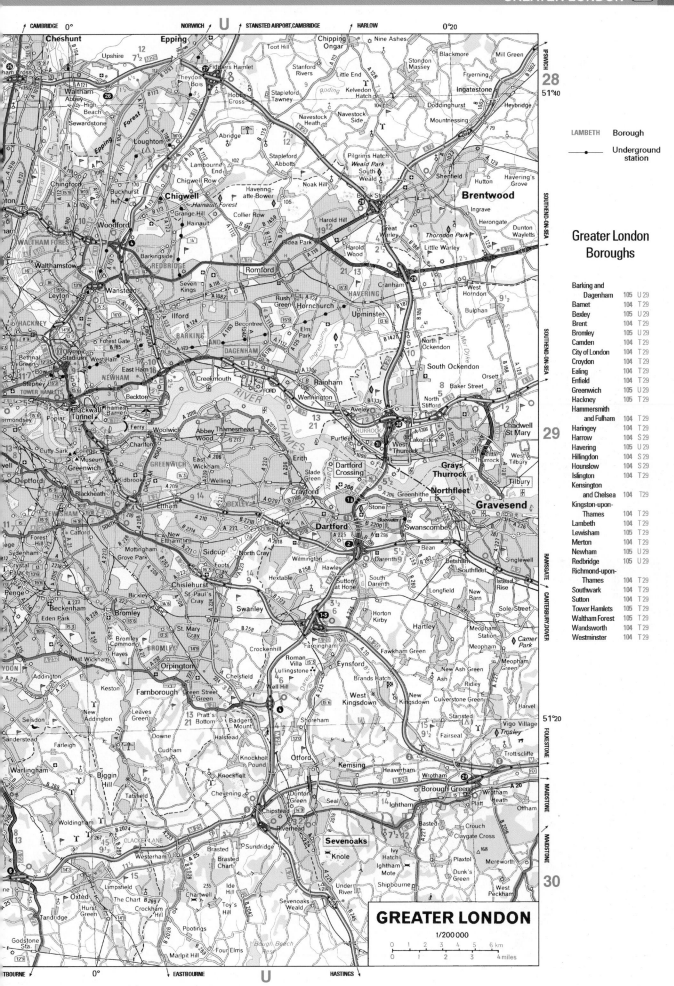

LAMBETH Borough

•━━━• Underground station

Greater London Boroughs

Barking and		
Dagenham	105	U 29
Barnet	104	T 29
Bexley	105	U 29
Brent	104	T 29
Bromley	105	U 29
Camden	104	T 29
City of London	104	T 29
Croydon	104	T 29
Ealing	104	T 29
Enfield	104	T 29
Greenwich	105	U 29
Hackney	105	T 29
Hammersmith		
and Fulham	104	T 29
Haringey	104	T 29
Harrow	104	S 29
Havering	105	U 29
Hillingdon	104	S 29
Hounslow	104	S 29
Islington	104	T 29
Kensington		
and Chelsea	104	T 29
Kingston-upon-		
Thames	104	T 29
Lambeth	104	T 29
Lewisham	105	T 29
Merton	104	T 29
Newham	105	U 29
Redbridge	105	U 29
Richmond-upon-		
Thames	104	T 29
Southwark	104	T 29
Sutton	104	T 29
Tower Hamlets	105	T 29
Waltham Forest	105	T 29
Wandsworth	104	T 29
Westminster	104	T 29

GREATER LONDON

1/200 000

0	1	2	3	4	5	6 km
0		1	2		3	4 miles

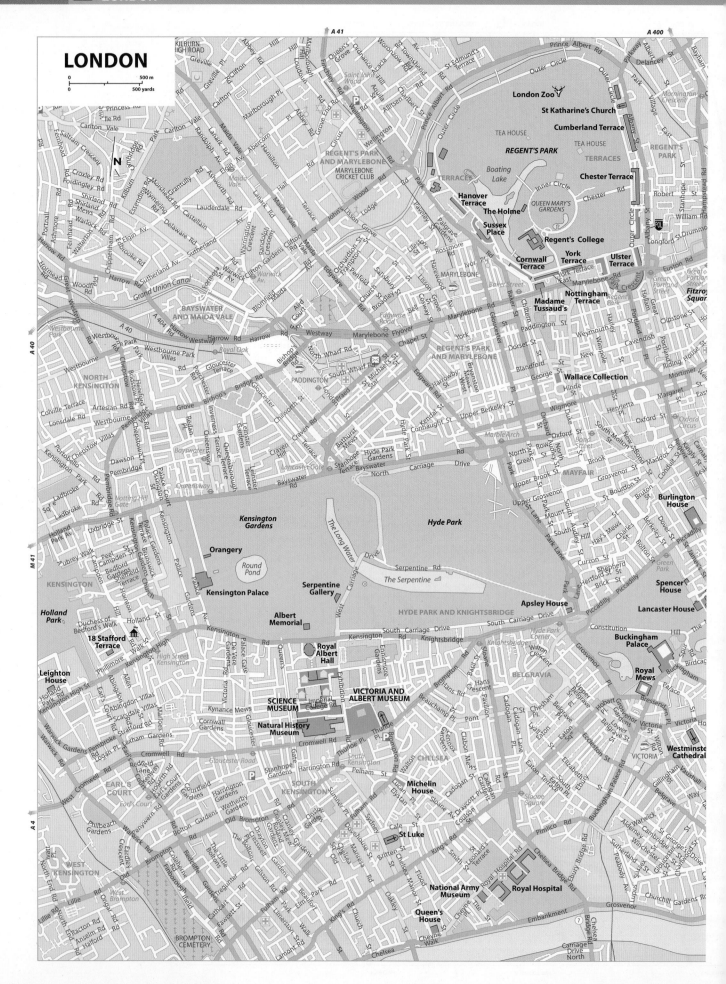

LONDON

0 ___ 500 m
0 ___ 500 yards

NEWCASTLE UPON-TYNE

TYNEMOUTH

SOUTH SHIELDS

GATESHEAD

SUNDERLAND

Whitley Bay

Wallsend

Jarrow

Washington

Stanley

Chester-le-Street

Seaham

Peterlee

HARTLEPO

Stockton-on-Tees

MIDDLESBROUGH

NEWCASTLE UPON TYNE

0   150 m
0   150 yards

EXHIBITION PARK

Great North Museum

St James Park

Laing Art Gallery and Museum

ELDON SQUARE SHOPPING CENTRE

Grey's Monument

Blackfriars

SAINT NICHOLAS CATHEDRAL

All Saints

Black Gate
Bessie Surtee's House

Castle Keep

Guildhall

Sage

Discovery Museum

Centre for Life

GATESHEAD MILLENNIUM BRIDGE BALTIC CENTRE

Quayside

Swing Bridge

High Level Bridge

Tyne Bridge

A 692, CONSETT
A1 (M), DURHAM

SUNDERLAND, A 184

DURHAM TEES VALLEY AIRPORT

Seaton Carew

Tees Bay

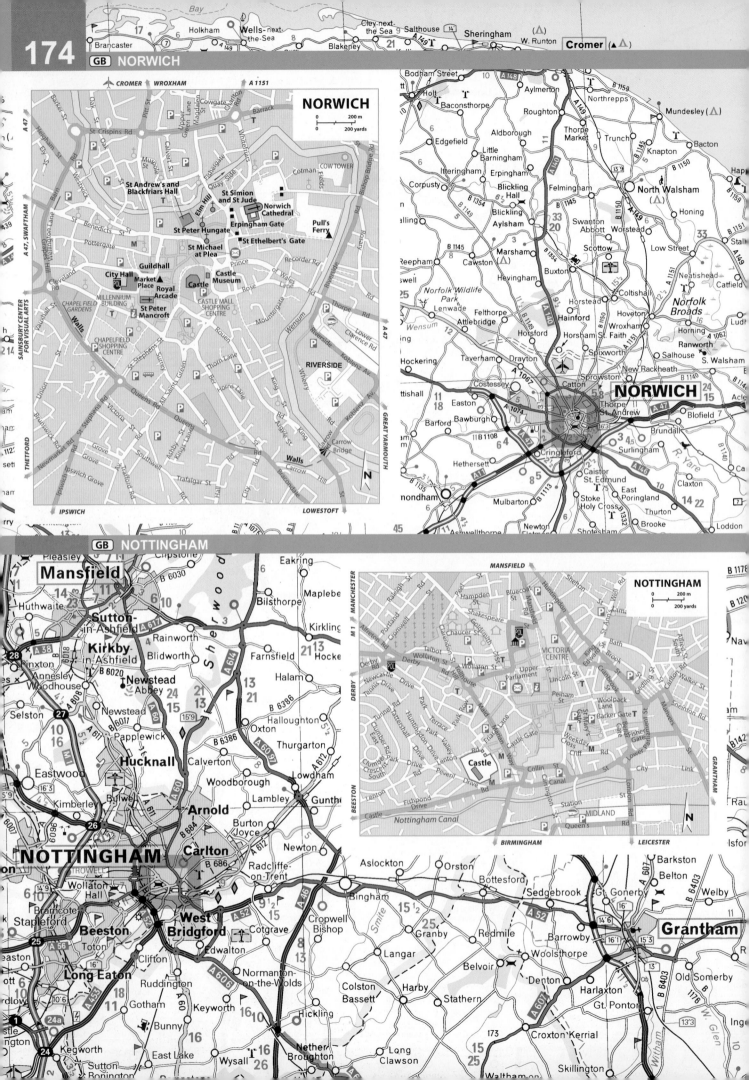

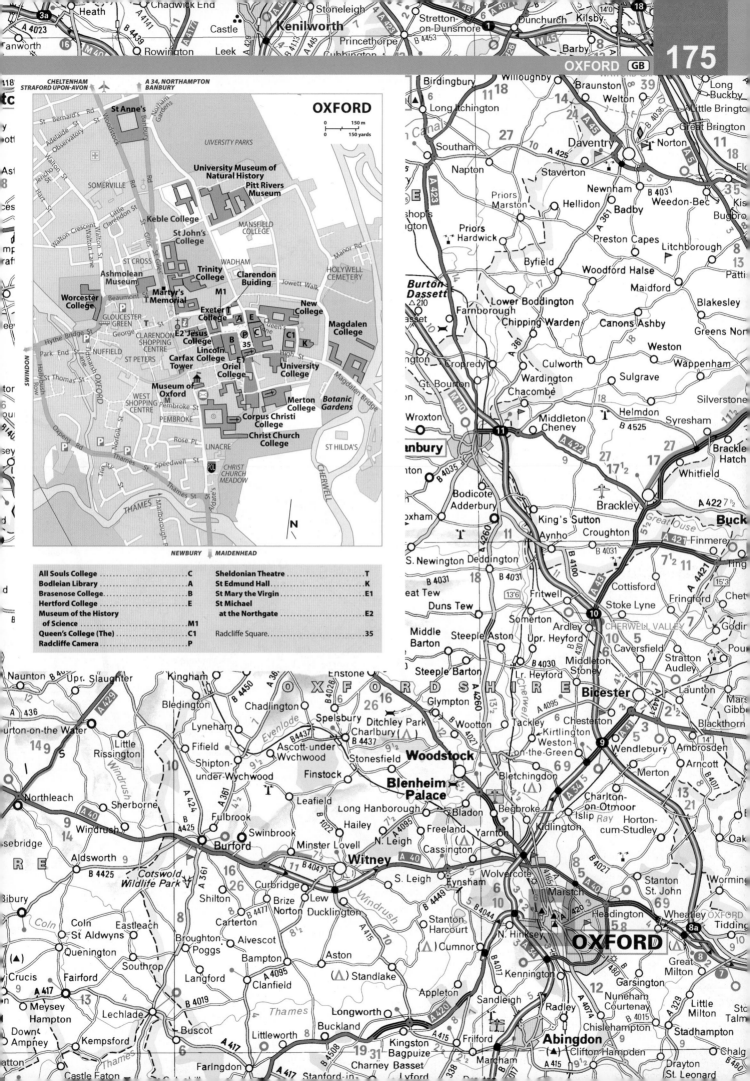

OXFORD

0 — 150 m
0 — 150 yards

All Souls College C
Bodleian Library .... A
Brasenose College .... B
Hertford College .... E
Museum of the History
  of Science M1
Queen's College (The) C1
Radcliffe Camera .... P

Sheldonian Theatre .... T
St Edmund Hall .... K
St Mary the Virgin E1
St Michael
  at the Northgate E2
Radcliffe Square 35

NEWBURY   MAIDENHEAD

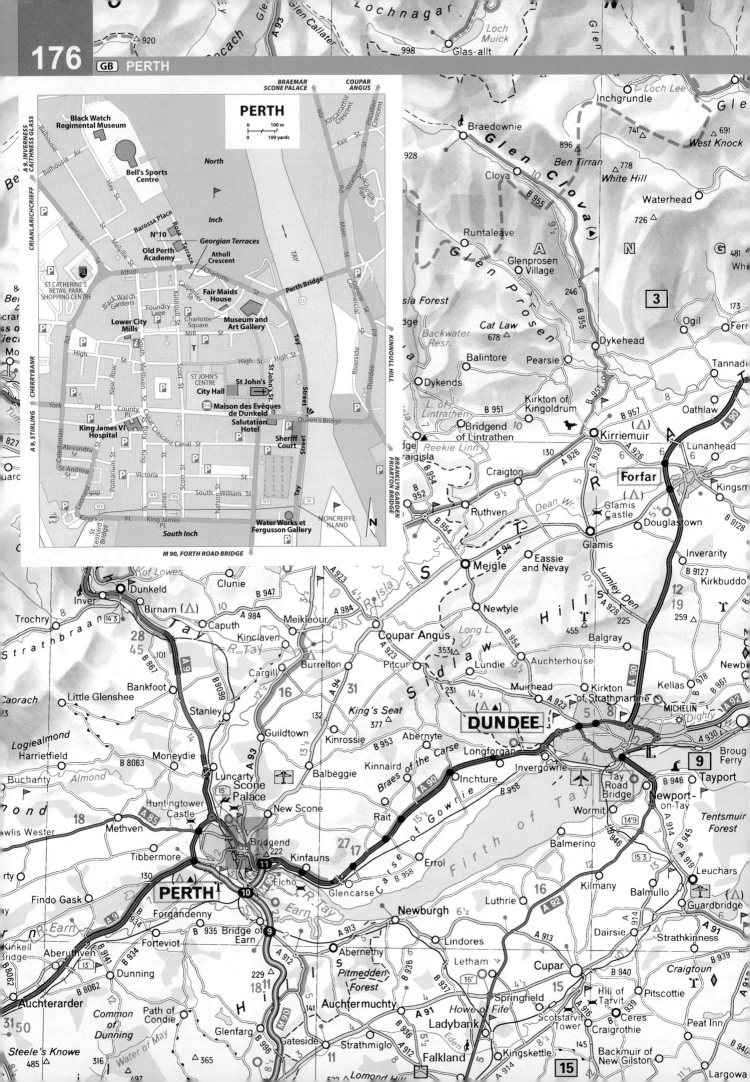

CHARLES DICKENS' BIRTHPLACE MUSEUM
CHICHESTER, M27, SOUTHAMPTON, LONDON

Mary Rose Museum
HMS VICTORY
National Museum of The Royal Navy
Action Stations
HMS Warrior 1860
HARBOUR
GUNWHARF QUAYS SHOPPING CENTRE
Spinnaker Tower
MARINA
The Point
OUTER CAMBER
Round Tower
Square Tower
Royal Garrison Church
OLD PORTSMOUTH
KING'S BASTION
St Thomas Cathedral
City Museum
PORTSEA
VICTORIA PARK
ST. JOHN R.C. CATHEDRAL
CASCADE CENTRE
TOWN
LANDPORT GATE
Landport Gate
SOUTHSEA
ENGLISH CHANNEL
HOVERPORT
SOUTHSEA COMMON
Southsea Terrace
Blue Reef Aquarium
D-Day museum
Southsea Castle
ROYAL MARINES MUSEUM

PORTSMOUTH

0   200 m
0   200 yards

N

ROYAL NAVY SUBMARINE MUSEUM, GOSPORT & EXPLOSION
ISLE OF WIGHT
A27, M27
A2030

A4
Shaw   Thatcham   Cold Ash   13   Sulhamstead   Burghfield   46   11   Shinfield   A329   Wokingham

Padworth   Swallowfield   Finchampstead   Sandhurst

Silchester   Stratfield Saye   Heckfield   Eversley   Yateley   A3272   11⁹

Tadley   Bramley   Stratfield Turgis   23   14   Hartley Wintney   FLEET   14   A327

Camber End   Sherfield on Loddon   Mattingley   9   Fleet   4a

Sherborne St. John   Hook   A30   Winchfield   Crookham Village   Church Crookham

Basing   5   N.   Warnborough   5   Odiham   Aldershot

oke   6   8   Upton Grey   A287   Upper Hale

7   5   Herriard   S. Warnborough   Crondall   10   Farnham

2   11   Bentley   Birdworld   Frensham

Preston Candover   B3349   11   17   Alton   Binsted

Bentworth   Holybourne   Kingsley   A325

Medstead   B3004   Bordon   Headley

Old Alresford   Four Marks   Whitehill   19   12

ford   Ropley   Selborne   Greatham   Liphook

E. Tisted   Liss   Rake   Mill

17   27   Bramdean   A32   Steep   Rogate

19   W. Meon   24   Langrish   16   Petersfield   11   17

Warnford   East Meon   25   Rogate   Stedh

uth   Downs   Queen Elizabeth   Elsted   Harting

Corhampton Meonstoke   Clanfield   National S

Droxford   Hambledon   Compton

N. Baddesley   ROWNHAMS   Upham   Bishop's Waltham   Cowplain   Rowland's Castle   Stoughton

Eastleigh   Fair Oak   Denmead   Havant   Funtington

Ower   Rownhams   Swaythling   Curdridge   Shedfield   Waterlooville   Westbourne   Southbourne

Totton   W. End   Hedge End   Botley   Wickham   Forest of Bere   Southwick Widley   Purbrook   Emsworth   Bosham

Cadnam   Netley Marsh   Eling   Bursledon   Sarisbury   Fareham   Portchester   Cosham   W Thorney   Fishbour

SOUTHAMPTON   Abbey Hound   Netley   Park Gate   Castle   Bridgemary   Emsworth

Ashurst   Marchwood   Hamble   Titchfield   Portsmouth Harbour   Langstone Harbour   Chichester Harbour   Birdham

Hythe   Warsash   Stubbington   Bosham

Holbury   National Motor Museum   Fawley   Lee on-the-Solent   Hayling Island   W Thorney

Beaulieu   Blackfield   Gosport   South Hayling   W. Wittering

Boldre   Bucklers Hard   Lepe   Southsea   E. Wittering

Lymington   Cowes   PORTSMOUTH   Selsey

Milford-on-Sea   Gurnard   Osborne House   Spithead   Ryde

Whippingham   Fishbourne   Quarr   Seaview

Parkhurst   Wootton Bridge

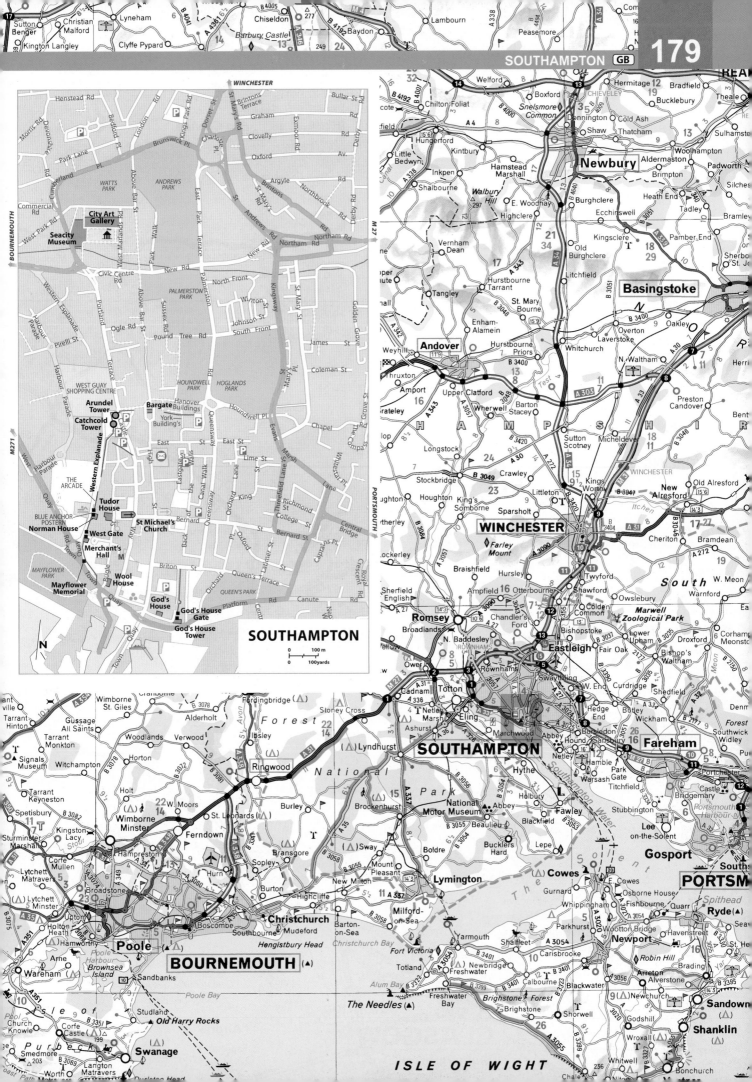

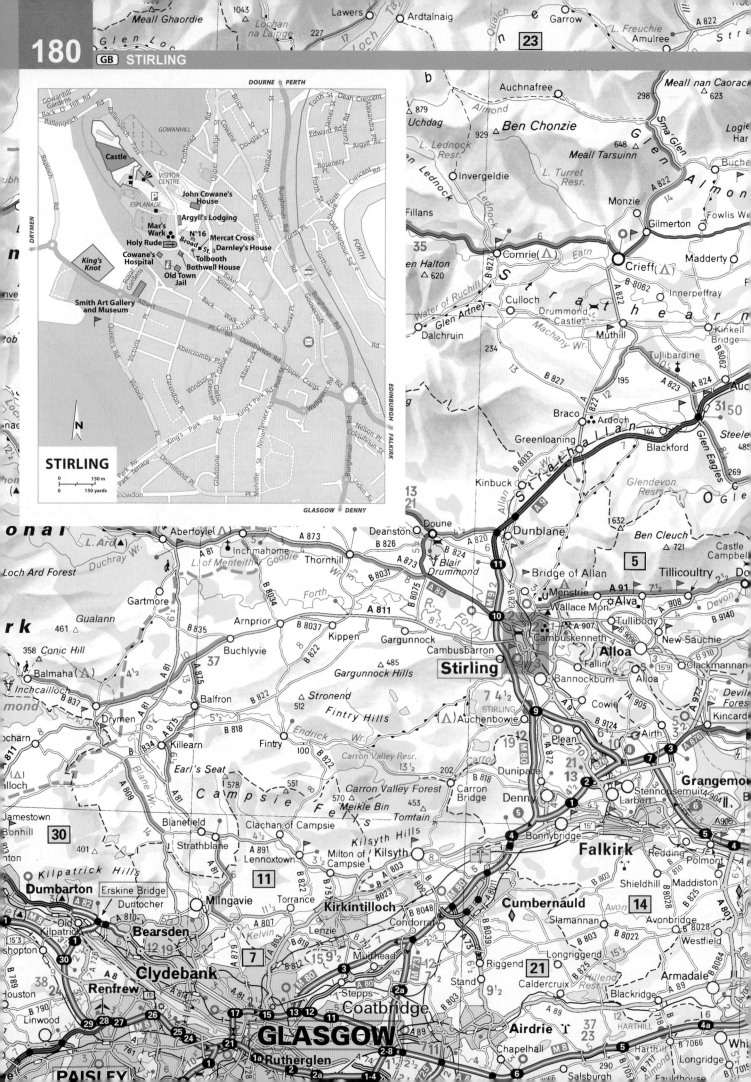

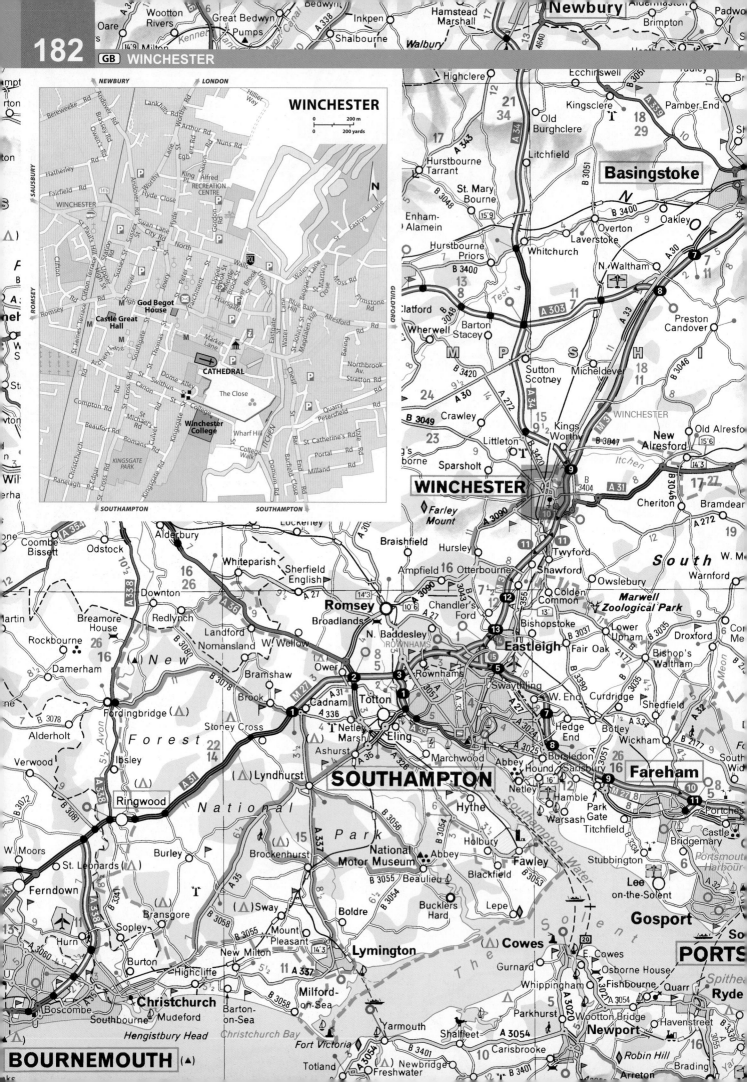

WINDSOR

Eton College
Home Park
M4
Meadow Lane
South Meadow Lane
Keats Lane
WINDSOR AND ETON RIVERSIDE
LEISURE CENTRE
CLEWER PARK
CLEWER
THAMES
ALEXANDRA GARDENS
Stovell Rd
WINDSOR ROYAL STATION
CENTRAL
WINDSOR CASTLE
ST GEORGE'S CHAPEL
Datchet Rd
Romney Lock Rd
King Edward VII Av
Prince Albert's Walk
The Long Walk
KING EDWARD COURT CENTRE
Oxford Rd
Albert St
Bexley St
Clarence Rd
Clarence Rd
Victoria St
Sheet St
Peascod St
High St
POL
King's Rd
St Mark's Rd
Grove Rd
Alma Rd
Frances Rd
CLEWER WITHIN
College Crescent
Osborne Rd
Bolton Rd
Bolton Crescent
Fountain Gardens
Home Park
FROGMORE
MAIDENHEAD
St Leonard's Rd
A322
STAINES-UPON-THAMES
N

Loudwater · Chalfont St. Peter · Harefield · Stanmore · Tottenham
Flackwell Heath · Beaconsfield · Pinner · Wealdstone · HARINGEY
HARROW
Cookham Dean · Cookham · Cliveden · Stoke Poges · Iver Heath · HILLINGDON · Wembley · BRENT · CAMDEN · ISLINGTON · HACKNEY
Maidenhead · Burnham · Farnham Royal · Slough · Wexham Street · Iver · EALING · HAMMERSMITH AND FULHAM
Taplow · Bray · Langley · HESTON · Heston · L·O·N·D·O·N · NEWHAM · Blackwall Tunnel
Eton · Datchet · HEATHROW AIRPORT · Kew · TOWER HAMLETS · Beckton
Windsor · Old Windsor · Staines · Stanwell · Isleworth · RICHMOND UPON THAMES · Putney · LAMBETH · LEWISHAM
Winkfield · Windsor Great Park · Egham · Ashford · Feltham · Twickenham · Wimbledon · WANDSWORTH · Streatham · Sydenham
Ascot · Englefield Green · Sunbury · Hampton Court · KINGSTON UPON THAMES · Mitcham · Croydon
Bracknell · Sunninghill · Sunningdale · Virginia Water · Chertsey · Shepperton · Walton-on-Thames · Esher · Cheam · Carshalton · West Wickham
Windlesham · Addlestone · Weybridge · Claygate · Chessington · SUTTON · Wallington · Sanderstead · New Addington
Crowthorne · Bagshot · Lightwater · Chobham · Byfleet · Cobham · Oxshott · Ewell · Epsom · Banstead · Warlingham
Royal Military Academy · Camberley · Horsell · Wisley · Leatherhead · Ashtead · Tadworth · Chipstead · Kingswood · Caterham
Blackwater · Frimley · Bisley · Knaphill · Woking · Ripley · Ockham · Fetcham · Great Bookham · Woldingham
Mytchett · Pirbright · Maybury · East Horsley · Polesden Lacey · Box Hill · Godstone · Oxted · Limpsfield
Farnborough · Worplesdon · Clandon Park · SURREY · South Nutfield · Redhill
Stoughton · Burpham · Roman Villa · Normandy · Ash · Tongham · Onslow Village · Guildford · Gomshall · Abinger Hammer · Dorking · Reigate
SOUTH DOWNS · Charlton · Bignor · Bury · Amberley · Washington · South Downs Way · Steyning

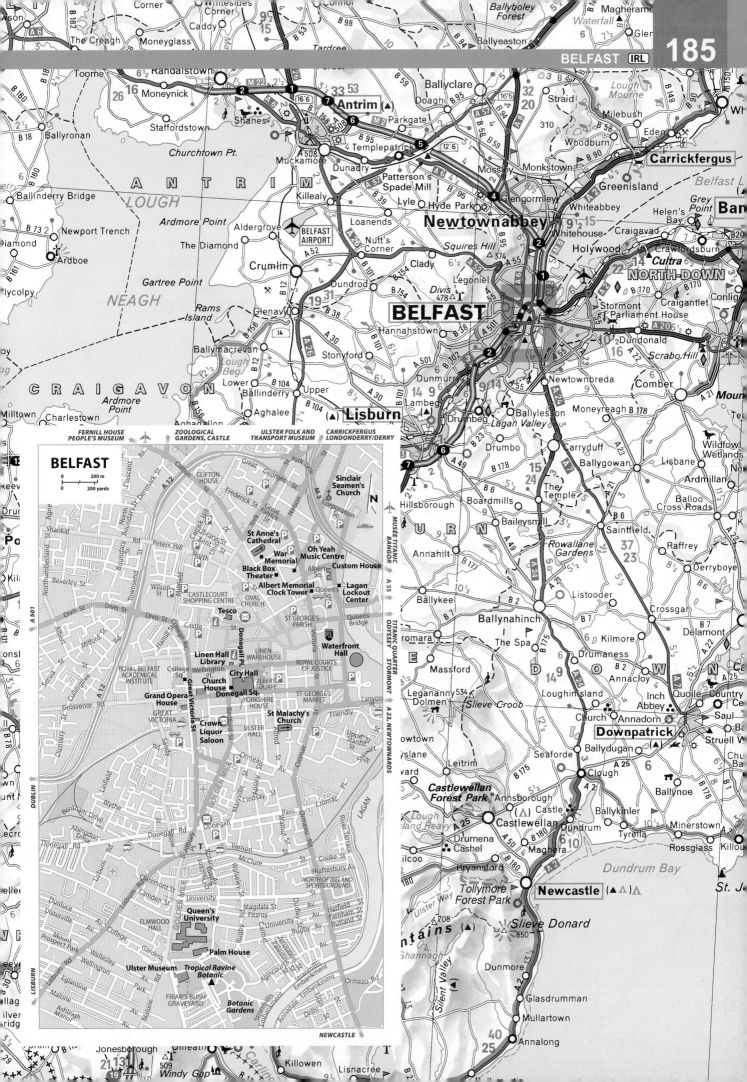

BELFAST

FERNILL HOUSE PEOPLE'S MUSEUM
ZOOLOGICAL GARDENS, CASTLE
ULSTER FOLK AND TRANSPORT MUSEUM
CARRICKFERGUS LONDONDERRY/DERRY

0 — 200 m
0 — 200 yards

N

CLIFTON HOUSE

Sinclair Seamen's Church

St Anne's Cathedral

Oh Yeah Music Centre

War Memorial

Black Box Theater

Custom House

Albert Memorial Clock Tower

Lagan Lookout Center

CASTLECOURT SHOPPING CENTRE

OVAL CHURCH

Tesco

DONEGALL WAREHOUSE

LINEN WAREHOUSE

ST GEORGE'S PARISH

Waterfront Hall

Linen Hall Library

ROYAL COURTS OF JUSTICE

City Hall

Church House

Donegall Sq.

ROYAL BELFAST ACADEMICAL INSTITUTE

ALBERT SQUARE

ST-GEORGE'S MARKET

Grand Opera House

YORKSHIRE HOUSE

St Malachy's Church

Crown Liquor Saloon

ULSTER HALL

NORTH OF IRELAND SPORTS GROUND

University

Queen's University

ELMWOOD HALL

Palm House

Ulster Museum

Tropical Ravine Botanic

FRIAR'S BUSH GRAVEYARD

Botanic Gardens

MUSÉE TITANIC BANGOR
TITANIC QUARTER ODYSSEY STORMONT A23, NEWTOWNARDS

NEWCASTLE

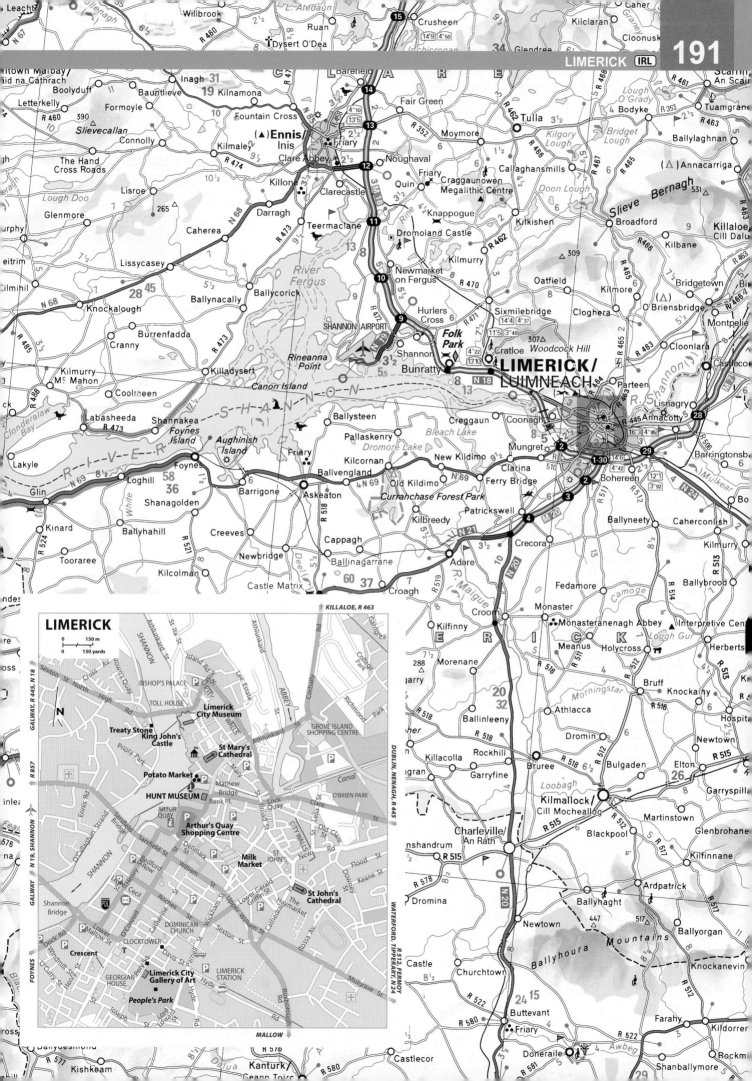

Eochair

Bóithre

Mótarbhealach - Limistéar seirbhíse
Carrbhealach dúbailte le saintréithe mótarbhealaigh
Acomhail mótarbhealaigh: iomlán - teoranta
Vimhreacha ceangail
Líonra idirnáisiúnta agus náisiúnta bóithre
Bóthar idir-réigiúnach nach bhfuil chomh plódaithe
Bóthar nuadheisithe - gan réitiú
Cosán - Conair mharcáilte / Cosán marcaíochta
Mótarbhealach, bóthar á dhéanamh
(an dáta oscailte sceidealta, mas eol)

Leithead bóithre

Carrshlí dhéach
4 lána - 2 leathanlíse
2 lána - 2 chunglána

Fad bóthar (iomlán agus meánfhad)

Bhóithre dola ar an mótarbhealach
Saor ó dhola ar an mótarbhealach
i mílte - i gciliméadair
ar an mbóthar

Aicmiú oifigiúil bóithre

Mótarshl - GB: Priomhbhealach

IRL: Bóithre eile ,

Priomhbhóithre agus fobhóithre náisiúnta
Ceann scríbe ar ghréasán bóithre priomha

Constaicí

Timpeall - Beamas agus a airde os cionn leibhéal na mara (í méadair)
Fána ghéar (suas treo an gha)
IRL: Bealach deacair nó baolach
Bóthar cúng le hionaid phasála (in Albain)
Crosaire comhréidh: iamród ag dul, faoi bhóthar, os cionn bóthair
Bóthar toirmeasctha - Bóthar faoi theorannú
Bacainn dola - Bóthar aonsli
(Ar phríomhbhóithre agus ar bhóithre réigiúnacha)
Teorainneacha airde (faoi 15'6" IRL, faoi 16'6" GB)
Teorainn Mheáchain (faoi 16t)

Iompar

Leithead caighdeánach - Staisiún paisinéiri
Aerfort - Aerpháirc
Longsheirbhísí : (Seirbhísí séasúracha: dearg)
Árthach foluaineach - Bád
Fartha (uas - ulach : tonnaí méadracha)
Coisithe agus lucht rothar

Lóistín - Riarachán

Teorainneacha riaracháin
Teorainn na hAlban agus teorainn na Breataine Bige

Teorainn idirnáisiúnta - Custam

Áiseanna Spóirt agus Súgartha

Machaire Gailf - Ráschúrsa
Timpeall rásaíochta - Cuan bád aeraíochta
Láthair champa , láthair charbhán
Conair mharcáilte - Páirc thuaithe
Zú - Tearmannéan mara
IRL: Lascaireacht - Ráschúrsa con Larnród theain ghaile
Traein cábla
Carr cábla , cathaoir cábla

Amhairc

Príomhradharcanna :
féach AN EOLAÍ UAINE
Bailte nó áiteanna inspéise, baill lóistín
Foirgneamh Eaglasta - Caisleán
Fothrach - Leacht meigilíteach - Pluais
Páirc, Gáirdíní - Ionaid eile spéisiúla
IRL: Dunfort - Cros Cheilteach - Cloigtheach
Lánléargas - Cothrom Radhairc - Bealach Aoibhinn

Comharthaí Eile

Cáblashlí thionsclaíoch
Crann teileachumarsáide - Teach solais
Stáisiún Giniúna - Cairéal
Mianach - Tionsclaíoch
Scaglann - Aill
Páirc Fhoraoise Naisiúnta - Páirc Naisiúnta

Allwedd

Ffyrdd

Trafford - Mannau gwasanaeth
Ffordd ddeuol â nodweddion traffordd
Cyfnewidfeyd: wedi'i chwblhau - cyfyngedig
Rhifau'r cyffyrdd
Fford ar rwydwaith rhyngwladol a chenedlaethol
Ffordd rhyngranbarthol a llai prysur
Ffordd ac wyneb iddi - heb wyneb
Llwybr troed - Llwybr troed ag arwyddion / Llwybr ceffyl
Trafford - ffordd yn cael ei hadeiladu
(Os cyfodi yr achos: dyddiad agor disgwyliedig)

Ffyrdd

ffordd ddeuol
4 lôn - 2 lôn lydan
2 lôn - 2 lôn gul

Pellter (cyfanswm a'r rhyng-bellter)

Tollffyrdd ar y draffordd
Rhan di-doll ar y draffordd
mewn miltiroedd - mewn kilometrau
ar y ffordd

Dosbarthiad ffyrdd swyddogol

Traffordd - GB : Prif ffordd

IRL: Prif ffordd genedlaethol a ffordd eilradd

Ffyrdd eraill
Cylchfan ar rwydwaith y prif ffrydd

Rhwystrau

Cylchfan - Bwlch a'i uchder uwchlaw lefel y môr (mewn metrau)
Rhiw serth (esgyn gyda'r saeth)
IRL: Darn anodd neu beryglus o ffordd
Yn yr Alban : ffordd gul â mannau pasio
Croesfan rheilffordd: croesfan rheilffordd, o dan y ffordd, dros y ffordd
Ffordd waharddedig - Ffordd a chyfyngiadau arni
Rhwystr Toll - Unffordd
(Ar brif ffyrdd a ffyrdd rhanbarthol)
Terfyn uchder (llai na 15'6" IRL, 16'6" GB)
Terfyn pwysau (llai na 16t)

Cludiant

Lled safonol - Gorsaf deithwyr
Maes awyr - Maes glanio
Llongau ceir: (Gwasanaethau tymhorol: mewn coch)
Ilong hofran - Ilong
Fferi (llwyth uchaf: mewn tunelli metrig)
Teithwyr ar droed neu feic yn unig

Llety - Gweinyddiaeth

Ffiniau gweinyddol
Ffin Cymru, ffin yr Alban

Ffin ryngwladol - Tollau

Cyfleusterau Chwaraeon a Hamdden

Cwrs golff - Rasio Ceffylau
Rasio Cerbydau - Harbwr cychod pleser
Leoedd i wersylla
Llwybr troed ag arwyddion - Parc gwlad
Parc saffari, sw - Gwarchodfa natur
IRL: Pysgota - Maes rasio milgwn
Trên twristiaid
Rhaffordd, car cêbl, cadair esgyn

Golygfeydd

Gweler Llyfr Michelin

Trefi new fannau o ddiddordeb, mannau i aros
Adeilag eglwysig - Castell
Adfeilion - Heneb fegalithig - Ogof
Gerddi, parc - Mannau eraill o ddiddordeb
IRL: Caer - Croes Geltaidd - twr crwn
Panorama - Golygfan - Ffordd dygfeydd

Symbolau eraill

Lein gêbl ddiwydiannol
Mast telathrebu - Goleudy
Gorsaf bwer - Chwarel
Mwyngloddio - Gweithgarwch diwydiannol
Purfa - Clogwyn
Parc Coedwig Cenedlaethol - Parc Cenedlaethol

Comnarthaí ar phleanna bailte

Ionaid inspéise

Ionad inspéise agus

Ionad inspéise adhartha

Bóithre

Mótarbhealach, carrbhealach dúbailte le saintréithe mótarbhea

Acomhail mótarbhealaigh : iomlán - teoranta

Priomh-thrébhealach

Sráid: neamhoiriúnach do thrácht, ach í stáit speisialta

Sráid: coisithe

Carrchlós

Comharthaí Éagsúla

Aerfort

Leithead caighdeánach - Staisiún paisinéiri

Ionad eolais turasóireachta - Ospidéal

Gairdín, páirc, coill - Reilig

Staidiam

Galfchúrsa

Stáisiún traenach faoi thalamh

Príomhoifi g phoist le poste restante

Foirgneamh poibli curtha in iúl le litir thagartha:

Músaem

Amharclann

Póitíní (ceanncheathrú)

Symbolau ar gynlluniau'r trefi

Golygfeydd

Man diddorol

Lle diddorol o addoliad

Ffyrdd

Trafford, ffordd ddeuol

Cyfnewidfeyd : wedi'i chwblhau - cyfyngedig

Prif ffordd drwodd

Stryd : Anaddas i draffi g, cyfyngedig

Stryd: Cerddwr

Parc ceir

Arwyddion amrywiol

Maes awyr

Lled safonol - Gorsaf deithwyr

Canolfan croeso - Ysbyty

Gardd, parc, coedwig - Mynwent

Stadiwm

Cwrs golff

Gorsaf danddaearol

Prif swyddfa bost gyda poste restante

Adeilad cyhoeddus a ddynodir gan lythyren:

Amgueddfa

Theatr

Yr Heddlu (pencadlys)